Social Psychology and Organizations

ORGANIZATION AND MANAGEMENT SERIES

Series Editors

Arthur P. Brief, University of Utah
Kimberly D. Elsbach, University of California, Davis
Michael Frese, National University of Singapore
and University of Luneburg

B. Ashforth, *Role Transitions in Organizational Life: An Identity-Based Perspective* (Psychology Press).

C. A. Bartel, S. Blader, & A. Wrzesniewski (Eds.), *Identity and the Modern Organization* (Psychology Press).

J. Bartunek, *Organizational and Educational Change: The Life and Role of a Change Agent Group* (Psychology Press).

L. R. Beach (Ed.), *Image Theory: Theoretical and Empirical Foundations* (Routledge).

J. Brett & F. Drasgow (Eds.), *The Psychology of Work: Theoretically Based Empirical Research* (Psychology Press).

J. Brockner, *A Contemporary Look at Organizational Justice: Multiplying Insult Times Injury* (Routledge).

J. S. Chhokar, F. C. Brodbeck, & R. J. House (Eds.), *Culture and Leadership Across the World: The GLOBE Book of In-Depth Studies of 25 Societies* (Psychology Press).

J. M. Darley, D. M. Messick, & T. R. Tyler (Eds.), *Social Influences on Ethical Behavior in Organizations* (Psychology Press).

D. De Cremer, J. K. Murnighan, & R. van Dick (Eds): *Social Psychology and Organizations* (Psychology Press).

D. R. Denison (Ed.), *Managing Organizational Change in Transition Economies* (Psychology Press).

J. E. Dutton & B. R. Ragins (Eds.), *Exploring Positive Relationships at Work: Building a Theoretical and Research Foundation* (Psychology Press).

K. D. Elsbach, *Organizational Perception Management* (Lawrence Erlbaum Associates).

P. C. Earley & C. B. Gibson, *Multinational Work Teams: A New Perspective* (Psychology Press).

R. Garud & P. Karnoe (Eds.), *Path Dependence and Creation* (Psychology Press).

M. M. Harris (Ed.), *Handbook of Research in International Human Resource Management* (Psychology Press).

S. M. Jacoby, *Employing Bureaucracy: Managers, Unions, and the Transformation of Work in the 20th Century, Revised Edition* (Psychology Press).

E. E. Kossek & S. J. Lambert (Eds.), *Work and Life Integration: Organizational, Cultural and Individual Perspectives* (Psychology Press).

R. M. Kramer, A. E. Tenbrunsel, & M. H. Bazerman (Eds.), *Social Decision Making: Social Dilemmas, Social Values and Ethical Judgments* (Psychology Press).

J. Lampel, J. Shamsie, & T. K. Lant (Eds.), *The Business of Culture: Strategic Perspectives on Entertainment and Media* (Lawrence Erlbaum Associates).

T. K. Lant & Z. Shapira (Eds.), *Organizational Cognition: Computation and Interpretation* (Psychology Press).

R. G. Lord & D. J. Brown, *Leadership Processes and Follower Self-Identity* (Psychology Press).

J. D. Margolis & J. P. Walsh, *People and Profits? The Search Between a Company's Social and Financial Performance* (Psychology Press).

M. P. Miceli, J. P. Dworkin, & T. M. *Near, Whistle-blowing in Organizations* (Psychology Press).

D. M. Messick & R. M. Kramer (Eds.), *The Psychology of Leadership: Some New Approaches* (Psychology Press).

J. L. Pearce, *Organization and Management in the Embrace of the Government* (Psychology Press).

R. S. Peterson & E. A. Mannix (Eds.), *Leading and Managing People in the Dynamic Organization* (Psychology Press).

A. Rafaeli & M. G. Pratt (Eds.), *Artifacts and Organizations: Beyond Mere Symbolism* (Lawrence Erlbaum Associates).

R. E. Riggio, S. E. Murphy, & F. J. Pirozzolo (Eds.), *Multiple Intelligences and Leadership* (Psychology Press).

L. M. Roberts & J. E. Dutton (Eds): *Exploring Positive Identities and Organizations: Building a Theoretical and Research Foundation* (Psychology Press).

B. Schneider & D. B. Smith (Eds.), *Personality and Organizations* (Psychology Press).

D. B. Smith (Ed.), *The People Make the Place: Dynamic Linkages Between Individuals and Organizations* (Psychology Press).

H.-S. Choi & L. L. Thompson (Eds.), *Creativity and Innovation in Organizational Teams* (Lawrence Erlbaum Associates).

J. M. Thompson, L. L. Levine, & D. M. Messick (Eds.), *Shared Cognition in Organizations: The Management of Knowledge* (Psychology Press).

Social Psychology and Organizations

David De Cremer
Erasmus University

Rolf van Dick
Goethe University

J. Keith Murnighan
Northwestern University

Routledge
Taylor & Francis Group
New York   London

Routledge
Taylor & Francis Group
711 Third Avenue, 8th Floor
New York, NY 10017

Routledge
Taylor & Francis Group
27 Church Road
Hove, East Sussex BN3 2FA

© 2011 by Taylor and Francis Group, LLC
Routledge is an imprint of Taylor & Francis Group, an Informa business

Transferred to digital print 2012

First issued in paperback 2012

International Standard Book Number: 978-1-84872-856-1 (Hardback) 978-0-415-65182-0 (Paperback)

Library of Congress Cataloging-in-Publication Data

Social psychology and organizations / editors, David De Cremer, Rolf van Dick, J.
Keith Murnighan.
p. cm. -- (Organization and management series)
Includes bibliographical references and index.
ISBN 978-1-84872-856-1 (hardcover : alk. paper)
ISBN 978-0-415-65182-0 (pbk)
1. Social psychology. 2. Control (Psychology) 3. Leadership. 4. Organizational
behavior. I. De Cremer, David. II. Van Dick, Rolf. III. Murnighan, John Keith.

HM1033.S643 2010
303.3'4--dc22   2010025159

**Visit the Taylor & Francis Web site at
http://www.taylorandfrancis.com**

**and the Psychology Press Web site at
http://www.psypress.com**

We dedicate this book to

*My buddies Alain, Dirk, and Jeroen, who helped me return
to my roots while working on this book. (DDC)*

*My wife, Steffi, and my children, Jan, Lucia, and Lennart. Every
minute spent on this book was one not spent with you—but every
minute spent with you is inspiration for the next book! (RVD)*

*My children, Jack, Erik, Kate, Annie, and Will, who have all given
me great insights into social psychology and who have, with love,
made sure that I was more attuned to organization. (KM)*

Contents

Chapter 9   The Repair of Trust: Insights From Organizational
Behavior and Social Psychology.................................... 211

Kurt T. Dirks and David De Cremer

Chapter 10 Give and Take: Psychological Mindsets in Conflict.... 231

Francis J. Flynn

Series Foreword

Art Brief, Kim Elsbach, and Michael Frese
Series Editors

Since its emergence as an identifiable area of inquiry, organizational behavior has looked to social psychology for theoretical and methodological inspiration. Perhaps this is truer today than ever before. David De Cremer, Rolf van Dick, and Keith Murnighan's edited volume can be thought of as a taking stock of this collaboration.

They selected traditional organizational topics to assess (e.g., power, leadership, conflict, trust) as well as some that have received less attention (e.g., normative influences, entrepreneurship, antisocial behavior, immorality). In all cases, the authors chosen are superb scholars: Adam Galinsky, Tom Tyler, Robert Cialdini, Rod Kramer, Karen Jehn, Carsten De Dreu—the list goes on and on.

Readers will leave the volume with appreciation of what a social psychological approach to organizations has accomplished and a clear sense of the promise the future holds. We thank De Cremer, van Dick, and Murnighan for this fine contribution to our series.

About the Editors

David De Cremer is a professor of behavioral business ethics at Rotterdam School of Management in the Netherlands, scientific director of the Erasmus Center of Behavioral Ethics and visiting professor at the London Business School in the United Kingdom, and Ghent University in Belgium. He is the recipient of the British Psychology Society (BPS) award for Outstanding PhD in Social Psychology (2000), the Jos Jaspars Early Career Award for Outstanding Contributions to Social Psychology (awarded by the European Association of Experimental Social Psychology, 2005), the Comenius European Young Psychologist Award (awarded by the European Federation of Psychology, 2007), and the International Society for Justice Research Early Career Contribution Award (2008). He is a member of the Young Academy of Sciences in the Netherlands (Royal Netherlands Academy of Arts and Sciences, De Jonge Akademie, KNAW). De Cremer's work has been published in the top journals in both basic and applied psychology (*Journal of Experimental Social Psychology, Journal of Personality and Social Psychology, Personality and Social Psychology Bulletin, Psychological Science, Journal of Applied Psychology, Organizational Behavior and Human Decision Processes*, and *Leadership Quarterly*). His books include *Social Psychology and Economics* (Lawrence Erlbaum, 2006), *Advances in the Psychology of Justice and Affect* (Information Age Publishing, 2007), and *Psychological Perspectives on Ethical Behavior and Decision Making* (Information Age Publishing, 2009).

Rolf van Dick is a professor of social psychology at Goethe University in Frankfurt, Germany, and currently serves as associate dean. Prior to his current position, van Dick was professor of social psychology and organizational behavior at Aston Business School in Birmingham, United Kingdom. He was visiting professor at the University of Alabama (2001), the University of the Aegean in Rhodes, Greece (2002), and Kathmandu, Nepal (2009). His research interests center on the application of social identity theory in organizational settings. In particular, he is interested in identity processes in highly diverse teams and organizations. He is applying identity research in the area of mergers and acquisitions and is currently investigating leadership and identity in the field and the laboratory. Van Dick served as associate editor of *European Journal of Work & Organizational Psychology* and is or has been editor-in-chief of *British Journal of Management* and *Journal of Personnel Psychology*. He has published more than 40 books and book chapters and 70 papers in academic journals including *Academy of Management Journal, Journal of Organizational Behavior, Journal of Applied Psychology, Journal of Marketing, Journal of Vocational Behavior,* and *Journal of Personality and Social Psychology.*

J. Keith Murnighan is the Harold H. Hines Jr. Distinguished Professor of Risk Management in the Kellogg School of Management at Northwestern University. He earned his PhD and MS degrees in social psychology and a BS in psychology and math from Purdue University. Prior to joining Kellogg in 1996, he taught at the Universities of Illinois and British Columbia. He has also had visiting appointments at the London Business School, the Center for Advanced Study in the Behavioral Sciences at Stanford University, the University of Warwick in Coventry, England, the Ecole Superieure des Sciences Economiques et Commerciales (ESSEC) outside Paris, and the Fuqua School of Business at Duke University. In August 2006 he received the Distinguished Educator Award from the Academy of Management, a Career Achievement Award. His research has been published in many different academic journals, primarily in organizational behavior, psychology, and economics. His books include *The Dynamics of Bargaining Games* (Prentice Hall, 1991), *Bargaining Games: A New Approach to Strategic Thinking in Negotiations* (William Morrow, 1992), *Social Psychology in Organizations: Advances in Theory and Research* (Prentice Hall, 1993), and *The Art of High-Stakes Decision-Making: Tough Calls in a Speed-Driven World* (with John Mowen; John Wiley & Sons, 2002). His fifth book is *Social Psychology and Economics* (with David De Cremer and Marcel Zeelenberg; Lawrence Erlbaum, 2006).

About the Contributors

Karl Aquino is the Richard Poon Professor of Organizations and Society in the Organizational Behavior and Human Resources Management Division at the Sauder School of Business. His work is devoted to understanding the moral foundations of organizational and social life. His current interests are exploring how moral identity influences morally relevant cognitions, emotions, and behavior. He also studies the coping strategies people use when they have been mistreated by others, the antecedents and consequences of workplace victimization, and the role of status, power, and dominance on organizational process. Dr. Aquino's work has appeared in leading journals in management, psychology, marketing, and political science including *Academy of Management Journal, Journal of Applied Psychology, Organizational Behavior and Human Decision Processes, Journal of Marketing, Journal of Personality and Social Psychology, Journal of Experimental Social Psychology, Personnel Psychology, Organization Science, Journal of Conflict Resolution*, and *Journal of Political Psychology*. He received his PhD in organizational behavior from Northwestern University.

Matthijs Baas is an assistant professor of psychology at the University of Amsterdam. He has taught academic courses on methods and research designs in organizational psychology. His research concerns the influence of mood and motives on creativity and has been published in a number of premier outlets, including *Journal of Personality and Social Psychology* and *Psychological Bulletin*.

Robert B. Cialdini is currently Regents' Professor of Psychology and Marketing at Arizona State University, where he has also been named Distinguished Graduate Research Professor. He has held visiting scholar appointments at The Ohio State University, the Universities of California at San Diego and Santa Cruz, the Annenberg School for Communications, and both the psychology department and the Graduate School of Business at Stanford University. He has been elected president of the Society of Personality and Social Psychology. Dr. Cialdini has authored nearly 200 articles and book chapters and is the recipient of the Distinguished Scientific Achievement Award of the Society for Consumer Psychology, the Donald T. Campbell Award for Distinguished Contributions to Social Psychology, and the inaugural Peitho Award for Distinguished Contributions to the Science of Social Influence. He is widely recognized as one of the world's leading experts on social influence, authoring several books, including *Influence*, which has sold more than 1.5 million copies.

Carsten K.W. De Dreu is a professor of psychology at the University of Amsterdam. Before moving to Amsterdam, he was affiliated with the Yale School of Management, the University of Groningen, and the University of Geneva (Switzerland). His research concerns creativity and innovation, group decision making, and social conflict, and is published in academic journals such as *Journal of Applied Psychology, Organizational Behavior and Human Decision Processes, Journal of Personality and Social Psychology, Personality and Social Psychology Review*, and *Psychological Bulletin*. He serves on the editorial board of several of these journals and has been associate editor for *Personality and Social Psychology Bulletin* and *Journal of Organizational Behavior*. Dr. De Dreu's work has been recognized by several awards including the Early Career Award from the European Association for Experimental Social Psychology in 1996 and a Most Influential Article Award from the Academy of Management in 2009. He currently serves as the president of the *European Association for Social Psychology*.

Kurt T. Dirks is a professor of organizational behavior at the Olin Business School at Washington University in St. Louis. He received his PhD from the University of Minnesota. His research is focused on trust in the workplace, particularly as it relates to leaders and teams. His work has appeared in numerous journals and books including *Academy of Management Review*, the *Journal of Applied Psychology, Organizational Behavior and Human Decision Processes*, and *Organization Science*. Dr. Dirks serves on the editorial boards of *Journal of Applied Psychology, Organization Science, Organizational Behavior and Human Decision Processes*, and *Journal of Organizational Behavior*.

Francis J. Flynn received his PhD in organizational behavior from the University of California, Berkeley. From 2000 to 2006, he served as an assistant and then as an associate professor at Columbia Business School, joining the Stanford Graduate School of Business in September 2006. Flynn is a winner of multiple teaching awards, and his courses focus on leadership issues, particularly how young managers can learn to navigate complex political environments and build interpersonal influence. His research investigates issues of employee cooperation, social influence, and leadership in organizations. His recent work considers how employees can develop healthy patterns of cooperation and which employees tend to emerge as leaders in their firms. His scholarly articles have appeared in more than a dozen publications that span the fields of management and social psychology. He currently serves as associate editor for *Administrative Science Quarterly*. Flynn has worked for the Department of Commerce in the International Trade Administration, the Institute for Business and Economic Development, and the Institute for Urban and Regional Development. He has provided executive education and training for various companies, including Cisco, Johnson & Johnson, Standard & Poor's, Ixis Financial, LSI Logic, and M&T Bank, that focuses on improving employee decision-making and interpersonal leadership skills.

Michael Frese holds a joint appointment with the National University of Singapore and Leuphana, University of Lueneburg, Germany. Prior to this appointment, he taught in Berlin, at the University of Pennsylvania, at the Universities of Munich and Amsterdam, and at the University of Giessen and London Business School. He also served as president of the International Association of Applied Psychology. His research is in the area of personal initiative within a company and with entrepreneurship, both inside larger companies and in small start-ups. He leads the interdisciplinary research unit on evidence-based management and entrepreneurship at the University of Giessen and worked on several projects on entrepreneurship in Africa and other developing countries, such as China and East Germany. He is also involved in a comparative study on innovation between the United States and Germany. Recent publications include "Success and Failure of Microbusiness Owners in Africa: A Psychological Approach" and "The Psychology of Entrepreneurship" (SIOP Organizational Frontiers Series) as well as "Business Owners' Action Planning and Its Relationship to Business Success in Three African

Countries" (*Journal of Applied Psychology,* 2007). He has been editor of *Applied Psychology: An International Review,* is currently field editor of *Journal of Business Venturing,* and is on the editorial board of a number of journals including *Journal of Applied Psychology, Personnel Psychology,* and *Entrepreneurship Theory and Practice.*

Adam D. Galinsky is currently the Morris and Alice Kaplan Professor of Ethics and Decision in Management in the Kellogg School of Management at Northwestern University. He has published more than 75 scientific articles, chapters, and teaching cases in the fields of management and social psychology. Dr. Galinsky's research has received national and international recognition and attention in numerous media outlets including *The Economist, The New Yorker, The Financial Times, Wall Street Journal,* and National Public Radio. His work on auctions was selected as one of the Ideas of the Year in 2006 by *New York Times Magazine.* His dissertation received the award for the Most Outstanding Dissertation from the International Association for Conflict Management, and his work has received grants from the National Science Foundation and the American Psychological Association.

Noah J. Goldstein is assistant professor of human resources and organizational behavior in the Anderson School of Management at the University of California, Los Angeles. He has taught academic courses on a number of topics, including social psychology, management, leadership, and power and influence. His scholarly research and writing have been published in a number of premier outlets, including *Journal of Personality and Social Psychology, Psychological Science, Annual Review of Psychology,* and *Sloan Management Review.* He has also received grants from the National Science Foundation and National Institutes of Health for his research. In addition, he has consulted for a number of private and public institutions, including Accenture, the U.S. Forest Service, and the U.S. Census Bureau. Along with Drs. Cialdini and Martin, Dr. Goldstein recently coauthored a book titled *Yes!: 50 Scientifically Proven Ways to Be Persuasive* (Free Press, 2008).

S. Alexander Haslam is professor of social and organizational psychology at the University of Exeter and former Commonwealth Scholar at Macquarie University in Sydney and Jones Scholar at Emory University in Atlanta. He was associate editor of *British Journal of Social Psychology* from 1999 to 2001 and chief editor of *European Journal of Social Psychology* from 2001 to 2005. He is currently on the editorial board of eight journals including *European Journal of Social Psychology, Personality and Social Psychology Bulletin, British Journal of Management, Journal of Personality and Social Psychology,* and *Scientific American Mind.* At Exeter he is part of a team of internationally renowned researchers who conduct theory-driven research into a range of core social and organizational topics including leadership, motivation, stereotyping, group conflict, stress, and prejudice. Dr. Haslam is a fellow of the Canadian Institute of Advanced Research and a recipient of EAESP's Kurt Lewin Award.

Karen A. Jehn is professor of management at the Melbourne Business School. Her research examines intragroup conflict, group composition, and lying in organizations. Dr. Jehn has authored numerous articles in these areas that have been published in numerous journals including *Academy of Management Journal, Administrative Science Quarterly, Journal of Personality and Social Psychology,* and *Journal of Business Ethics.* She has served as director of the Solomon Asch Center for the Study of Ethnopolitical Conflict and the Sloan Foundation's Diversity Research Network. Her most recent area of interest is in asymmetric perceptions within workgroups.

Roderick M. Kramer is currently a visiting professor at Harvard's Kennedy School's Center for Public Leadership. He is on leave from the Stanford Business School, where he is the William R. Kimball Professor of Organizational Behavior. He is the author or coauthor of more than 100 scholarly articles and essays. His work has appeared in leading academic journals, such as *Journal of Personality and Social Psychology, Administrative Science Quarterly,* and *Academy of Management Journal.* He has also published in popular journals, such as the *Harvard Business Review.* He is also the author or coauthor of numerous books, including *Negotiation in Social Contexts; The Psychology of the Social Self; Trust in Organizations: Frontiers of Theory and Research, Power and Influence in Organizations; Psychology of Leadership, Trust and Distrust in Organizations; Misuses of Power: Causes and Correctives, Trust and Distrust;* and *Social Decision Making: Social Dilemmas, Social Values, and Ethical Judgments.* He also teaches at Harvard's Kennedy School of

Government and has been a visiting scholar at Oxford, London Business School, the Bellagio Center, and Hoover Institution. Dr. Kramer has consulted with a variety of organizations on issues of trust, leadership, power, group decision making, and creativity.

Joris Lammers is an assistant professor of social psychology at Tilburg University. He obtained his PhD in 2008 at the University of Groningen. He is currently working at the Tilburg Institute of Behavioral Economics Research (TIBER). His research is aimed at power and its effects on behavior and cognition, stereotyping, intergroup relations, and gender inequality. His research has appeared in *European Journal of Social Psychology, Journal of Experimental Social Psychology, Journal of Personality and Social Psychology*, and *Psychological Science.*

Sun Young Kim-Jun is pursuing a PhD in management and organizations in the Kellogg School of Management at Northwestern University. She received her MS in statistics from Stanford University and a BA in business administration from Hankuk University of Foreign Studies in Seoul, Korea. Interested in most aspects of culture, diversity, group processes, ethics, and decision making, some of her current research focuses on status and information sharing in groups, cultural differences of moral emotions, and the effects of gender in interpersonal and intergroup conflict. Her research on deception in groups has been published in the *Journal of Experimental Social Psychology.*

Kwok Leung obtained his PhD in social and organizational psychology from the University of Illinois at Urbana-Champaign and is currently a chaired professor of management at City University of Hong Kong. His major research interests include culture and behavior, international business, justice and conflict, and cross-cultural research methodology. He has published several books and over 100 articles in these various areas. He is currently senior editor of *Management and Organization Review* and former editor of *Asian Journal of Social Psychology*, deputy editor-in-chief of *Journal of International Business Studies*, and associate editor of *Journal of Cross-Cultural Psychology* and *Asia Pacific Journal of Management*. He is president-elect of the International Association for Cross-Cultural Psychology, fellow of the Association of Psychological

Science and Academy of International Business, and a member of the Society of Organizational Behavior.

Don A. Moore is an associate professor of organizational behavior at Carnegie Mellon University's Tepper School of Business and holds the chair of Carnegie Bosch Faculty Development. He received his PhD in organizational behavior from Northwestern University. His research interests include overconfidence; bargaining and negotiation; comparative judgment, especially with regard to when people believe themselves to be better or worse than others; decision making and decision-making biases; and ethical issues in business. His research has appeared in *Organizational Behavior and Human Decision Processes, Journal of Personality and Social Psychology, Organization Science, Experimental Economics*, and *Psychological Review*.

Michael W. Morris is the Chavkin-Chang Professor of Leadership in the Columbia Business School as well as professor in the psychology department at Columbia University. Dr. Morris has published on topics such as individual decision making, interpersonal influence, and social networks, with a particular emphasis on the influence of culture. His work has received many awards from scholarly societies for its originality and influence, including Outstanding Dissertation Award from the Society for Experimental Social Psychology (1993), biennial Einhorn Award for the best early career research on decision making from the Society for Judgment and Decision Making (1996), the Klineberg Intercultural and International Relations Award from the Society for Psychological Study of Social Issues (2001), and the Misumi Award from the Asian Society of Social Psychology (2004).

Bernard A. Nijstad is a professor of decision making and organizational behavior in the Faculty of Economics and Business at the University of Groningen. He received his PhD from Utrecht University and was previously affiliated with the University of Amsterdam. His research interests include individual and group creativity, individual and team innovation, decision making, and indecision. He has published about these topics in journals such as *Journal of Personality and Social Psychology, Personality and Social Psychology Review, Psychological Bulletin, Journal of Experimental Social Psychology*, and *Organizational Behavior and*

Human Decision Processes. He has also published two books: *Group Creativity* (Oxford University Press, 2003, with Paul B. Paulus) and *Group Performance* (Psychology Press, 2009).

Jane O'Reilly is a PhD student in the organizational behavior and human resources division of the Sauder School of Business at the University of British Columbia. Her research is directed at understanding both the negative and positive sides of interpersonal relationships and interactions in organizations. Specifically, her work has investigated why people mistreat one another in organizations and the harmful impact of this mistreatment. She has also investigated the unique effects of social exclusion at work. On the positive side, her work has looked at the reasons why third parties will intervene to help the victims of workplace mistreatment.

Katherine W. Phillips is associate professor of management and organizations in the Kellogg School of Management. Dr. Phillips received her PhD from the Stanford Graduate School of Business in 1999 and a BA in psychology from the University of Illinois, Urbana-Champaign. Her research focuses on understanding the impact of social and task-relevant diversity on group functioning. She has looked at the impact of gender on the use of expertise and the impact of race and other social distinctions on information sharing in groups. Generally speaking, her work seeks to understand how to get any group of people to share, listen to, and successfully integrate the ideas and information possessed by all members of the group. Dr. Phillips has published in several scholarly outlets including *Personality and Social Psychology Bulletin, Journal of Experimental Social Psychology, Organizational Behavior and Human Decision Processes, Journal of Applied Psychology,* and *Research in Organizational Behavior.*

Madan M. Pillutla is professor and chair of the organizational behavior group at the London Business School. In his current research, he focuses on the neural correlates of fair behaviors in bargaining games, incentives in groups, and the rebuilding of trust following transgressions. Recent papers include "Constrained Behavior: A Cultural Analysis of Reward Allocations in Chinese Groups" (with Farh, Lee, and Lin, *Groups and Organizational Management,* 2007) and "Power Gained, Power Lost" (with Sivanathan and Murnighan, *Organizational Behavior and Human Decision Processes,* 2008). Dr. Pillutla serves on the editorial board of

Administrative Science Quarterly, Academy of Management Review, and *Organizational Behavior and Human Decision Processes.*

Sonja Rispens is an assistant professor in the Faculty of Technology Management at the Eindhoven University of Technology in the Netherlands. She obtained her PhD in social and organizational psychology from Leiden University in the Netherlands. Her research focuses on interpersonal and intrateam conflict, aversive leadership, and the consequences of asymmetric perceptions in groups and dyads. Rispens currently serves as associate editor of *Negotiation and Conflict Management Research.* Dr. Rispens has published in several academic books and journals including *Academy of Management Journal.*

Diana Rus is assistant professor in social and organizational psychology at the University of Groningen in the Netherlands. She obtained her PhD in management from the Rotterdam School of Management at Erasmus University. Her research interests revolve primarily around issues of leadership and power as well as procedural justice and perspective taking. Some of her work on leadership has been published in the *Leadership Quarterly.*

So-Hyeon Shim is currently a PhD student of management and organizations in the Kellogg School of Management at Northwestern University. She received her BA in psychology from Korea University. Her research focuses on diversity, status, power, and trust in groups and in interpersonal relationships. Her current work explores how diversity affects people's perceptions of others' status and how this perception of status affects group members' emotions, cognition, and behavior in group decision-making contexts. She also studies the impact of unconscious thought on individuals' ethical decisions and the role of motivation on individuals' judgments and choices.

Samuel A. Swift is pursuing a PhD in organizational behavior and theory in the Tepper School of Business at Carnegie Mellon University. He received his BS in decision science as one of the first graduating classes from Carnegie Mellon's Department of Social and Decision Sciences. His research interests include subjective utility in negotiation, attribution errors in selection decisions, and the subjective utility maximizing properties of human decision making. His work has been published in *Personality and Social Psychology Bulletin*.

Tom R. Tyler is a professor of psychology in the Department of Psychology at New York University. His research interests are concerned with authority dynamics within organized groups. In particular, he has studied the role judgments about the fairness of outcomes and the justice of procedures play in shaping people's reactions to decisions made by authorities. His work demonstrates that the legitimacy of authorities is strongly linked to judgments about their fairness. More recently he has been concerned with understanding why people care about their treatment by others and has examined that issue in a variety of organizational contexts. He has also studied the implications of diversity and multiculturalism for the operation of rule and authority systems in organizations.

Section I

Introduction

1

On Social Beings and Organizational Animals: A Social Psychological Approach to Organizations

David De Cremer
Rotterdam School of Management, Erasmus University

Rolf van Dick
Department of Social Psychology, Goethe University

J. Keith Murnighan
Kellogg School of Management, Northwestern University

One of the most important ways to advance scientific thinking is to engage in interdisciplinary collaborations rather than working solely within the core of a subfield. Having people from within and outside a field analyze and evaluate knowledge has a host of benefits: It stimulates questions that might never come up while working within a single framework; it introduces new and alternative ways of looking at old problems; and it provides all sorts of unexpected and otherwise unlikely insights.

In a similar vein, this book presents an attempt to integrate the fields of social psychology and organizations/management. In March 2009, we organized a conference on "Social Psychology and Organizations" in the Kellogg School of Management at Northwestern University, sponsored by the Kellogg School and three of its centers (the Dispute Resolution Research Center, the Center for Executive Women, and the Kellogg Teams and Groups Center), as well as the Erasmus Center of Behavioral Ethics at Rotterdam School of Management and the Department of Social Psychology at Goethe University, Frankfurt. Our goal was to bring together accomplished researchers in social psychology and organizations/

management to hear about each other's work and, even more importantly, to discuss and think about research projects that were conducted in each of the two fields but that, too often, were treated as unique to one field or the other. The meeting stimulated a tremendously positive atmosphere of intellectual exchange, making the conference a complete success and making us even more enthusiastic about this volume. We have high hopes that this simple beginning encourages similar interactions and insights, for these two fields each have the potential to make enormous contributions to the other.

This book presents an overview of conference participants' research. Many of these scholars have provided a chapter that addresses why they are interested in their research field (social psychology or organizations/management) and in the topics they study and how they might relate to the other of the two fields. Each chapter indicates that the discourse and practice of management and organizational behavior has much to do with social psychology. A slightly altered converse is also true: Many of the ideas expressed and investigated in social psychology concern issues that are centrally relevant to management and organizations. Both fields share many points of view and interests, even though cross-fertilization of the two fields has hardly begun. Thus, increasing the communication between the fields would be particularly fruitful—but a change of attitude within each field, toward each other, may be needed first. Although the two fields have been collaborating, inspiring, and motivating each other, in many ways these interactions are often implicit. The aim of the present book is to make this mutual influence more explicit and to shape and encourage integrative thinking in both fields.

SOCIAL PSYCHOLOGY AND ORGANIZATIONS: UNDERSTANDING WORK LIFE

We spend many of our waking hours at work and much of our work life in organizations. Like any other social context, a variety of social influence mechanisms—which we are sometimes aware of and sometimes not—affect us at work. Our social–work contexts influence our minds, feelings, behaviors, and decisions. Attempts to understand how social influences affect our employees, our managers, and our organizations open up a diverse, dynamic array of important questions. In particular, as social scientists, it is incumbent upon us to understand how social elements influence individuals and how individuals influence their social relationships. The field of social psychology is well suited to meet these challenges.

William James (1890) defined the broad field of psychology as "the description and explanation of states of consciousness in human beings … the study of … sensations, desires, emotions, cognitions, reasonings, decision, volitions, and the like" (p.i.). Social psychology extends this approach, defining itself as a "scientific attempt to understand and explain how the thoughts, feelings, and behaviors of individuals are influenced by the actual, imagined, or implied presence of other human beings" (Allport, 1954, p. 5). Thus, social psychologists are primarily concerned with individuals (affect, motivations, and cognition) and groups (individuals' interactions). Social situations (including social others) affect individuals and individuals affect social situations. As Kelley (2000, p. 11) noted, "the proper study of social psychology is the study of interaction and its immediate determinants and consequences."

Organizations are, obviously, entities that include individuals, groups, interactions, and all that accompanies them. They are also repositories of uncertainty: They present people with challenges, dilemmas, and conundrums. At the same time, they engage people positively, in centrally important personal ways, often providing them with important elements of their personal identities. Organizations are also eminently social entities that have important pasts and hopeful futures (just like people do).

More obviously, and centrally, individuals populate, run, and confuse organizations, making their analysis, *in situ*, eminently critical for understanding organizational effectiveness and success as well as individual satisfaction and well-being. In addition, understanding how people react to their organizations' challenges and how managers can encourage and lead organizational members toward actions that benefit the organization and all of its members requires singular insights into how and why people respond to uncertainty. More pointedly, socio-organizational scientists need to pursue an understanding of the influence of social processes on perceptions of uncertainty, conflict, cooperation, and ambiguity and how we can deal with these perceptions effectively. Social psychology provides conceptual tools and theories to tackle these managerial and organizational challenges: It can help identify the questions that need to be addressed and for which deeper insights and theories are required.

SOCIAL/ORGANIZATIONAL RESEARCH THEMES

As editors of this volume, we wanted to include authors who have done exciting, path-breaking research in these two fields—according to us. Thus, our selections convey an implicit message about our research values. As we put this volume together, we realized that embedded within our values are a series of research themes.

A first theme concerns how individual employees perceive organizations and organizational phenomena and how their perceptions provide a basis for understanding their organization-related behavior. This theme clearly requires an integrative approach that would use psychological insights to build an understanding of the minds of organizational members. Theories of individuals such as attribution theory, cognitive dissonance, psychological reactance, and theories of attitudes and persuasion can all contribute and guide explorations into an individual's work motivations, perceptions, and attributions—concepts that are immediately relevant for situations like job interviews or performance evaluations.

A second theme concerns how individual organizational members interact in highly interdependent settings, resulting in competitive, cooperative, or conflict relationships. This theme could employ social psychological theories on cooperation, aggression, justice and fairness, and affiliation to help explain how people interrelate. Specific issues might include how people approach and achieve smooth and effective management in organizations. On one hand, leaders and managers may develop more personal relationships to manage their individual employees (e.g., Leader–Member Exchange Theory, Graen & Uhl-Bien, 1995); on the other hand, management and leadership in organizations are usually accomplished within teams. Theories of groups have provided a long-term, central interest in social psychology (Moreland, Hogg, & Hains, 1994), an interest that waned in the 1970s and 1980s but that has now been supplanted and expanded by increasing interest from scholars in business schools (e.g., Phillips et al.'s chapter in this volume). Theories of in-group interactions now address, among other issues, social influence, social identity, intergroup behavior, and faultlines, all of which have obvious relevance for organizations.

A related issue that also emphasizes interactions might use the conceptual analyses of social psychology not only to open a window into leadership and management effectiveness but also to understand the dynamics of cooperation and conflict within and between groups (e.g., Bornstein, 2003). In fact, how organizations and their managers can handle conflict so that all interaction partners take responsibility and create trustworthy and fair climates is a central aspect in leadership. When entire organizations act as groups during mergers and acquisitions, for example, their interactions have a huge impact on all of the organizations' individual members. Under such circumstances, it is crucial to maintain, build, and restore trust; it is also crucial that leaders use fair and legitimate decision-making procedures.

A third theme concerns the social context and the culture of the workplace. Organizations differ in the goals and values they stress and in how they move to achieve them. Beliefs, both individual and cultural, are important social influencers, and so are groups, especially in organizations. It is imperative for organizations to understand and value the broad variation in individual beliefs and team and group cultures so that they can effectively coordinate their efforts. Also, when individual beliefs differ from organizational beliefs, it becomes critical to know how to merge those beliefs into a central, motivating culture: Accommodation then becomes an important internal challenge for contemporary organizations. Social psychology has the potential to contribute to our understanding of these influences as well, as psychologists have often studied societal and cultural influences on individuals' everyday attitudes and behavior as well as their cross-cultural interactions (e.g., Nisbett, Peng, Choi, & Norenzayan, 2001).

To summarize, we put this book together to provide an overview of recent developments in social psychological theory with a particular focus on their application to organizational issues. We hope that you are inspired by its content.

OUTLINE OF THE BOOK

Following this introductory chapter, the book is divided into three parts.

Section II

The first group of chapters focuses on leadership, power, and social influence. It starts with chapter 2 by Adam Galinsky, Diana Rus, and Joris Lammers, who review a wide array of research on the effects of power and powerlessness on individuals' basic cognitive processes. Perceptions of power have many positive effects, but some are negative; perceptions of powerlessness have many negative effects, but some are positive. The chapter argues that people are fundamentally affected by whether they feel powerful. Not surprisingly, this has significant consequences for organizational life, and the last half of the chapter explores these effects, with a special emphasis on how the positive effects of hierarchy can be harnessed to achieve great organizational outcomes while minimizing hierarchy's deleterious effects.

Chapter 3, on justice and leadership, by David De Cremer and Tom Tyler, makes the point that, although the leadership and procedural justice literatures have much in common, little exchange and communication has taken place between both research fields. These authors therefore discuss a contingency approach in which it is shown that the effects of procedural justice in organizations (and the reasons why they exert such influence) depend on the specific leadership style adopted by the enacting leader.

Chapter 4, on social influence, by Noah Goldstein and Robert Cialdini, reviews the social psychological literature on how social norms motivate and guide people's actions, concentrating primarily on the focus theory of normative conduct. The chapter discusses how social psychological theories and findings in the domain of social norms can contribute to an understanding of organizational behavior, focusing primarily on descriptive norms (what most people do) and injunctive norms (what most people approve or disapprove). The chapter indicates how the use (or unintentional misuse) of social norms in an organization's internal communications can motivate those in the workplace to behave in ways that are consistent with (or counter to) organizational goals.

Chapter 5, on entrepreneurship, by Michael Frese, addresses a variety of questions within the umbrella of action theory. The chapter focuses first on a series of questions, including a discussion of the personality, educational, and cultural factors that facilitate the emergence of entrepreneurs. The chapter then discusses psychological theories on self-management, self-regulation, and social learning processes to understand how would-be entrepreneurs make the decision to start an organization. The chapter shows clearly how an action regulation perspective provides a particularly useful foundation for understanding the processes that result in the founding of a company.

Section III

The next group of chapters focuses on conflict, cooperation, and decision making and begins with Chapter 6, on responsive leaders and their reactions to identity threats, by Roderick Kramer. The chapter reviews the importance of identity for leaders (how they are socially constructed and negotiated and how they can be restored or repaired). The chapter centers on the relevance of self-presentation and impression management skills for a leader's persuasion, influence, and negotiation skills. The focus highlights the importance of identity-threatening predicaments and uses qualitative data to inductively investigate how several notable leaders responded to these risks.

Chapter 7, on negotiation and individual decision making, by Don Moore and Samuel Swift, centers its attention on the negative organizational effects of overconfidence, including stock market bubbles. The chapter uses the benefits of confidence, such as motivating and inspiring others and promoting both persistence and positive psychological adaptation, as a foundation to explore the psychology of confidence. The discussion notes both benefits and costs, identifies organizational implications, and indicates when confidence becomes overconfidence. The chapter suggests that understanding the organizational implications of confidence depends fundamentally on understanding the three different forms of overconfidence: overestimation, overplacement, and overprecision.

Chapter 8, on conflict, by Sonja Rispens and Karen Jehn, describes the ongoing debate in the organizational literature about whether and under what conditions conflict in workgroups might be beneficial. Theory from both social and cognitive psychology informs this debate. One of the shortcomings of past conflict research is that it often assumes that all group members perceive the same amount of conflict, without acknowledging that members may have different perceptions about the amount of conflict within their group. In addition, whether individuals perceive conflict as a threat or challenge can determine whether it is beneficial or detrimental. This chapter also discusses the research on constructive and destructive conflict and presents a new framework of asymmetric perceptions to inform the organizational research on workgroup conflict.

Chapter 9, on trust and repairing trust, by Kurt Dirks and David De Cremer provides a scientific explanation of trust and its operation. The chapter reviews research that addresses a series of fundamental questions:

What benefits accrue from trust and when are they realized? What are the psychological processes that govern the establishment or destruction of trust? When trust is damaged, how can it be repaired?

Chapter 10, on prosocial behavior in organizations, by Francis Flynn, argues that helping behavior is the main key to personal and organizational effectiveness. To defend this claim, the chapter summarizes and integrates findings from a series of studies of everyday helping behavior and employee cooperation. Taken together, this work paints a compelling picture of giving and receiving help—not as an obligation but as an opportunity.

Section IV

These chapters center on what we call "contemporary issues." The topics covered in part 4 vary widely and span a range of important and timely areas such as diversity, negative behavior, creativity, stress, and culture. The central question of Chapter 11, on diversity, by Katherine Phillips, Sun Young Kim-Jun, and So-Hyeon Shim, concerns the means by which diversity affects the process and performance of groups. Although this may seem like a simple question, the dynamics of diversity create a variety of complications. The chapter reviews the diversity research of both organizational and social psychological scholars and highlights its most recent perspectives. The common wisdom that diversity is beneficial because people who are "different" will bring different perspectives to the table is systematically examined and shown to fall short in explaining the benefits of diversity. Instead, it appears that sociocognitive and motivational processes drive individuals' behavior in diverse settings.

Chapter 12, on antisocial and negative behavior in organizations, by Karl Aquino and Jane O'Reilly, attempts to synthesize a program of 15 years of research on various forms of antisocial behavior in organizations—that is, actions performed by employees that have the potential to harm other employees or the organization. The chapter focuses on both individual- and organizational-level predictors of such behaviors and illustrates how social psychological theories can help explain the causes of such behaviors and also provide insights into how they might be minimized. The chapter also situates this work within the broader research stream of antisocial behavior in organizations to suggest new directions for future research and to draw both managerial and practical implications from it.

Chapter 13, on creativity, by Carsten De Dreu, Bernard Nijstad, and Matthijs Baas, integrates a large social psychological literature on individual and group creativity with an equally large but thus far disconnected literature on team and organizational innovation. The chapter summarizes research in the laboratory and in organizational field settings to illustrate how applied work on team innovation benefits from basic social psychological experiments on individual and group creativity while recognizing important boundary conditions. The discussion concludes by identifying new avenues for research and more fine-tuned implications for practice.

Chapter 14, on social identity at work, by Alexander Haslam and Rolf van Dick, aims to demonstrate the relevance and usefulness of social identity principles to the analysis of occupational health and stress. The chapter briefly outlines the social identity approach and summarizes existing research that has explored the relationship between social identity and stress at work. Existing evidence points to the positive role that social identification can play in buffering employees from the negative effects of stress—in particular, because it serves as a basis for social support and collective resistance. However, evidence also points to problems associated with high levels of identification that can contribute to both exhaustion and bullying. The discussion focuses on how the positive potential of social identities can be realized; it also points to a range of complexities surrounding both the conceptualization and management of stress at work.

Chapter 15, on ethics in organizations, by Madan Pillutla, first suggests that work groups are central to organizational behavior and that, as a result, they must also be central to ethical behavior at work. The chapter uses an appreciation of the social psychology of groups to develop a model of unethical behavior by individuals within organizations that focuses on individual status, feelings of inclusion within groups, and group cohesion. Research suggests when and how these three factors either facilitate or inhibit ethical action in organizations.

The final chapter, Chapter 16, on culture and innovation, by Kwok Leung and Michael Morris, notes that even though there is considerable research on creativity in organizations, little research has explored the relationship between national culture and innovativeness in the workplace. The influence of national culture is at least twofold. First, culture can influence the definition of innovativeness, and what is regarded as innovative in one culture may not be regarded as so in a different culture. Second, some cultural elements may promote innovativeness, while others may discourage it. For instance, innovativeness may be less encouraged in collectivist than in individualist cultures. The chapter evaluates the validity of these two propositions based on findings from diverse settings and develops a model of culture and innovativeness for the workplace that takes into account implicit theories of innovativeness and the dynamics underlying the intention to develop novel ideas and products. Culture is assumed to influence the definition of innovativeness, creative self-efficacy, and the importance attached to a creative role, which in turn influence the intention to be innovative.

In conclusion, we hope that readers of these chapters will feel that the social psychology lens makes every analysis of organizations more complete. We as editors feel that what our colleagues have presented in their respective chapters is groundbreaking and will inspire future research and theory building alike. We are extremely grateful to all contributors for their input in this enterprise and for their prompt responses to all our requests. We also want to thank various people who helped with reviewing the chapters, particularly Johannes Graser, Tina Tai-Chi Wu, and Sebastian Stegmann, and also those who made the conference a success with their perfect organizational skills, particularly Andrew Marfia. Finally, we would like to thank the people at Psychology Press, namely, Anne Duffy and Erin Flaherty for their encouragement and help throughout the project.

REFERENCES

Allport, G. W. (1954). The historical background of modern social psychology. In G. Lindzey (Ed.), *Handbook of social psychology* (Vol. 1, pp. 3–56). Reading, MA: Addison-Wesley.

Bornstein, G. (2003). Intergroup conflict: Individual, group, and collective interests. *Personality and Social Psychology Review, 7*, 129–145.

James, W. (1890). *The principles of psychology.* New York: Holt and Macmillan.

Graen, G. B., & Uhl-Bien, M. (1995). Relationship-based approach to leadership: Development of leader–member exchange (LMX) theory of leadership over 25 years: Applying a multi-level multi-domain perspective. *Leadership Quarterly, 6*, 219–247.

Kelley, H. H. (2000). The proper study of social psychology. *Social Psychology Quarterly, 63*, 3–15.

Moreland, R. L., Hogg, M. A., & Hains, S. C. (1994). Back to the future: Social psychological research on groups. *Journal of Experimental Social Psychology, 30,* 527–555.

Nisbett, R. E., Peng, K., Choi, I., & Norenzayan, A. (2001). Culture and systems of thought: Holistic vs. analytic cognition. *Psychological Review, 108,* 291–310.

Section II

Leadership, Power, and Social Influence

2

Power:
A Central Force Governing Psychological, Social, and Organizational Life

Adam D. Galinsky
Northwestern University

Diana Rus
University of Groningen

Joris Lammers
Tilburg University

Who has power, who is affected by power, and how power is acquired and exercised provide the foundation for understanding human relations (Russell, 1938/1960). Indeed, to truly understand the dynamics of any organization or firm requires knowing where power resides and where influence flows. The dispersion of power within and between organizations can emerge from formal systems or through the process of informal interaction and is typically conveyed through organizational charts or network maps. In this chapter, we move beyond research exploring how power is achieved and represented in organizational forms and focus on how having or lacking power fundamentally alters basic thought, emotion, and behavior (Keltner, Gruenfeld, & Anderson, 2003; Kipnis, 1972).

We define power as asymmetric control over valued resources in social relations (Fiske, 1993; Magee & Galinsky, 2008; Thibaut & Kelley, 1959). In any given interaction, one party has more control over and access to some resource that can range from material goods, services, and currency to more intangible elements such as information or affection. This definition of power captures an underlying asymmetry in dependence between those who possess power and those who do not, effectively framing it as an inherently social variable.

Although power emerges in a specific social context, the experience of power also fundamentally transforms an individual's psychological states and processes. The idea that power has metamorphic effects has already been professed in the ground-breaking work of Kipnis (1972, 1976) and has been substantiated in more recent power research (e.g., Galinsky, Gruenfeld, & Magee, 2003; Keltner et al., 2003). Indeed, it has been argued that power and its effects can become a psychological property of the individual (e.g., Bargh, Raymond, Pryor, & Strack, 1995; Chen, Lee-Chai, & Bargh, 2001; Galinsky et al., 2003), allowing the effects of power to endure beyond the particular social context where it was initially experienced (Anderson & Galinsky, 2006; Chen et al., 2001; Gruenfeld, Inesi, Magee, & Galinsky, 2008; Guinote, 2007a; Smith & Trope, 2006). Consequently, power's psychological effects can be activated by having actual control over resources (Anderson & Berdahl, 2002), by recalling a time when one had power over others (Galinsky et al., 2003), or by being exposed, even subliminally, to words related to power (Bargh et al., 1995; Zhong, Galinsky, Magee, & Maddux, 2009). Each of these methods for activating the experience and concept of power demonstrates remarkably similar effects.

The most influential theory for articulating how power transforms its possessors is the Power-Approach Theory (Keltner et al., 2003). This theory states that power triggers the behavioral approach system, which is posited to increase sensitivity to rewards, such as food, achievement, sex, and social bonding, whereas powerlessness activates the behavioral inhibition system, an alarm system that triggers anxiety, avoidance, and response inhibition. Because of the relative activation of these two complementary neurobiological systems, power has a number of predictable effects on cognition and behavior.

In the ensuing sections of this review, we will discuss how the experience of power has three main effects: (1) power affects social attentiveness; (2) power makes the person; and (3) power reveals the person (both the person's personality and culture). Although scholars as well as laypeople often portray the effects of power as being predominantly negative, in this chapter we will discuss how these effects can be either constructive or pernicious depending on the person and on the situation and the larger context within which these effects play out.

Each of these separate streams of power's effects can be united by the robust finding that power increases a focus on goals and facilitates goal-directed behavior (Galinsky et al., 2003; Guinote, 2007a; Smith, Jostmann, Galinsky, & van Dijk, 2008). The power-induced focus on goals explains how the powerful ignore the perspective of others while shifting their attention to instrumental others who will allow the powerful to achieve their goals. The prominence of goals can elucidate how power both trans-forms people into optimistic, abstract-thinking, action-oriented individuals while also revealing the person's personality and magnifying culture differences. Finally, we discuss how appreciating that current goals carry greater psychological weight for the powerful can add insight into how power can be harnessed in the service of leadership.

POWER AFFECTS SOCIAL ATTENTIVENESS

The statement that the powerful pay less attention to others has almost become a truism. By definition, those who hold the reigns of power are less dependent on others, capable of satisfying their own needs and desires without relying on or needing anyone's resources but their own. Because of this relative independence, the powerful are less concerned with how others see them or judge their actions and are less attentive to others' internal experiences (e.g., Galinsky, Magee, Inesi, & Gruenfeld, 2006; Galinsky, Magee, Gruenfeld, Whitson, & Liljenquist, 2008; van Kleef, De Dreu, Pietroni, & Manstead, 2006). In contrast, those who lack social con-trol are motivated to understand the needs of their more powerful coun-terparts and the shifting sands of their environment, which leads them to systematically consider the factors and forces that compel others to act as they do (Keltner et al., 2003). To be in power means that more eyes are focused on you, yet the powerful feel relatively immune to these stares, acting as if they are invisible.

Power has been associated with two broad effects on social attention. First, power decreases the tendency to step into others' shoes and view the world from their vantage point or identify and connect with their emotions (e.g., Galinsky, Magee, Inesi, & Gruenfeld, 2006; van Kleef, Oveis, van der Löwe, LuoKogan, Goetz, & Keltner, 2008). Second, power increases instrumental attention to others, leading the powerful to view their social interaction partners through a lens of self-interest (e.g., Gruenfeld et al., 2008; Overbeck & Park, 2006).

Power Reduces Perspective Taking, Compassion, and Conformity

Converging research evidence paints an image of the powerful as being notoriously poor perspective takers. Indeed, power seems to lock individuals into their own myopic perspectives, placing a blind spot on considering the unique viewpoints of others. Galinsky and colleagues (2006) demonstrated that possessing power seems to impair the ability to take others' perspectives and to form an accurate understanding of how others experience the world. In their studies, the powerful were less likely than the powerless to spontaneously take the visual perspective of others, to take others' background knowledge into account, and to correctly identify others' emotional expressions. In one study, Galinsky et al. had participants draw the capital letter "E" on their foreheads with a marker. One way to complete the task is to draw an "E" as though the self is reading it, which leads to a backward and illegible "E" from the perspective of another person. The other way to approach the task is to draw the "E" as though another person is reading it, which leads to production of an "E" that is backward to the self. Powerful individuals were three times more likely to draw a self-focused "E." Experiencing power seems to almost instantly impair the ability to see things from other people's points of view.

Power also leads to increased difficulty recognizing and adjusting for the fact that others do not share their privileged perspective. For example, the same semantic content (e.g., "Nice suit!") can be received as a compliment or as a thinly veiled insult, depending on knowledge of the speaker's tastes and previous interactions. Galinsky et al. (2006) presented participants with a message that on its face seemed sincere ("About the restaurant, it was marvelous, just marvelous"), but privileged background knowledge about the speaker's intentions suggested a sarcastic interpretation (the person had a very bad experience). The powerful inaccurately predicted that others would see the world as they saw it (i.e., that the message was sarcastic) even though these others lacked access to the private knowledge of the disappointing experience.

These studies all demonstrate that the powerful anchored more heavily on their own points of view and were less accurate than less powerful individuals in assessing others' thoughts. Taking this line of reasoning one step further, Lammers, Gordijn, and Otten (2008) showed that, because the powerful are less concerned with taking others' perspectives and understanding what others think about them, they are less likely to activate and use metastereotypes in intergroup situations. Metastereotypes are stereotypical assessments about an out-group's perception of the in-group: "How do I think that they think we are alike." Typically, metastereotypes are used to understand and make sense of other people's behaviors and intentions, especially when more fine-grained individuating information is unavailable. In these cases, people should be motivated to try to see what other people think of them. However, across four experiments, Lammers et al. found that whereas the powerless, who are after all more motivated to understand how others see them, engaged in significant amounts of metastereotyping, the powerful did not.

Power also impairs emotional identification and social connection. For example, the powerful were less accurate in comprehending others' emotional states in Galinsky et al.'s (2006) studies. Similarly, in research by van Kleef et al. (2008) power was associated with diminished reciprocal emotional responses to another person's suffering (feeling distress at another person's distress) and with less compassion. They found that this emotional disengagement was driven by power-related differences in the motivation to affiliate with and connect with others. A similar finding was found by Kipnis (1972), who found that, when offered an opportunity to meet their subordinates for refreshments after the experiment was completed, participants who had played the role of manager in the power condition (i.e., who were given institutional means of rewarding and punishing their employees) expressed less interest than managers in the no-power condition (i.e., who had to rely on their powers of persuasion to influence their employees). These results all provide further support that power creates a psychological distance from others.

The fact that the powerful turn a blind eye to other people is not necessarily negative. For example, power immunizes negotiators from the influence of their opponents' emotional displays, with low-power negotiators conceding more to an angry opponent compared with high-power negotiators (van Kleef et al., 2006). Power protects negotiators from being swayed by the strategic displays of emotions that are designed to induce concessions.

Possessing power shields the individual not only from being influenced by the displays of others' emotion but also from the conforming pressure of their attitudes. For example, Briñol, Petty, Valle, Rucker, and Becerra (2007) found that power protected the individual from falling prey to others' attempts to influence them. Briñol and colleagues presented high- and low-power participants with persuasive messages for a new cell phone and asked them to report their attitudes toward the product; they found that high-power participants' attitudes were not affected by the persuasive message, whereas low-power participants held more favorable attitudes toward the product (but only when presented with a strong message compared with a weak message). Galinsky and colleagues (2008) also showed that power protects individuals from succumbing to peer conformity pressure. Participants in one of the Galinsky et al. studies first completed a relatively boring task and then were presented with other participants' favorable (bogus) task ratings. If power shields individuals from the influence of others' opinions, then powerful participants should be more likely to express their true attitudes and rate the task less favorably. That is exactly what Galinsky and colleagues found: High-power participants' task ratings were less favorable than low-power participants', suggesting that the powerful can successfully resist the pernicious pressure to act like the rest of the "herd."

In sum, the powerful tend to myopically see the world through their own eyes, to be less concerned with how others see them or judge their actions, and to ignore others' opinions and emotions. This can have both negative as well as positive consequences depending on the context and the task at hand. Although power seems to reduce overall social attention, it in fact focuses it in very specific ways, a topic we turn to now.

Power Increases Instrumental Attention

Power makes people more inclined to view others in an instrumental manner, as a tool toward the achievement of their own goals. For example, a series of studies by Overbeck and Park (2006) showed that when the powerful are pursuing "people-centered" goals they individuate their targets by paying increased attention to and remembering more unique information about them, but if they are pursuing "product-centered" goals they recall less correct unique information about their subordinates. The goals of the powerful directed their social attention.

A second line of studies by Gruenfeld and colleagues (2008) further added to this idea that power increases objectification, which they define as the process of relating to social targets as though they were objects based on the utility of their goal-relevant attributes. Gruenfeld and colleagues asked high-ranking senior executives and MBA students to describe either a relationship with a subordinate (high power) or a relationship with a peer (equal power) at work. Subsequently, participants had to rate their perceptions of the described relationship on an objectification scale (e.g., "I tend to contact this person only when I need something from him/her"). Both senior executives and MBA students reported greater objectification in their relationships with a subordinate than with a peer. Similarly, senior executives, who arguably are more powerful than MBA students, tended to view both relationships with subordinates as well as peers in more instrumental terms. Therefore, greater personal power was associated with greater objectification independent of relationship type. In essence, power increases the tendency to view others through an instrumental lens and focuses one's attention on those aspects of others that serve one's salient interests or goals. Consequently, powerful individuals approach and attend to useful others who will help them complete these goals (Gruenfeld et al., 2008).

This tendency to view others in an instrumental manner can have both positive and negative consequences for the organization and for others. For example, Gruenfeld et al. (2008) found that power-induced tendencies toward objectification can increase organizational efficiency. They created a hiring situation in which some job candidates were better fits for specific positions (e.g., a salesperson needed to be extroverted). In this situation high-power individuals were better able to select the candidate whose attributes best matched the hiring criterion. Similarly, Lammers and Stapel (2009b) found that, in a medical simulation, high-power senior surgeons' more object-like view on patients helped them to administer a painful but effective medical treatment. Low-power nurses and junior surgeons were hindered in doing so, because they focused too much on the pain and suffering caused by it, preferring instead a painless but less effective medical treatment. A different way instrumental attention can have positive consequences is that, because the powerful have a more object-like focus on other people, they are also better able to ignore individual idiosyncrasies that people have to deviate from preestablished rules and to make exceptions. Lammers and Stapel (2009a) demonstrated this by testing the effect of power on moral reasoning and showing that low-power individuals get influenced by the needs and suffering of single individuals that lead them to make exceptions to help these individuals. The instrumental view on others by the powerful makes it much easier for them to ignore idiosyncrasies and to stick to formal rules. This relationship between power and objectification might be dysfunctional in the realm of social relationships (leading people to feel as if their full humanity is being minimized) but is functional for the attainment of organizational goals.

POWER MAKES THE PERSON

The previous section suggested that power fundamentally alters how people perceive and relate to other individuals. Other works suggests that power transforms individuals, producing predictable effects on thought and behavior. A deluge of recent research directly following from the Power-Approach Theory (Keltner et al., 2003) has unearthed a variety of power-induced effects that can all be classified as altering basic neuropsychological processes. Based on this research, the powerful appear to be optimistic, action-oriented individuals with broad visions of the future. On the flipside of the coin they also seem to be overconfident risk takers who are prone to illusions of control.

Power Increases Assertive Action

The possession or experience of power has been shown to directly lead to the taking of assertive action in a variety of contexts. For example, Galinsky et al. (2003) had participants first recall an incident where they had power over someone else (i.e., high power) or where someone else had power over them (i.e., low power). Subsequently, participants were led into a different room to complete some others tasks and were placed at a desk where a fan was blowing directly onto them. In this situation where it was unclear to participants whether they were allowed to act upon this annoying stimulus, the powerful were more likely than the powerless to take assertive action and either turn off or remove the fan.

Similarly, in a bargaining context, high-power negotiators were more likely to both initiate a negotiation and to make a first offer compared with their less powerful partners (Magee, Galinsky, & Gruenfeld, 2007). Congruent with previous research showing that both of these assertive strategies are beneficial to the accumulation of resources (Babcock & Laschever, 2003; Galinsky & Mussweiler, 2001), powerful negotiators in the Magee et al. (2007) studies garnered a distinct financial advantage from initiating negotiations and making first offers.

Not only are the powerful more likely to take assertive action to ensure their own well-being (i.e., get rid of the annoying fan), but also this action orientation can lead to good outcomes for others and for communities. For example, the powerful are also more likely to race to the help of those in distress in emergency situations (Whitson, Galinsky, Magee, Gruenfeld, & Liljenquist, 2007). Whitson et al. (2007) found that high-power participants were more likely to spring into action and rush to the help of a confederate that had fallen off a ladder in contrast to their low-power counterparts. Similarly, Galinsky et al. (2003) presented participants with a public-goods dilemma task and measured the amount of resources they chose to contribute to replenish a dwindling resource pool. They found that the powerful were more likely to contribute to and therefore to preserve a public good and community-shared resource compared with powerless or control participants. Here again, the tendency toward action has constructive or destructive consequences depending on the goals of the powerful.

POWER INCREASES OPTIMISM AND RISK TAKING

The psychological experience of power increases a general sense of optimism. For example, Anderson and Galinsky (2006) found that more powerful individuals tended to believe that their futures held both more positive (e.g., enjoying a job after graduation) and less negative events (e.g., having gum problems) in store for them. Interestingly, these optimistic views of their own future extended to events outside of participants' actual control (e.g., avoiding an encounter with a dangerous snake on vacation; having their home's value double in 10 years). Finally, the powerful are more likely not only to see their own futures clad in opportunities and devoid of danger but also to see the world as being less dangerous and filled with fewer risks. In a different study, Anderson and Galinsky

(2006) asked participants to estimate the number of fatalities per year in the United States due to various causes of death (e.g., plane crashes, lung cancer). Consistent with the idea that the powerful pay more attention to positive than to negative aspects of the world, high-power participants underestimated the number of fatalities connected to the various causes of death compared with low-power participants.

Feeling powerful not only makes individuals more prone to seeing the world through rose-colored glasses, but it also increases their attraction to risk, both in terms of exhibiting greater risk preferences as well as of making riskier choices (Anderson & Galinsky, 2006; Maner, Gailliot, Butz, & Peruche, 2007). Because powerful people tend to inhabit reward-rich environments where they are relatively unencumbered by the specter of punishment, they focus their attention on potential rewards and are less sensitive to potential threats in their surroundings. When presented with a risky choice, they are therefore more likely to "see" the potential gains and to turn a blind eye to the potential losses associated with the risky course of action. Anderson and Galinsky (2006) found powerful individuals were more likely to be risk seeking in their choices, to see less danger in unprotected sex, and to exhibit a greater willingness to engage in these risky behaviors as well as to resort to risky information-sharing tactics by divulging their personal interests in a negotiation context.

Power Increases Illusions of Control

Possessing or experiencing power not only transforms individuals into optimistic assertive doers but also increases their general sense of control, even in situations where this control is illusory. Participants in a study by Fast, Gruenfeld, Sivanathan, and Galinsky (2009) were promised a reward for correctly predicting the outcome of a single roll of a six-sided die and were given a choice of rolling the die themselves or of having someone else roll it for them. Deciding to roll the die is indicative of an illusory sense of control because it suggests that the actor believes he or she can influence the outcome of a random event. Consistent with the notion that power increases a sense of control, more (100%) high-power participants chose to roll the die than did low-power participants (58%) or those in a control condition (69%). Moreover, Fast et al. found converging evidence that this power-induced sense of control mediates the relationship between power and action as well as between power and optimism. In other words, powerful people are more optimistic and take more assertive action because they experience a heightened sense of control.

Having a sense of control can result in both positive and negative downstream consequences. A perceived sense of control can shield the individual from falling prey to the demons of depression (e.g., Abramson, Seligman, & Teasdale, 1978) or from developing superstitious beliefs based on seeing illusory patterns in their environment (Whitson & Galinsky, 2008). These optimistic illusions of control can allow the powerful to achieve unimaginable accomplishments by embarking on low-probability journeys and persisting when others would give up (Taylor & Brown, 1988), leading the powerful to make the seemingly impossible possible. But the relationship between power and illusory control might also contribute to escalation of commitment, leading themselves and others down disastrous paths of entrapment.

Power Increases Abstract Thinking

Power fundamentally shapes the way individuals construe the world by leading them to process information more abstractly, to see the forest beyond the trees. For example, Smith and Trope (2006) found this direct link between power and abstract thinking: The powerful in their studies generated more abstract representations of stimuli, were better at perceiving structure and patterns, and were more likely to focus on central aspects and to capture the gist of information. The powerful thus tend to process information differently from the powerless by focusing their attention on global rather than on local features of stimuli (Guinote, 2007b). This power-induced tendency to see the "big picture" and to abstract away from specific details has also been replicated in a field study by Milliken, Magee, Lam, and Menezes (2008). The authors analyzed media statements immediately in the aftermath of Hurricane Katrina and found that government officials described the events in more abstract terms than did volunteers or powerless victims. This tendency toward more abstract thinking can be linked back to power's effects on illusion of control and optimism. Greater abstraction in thought has been linked to the tendency to focus on desirable features of the environment and less on what makes a plan feasible (Trope & Liberman, 2003).

The tendency exhibited by the powerful to focus on the general picture and to address problems at a higher level of abstraction can easily lead to communication distortions between high- and low-power individuals.

Whereas the powerful may feel that they are addressing the root of the problem, the powerless may feel that their specific interests and perspectives are not being taken into account. On a more positive note, this propensity to detach oneself from the here and now and to keep an eye on the broader picture can result in the creation of grand visions for the future that can both motivate and inspire and allow people to chart a steady course of action less likely to be derailed by minor adversities.

The positive relationship between power and illusions of control, optimism, risk taking, and abstraction carries the seed of understanding for both how power begets more power as well as for how power begets its loss. As Anderson and Galinsky (2006) duly note, by taking risks that others avoid, the powerful can take advantage of low-probability opportunities and snatch victory from the jaws of despair, thereby increasing their power. Overconfidence and illusory positive thinking combined with risky choices can, however, also lead to public embarrassment (e.g., the Enron case) and ultimately to the loss of power and status. Miscommunication driven by power-induced abstraction may lead to perceptions of ineffectiveness and, in democratic systems, could ultimately lead to the loss of power. The very forces that allow those in power to maintain their grip on resources can, when unchecked, lead to the loss of power. This is certainly a topic worthy of more research in both social psychology and organizational behavior.

POWER REVEALS THE PERSON

The possession of power frees the individual from the shackles of normative constraints that usually govern thought, expression, and behavior (Keltner et al., 2003). The domineering press of the situation recedes, allowing a person's true nature to emerge. Essentially, power increases the correspondence between individual traits and behavior (Bargh et al., 1995; Chen et al., 2001; Galinsky et al., 2008), with their personalities being better predictors of their thoughts and behaviors than are the personalities of the powerless. That is, power reveals a person's true nature, lending credence to Abraham Lincoln's intuition that "nearly all men can stand adversity, but if you want to test a man's character, give him power." Power makes you more like yourself.

But if power reveals the true self, then the effects of power should also differ across cultures, which vary in their conceptualizations of power and different propensities to define the chronic self (Zhong et al., 2009). Thus, power should increase the association between cultural differences and behavior, or, in other words, power should make you more like your culture.

Power Makes You More Like Yourself

A fair number of recent studies have provided support for the idea that power reveals the person's true nature. Chen et al. (2001) found that communally oriented participants acted more selflessly and exchange-oriented participants acted more selfishly under the sway of power. The authors argued that power activated social responsibility goals in communals and self-interest goals in exchangers, thus leading to different behavioral outcomes. Similarly, Bargh et al. (1995) showed that the activation of the concept of power in men who had a predisposition toward sexual harassment led to an automatic triggering of sex-related concepts and consequently to viewing female discussion partners as sexual objects. More recently, Galinsky et al. (2008) found that, in a negotiation task, high-power participants' social value orientations were better predictors of their interest in trusting and building a relationship with their negotiation partner than their partners' reputations. In contrast, baseline participants' interest in relationship building was more a function of their partner's reputation than of their social value orientations.

In sum, the behaviors of the powerful are more in line with their intrapsychic states, trait propensities, and idiosyncratic tendencies. With power the aggressive become more fierce, the generous more magnanimous, and the flirtatious even more amorous.

Power Makes You More Like Your Culture

The idea that power is a chief shaper and propellant of cognitions and behavior seems to suggest invariant effects across cultures. However, cultures vary both in their conceptualizations of power as well as in their definitions of the "self." Therefore, the effects of power on assertive action and attention to rewards are bound to be culturally circumscribed (Zhong et al., 2009). Whereas Western cultures tend to place a premium on understanding power as freedom from external constraints and the capacity to satisfy one's own desires, Eastern cultures highlight the virtue of restraint and responsibility on the part of the powerful. Congruent with this view, Zhong et al. found that culture determined individuals' primary associations with power. Westerners subliminally primed with the word *power* (vs. the word *paper*) responded more quickly to reward-related words but more slowly to responsibility-related words. In contrast, East Asians exhibited greater accessibility of responsibility-related words and weaker accessibility to reward-related words.

Furthermore, members of Western and Eastern cultures differ in their construal of the "self." In Western cultures, the prevailing view of the self is that of a unique entity with an individuated repertoire of internal attributes such as feelings, cognitions, and motivations (Markus & Kitayama, 1991). This view stresses the autonomy and separateness of the self. In contrast, members of East Asian cultures tend to have interdependent self-construals that emphasize the importance of social connectedness and of being embedded in larger groups. Thus, powerful members of cultures stressing interdependent self-construals should engage in more cooperative behaviors than powerful members of cultures emphasizing independent self-construals. Galinsky and colleagues (2003) found that among Westerners power increases self-interested claiming in a common dilemma. In contrast, Zhong et al. (2009) showed that among East Asians power led to reduced claiming from a commonly shared resource pool. In a different study, Zhong and colleagues measured Caucasian (independent culture) and East Asian (interdependent culture) participants' sense of power and had them play two rounds of a prisoner's game dilemma. In line with the prediction that power increases the correspondence between one's culture and one's behavior, powerful members of independent cultures defected more than powerful members of interdependent cultures. In sum, these findings support our contention that power not only makes you more like yourself but also makes you more like your culture.

HARNESSING POWER IN THE SERVICE OF LEADERSHIP

Despite the considerable progress made in depicting power as both a constructive and a corrupting force, one important theoretical and practical question—how to mitigate negative effects of power while simultaneously harnessing its positive effects—remains largely unstudied. That is, how can power be transformed into leadership? Although there is an almost natural association between power and leadership, the two are not the same (Goodwin, 2003). Merely possessing power does not make one a leader, and being a leader does not necessarily require the possession of power. Whereas we have defined power as asymmetric control over valuable resources in social relations, we conceptualize leadership as influencing, motivating, and directing group members' efforts toward the achievement of commonly shared goals (Farmer & Aguinis, 2005; Hollander, 1980; Yukl & van Fleet, 1992; Yukl, Wall, & Lepsinger, 1990). Power and leadership are similar in that they both involve influence as well as a focus on goals. However, they also differ on a number of key dimensions: (1) the source of influence; (2) the ultimate purpose of wielding influence; and (3) the consequences of influence.

First, power derives its influence from the ability to provide or withhold valuable resources or administer punishments (Keltner et al., 2003). Leadership, on the other hand, derives its influence from inspiring and motivating others through rhetoric, intellectual stimulation, and the modeling of desired behavior (Avolio & Bass, 1988; Bass, 1990). Whereas the powerful influence others by wielding carrots and sticks, leaders influence by transforming others to share their visions. Thus, the influence of power is exogenous to the target (the target complies because he or she has to), while the influence of leadership is endogenous (the target complies because he or she wants to). Second, power and leadership usually diverge in terms of the ultimate goal of exercising one's influence. Whereas the powerful influence others to satisfy personal interests and desires (Keltner et al., 2003; Kipnis, 1972), leaders wield their influence to achieve group goals (Yukl & van Fleet, 1992). Third, the consequences of influence deriving from power and leadership will differ both for the targets as well as for the influence wielders. The powerful are more likely to myopically focus on their idiosyncratic vantage points and thereby to treat their subordinates as tools toward the achievement of their personal goals. Therefore, their targets of influence are more likely to feel used and underappreciated. Thus, the powerful may earn others' opprobrium rather than praise. In contrast, leaders concerned with the well-being of their groups are more likely to consider their subordinates' needs and perspectives and to treat them with dignity and respect. This in turn should render their subordinates more likely to confer them status and respect.

Our preceding discussion of the psychological effects of power suggests that it can lead to both constructive as well as to negative social and organizational outcomes. For example, power increases assertive action, agency, optimism, confidence, and abstract thinking. In a leadership context, this ability to see the big picture coupled with optimistic confidence can be used to generate and successfully communicate grand visions for the future and thereby to motivate subordinates to relentlessly pursue a common goal. In addition, power wielders' action orientation could inspire subordinates to mimic such behaviors and to increase their propensity to assertively engage in goal-directed behavior. However, power-induced illusions of control, hubristic overconfidence, and a proclivity for potentially fateful risks would need to be harnessed for power to be successfully transfigured into leadership. Likewise, the myopic egocentric focus induced by elevated power that impels individuals to pursue the achievement of their personal goals would need to be tempered. In addition, for power to morph into effective leadership, the tendency to objectify and dehumanize subordinates by treating them as tools devoid of unique human characteristics would have to be muzzled without negatively impacting its relationship to efficiently pursue group goals.

In the following sections, we will elaborate on how power can be harnessed in the service of effective leadership. We focus specifically on how insights gained from research demonstrating that power both reveals and transforms people and can inform leadership selection (picking individuals who will be positively affected by power) and leadership creation (organizational structures and contexts that will maximize the leadership possibilities inherent in the effects of power).

Leadership Selection

Given that power reveals who people really are, making their personalities and predilections potent predictors of their own behavior, organizations need to be careful in whom they select to hold positions of power. Power effectively licenses people to act like their true selves, so organizations need to diagnose who each person's true self is and who and what will emerge and be unleashed under the sway of power. Identifying who are the selfish, the harassing, the volatile will be critical for creating efficient and effective organizations.

Promoting people into positions of power depends not only on technical expertise or analytic skill but also on the nature of the person. This review suggests that who the person is and not just how he or she performs should be essential guides for leadership selection.

Leadership Creation

We argue that perspective taking can successfully harness power's positive consequences as well as mitigate its more destructive consequences and, thus, can transform power into effective leadership. Perspective taking—the ability to step into someone else's shoes—has been related to smoother social functioning (Davis, 1980; Mead, 1934; Piaget, 1932). It has been shown to increase helping and cooperative behaviors in organizational settings (Parker & Axtell, 2001), the accuracy of perception of others' interests (Eisenberg, Murphy, & Shepard, 1997), empathic feeling (Betancourt, 1990; Coke, Batson, & McDavis, 1978), and altruistic motivation (Batson, 1991) while reducing stereotyping (Galinsky & Moskowitz, 2000) and a number of egocentric biases in judgment (Galper, 1976; Regan & Totten, 1975; Wade-Benzoni, Tenbrunsel, & Bazerman, 1996).

We offer the metaphor of driving a car to understand how power can be transformed into effective individual and group outcomes. The assertiveness of power is akin to pressing the gas pedal. Without acceleration, one is left standing still, unable to move forward. But one also needs a steering wheel and the acumen for how to use it, to avoid crashing into obstacles along the way. We propose that, in social interaction, perspective taking is that steering wheel, giving individuals the capacity to focus not only on their own ideas and goals but also on the ideas and goals of others. Perspective taking without assertiveness is ineffective for accomplishing goals, and assertiveness without perspective taking is dangerous and irresponsible. Effective leaders require acceleration and prudent steering—power coupled with perspective taking.

We propose that the combined effects of power and perspective taking should lead to superior outcomes on a number of dependent variables related to the complexity of thought and decision effectiveness at both the individual as well as at the group level. For example, a common problem identified in decision-making groups dealing with distributed information is that they often fail to discuss information that only one of the group members possesses (Gruenfeld, Mannix, Williams, & Neale,

1996; Stasser & Titus, 1985; Wittenbaum & Stasser, 1996), which in turn results in suboptimal decision quality. There is some evidence suggesting that group leadership may affect the discussion of unique information; however, to date the results are inconclusive about how leaders can lead group members to discuss more distributed information and make higher-quality decisions (see Larson, Christensen, Abbott, & Franz, 1996; Larson, Christensen, Franz, & Abbott, 1998; Larson, Foster-Fishman, & Franz, 1998; Wittenbaum & Park, 2001).

Recent experiments support the claim that powerful individuals who take their group members' perspectives are more likely both to share as well as to elicit the sharing of unique information from their team members compared with powerful individuals who fail to take their group members' perspectives. In addition, this increased sharing of distributed information increased the likelihood that groups led by high perspective-taking individuals reached higher-quality decisions than groups led by individuals who are low in perspective taking (Rus, Galinsky, & Magee, 2009).

One possible way to increase perspective taking would be to hold the powerful accountable (Tetlock, Skitka, & Boettger, 1989). Powerful individuals who know that they will have to justify their actions are more likely to consider the social consequences of their decisions and to take others' interests into account (Lerner & Tetlock, 1999; Tetlock, 1992). For example, U.S. presidents exhibit greater cognitive complexity after having been elected, when they become accountable to a variety of constituents, than before election (Tetlock, 1981). Because they have to justify their decisions and policies to a wide array of different interest groups, the elected presidents are more likely to consider the perspectives of these various groups and how their decisions will affect them.

Another way to increase perspective taking in organizational settings, and thereby to turn power into leadership, would be to have procedural justice systems in place (Rus, van Knippenberg, & Wisse, 2009). For example, if subordinates are afforded voice (Thibaut & Walker, 1975) regarding decisions that affect them, the powerful will be more likely to consider their employees' various perspectives and interests in the decision-making process. Thus, more democratic decision-making systems could serve to increase perspective taking by the powerful and aid in turning power into leadership.

To become true leaders, the powerful will need to learn how to harness the constructive forces bestowed upon them by power while at the same time mitigating its more dysfunctional effects. By understanding the systematic ways that power both makes and reveals individuals, organization can capture leadership and longevity, propelling organizations toward brighter futures.

REFERENCES

Abramson, L. Y., Seligman, M. E. P., & Teasdale, J. D. (1978). Learned helplessness in humans: Critique and reformulation. *Journal of Abnormal Psychology, 87,* 49–74.

Anderson, C., & Berdahl, J. L. (2002). The experience of power: Examining the effects of power on approach and inhibition tendencies. *Journal of Personality and Social Psychology, 83,* 1362–1377.

Anderson, C., & Galinsky, A. D. (2006). Power, optimism, and risk-taking. *European Journal of Social Psychology, 36,* 511–536.

Avolio, B. J., & Bass, B. M. (1988). Transformational leadership, charisma, and beyond. In J. G. Hunt, B. R. Baliga, H. P. Dachler, & C. A. Schriesheim (Eds.), *Emerging leadership vistas* (pp. 29–49). Lexington, MA: Lexington Books.

Babcock, L., & Laschever, S. (2003). *Women don't ask: Negotiation and the gender divide.* Princeton, NJ: Princeton University Press.

Bargh, J. A., Raymond, P., Pryor, J. B., & Strack, F. (1995). Attractiveness of the underling: An automatic power–sex association and its consequences for sexual harassment and aggression. *Journal of Personality and Social Psychology, 68,* 768–781.

Bass, B. M. (1990). From transactional to transformational leadership: Learning to share the vision. *Organizational Dynamics, 18,* 19–31.

Batson, C. D. (1991). *The altruism question: Toward a social–psychological answer.* Hillsdale, NJ: Erlbaum.

Betancourt, H. (1990). An attribution-empathy model of helping behavior: Behavioral intentions and judgments of help-giving. *Personality and Social Psychology Bulletin, 16,* 573–591.

Briñol, P., Petty, R. E., Valle, C., Rucker, D. D., & Becerra, A. (2007). The effects of message recipients' power before and after persuasion: A self-validation analysis. *Journal of Personality and Social Psychology, 93,* 1040–1053.

Chen, S., Lee-Chai, A. Y., & Bargh, J. A. (2001). Relationship orientation as moderator of the effects of social power. *Journal of Personality and Social Psychology, 80,* 173–187.

Coke, J. S., Batson, C. D., & McDavis, K. (1978). Empathic mediation of helping: A two-stage model. *Journal of Personality and Social Psychology, 36,* 752–766.

Davis, M. H. (1980). A multidimensional approach to individual differences in empathy. *JSAS: Catalog of Selected Documents in Psychology, 10,* 85.

Eisenberg, N., Murphy, B.C., & Shepard, S. (1997). The development of empathic accuracy. In W. J. Ickes (Ed.), *Empathic accuracy* (pp. 73–116). New York: Guilford Press.

Farmer, S. M., & Aguinis, H. (2005). Accounting for subordinate perceptions of supervisory power: An identity-dependence model. *Journal of Applied Psychology, 90*, 1069–1083.

Fast, N., Gruenfeld, D., Sivanathan, N., & Galinsky, A. (2009). Illusory control: A generative force behind power's far-reaching effects. *Psychological Science, 20*, 502–508.

Fiske, S. T. (1993). Controlling other people: The impact of power on stereotyping. *American Psychologist, 48*, 621–628.

Galinsky, A. D., & Moskowitz, G. B. (2000). Perspective-taking: Decreasing stereotype expression, stereotype accessibility, and in-group favoritism. *Journal of Personality and Social Psychology, 78*, 708–724.

Galinsky, A. D., & Mussweiler, T. (2001). First offers as anchors: The role of perspective-taking and negotiator focus. *Journal of Personality and Social Psychology, 81*, 657–669.

Galinsky, A. D., Gruenfeld, D. H, & Magee, J. C. (2003). From power to action. *Journal of Personality and Social Psychology, 85*, 453–466.

Galinsky, A. D., Magee, J. C., Gruenfeld, D. H., Whitson, J., & Liljenquist, K. (2008). Power reduces the press of the situation: Implications for creativity, conformity, and dissonance. *Journal of Personality and Social Psychology, 95*, 1450–1466.

Galinsky, A. D., Magee, J. C., Inesi, M. E., & Gruenfeld, D. H. (2006). Power and perspectives not taken. *Psychological Science, 17*, 1068–1074.

Galper, R. E. (1976). Turning observers into actors: Differential causal attributions as a function of "empathy." *Journal of Research in Personality, 10*, 328–335.

Goodwin, S. A. (2003). Power and prejudice: A social-cognitive perspective on power and leadership. In D. van Knippenberg & M. A. Hogg (Eds.), *Leadership and power: Identity processes in groups and organizations* (pp. 138–152). London: Sage Publications.

Gruenfeld, D. H, Inesi, M. E., Magee, J. C., & Galinsky, A. D. (2008). Power and the objectification of social targets. *Journal of Personality and Social Psychology, 95*, 111–127.

Gruenfeld, D. H., Mannix, E. A., Williams, K. Y., & Neale, M. A. (1996). Group composition and decision making: How member familiarity and information distribution affect process and performance. *Organizational Behavior and Human Decision Processes, 67*, 1–15.

Guinote, A. (2007a). Power and goal pursuit. *Personality and Social Psychology Bulletin, 33*, 1076–1087.

Guinote, A. (2007b). Power affects basic cognition: Increased attentional inhibition and flexibility. *Journal of Experimental Social Psychology, 43*, 685–697.

Hollander, E. P. (1980). Leadership and social exchange processes. In K. J. Gergen, M. S. Greenberg, & R. H. Willis (Eds.), *Social exchange: Advances in theory and research* (pp. 103–18). New York: Plenum Press.

Keltner, D., Gruenfeld, D. H., & Anderson, C. (2003). Power, approach, and inhibition. *Psychological Review, 110*, 265–284.

Kipnis, D. (1972). Does power corrupt? *Journal of Personality and Social Psychology, 24*, 33–41.

Kipnis, D. (1976). *The powerholders*. Chicago: University of Chicago Press.

Lammers, J., Gordijn, E. H., & Otten, S. (2008). Looking through the eyes of the powerful. *Journal of Experimental Social Psychology, 44*, 1229–1238.

Lammers, J., & Stapel, D.A. (2009a). How power influences moral thinking. *Journal of Personality and Social Psychology, 97*, 279–289.

Lammers, J., & Stapel, D.A. (2009b). *Power increases everyday dehumanization*. Manuscript submitted for publication. Tilburg University.

Larson, J. R., Christensen, C., Abbott, A. S., & Franz, T. M. (1996). Diagnosing groups: Charting the flow of information in medical decision-making teams. *Journal of Personality and Social Psychology, 71*, 315–330.

Larson, J. R., Jr., Christensen, C., Franz, T. M., & Abbott, A. S. (1998). Diagnosing groups: The pooling, management, and impact of shared and unshared case information in team-based medical decision making. *Journal of Personality and Social Psychology, 75*, 93–108.

Larson, J. R., Foster-Fishman, P. G., & Franz, T. M. (1998). Leadership style and the discussion of shared and unshared information in decision-making groups. *Personality and Social Psychology Bulletin, 24,* 482–495.

Lerner, J. S., & Tetlock, P. E. (1999). Accounting for the effects of accountability. *Psychological Bulletin, 125*, 255–275.

Magee, J. C., & Galinsky, A. D. (2008). Social hierarchy: The self-reinforcing nature of power and status. *Academy of Management Annals, 2,* 351–398.

Magee, J. C., Galinsky, A. D., & Gruenfeld, D. H. (2007). Power, propensity to negotiate, and moving first in competitive interactions. *Personality and Social Psychology Bulletin, 33,* 200–212.

Maner, J. K., Gailliot, M. T., Butz, D., & Peruche, B. M. (2007). Power, risk, and the status quo: Does power promote riskier or more conservative decision making? *Personality and Social Psychology Bulletin, 33,* 451–462.

Markus, H., & Kitayama, S. (1991). Culture and the self: Implications for cognition, emotion, and motivation. *Psychological Review, 98,* 224–253.

Mead, G. H. (1934). *Mind, self and society.* Chicago: University of Chicago Press.

Milliken, F. J., Magee, J. C., Lam, N., & Menezes, D. (2008). *Seeing through the lens of power: Sense-making and communication in the aftermath of Hurricane Katrina.* Manuscript submitted for publication.

Overbeck, J. R., & Park, B. (2006). Powerful perceivers, powerless objects: Flexibility of powerholders' social attention. *Organizational Behavior and Human Decision Processes, 99*, 227–243.

Parker, S. K., & Axtell, C. M. (2001). Seeing another viewpoint: Antecedents and outcomes of employee perspective taking. *Academy of Management Journal, 44,* 1085–1100.

Piaget, J. (1932). *The moral judgment of the child.* London: Paul Kegan.

Regan, D. T., & Totten, J. (1975). Empathy and attribution: Turning observers into actors. *Journal of Personality and Social Psychology, 32,* 850–856.

Rus, D., Galinsky, A. D., & Magee, J. C. (2009). *Acceleration with steering: How power and perspective-taking combined create exceptional outcomes.* Manuscript in preparation.

Rus, D., van Knippenberg, D., & Wisse, B. (2009). *Myopia of power: Procedural justice systems, perspective-taking and leader self-serving behaviors.* Manuscript submitted for publication.

Russell, B. (1938/1960). *Power: A new social analysis.* New York: W. W. Norton.

Smith, P. K., Jostmann, N. B., Galinsky, A. D., & van Dijk, W. W. (2008). Lacking power impairs executive functions. *Psychological Science, 19,* 441–447.

Smith, P. K., & Trope, Y. (2006). You focus on the forest when you're in charge of the trees: Power priming and abstract information processing. *Journal of Personality and Social Psychology, 90,* 578–596.

Stasser, G., & Titus, W. (1985). Pooling unshared information in group decision making: Biased information sampling during discussion. *Journal of Personality and Social Psychology, 48,* 1467–1478.

Taylor, S. E., & Brown, J. D. (1988). Illusion and well-being: A social psychological perspective on mental health. *Psychological Bulletin, 103,* 193–210.

Tetlock, P. E. (1981). Pre- to post-election shifts in presidential rhetoric: Impression management or cognitive adjustment? *Journal of Personality and Social Psychology, 41,* 207–212.

Tetlock, P. E. (1992). The impact of accountability on judgment and choice: Toward a social contingency model. *Advances in Experimental Social Psychology, 25,* 331–376.

Tetlock, P. E., Skitka, L., & Boettger, R. (1989). Social and cognitive strategies for coping with accountability: Conformity, complexity, and bolstering. *Journal of Personality and Social Psychology, 57,* 632–640.

Thibaut, J. W., & Kelley, H. (1959). *The social psychology of groups.* New York: John Wiley.

Thibaut, J., & Walker, L. (1975). *Procedural justice: A psychological analysis.* Hillsdale, NJ: Erlbaum.

Trope, Y., & Liberman, N. (2003). Temporal construal. *Psychological Review, 110,* 403–421.

van Kleef, G. A., De Dreu, C. K. W., Pietroni, D., & Manstead, A. S. R. (2006). Power and emotion in negotiation: Power moderates the interpersonal effects of anger and happiness on concession making. *European Journal of Social Psychology, 36,* 557–581.

van Kleef, G. A., Oveis, C., van der Löwe, I., LuoKogan, A., Goetz, J., & Keltner, D. (2008). Power, distress, and compassion: Turning a blind eye to the suffering of others. *Psychological Science, 19,* 1315–1322.

Wade-Benzoni, K. A., Tenbrunsel, A. E., & Bazerman, M. H. (1996). Egocentric interpretations of fairness in asymmetric environmental social dilemmas: Explaining harvesting behavior and the role of communication. *Organizational Behavior and Human Decision Processes, 67,* 111–126.

Whitson, J. A., & Galinsky, A. D. (2008). Lacking control increases illusory pattern perception. *Science, 322,* 115–117.

Whitson, J. A., Galinsky, A. D., Magee, J. C., Gruenfeld, D. H, & Liljenquist, K. A. (2007). *Power and overcoming obstacles: Implications for obedience and bystander intervention.* Manuscript submitted for publication.

Wittenbaum, G. M., & Park, E. S. (2001). The collective preference for shared information. *Current Directions in Psychological Science, 10,* 70–73.

Wittenbaum, G. M., & Stasser, G. (1996). Management of information in small groups. In J. L. Nye & A. R. Brower (Eds.), *What's social about social task representations? Research on socially shared task representations in small groups* (pp. 3–28). Thousand Oaks, CA: Sage.

Yukl, G. A., & van Fleet, D. D. (1992). Theory and research on leadership in organizations. In M. D. Dunnette & L. M. Hough (Eds.), *Handbook of industrial and organizational psychology* (Vol. 3, pp. 147–197). Palo Alto, CA: Consulting Psychologists Press.

Yukl, G. A, Wall, S., & Lepsinger, R. (1990). Preliminary report on the validation of the management practices survey. In K. E. Clark & M. B. Clark (Eds.), *Measures of leadership* (pp. 223–237). West Orange, NJ: Leadership Library of America.

Zhong, C., Galinsky, A. D., Magee, J. C., & Maddux, W. W. (2009). The cultural contingency of power: Conceptual associations and behavioral consequences. Manuscript submitted for publication.

3

On Being the Leader and Acting Fairly: A Contingency Approach

David De Cremer
Rotterdam School of Management, Erasmus University

Tom R. Tyler
New York University

Justice is of considerable importance to the members of contemporary groups, organizations, and societies (Tyler, Boeckmann, Smith, & Huo, 1997). In fact, relationships within these social entities are characterized by people's concerns about whether the allocations of outcomes between the interaction partners are fair, whether people are treated fairly and respectfully by the others, and whether the group is perceived to be trustworthy and ethical (De Cremer & Tyler, 2005a; Folger & Cropanzano, 1998; Miller, 2001; Walster, Walster, & Berscheid, 1978). Thus, justice is an important concern that is evoked in most interpersonal relationships within social groups (Greenberg, 1996), and one common type of justice that has profound implications for such within group relationships is *procedural fairness* (Tyler & Lind, 1992). Procedural fairness is referred to as the justice of the procedure used when making allocation decisions—although some also argue that the quality of interpersonal treatment is also a procedural justice issue (Bies, 2005; Blader & Tyler, 2003a, 2003b).

Fair enactment of procedures has been shown to lead to a variety of important consequences such as influencing support for and legitimacy of authorities (Tyler, 1989), cooperation (De Cremer & Tyler, 2005a), fairness and outcome judgments (van den Bos, Lind, Vermunt, & Wilke, 1997), self-evaluations (De Cremer & Sedikides, 2005; Koper, van Knippenberg, Bouhuijs, Vermunt, & Wilke, 1993), and emotions (De Cremer, 2004; van den Bos & Miedema, 2000). All these studies can as such be seen as demonstrating a fairness principle, referred to as the "fair process" effect (Folger, 1977; van den Bos, 2005)—that is, that procedural fairness positively affects a wide range of human reactions.

A common feature of most of these procedural fairness studies is that authorities enact procedures. The presence of an authority in this fair process effect is, for example, explicitly emphasized by the name of one of the more influential procedural justice theories: the *relational model of authority* (Tyler & Lind, 1992). What is interesting from this perspective is that, although the issue of procedural fairness is quite often applied to authorities and group leaders, it is also clear that insights from the procedural fairness literature are rarely used in the existing leadership literature and vice versa. In other words, it is noteworthy that both scientific fields do not seem to communicate with one another, despite their common interest in authority issues. Recently, Bies (2005, p. 105) made a similar argument when noting that "why justice is no longer a figural element in the dominant models of leadership and management today emerges as an intriguing question." Moreover, De Cremer, van Knippenberg, van Knippenberg, Mullenders, and Stinglhamber (2005, p. 3) more explicitly noted with respect to the issue of procedural fairness that "it is surprising that [a] leader's procedural fairness is not included as a leadership feature in the existing leadership literature."

This observation can be seen as regretful, because, as Colquitt and Greenberg (2003, p. 196) argue, "perhaps the most natural connection can be made between justice and leadership." Thus, the integration between both fields of research has not happened yet, which is illustrated by, for example, the argument that "the role that justice plays ... in paradigms of leadership ... has only recently begun to receive research attention" (Pillai, Scandura, & Williams, 1999, p. 763). A possible reason for this may be that, as Tyler (2001, p. 71) notes, "social justice research typically has not been thought of as being research about social influence," whereas an essential characteristic of leadership is influence over others (Chemers, 2001). Leaders are expected to motivate organizational members to go beyond their own self-interest by fostering affiliations between the leader and followers (Bass, 1985; Burns, 1978). It is therefore an important scientific task to create a theoretical and empirical integration between the procedural fairness and leadership literatures.

THE RELATIONSHIP BETWEEN FAIRNESS AND LEADERSHIP

Have both scientific fields always been so separate? When speaking of fairness more broadly than only procedural fairness it becomes clear that fairness has always been an aspect of leadership and management (sometimes a more central one, sometimes a more peripheral one). Indeed, several centuries ago Niccolo Machiavelli noted that the issue of fairness mattered a great deal because followers believed that it would matter (Machiavelli, 1991). Further, the philosopher John Rawls (1971, p. 111) notes that "justice is the first virtue of social institutions.... Laws and institutions no matter how efficient or well-arranged must be reformed or abolished if they are unjust."

More recently, these ideas have shaped early leadership theories. For example, ever since the famous "Ohio Studies" (Stogdill, 1974), fair behavior by the leader has always, although mostly implicitly, been part of the leadership concept (Kouzes, Posner, & Peters, 1996). McGregor (1960), in his Theory Y management, included a focus on justice by noting that subordinate perceptions of justice are based on the integrity and fairness of the behaviors that the leader displays and the extent to which the leader cares about the interests and goals that the followers pursue. These early approaches demonstrate an interest by management scholars in the issue of fair treatment and the just enactment of procedures.

Thus, in the past, the concepts of fairness and of leadership have been discussed together rather than viewed as being independent. However, as Bies (2005, p. 105) notes, somewhere "justice got 'lost' in more recent models of leadership." Indeed, over the years, only a limited number of studies in the field of social psychology and organizational behavior have looked at a potential relationship among fairness, justice, and leadership. Importantly, the bulk of these studies have focused primarily on using leadership and fairness/justice as dependent measures. However, as can be seen from our brief review, fairness and leadership share a common history, being widely viewed as linked in philosophy, psychology, and early discussions of leadership. In our view this relationship is particularly central to the recent importance of work on procedural fairness.

THE CONNECTION OF LEADERSHIP TO PROCEDURAL FAIRNESS

The case for connecting procedural fairness with leadership comes from research conducted during the formative years of procedural justice research. In their classic studies of procedural fairness, Thibaut and Walker (1975) explored people's reactions to third-party dispute resolution procedures involving judges. While authorities—in this case, judges—were central to the procedures that Thibaut and Walker studied, their work did not consider reactions to those authorities to be a key issue. So, for example, in the work of Thibaut and Walker, participants were not asked to evaluate the judge. They were asked to evaluate the decision that the judge made.

The connection between procedural fairness and leadership developed through studies in the 1980s showing that the procedural fairness of leaders shaped reactions to their decisions. Tyler and Caine's (1981) work is one example. This study explored the basis of support for teachers and political leaders. Two studies were conducted involving each type of leader. In the first study respondents reacted to a hypothetical scenario in which the favorability of the outcome they received and the procedural fairness of the allocation process used by the authority were experimentally varied. The results indicated that leadership endorsement was shaped by both outcomes and procedural fairness. A second type of study, again involving both types of leaders, explored the antecedents of leadership in field settings. This study suggested that procedural fairness was the primary factor shaping leadership endorsement when people were reacting to actual allocation decisions.

The argument that procedural fairness was the primary factor shaping evaluations of leaders is striking. It has since received widespread support. For example, Tyler, Rasinski, and McGraw (1985) used survey-based data to explore the antecedents of support for political leaders. Their results again suggested that procedural fairness shaped evaluations of both incumbent political leaders (e.g., the president) and political institutions. Hence, the range of procedural fairness influences on leadership endorsement was found to be broad.

In subsequent studies of legal (Lind & Tyler, 1988; Tyler, 1990; Tyler & Huo, 2002), political (Gibson, 2002; Kershaw & Alexander, 2003), and managerial leadership (Kim & Mauborgne, 1993; Tyler & Blader, 2000), studies consistently suggested that people's reactions to leaders were strongly based on evaluations of the fairness of the procedures through which those leaders exercised their authority. This strong connection between procedural fairness and leadership underlies the argument that the neglect of procedural fairness in the study of leadership does not seem logical or helpful.

In addition, other correlational research in the 1980s also demonstrated that positive interpersonal relationships between the leader and the follower promote procedural fairness perceptions (Vecchio, Griffeth, & Hom, 1986). Subsequently, in the 1990s, leadership researchers used the concept of fairness by showing that leadership in which decisions were fairly enacted results in higher perceptions of procedural and distributive justice (Cobb & Frey, 1996), that higher levels of Leader Member Exchange (LMX) were positively related to subordinate perceptions of procedural fairness (Mansour-Cole & Scott, 1998), and that empowering leadership practices were positively related to subordinate perceptions of supervisor fairness (Keller & Dansereau, 1995).

The second aspect of the connection between procedural fairness and leadership is an examination of research on why this connection exists. Tyler and Lind (1992) proposed a relational model of leadership. They argued that the actions of leaders (i.e., the way they exercised authority) communicated a social message that told people about their status in the groups to which they belonged. This message was communicated by three aspects of procedural fairness: the neutrality of decision making; the trust that people had in the motives of the decision maker; and the politeness and courtesy that people experienced when dealing with authorities. The first of these criteria, neutrality, corresponds to early work on justice in decision making. The last criterion, politeness and courtesy, connects to the issues of interpersonal treatment also noted in early work on leadership.

Several types of evidence support a relational perspective on authority. First, although Thibaut and Walker (1975) suggested that people value having an opportunity to deal with a leader to the degree that they believed they were shaping that person's decisions, subsequent research suggests that people had a more relational perspective on their connection with authorities. They valued the opportunity to speak to leaders even when they did not think they were necessarily shaping outcomes (Tyler, Rasinski, & Spodick, 1985). Their primary concern was with whether the leader considered their arguments when decisions were being made (Tyler, 1987).

In addition, studies that examined the criterion used to evaluate the justice of the procedures used by leaders indicate that people used relational criteria—neutrality, trust, quality of interpersonal treatment—rather than focusing only or even primarily on opportunities for participation (Tyler, 1988). In fact, studies suggested that issues of participation might be subsumed within relational judgments (Lind, Tyler, & Huo, 1997). In any event the relational criteria were the primary drivers of judgments of procedural justice, of leadership evaluations, and of willingness to defer to leaders (Tyler & Lind, 1992).

The argument that people valued relational judgments because they used feedback drawn from the behavior of leaders to shape their judgments of their status in groups also drew support from studies showing that people were more interested in relational information when status issues were more salient. This has been shown in several experimental studies (De Cremer & Sedikides, 2008; Smith & Tyler, 1997; Smith, Tyler, Huo, Ortiz, & Lind, 1998) as well as in field studies (Huo, Smith, Tyler, & Lind, 1996; Smith & Tyler, 1996; Tyler & Degoey, 1995). These field studies demonstrated that people's willingness to defer to leaders was more strongly based on procedural justice judgments when people identified more strongly with the groups those leaders represent. This connection was directly demonstrated by Tyler and De Cremer (2005) in a study showing that people were more willing to accept decisions made by leaders for procedural fairness reasons when they identified with a group.

The exercise of authority and leadership all show important effects of procedural fairness both in terms of showing that procedural fairness shapes reactions to authorities and in demonstrating the relational roots of procedural fairness. Moreover, in the development of the procedural fairness literature, the perspective of leadership always seems to have been taken into account. For these reasons, it seems clear that both the procedural fairness and the leadership literature do have common interests and that an integration between the insights derived from both fields should be encouraged. Several ways of achieving this type of integration may be possible. The present chapter presents one such specific approach. In the following sections, we will direct our attention to how leadership can be looked upon and how procedural fairness may have its place in this perspective.

DOES LEADERSHIP HAVE A FOCUS ON FAIRNESS?

At the start of the twenty-first century, the field of social psychology started to direct its attention more explicitly to the issue of leadership (see De Cremer & van Vugt, 2002; Haslam, 2001; Hogg & van Knippenberg, 2003; Tyler & De Cremer, 2005; van Knippenberg & Hogg, 2003). Consequently, interest in the relationship between fairness and leadership seemed to grow as well (e.g., De Cremer, 2006, 2007; De Cremer & den Ouden, 2009; De Cremer, van Dijke, & Bos, 2004; De Cremer & van Knippenberg, 2002; Ullrich, Christ, & van Dick, 2009). Indeed, the introduction to a special issue on leadership, self, and identity in *Leadership Quarterly* noted that this topic "also highlight another important theme that emerges from the current set of studies: the role of leader fairness" (van Knippenberg, van Knippenberg, De Cremer, & Hogg, 2004, p. 497). Further, Lord and Brown (2004, p. 175) also note that "many important work outcomes may require an understanding of organizational justice processes for leaders to be effective." Finally, responding to these calls, a recent special issue in *European Journal of Work and Organizational Psychology* focused explicitly on the issue of leader fairness (van Knippenberg & De Cremer, 2008).

To summarize, it seems that the time is right to highlight the importance of looking at insights derived from both the fairness and leadership literature and to explore whether they may help each other in addressing several questions about the effectiveness and influence of authorities in groups, organizations, and society. To date, however, it seems that, as our brief review shows, most studies have treated the use of fair procedures and treatment as distinct from leadership. We believe that procedural fairness can be seen as leadership: something that can be referred to as process-based leadership (De Cremer, van Dijke, & Bos, 2007; Tyler, 2004).

In the present chapter, we review a series of recent studies showing that leadership behaviors and characteristics accompany the enactment of fair procedures in such a way that the effects of procedural fairness on group, team, and organizational members becomes more pronounced or diminished depending on other factors involved in the enactment of procedures.

It is important to note that in this approach we do not wish to make the claim that our studies and our advocated perspective addresses all the complexities of leadership (it does not!); rather, we wish to illustrate the idea that specific leadership styles and characteristics (elements of leadership; see Judge & Bono, 2000) may interact with the formal procedural rules as identified by Leventhal (1980). Identifying consistent interactive effects between these two types of variables can then be seen as empirical support for the argument that the relationship between the fairness and leadership literature deserves more attention than it has received to date. Of course, our so-called interactive approach represents one way of examining insights from both types of literature, whereas other approaches are also possible. For the purpose of the present chapter, however, our primary aim lies in showing the necessity of examining both aspects.

LEADERSHIP AND PROCEDURAL FAIRNESS: A CONTINGENCY APPROACH

Leadership has been defined in many ways. This motivated Stogdill (1974, p. 259) to note that "there are almost as many definitions of leadership as there are persons who have attempted to define the concept." Here, we will not attempt to create a new definition; rather, we will rely on the more current (and social psychological) conceptualization of leadership as a process of influence (Chemers, 2001). Recent approaches to leadership have focused on how leaders have impact and change the way followers feel, think, decide, and act (Lord & Brown, 2004). Indeed, from a social psychological point of view, leadership can be seen as a psychological process that transpires between leader and follower and in which followers become aroused in such a way that how they feel, view themselves, make decisions, and act is shaped by the influence that a leader exerts (see Messick & Kramer, 2005). Bryman (1996, p. 276), for example, also noted that leadership involves a "process of influence whereby the leader has an impact on others by inducing them to behave in a certain way." Leadership, in other words, is the ability to influence others.

Interestingly, because leaders are seen as having such an important influence on followers, they are expected to *do* the *right things*. In the literature, management is often referred to as the process of *doing things right*—that is, acting to create order, predictability, and regularity in organizations (Kotter, 1982). Leadership, in contrast, is more about doing the right things, or, as Chemers (2001, p. 378) argues, "leadership is one of the major vehicles by which organizations achieve the functions" of "integrity and reliability" (p. 377). Thus, leaders need to set out directives and procedures that are fair and ethical (Northouse, 2001), but in this process it is important to point out that they need to posses the qualities and actions that lead others to want to direct their own attention to these directives and procedures (cf. Hackman & Walton, 1986). Thus, for the purpose of the present chapter, it becomes clear that leaders enact fair procedures but that, at the same time, they have to take care that the enactment of these procedures influences the emotions, self-esteem, decisions, and actions of the followers. This line of reasoning implies that the specific behaviors and characteristics that the enacting leader possesses or displays may help in promoting versus softening (or even eliminating) the influence that procedural justice exerts on others. Leadership style, in other words, interacts with procedural justice (see De Cremer, 2006; De Cremer & van Knippenberg, 2002; De Cremer et al., 2005).

Examining and identifying such a contingency approach may help us in further understanding how and when procedural fairness can exert influence on followers. Organizations wish to create a fair culture and due to this organizational orientation toward culture leaders have the important task of ensuring that the influence of fair procedures is optimal. It is also interesting and important to highlight that our proposed contingency approach, which suggests that leadership styles may direct followers' attention toward or away from justice issues and consequently alter the influence of procedural fairness, aligns well with other perspectives in the leadership literature. For example, Burns (1978) argued that transformational leaders encourage followers to embrace moral values such as justice, equality, and the interests of the collective, suggesting that transformational leaders "move followers to higher stages of moral development, by directing their attention to important principles and end values such as justice and equality" (Brown & Trevino, 2003, p. 158). Thus, this argument also holds that specific leadership styles make followers focus more strongly on fairness issues—a process that, according to us, will enhance the influence of procedural fairness (see De Cremer & Den Ouden, 2009, for evidence).

EMPIRICAL EVIDENCE OF A CONTINGENCY APPROACH

In the following sections, a series of studies are presented to illustrate our advocated contingency approach. More precisely, the effectiveness of leadership behaviors such as displaying self-confidence and advocating a self-rewarding style will be examined as moderators of procedural fairness. In addition, evidence will be shown that even social features associated with the act of leadership, such as how the leader is selected, will affect the influence of procedural fairness.

Such a contingency approach also emerges in the leadership literature. In that literature it is argued that the effectiveness of leadership styles or behavior may be contingent on a host of personal, situational, and organizational characteristics (for reviews, see, e.g., Bass, 1985; Yukl, 1994) and, in particular, other leader behaviors (see Casimir, 2001; De Cremer & van Knippenberg, 2004). In a similar vein, in the present chapter we argue that when it comes to the effectiveness of procedural fairness in affecting other's reactions it is necessary to examine the extent to which procedural fairness effects are contingent on leader behaviors and characteristics.

The Case of Self-Confident Leaders

When authorities monitor tasks within groups and teams, procedural fairness is an especially important organizational service because it is necessary to make sure that rewards and bonuses derived from the hard work are allocated in a fair way. As such, fair procedures are needed so that these allocations happen in a fair manner (e.g., by giving voice to the team members involved in the different tasks). Of course, under such circumstances, followers prefer leaders who know what they are dealing with and who have confidence in their own abilities to monitor and evaluate tasks.

In other words, leaders exhibiting self-confidence are often preferred by organizational members. Indeed, leader display of self-confidence has been identified in a number of theoretical analyses of charismatic leadership as an important factor in leadership effectiveness and as an antecedent of attributions of charisma (e.g., Conger & Kanungo, 1987; House, 1977; Shamir, House, and Arthur, 1993). Observations from the field seem to corroborate this analysis (Conger, 1989; Khurana, 2002). Self-confident leaders communicate the expectation of success, consequently rendering the leader more attractive and able to motivate involvement in the job (cf. Bandura, 1986; Vroom, 1964). The reason for this is that the expectation of success communicated by leader self-confidence strongly affects follower's perceptions of control and self-efficacy (cf. Shamir et al., 1993; Shea & Howell, 1999). As a result, those followers led by a self-confident leader may feel more motivated to voice their opinion because they feel more in control.

Following from this line of reasoning, De Cremer and Wubben (2010) reasoned that if a team leader exhibited self-confidence the members of the team would be focused more on the procedural element of voice, because due to their enhanced feeling of self-efficacy and control they would feel a stronger need to express their ideas and opinions. This idea also follows closely from the findings of research by Brockner and colleagues (1998), in which they showed that people high in self-esteem cared more about voice (relative to no voice) than those low in self-esteem. The reason for this was that those high in self-esteem had higher perceptions of self-efficacy and as a consequence were more motivated to exert control over the decision-making process. This line of reasoning builds upon the instrumental models of procedural fairness—models claiming that people prefer fair procedures to exert control over their outcomes (Leventhal, 1980; Thibaut & Walker, 1975).

To examine the impact of this control motive in shaping the interactive effect between leader self-confidence and the enactment of procedural fairness, De Cremer and Wubben (2010) used a paradigm developed by Lind, Kanfer, and Earley (1990). Lind and colleagues used a clever experimental design to disentangle instrumental and relational motives. In their experiment on goal setting, participants received an opportunity to voice their opinion before the experimenter had decided on the goal (predecision voice), after the experimenter had already decided on the goal (postdecision voice), or not at all (no voice). If people cared about voice because of instrumental or control concerns then a difference between predecision voice and postdecision voice should be found. However, if control concerns were not the driving force (but rather relational motives such as receiving respect), then no difference should be found between those two voice conditions. Interestingly, the results showed (among other things) that perceptions of fairness were enhanced by the possibility of voice, but more so in the predecision voice condition than in the postdecision voice condition. This provided some evidence for the control component. Importantly, relational concerns also played a role, because postdecision voice was better than no voice at all.

Building on this type of research, De Cremer and Wubben (2010) argued that leaders who were high in self-confidence should also motivate followers to attend more closely to procedural fairness practices (due to the enhanced control motive) in such a way that they care more about voice opportunities in which they are able to influence the decision (predecision voice) relative to voice opportunities in which no control over the decision can be exerted anymore (postdecision voice) or where no voice is given at all. The results revealed that when the leader displayed high self-confidence, negative emotions and exit reactions were lower in the predecision condition relative to the postdecision and no-voice conditions. However, when the leader displayed low self-confidence, negative emotions and exit reactions did not differ between the predecision and postdecision condition (both conditions did differ from the no-voice condition). These results are thus in line with the contingency approach presented in the introduction. Self-confident leaders make followers attend to how fair procedures are enacted, and the psychological process underlying this effect seems to be the control motive.

The Case of Self-Rewarding Leaders

A strong focus within the recent organizational behavior literature is on how leaders and organizations can empower their employees. One aspect of empowerment is to increase motivation by enabling employees to commit to and assign meaning to their tasks and jobs (Conger, 2004). Empowerment is a good thing for both employees and organizations because it leads to greater work satisfaction, effectiveness, and innovation at work (Spreitzer, 1995). De Cremer et al. (2005) related this notion to leadership and argued that empowerment refers to specific leadership behaviors that activate a process in which a leader creates conditions for the followers to develop and promote their sense of competence and self (see, e.g., Conger, 2004). More precisely, they suggested that empowerment influences individuals' sense of competence, which, consequently, fosters their sense of self-confidence (see also Spreitzer, 1995).

Pearce and Sims (2002) presented a list of empowerment leadership styles representative of behaviors promoting people's self. One style that particularly builds confidence and competence among followers, consequently influencing self-esteem, is the rewarding leadership style (see also Arnold, Arad, Rhoades, & Drasgow, 2000). This leadership style comprises behaviors of complimenting followers with their achievements and motivating them to reward themselves after a job well done. As such, by means of using this behavior the successful performance of the follower is clearly attributed by the leader to the efforts of the follower, and, in addition, is reinforced by rewarding this successful performance by means of something that the followers choose themselves. The establishment of such a positive outcome has been shown to foster people's feelings of confidence and competence and, ultimately, promote people's self-esteem (Deci & Ryan, 2000). Thus, leaders high in rewarding leadership style are typical examples of empowerment leadership as they motivate the follower to manage his or her own self-regard and worth (i.e., encouraging a link between self-regard and successful performance; see Pearce & Sims, 2002).

Building on this literature, De Cremer and colleagues (2005) argued that a leader high in rewarding style should promote feelings of competence among followers. In turn, due to such an enhanced sense of competence, participants should be more sensitive to voice procedures, since feelings of competence are related to feelings of self-efficacy and, following Brockner et al. (1998), since such feelings should motivate people to be more willing to voice their opinion. Thus, following a contingency approach, it was expected that a rewarding leadership style should enhance the influence of procedural fairness on others' reactions. The results indeed showed that when the leader was high in self-rewarding style, participants felt less valued when receiving no voice relative to receiving voice. In case of a leadership style that was low in self-reward, no difference between the voice and no-voice conditions was found.

The Case of Selecting a Leader

As leadership entails influence (Chemers, 2001), it has the potential to direct followers' attention toward or away from procedural fairness. An important feature of established leadership, however, is that group members need to acquire the status of leader. One important leadership element related to status emergence is the selection procedure (i.e., appointment and election) through which people occupy leadership positions (Julian, Hollander, & Regula, 1969).

Although procedural fairness has been argued to have a profound effect on relationships within groups, teams, and organizations, this literature largely ignores the fact that group members will attend to procedural issues only if they have an interest in or are committed to the leader in charge. In this respect, how the leader obtained his or her position becomes an important focus. Indeed, research has shown that the selection of leaders influences how leadership is able to communicate information like procedural fairness, particularly because it (1) influences the quality of the relationship between the group leader and the others (Hollander & Julian, 1970), (2) provides a basis for continuity of leadership (Cohen & Bennis, 1961), and (3) creates different social environments consequently affecting the importance of different leadership behaviors and communications (Hollander, 1985).

De Cremer and Alberts (2004) addressed the research question of how leadership selection moderates the influence of procedural fairness. In doing this, these authors used the traditional distinction between an appointed and an elected leader (see Hollander, 1985). First of all, when a leader is *appointed* (e.g., by an external authority), they reasoned that followers would have no clear conception about what to expect from this leader and, therefore, would be likely to use any other leader information as a reference point for their subsequent judgments and reactions. Such other leadership information may include the fairness of procedures. Thus, if the appointed leader provides voice to the other group members, this leader should be perceived as fair and ultimately be seen as a good choice of leader (i.e., probably one they would have chosen themselves). If this leader, however, provides no voice, this negative information should result in less support and more negative reactions. Therefore, under circumstances of an appointed leader, a stronger voice effect is expected than would be found with an elected leader who has already been legitimated by the procedure by which they became the leader.

What about an *elected* leader? In examining this possibility, De Cremer and Alberts (2004) distinguished between two different types of elected leaders. The first situation is the one found most commonly in the leadership literature, that is, an elected leader who is supposedly supported by the whole of the group (including oneself). Under such circumstances, an elected leader is expected to fulfill leadership functions (like fair treatment) very well, or, as Hollander and Julian (1970) argued, "election builds higher demands on the leadership role" (p. 66). Moreover, because this elected leader reflects people's own choice, feelings of support for and responsibility upon the leader will be enhanced (Julian et al., 1969). Therefore, under such circumstances leaders are expected to use fair procedures. If voice is then given, people's choice will be valid, and hence they should perceive this leader as fair. However, when no voice is given, people will feel disappointed, and negative reactions should emerge.

The other type of elected leader is one in which the leader is elected, but this leader is not the participants' personal favorite. In other words, the majority has chosen this leader, but you would choose someone else. De Cremer and Alberts (2004) reasoned that if people are given an opportunity to select a leader but if they notice that their vote was not for the person chosen (i.e., another leader is selected), they might feel frustrated (cf. Folger, 1977) about this outcome and consequently care less about the actions of the leader. In other words, people will experience feelings of exclusion, since their choice did not seem to matter and did not fit well with the choice of the others. As a result, low feelings of commitment to the leader and his or her actions are most likely to emerge. As a consequence, fair treatment enacted by such an authority will not be perceived as desirable. Therefore, it can be expected that under such circumstances, voice would not reveal the same strong effect that would otherwise be found.

The results revealed that procedural fairness influenced participants' positive emotions (i.e., higher positive emotions when voice was given relative to no voice) when the leader was appointed or elected by the whole group (including oneself). Procedural fairness was not found to affect participants' emotions when the elected leader was not one's personal favorite. Even more importantly, however, this interaction effect emerged only among participants who were classified as high in need to belong relative to low in need to belong (before starting the study, participants had filled out Leary, Kelly, Cottrell, and Schreindorfer's [2001] 10-item need to belong scale). More precisely, if participants felt the inner drive to feel accepted and included by the group and the representative authority, then procedural fairness exerted influence on positive emotions as a function of leadership selection. However, this was not the case when the need to feel accepted was low.

The emergence of this moderating effect of need to belong is interesting for procedural fairness research because recently Cropanzano, Byrne, Bobocel, and Rupp (2001, p. 177) concluded that "the need for belonging could serve as one mechanism for the relational model of authority (Tyler & Lind, 1992)." In addition, De Cremer and Blader (2006) provided empirical evidence (across three studies) that the need to belong moderates procedural fairness effects, primarily because having such a strong need to affiliate makes people more attentive to procedural fairness information.

According to De Cremer and Alberts (2004), a possible reason need to belong moderates the relationship between procedural fairness and leadership selection is that procedural fairness influences people's reactions most strongly when people are high in need to belong and, as a result, care about receiving feedback that will enhance or sustain their feelings of belonging within the group. If such a possibility does not exist because members feel excluded and no longer committed to the leader, for example, because the leader is not someone whom they have chosen, procedural fairness is less likely to exert influence or may even have no influence at all.

Summary

Taken together, our studies illustrate the usefulness and importance of integrating leadership insights with the knowledge derived from procedural fairness research. In fact, realizing that both fairness and leadership can be seen as social events taking place at a relational and interpersonal level (Greenberg, 1996; Tyler & Lind, 1992), it is clear that both fields have much to talk about. Therefore, it is rather surprising that (1) procedural fairness is often not included as a leadership feature in the existing leadership literature and that (2) the procedural fairness literature has drawn hardly any relationships between the concepts of fairness and leadership styles. Fortunately, this situation seems to be changing. Indeed, in their leadership article on the Ohio State factors of initiation and structure, Judge, Piccolo, and Ilies (2004) suggested that "the integration of the Ohio State factors with justice theory is an important area for future research" (p. 45), as such acknowledging that leadership styles (derived and taken from the Ohio State factors throughout the years) have to be examined in tandem with justice issues (see De Cremer et al., 2007, for a recent demonstration).

The studies that we just reviewed present one possible approach to the integration between leadership styles and one aspect of fairness, that is, procedural fairness. Adopting a contingency approach, we were able to demonstrate that leadership styles and features associated with leadership emergence moderate the influence of procedural fairness. Why do these interactive effects emerge?

In the following paragraphs, we would like to elaborate on this question by focusing on the role of self and needs and thereby presenting a *motivational* analysis of leadership and procedural fairness. Indeed, the studies presented in the present chapter clearly imply an important role for human needs. For example, self-rewarding (De Cremer et al., 2005) and self-confident leadership (De Cremer & Wubben, 2008) seem to reveal effects because they promote a stronger sense of competence among followers—a need that can be met by giving them an opportunity to voice their opinion and thus to show their competence. Further, the need to belong also seems to play a role in explaining interactive effects between leadership and procedural fairness. In addition, needs are important in regulating people's reactions as a function of one's self-involvement (Ryan & Deci, 2003). That is, if one does not evaluate the social situation at hand to be relevant to shape one's self-view and identity, situational and interactional features such as leadership and fairness will not exert much influence on the satisfaction of one's needs and goals.

Interestingly, this focus on the importance of needs and the self is something that recent analyses of leadership also emphasize. That is, leaders are now also seen as group members that are subject to the same normative and social influences as the followers are (De Cremer & van Vugt, 2002; van Knippenberg & Hogg, 2003). As a result, leaders have become symbols of their own group, and because of this position they are believed to be able to influence the self and identity, and, consequently, the self-esteem of followers (e.g., van Knippenberg et al., 2004; Wieseke, Ahearne, Lam, & van Dick, 2009). Thus, one possible explanation why leadership styles moderate the influence of procedural fairness relates to the importance of human needs and its relevance for oneself.

THE ROLE OF NEEDS IN OUR CONTINGENCY APPROACH

As we mentioned earlier, social and interactional features such as leadership can make followers self-involved (e.g., van Knippenberg et al., 2004) or, in other words, can make the self more accessible by letting people focus on their internal values, goals, and motives. Indeed, the self is the cognitive-affective apparatus that allows people to engage in abstract, symbolically mediated thought and reflection about themselves (Leary, 2002b). Through this process of self-reflection, one is able to think about one's motives and needs (Leary, 2002a). In fact, Sedikides and Gregg (2003) argued that the self is immersed in a variety of motives, and social psychologists have even proposed a taxonomy of self-motives (see Deci & Ryan, 2000). Thus, reinforcing a focus on the self (by means of leadership) may make salient the needs and motives that people wish to achieve. According to us, procedural fairness then can serve as a psychological tool that meets these needs.

Following Self-Determination Theory (SDT; Deci & Ryan, 2000) it is proposed that humans have basic psychological needs for autonomy, competence, and relatedness. SDT defines needs as universal necessities, as the nutriments that are essential for optimal human development and integrity (Ryan, Sheldon, Kasser, & Deci, 1996), which involves a positive influence on emotional well-being, intrinsic motivation, and self-views and self-evaluations. For example, Gagne and Deci (2005, p. 336) noted that "satisfaction of basic psychological needs provides the nutriments for intrinsic motivation." In a similar vein, satisfaction of these needs thus also can be nutriment for emotions, cooperation, and self-esteem. Interestingly, procedural fairness has been shown to reveal positive effects on emotions (De Cremer, 2004; van den Bos & Miedema, 2000), cooperation (De Cremer & Tyler, 2005a), and self-esteem (De Cremer & Sedikides, 2005; De Cremer, van Knippenberg, van Dijke, & Bos, 2004; Koper et al., 1993).

Building on these insights, we suggest that leadership styles elicit self-focus: a process that makes people more attentive to their needs and motives. In turn, these salient needs may be addressed by means of the enactment of fair procedures. Indeed, the three needs of autonomy, competence, and relatedness show close resemblance to the motives that have been suggested in the literature to account for the procedural fairness effect. That is, on one hand, the control-based models argue that procedures enable people to exert control over outcomes (Leventhal, 1980; Thibaut & Walker, 1975), which highlights the importance of competence and autonomy. On the other hand, relational models of procedural fairness emphasize the importance of procedures in communicating information relevant to respect and acceptance (De Cremer & Tyler, 2005a, 2005b; Tyler & Lind, 1992). Thus, if one is treated fairly the associated feelings of belonging will satisfy the reinforced need of relatedness (De Cremer & Blader, 2006).

Thus, by stressing the pivotal role of self-focus and reinforcement of people's basic needs, it may be possible to explain (at least to some extent) interactive effects between leadership styles and procedural fairness. For example, rewarding behavior seems to be a specific instance of empowerment as it influences the management of followers' self-concept (Bass, 1998; Pearce & Sims, 2002). Therefore, leadership styles, like rewarding behavior, create a focus on the self and its associated needs of competence and self-confidence (see Conger, 2004; Spreitzer, 1995)—a situation that consequently will allow fair procedures to more strongly influence followers' reactions as predicted by a control perspective (and not a relational perspective). In a similar vein, an empowering leadership style such as encouragement of self-development (Yukl, 1994) relates to the need of autonomy, which will again lead to a stronger influence of procedural fairness via the psychological mechanisms outlined by the control perspective.

THE VALUE OF THE CONTINGENCY APPROACH

In our view, research examining the relationship between leadership elements such as styles and characteristics and procedural fairness may benefit greatly from a motivational model (as discussed in the present chapter) in which the self and a focus on its associated motives and needs is taken into account. This idea of a motivational account of leadership and procedural fairness is appealing, particularly since many procedural fairness models have shown a tendency to focus solely on the role that cognitive factors play in responding to variations in procedural fairness (see, e.g., Folger, 1986; Folger & Cropanzano, 1998; Lind, 2001; van den Bos, Lind, & Wilke, 2001).

For example, Lind (2001), in his fairness heuristic theory, advocates the use of a more cognitive analysis of fairness judgment processes when he describes the use of fair procedures in terms of heuristics, and Folger and Cropanzano (1998), in their fairness theory, explain justice effects by referring to the impact of attribution-based cognitive analyses. Although these models have been very effective in unraveling justice problems and stimulating exciting experimental and field studies, here we wish to suggest that a cognitive framework is too limited and that motivational accounts of procedural fairness also need to be examined. After all, both cognition and motivation act in tandem when it comes to predicting people's affective and social lives (Higgins & Kruglanski, 2001).

Further, a focus on leadership by using a contingency approach is also useful for deepening our understanding of when procedural fairness matters most. That is, a basic assumption of our contingency approach is that the strength of the influence of procedural fairness on employees' reactions depends on how a leader acts when employing decision-making procedures. As such, leadership styles and characteristics can be seen as an important class of moderators that can be examined in the procedural fairness literature.

Recently, Colquitt, Greenberg, and Scott (2005) noted that moderator variables play an important role in the building of justice theories and therefore suggested that moderator variables need to be identified based on systematic and sound reasoning. In line with this view, we think that it seems clear that leadership constitutes an important moderator variable, particularly because the integration between leadership and procedural fairness is based on a strong historical line of research and sound theoretical reasoning.

Also, by exploring the relationship between procedural fairness and leadership, the present chapter points out a valuable direction for future research. At the same time, however, it also makes the claim that the intuitive link between fairness and leadership (see Colquitt & Greenberg, 2003) does not just include the concept of interpersonal justice (see, e.g., De Cremer et al., 2007). Indeed, Bies (2005, p. 99) recently argued, "Directions for future research on interpersonal justice include leadership." We hope that the previous analysis makes clear that for future fairness research it may be beneficial to examine the relationship between leadership and both the decision-making and interpersonal aspects of procedural fairness. Interestingly, in 1988, Lind and Tyler had already noted that procedural justice can "specify the authority relations and the formal and informal social processes that regulate much of the group's activity" (p. 231).

Finally, by exploring the relationship between procedural fairness and leadership, our research further illustrates the importance of fairness for organizations. Indeed, some justice scholars (see Greenberg & Colquitt, 2005) noted that we still need to embark on the scientific journey to demonstrate that justice is really as important as we usually claim. In our opinion, the value of and importance of fairness to organizations can also be demonstrated by pointing out the relationship that fairness (e.g., procedural and interpersonal fairness) has with other established organizational variables such as leadership. Thus, research on the relationship between fairness and leadership may also fulfill part of this important task.

CONCLUSION

To conclude, the main message of the present chapter is that leadership and procedural fairness have much in common and that more research is needed to explore this relationship in greater detail. Here, we have presented a contingency approach that advocates the use of zooming in on leadership styles and characteristics that affect when and to what extent procedural fairness will impact employees' reactions. In addition, the value of such an approach is outlined. We hope that our investigation will spark additional forays into the relation between leadership and procedural fairness.

REFERENCES

Arnold, J. A., Arad, S., Rhoades, J. A., & Drasgow, F. (2000). The empowering leadership questionnaire: The construction and validation of a new scale for measuring leader behaviors. *Journal of Organizational Behavior, 21,* 249–269.

Bandura, A. (1986). *Social foundations of thought and action: Social cognitive theory.* Englewood Cliffs, NJ: Prentice Hall.

Bass, B. M. (1985). *Leadership and performance beyond expectations.* New York: Free Press.

Bass, B. M. (1998). *Transformational leadership: Industrial, military and educational impact.* Mahwah, NJ: Lawrence Erlbaum Associates.

Bies, R. J. (2005). Are procedural justice and interactional justice conceptually distinct? In J. Greenberg & J. A. Colquitt (Eds.), *Handbook of organizational justice* (pp. 85–112). Lawrence Erlbaum Associates.

Blader, S., & Tyler, T. R. (2003a). What constitutes fairness in work settings? A four-component model of procedural justice. *Human Resource Management Review, 13,* 107–126.

Blader, S., & Tyler, T.R. (2003b). A four-component model of procedural justice: Defining the meaning of a "fair" process. *Personality and Social Psychology Bulletin, 29,* 747–758.

Brockner, J., Heuer, L., Siegel, P. A., Wiesenfeld, B., Martin, C., Grover, S., et al. (1998). The moderating effect of self-esteem in reaction to voice: Converging evidence from five studies. *Journal of Personality and Social Psychology, 75,* 394–407.

Brown, M. E., & Trevino, L. K. (2003). Is values-based leadership ethical leadership? In S. W. Gilliland, D. D. Steiner, & D. P. Skarlicki (Eds.), *Emerging perspectives on values in organizations* (pp. 151–174). Greenwich, CT: Information Age Publishers.

Bryman, A. (1996). Leadership in organizations. In S. R. Clegg, C. Hardy, & W. R. Nord (Eds.), *Handbook of organization studies* (pp. 276–292). Thousand Oaks, CA: Sage.

Burns, J. M. (1978). *Leadership.* New York: Harper & Row.

Casimir, G. (2001). Combinative aspects of leadership style: The ordering and temporal spacing of leadership behaviors. *Leadership Quarterly, 12,* 245–278.

Chemers, M. M. (2001). Leadership effectiveness: An integrative review. In M. A. Hogg & R. S. Tindale (Eds.), *Blackwell handbook of social psychology: Group processes* (pp. 376–399). Oxford, UK: Blackwell.

Cobb, A. T., & Frey, F. M. (1996). The effects of leader fairness and pay outcomes on superior/subordinate relations. *Journal of Applied Social Psychology, 26,* 1401–1426.

Cohen, A. M., & Bennis, W. G. (1961). Continuity of leadership in communication networks. *Human Relations, 14,* 351–367.

Colquitt, J. A., & Greenberg, J. (2003). Organizational justice: A fair assessment of the state of the literature. In J. Greenberg (Ed.), *Organizational behavior: The state of the science* (pp. 165–210). Mahwah, NJ: Lawrence Erlbaum Associates.

Colquitt, J. A., Greenberg, J., & Scott, B. A. (2005). Organizational justice: Where do we stand? In J. Greenberg & J. A. Colquitt (Eds.), *Handbook of organizational justice* (pp. 589–619). Mahwah, NJ: Lawrence Erlbaum.

Conger, J. A. (1989). *The charismatic leader: Behind the mystique of exceptional leadership.* San Francisco: Jossey-Bass.

Conger, J. A. (2004). Motivate performance through empowerment. In E. A. Locke (Ed.), *Handbook of principles of organizational behavior* (pp. 137–149). Oxford, UK: Blackwell.

Conger, J. A., & Kanungo, R. N. (1987). Toward a behavioral theory of charismatic leadership in organizational settings. *Academy of Management Review, 12,* 637–647.

Cropanzano, R., Byrne, Z. S., Bobocel, D. R., & Rupp, D. (2001). Moral virtues, fairness heuristics, social entities, and other denizens of organizational justice. *Journal of Vocational Behavior, 58,* 164–209.

Deci, E. L., & Ryan, R. M. (2000). The "what" and "why" of goal pursuits: Human needs and the self-determination of behavior. *Psychological Inquiry, 11,* 227–268.

De Cremer, D. (2004). The influence of accuracy as a function of leader's bias: The role of trustworthiness in the psychology of procedural justice. *Personality and Social Psychology Bulletin, 30,* 293–304.

De Cremer, D. (2006). When authorities influence followers' affect: The interactive effect of procedural justice and transformational leadership. *European Journal of Work and Organizational Psychology, 15,* 322–351.

De Cremer, D. (2007). Emotional effects of distributive justice as a function of autocratic leader behavior. *Journal of Applied Social Psychology, 37,* 1385–1404.

De Cremer, D., & Alberts, H. (2004). When procedural fairness does not influence how good I feel: The effects of voice and leader selection as a function of belongingness needs. *European Journal of Social Psychology, 34,* 333–344.

De Cremer, D., & Blader, S. (2006). Why do people care about procedural fairness? The importance of belongingness in responding and attending to procedures. *European Journal of Social Psychology, 36,* 211–228.

De Cremer, D., & Den Ouden, N. (2009). "When passion breeds justice": Procedural fairness effects as a function of authority's passion. *European Journal of Social Psychology, 39,* 384–400.

De Cremer, D., & Sedikides, C. (2005). Self-uncertainty and responsiveness to procedural justice. *Journal of Experimental Social Psychology, 41,* 151–173.

De Cremer, D., & Sedikides, C. (2008). Reputational implications of procedural fairness for personal and relational self-esteem. *Basic and Applied Social Psychology, 30,* 66–75.

De Cremer, D., & Tyler, T. R. (2005a). Managing group behavior: The interplay between procedural fairness, sense of self, and cooperative behavior. In M. Zanna (Ed.), *Advances in experimental social psychology* (Vol. 37, pp. 151–218). New York: Elsevier.

De Cremer, D., & Tyler, T. R. (2005b). Am I respected or not?: Inclusion and reputation as issues in group membership. *Social Justice Research, 18,* 121–153.

De Cremer, D., van Dijke, M., & Bos, A. (2004). Distributive justice moderating the effects of self-sacrificial leadership. *Leadership and Organization Development Journal, 25,* 466–475.

De Cremer, D., van Dijke, M., & Bos, A. (2007). When leaders are seen as transformational: The effects of organizational justice. *Journal of Applied Social Psychology, 37,* 1797–1816.

De Cremer, D., & van Knippenberg, D. (2002). How do leaders promote cooperation? The effects of charisma and procedural fairness. *Journal of Applied Psychology, 87,* 858–866.

De Cremer, D., & van Knippenberg, D. (2004). Leader self-sacrifice and leadership effectiveness: The moderating role of leader self-confidence. *Organizational Behavior and Human Decision Processes, 95,* 140–155.

De Cremer, D., van Knippenberg, D., van Dijke, M., & Bos, A. (2004). How self-relevant is fair treatment? Social self-esteem moderates interactional justice effects. *Social Justice Research, 17,* 407–419.

De Cremer, D., van Knippenberg, B., van Knippenberg, D., Mullenders, D., & Stinglhamber, F. (2005). Effects of procedural fairness as a function of leadership style: Self-reward leadership and fair procedures as determinants of self-esteem. *Journal of Applied Psychology, 90,* 3–12.

De Cremer D., & van Vugt, M. (2002). Intergroup and intragroup aspects of leadership in social dilemmas: A relational model of cooperation. *Journal of Experimental Social Psychology, 38,* 126–136.

De Cremer, D., & Wubben, M. (2010). *Instrumental effects of procedural fairness as a function of self-confident leadership.* Unpublished manuscript, Erasmus University, the Netherlands.

Folger, R. (1977). Distributive and procedural justice: Combined impact of "voice" and improvement of experienced inequity. *Journal of Personality and Social Psychology, 35,* 108–119.

Folger, R. (1986). Rethinking equity theory: A referent cognitions model. In H. W. Bierhoff, R. L. Cohen, & J. Greenberg (Eds.), *Justice in social relations* (pp. 145–162). New York: Plenum Press.

Folger, R., & Cropanzano, R. (1998). *Organizational justice and human resource management.* Thousand Oaks, CA: Sage.

Gagne, M., & Deci, E. L. (2005). Self-determination theory and work motivation. *Journal of Organizational Behavior, 26,* 331–362.

Gibson, J. L. (2002). Truth, justice, and reconciliation: Judging the fairness of amnesty in South Africa. *American Journal of Political Science, 46,* 540–556.

Greenberg, J. (1996). *The quest for justice on the job.* Thousand Oaks, CA: Sage Publications.

Greenberg, J., & Colquitt, J. A. (2005). *Handbook of organizational justice.* Mahwah, NJ: Lawrence Erlbaum.

Hackman, J. R., & Walton, R. E. (1986). Leading groups in organizations. In P. S. Goodman et al., *Designing effective work groups* (pp. 72–119). San Francisco: Jossey-Bass.

Haslam, S. A. (2001). *Psychology in organisations: The social identity approach.* London: Sage.

Higgins, E. T., & Kruglanski, A. W. (2001). Motivational science: The nature and functions of wanting. In E. T. Higgins & A. W. Kruglanski (Eds.), *Motivational science: Social and personality perspectives* (pp. 1–20). New York: Psychology Press.

Hogg, M. A., & van Knippenberg, D. (2003). Social identity and leadership processes in groups. In M. P. Zanna (Ed.), *Advances in experimental social psychology* (Vol. 35, pp. 1–52). New York: Elsevier Science.

Hollander, E. P. (1985). Leadership and power. In G. Lindzey & E. Aronson (Eds.), *The handbook of social psychology* (pp. 485–537). New York: Random House.

Hollander, E. P., & Julian, J. W. (1970). Studies in leader legitimacy, influence, and innovation. *Advances in Experimental Social Psychology, 5,* 33–69.

House, R. J. (1977). A 1976 theory of charismatic leadership. In J. G. Hunt & L. L. Larson (Eds.), *Leadership: The cutting edge* (pp. 189–207). Carbondale: Southern Illinois University Press.

Huo, Y. J., Smith, H. J., Tyler, T. R., & Lind, E. A. (1996). Superordinate identification, subgroup identification, and justice concerns: Is separatism the problem, is assimilation the answer? *Psychological Science, 7,* 40–45.

Judge, T. A., & Bono, J. E. (2000). Five-factor model of personality and transformational leadership. *Journal of Applied Psychology, 85,* 751–765.

Judge, T. A., Piccolo, R. F., & Ilies, R. (2004). The forgotten ones? The validity of consideration and initiating structure in leadership research. *Journal of Applied Psychology, 89,* 36–51.

Julian, J. W., Hollander, E. P., & Regula, C. R. (1969). Endorsement of the group spokesman as a function of his source of authority, competence, and success. *Journal of Personality and Social Psychology, 11,* 42–49.

Keller, T., & Dansereau, F. (1995). Leadership and empowerment: A social exchange perspective. *Human Relations, 48,* 127–146.

Kershaw, T. S., & Alexander, S. (2003). Procedural fairness, blame attributions, and presidential leadership. *Social Justice Research, 16,* 79–93.

Khurana, R. (2002). The curse of the superstar CEO. *Harvard Business Review*, September, 60–66.

Kim, W. C., & Mauborgne, R. A. (1993). Procedural justice, attitudes, and subsidiary top management compliance with multinationals' corporate strategic decisions. *Academy of Management Journal, 36,* 502–526.

Koper, G., van Knippenberg, D., Bouhuijs, F., Vermunt, R., & Wilke, H. A. M. (1993). Procedural fairness and self-esteem. *European Journal of Social Psychology, 23,* 313–325.

Kotter, J. P. (1982). *The general managers.* New York: Free Press.

Kouzes, J. M., Posner, B. Z., & Peters, T. (1996). *The leadership challenge.* San Francisco: Jossey-Bass.

Leary, M. (2002a). The self as a source of relational difficulties. *Self and Identity, 1,* 137–142.

Leary, M. (2002b). When selves collide: The nature of the self and dynamics of interpersonal relationships. In A. Tesser, D. A. Stapel, & J. V. Wood (Eds.), *Self and motivation: Emerging psychological perspectives* (pp. 119–146). Washington, DC: American Psychological Association.

Leary, M. R., Kelly, K. M., Cottrell, C. A., & Schreindorfer, L. S. (2001). *Individual differences in the need to belong.* Unpublished manuscript, Wake Forest University, Winston-Salem, NC.

Leventhal, G. S. (1980). What should be done with equity theory? New approaches to the study of fairness in social relationships. In K. J. Gergen, M. S. Greenberg, & R. H. Willis (Eds.), *Social exchange: Advances in theory and research* (pp. 27–54). New York: Plenum.

Lind, E. A. (2001). Fairness heuristic theory: Justice judgments as pivotal cognitions in organizational relations. In J. Greenberg & R. Cropanzano (Eds.), *Advances in organizational justice* (pp. 56–88). Stanford, CA: Stanford University Press.

Lind, E. A., Kanfer, R., & Earley, P. C. (1990). Voice, control, and procedural justice: Instrumental and noninstrumental concerns in fairness judgments. *Journal of Personality and Social Psychology, 59,* 952–959.

Lind, E. A., & Tyler, T. R. (1988). *The social psychology of procedural justice.* New York: Plenum Press.

Lind, E. A., Tyler, T. R., & Huo, Y. J. (1997). Procedural context and conflict: Variation in the antecedents of procedural justice judgments. *Journal of Personality and Social Psychology, 73,* 767–780.

Lord, R. G., & Brown, D. J. (2004). *Leadership processes and follower self-identity.* Mahwah, NJ: Lawrence Erlbaum Associates.

Machiavelli, N. (1991). *The prince* (2nd ed.). London: W. W. Norton & Company.

Mansour-Cole, D. M., & Scott, S. G. (1998). Hearing it through the grapevine: The influence of source, leader-relations, and legitimacy on survivors' fairness perceptions. *Personnel Psychology, 51,* 25–54.

McGregor, D. (1960). *The human side of enterprise.* New York: McGraw-Hill.

Messick, D. M., & Kramer, R. M. (Eds.). (2005). *The psychology of leadership: New perspectives and research.* Mahwah, NJ: Lawrence Erlbaum.

Miller, D. T. (2001). Disrespect and the experience of injustice. *Annual Review of Psychology, 52,* 527–553.

Northouse, P. G. (2001). *Leadership: Theory and practice* (2nd ed.). Thousand Oaks, CA: Sage Publications.

Pearce, C. L., & Sims Jr., H. P. (2002). Vertical versus shared leadership as predictors of the effectiveness of change management teams: An examination of aversive, directive, transactional, transformational, and empowering leader behaviors. *Groups Dynamics: Theory, Research, and Practice, 6,* 172–197.

Pillai, R., Scandura, T. A., & Williams, E. A. (1999). Leadership and organizational justice: Similarities and differences across cultures. *Journal of International Business Studies, 30,* 763–779.

Rawls, J. (1971). *A theory of justice.* Cambridge, MA: Harvard University Press.

Ryan, R. M., & Deci, E. L. (2003). On assimilating identities to the self: A self-determination theory perspective on internalization and integrity within cultures. In M. R. Leary & J. P. Tangney (Eds.), *Handbook of self and identity* (pp. 253–272). New York: Guilford Press.

Ryan, R. M., Sheldon, K. M., Kasser, T., & Deci, E. L. (1996). All goals are not created equal: An organismic perspective on the nature of goals and their regulation. In P. M. Gollwitzer & J. A. Bargh (Eds.), *The psychology of action: Linking cognition and motivation to behavior* (pp. 7–26). New York: Guilford.

Sedikides, C., & Gregg, A. (2003). Portraits of the self. In M. A. Hogg & J. Cooper (Eds.), *Sage handbook of social psychology* (pp. 110–138). London: Sage Publications.

Shamir, B., House, R. J., & Arthur, M. B. (1993). The motivational effects of charismatic leadership: A self-concept based concept. *Organizational Science, 4,* 577–594.

Shea, C. M., & Howell, J. M. (1999). Charismatic leadership and task feedback: A laboratory study of their effects on self-efficacy and task performance. *Leadership Quarterly, 10,* 375–396.

Smith, H. J., & Tyler, T. R. (1996). Justice and power: When will justice concerns encourage the advantaged to support policies which redistribute economic resources and encourage the disadvantaged to willingly obey the law? *European Journal of Social Psychology,* 26, 171–200.

Smith, H. J., & Tyler, T. R. (1997). Choosing the right pond: The impact of group membership on self-esteem and group-oriented behaviors. *Journal of Experimental Social Psychology,* 33, 146–170.

Smith, H. J., Tyler, T. R., Huo, Y. J., Ortiz, D. J., & Lind, E. A. (1998). The self-relevant implications of the group-value model: Group membership, self-worth, and treatment quality. *Journal of Experimental Social Psychology, 34,* 470–493.

Spreitzer, G. M. (1995). Individual empowerment in the workplace: Dimensions, measurement, and validation. *Academy of Management Journal, 38,* 1442–1465.

Stogdill, R. M. (1974). *Handbook of leadership.* New York: Free Press.

Thibaut, J., & Walker, L. (1975). *Procedural justice.* Mahwah, NJ: Erlbaum.

Tyler, T. R. (1987). Conditions leading to value-expressive effects in judgments of procedural justice: A test of four models. *Journal of Personality and Social Psychology, 52,* 333–344.

Tyler, T. R. (1988). What is procedural justice?: Criteria used by citizens to assess the fairness of legal procedures. *Law and Society Review, 22,* 103–135.

Tyler, T. R. (1989). The psychology of procedural justice: A test of the group value model. *Journal of Personality and Social Psychology, 57,* 830–838.

Tyler, T. R. (1990). *Why people obey the law: Procedural justice, legitimacy, and compliance.* New Haven, CT: Yale University Press.

Tyler, T. R. (2001). Procedural strategies for gaining deference: Increasing social harmony or creating false consciousness? In J. M. Darley, D. M. Messick, & T. R. Tyler (Eds.), *Social influences on ethical behavior in organizations* (pp. 71–90). Mahwah, NJ: Lawrence Erlbaum Associates.

Tyler, T. R. (2004). Process based leadership: How do leaders lead? In D. Messick & R. Kramer (Eds.), *The psychology of leadership: New Perspectives and Research* (pp. 167–193). Mahwah, NJ: Lawrence Erlbaum Associates.

Tyler, T. R., & Blader, S. (2000). *Cooperation in groups: Procedural justice, social identity, and behavioral engagement.* Philadelphia: Psychology Press.

Tyler, T. R., Boeckmann, R. J., Smith, H. J., & Huo, Y. J. (1997). *Social justice in a diverse society.* Boulder, CO: Westview Press.

Tyler, T. R., & Caine, A. (1981). The influence of outcomes and procedures on satisfaction with formal leaders. *Journal of Personality and Social Psychology, 41,* 642–655.

Tyler, T. R., & De Cremer, D. (2005). Process-based leadership: Fair procedures and reactions to organizational change. *Leadership Quarterly, 16,* 529–545.

Tyler, T. R., & Degoey, P. (1995). Collective restraint in social dilemmas: Procedural justice and social identification effects on suport for authorities. *Journal of Personality and Social Psychology, 69,* 482–497.

Tyler, T. R., & Huo, Y. J. (2002). *Trust in the law: Encouraging public cooperation with the police and courts.* New York: Russell-Sage Foundation.

Tyler, T. R., & Lind, E. A. (1992). A relational model of authority in groups. In M. Zanna (Ed.), *Advances in Experimental Social Psychology* (Vol. 25, pp. 115–191). New York: Academic Press.

Tyler, T. R., Rasinski, K. A., & McGraw, K. M. (1985). The influence of perceived injustice on the endorsement of political leaders. *Journal of Applied Social Psychology, 15,* 700–725.

Tyler, T. R., Rasinski, K. A., & Spodick, N. (1985). Influence of voice on satisfaction with leaders: Exploring the meaning of process control. *Journal of Personality and Social Psychology, 48,* 72–81.

Ullrich, J., Christ, O., & van Dick, R. (2009). Substitutes for procedural fairness: Prototypical leaders are endorsed whether they are fair or not. *Journal of Applied Psychology, 94,* 235–244.

van den Bos, K. (2005). What is responsible for the fair process effect? In J. Greenberg & J. A. Colquitt (Eds.), *Handbook of organizational justice* (pp. 273–300). Mahwah, NJ: Lawrence Erlbaum Associates.

van den Bos, K., Lind, E. A., Vermunt, R., & Wilke, H. A. M. (1997). How do I judge my outcome when I do not know the outcome of others? The psychology of the fair process effect. *Journal of Personality and Social Psychology, 72,* 1034–1046.

van den Bos, K., Lind, E. A., & Wilke, H. A. M. (2001). The psychology of procedural and distributive justice viewed from the perspective of fairness heuristic theory. In R. Cropanzano (Ed.), *Justice in the workplace: From theory to practice* (pp. 49–66). Mahwah, NJ: Lawrence Erlbaum Associates.

van den Bos, K., & Miedema, J. (2000). Toward understanding why fairness matters: The influence of mortality salience on reactions to procedural fairness. *Journal of Personality and Social Psychology, 79,* 355–366.

van Knippenberg, D., & De Cremer, D. (2008). Leadership and fairness: Taking stock and looking ahead. *European Journal of Work and Organizational Psychology, 17,* 173–179.

van Knippenberg, D., & Hogg, M. A. (2003). A social identity model of leadership effectiveness in organizations. *Research in Organizational Behavior, 25,* 243–296.

van Knippenberg, D., van Knippenberg, B., De Cremer, D., & Hogg, M. A. (2004). Leadership, self, and identity: A review and research agenda. *Leadership Quarterly, 15,* 825–856.

Vecchio, R. P., Griffeth, R. W., & Hom, P. W. (1986). The predictive utility of the vertical dyad linkage approach. *Journal of Social Psychology, 126,* 617–625.

Vroom, V. H. (1964). *Work and motivation.* New York: Wiley and Sons.

Walster, E., Walster, G. W., & Berscheid, E. (1978). *Equity: Theory and research.* Boston: Allyn and Bacon.

Wieseke, J., Ahearne, M., Lam, S. K., & van Dick, R. (2009). The role of leaders in internal marketing. *Journal of Marketing, 73,* 123–145.

Yukl, G. A. (1994). *Leadership in organizations* (3rd ed.). Englewood Cliffs, NJ: Prentice Hall.

4

Managing Normative Influences in Organizations

Noah J. Goldstein
University of California, Los Angeles

Robert B. Cialdini
Arizona State University

For decades, social psychologists have debated the role of normative perceptions in individuals' everyday actions (e.g., Berkowitz, 1972; Darley & Latané, 1970; Fishbein & Ajzen, 1975; Sherif, 1936). However, it is now clear that, across a wide variety of domains, social norms direct the behavior of individuals in predictable ways within organizational contexts as well as outside of them (Aarts & Dijksterhuis, 2003; Bettenhausen & Murnighan, 1985; Feldman, 1984; Kerr, 1995; Schultz, 1999; Terry & Hogg, 2000; Turner, 1991). Understanding how social norms operate is important for better understanding organizational behavior because there are norms for nearly every behavior at work, including the hours employees work, the clothes they wear, how projects are carried out, how resources are allocated, how and how often employees communicate with and help one another, and even how often they interact outside of the work environment (Goodman, Ravlin, & Schminke, 1987).

To get a better grasp on the influence of social norms both within and outside of organizational contexts, it is useful to return to that old grade-school standby of *who, what, when, where, why,* and *how.* Having reached somewhat of a consensus on *what* norms are capable of doing, researchers have turned their attention to issues such as *when* and *where* their causal impact is likely to be largest, *how* and *why* different kinds of social norms influence behavior via disparate mediating mechanisms, and *who* is most likely to be influenced by social norms. Several theoretical perspectives have emerged to address these issues. Although our coverage of the normative literature in this chapter concentrates primarily on one of these perspectives—namely, the Focus Theory of Normative Conduct (Cialdini, Kallgren, & Reno, 1991; Cialdini, Reno, & Kallgren, 1990)—we will also discuss this literature from the perspective of social identity and self-categorization theories (e.g., Abrams & Hogg, 1990). In addition, we will examine the implications of social psychological research on social norms for how individuals behave in organizations and for how managers might go about shaping and communicating social norms to spur desirable behavior and to minimize undesirable behavior.

FOCUS THEORY OF NORMATIVE CONDUCT

Before we discuss the role norms play in influencing behavior within and outside of organizational contexts, it is important to understand what exactly we mean when we use the term *social norms*. The meaning of social norms has been somewhat amorphous over the last half a century (for a brief history, see Cialdini & Trost, 1998). However, looking both to clarify the definitional confusion that had clouded researchers' ability to understand the roles of social norms (see Shaffer, 1983) and to better predict when social norms will influence behavior, Cialdini and colleagues (Cialdini et al., 1990, 1991) developed the Focus Theory of Normative Conduct. Focus Theory has two central propositions. The first is that two different types of norms—descriptive and injunctive—can have considerably different effects on behavior. The second is that any given norm is likely to influence behavior directly to the extent that is it salient. We will consider the evidence for each of these propositions in turn.

Differentiating Between Descriptive and Injunctive Norms

Similar to the distinction that Deutsch and Gerard (1955) made between informational and normative influences, Cialdini et al. (1990) suggested that descriptive and injunctive norms influence conduct through separate sources of motivation. Akin to what Cialdini (2008) called "social proof," descriptive norms refer to what is commonly done in a given situation, and they motivate human action by informing individuals of what is likely to be effective or adaptive behavior in that situation. A wide variety of research shows that the behavior of others in the social environment shapes individuals' interpretations of and responses to the situation, especially in novel, ambiguous, or uncertain situations (Cialdini & Trost, 1998). Injunctive norms, on the other hand, refer to what is commonly approved or disapproved within the culture, and they motivate behavior through informal social sanctions. In brief, descriptive norms refer to perceptions of what *is* done, whereas injunctive norms refer to perceptions of what *ought to be* done. The two are often confused as a single construct because what is commonly approved within a culture is also what is commonly done in a culture. However, this is not always the case. For example, although most people probably believe that workers *should not* steal office supplies or pad expense reports (injunctive norm), it may very well be that most workers *actually engage* in this behavior (descriptive norm).

The mechanisms through which descriptive and injunctive norms spur and guide people's actions have remained relatively unexplored. However, Cialdini and colleagues (Cialdini, 2003; Cialdini et al., 2010) recently suggested that injunctive and descriptive norms influence behavior via different routes. They posited that individuals focusing on descriptive norms need not engage in elaborate cognitive processing of the relevant information because applying the heuristic rule "I should do what most others do" is based primarily on the simple observations of others' situation-specific behaviors. In contrast, acting on information provided by injunctive norms proves a more cognitively demanding route because it is based on an understanding of the culture's moral rules—that is, what others are likely to approve. To test whether these two types of norms are mediated through these different mechanisms, the researchers had participants watch public service announcements (PSAs) that featured both injunctive and descriptive norms in favor of recycling. Immediately after viewing the ads, participants completed a number of items that assessed their beliefs about recycling norms, their perceptions of the ads, and their recycling intentions. In support of the contention that descriptive and injunctive norms influence behavior through different levels of cognitive analysis, the relationship between recycling intentions and participants' perceptions that the ads conveyed approval for recycling (injunctive norm) was mediated by their cognitive evaluations of the ads' persuasiveness, whereas the effect of descriptive normative information on intentions was direct (i.e., unmediated by considerations of ad persuasiveness).

If the mechanism through which descriptive norms affect conduct is rooted more in perception than cognition, perhaps its power to motivate behavior might be limited to the setting in which it was originally perceived. Reno, Cialdini, and Kallgren (1993) contended that descriptive norms are more situation specific in the information they convey, as these norms communicate what others have felt is an effective course of action in that particular setting or situation. Thus, they suggested that the effect of the descriptive norm is less likely to transfer across situations than is the effect of injunctive norms. This is because injunctive norms more generally convey the kind of behavior that is approved or disapproved within a culture, which is subject to less variation across situations. Therefore, the influence of injunctive norms should transfer across a wide variety of environments. Reno et al. found that descriptive and injunctive norms against littering were equally successful at reducing littering when the opportunity for their participants to litter occurred in the same setting in which the norm was made salient. However, only the injunctive norm reduced littering rates when the opportunity to litter occurred in an environment that was different from the one in which the norm was made salient. Although it is somewhat speculative, these data suggest that injunctive norms are more likely to be consistent across organizational departments than are descriptive norms, a prediction that is open to empirical validation.

It is important to note that we are not arguing that descriptive norms never transfer across situations, environments, or contexts but rather that they are simply less likely to do so than are injunctive norms. Both types of norms are particularly likely to generalize to other situations and settings when they are associated with mnemonic cues that are also present in these other situations and settings, a hypothesis that we will return to later in the chapter.

The Importance of Focus

By now, it should be evident that descriptive and injunctive norms are orthogonal constructs that are capable of eliciting considerably different behaviors. However, given that countless social norms have the potential to operate in almost any setting or social situation within a given organization, what determines which norm or norms will have a direct influence on behavior? Recall that the second postulate of Focus Theory is that a norm will directly affect conduct to the extent that it is focal (i.e. salient) in consciousness.

Cialdini and colleagues (1990) tested this assertion within the context of littering behavior. Dormitory residents who found a flier in their mailboxes encountered an environment that was prearranged to contain no litter (the control condition), one piece of very conspicuous litter (a hollowed-out, end piece of watermelon rind), or an assortment of different kinds of litter, including the watermelon rind. The purpose of the large, eye-catching watermelon rind was to ensure that participants would focus on the descriptive norm in that setting regarding the typicality of littering behavior. Thus, when the environment's only blemish was the watermelon rind, participants would focus on the fact that, with the exception of the rind, littering is uncommon in that setting. On the other hand, when the environment was filled with rubbish in addition to the rind, participants would focus on the fact that littering is common in that setting. Consistent with predictions, the authors found that compared with the littering rate in the clean environment (10.7%) participants in the fully littered environment littered at a significantly higher rate (26.7%), whereas participants who encountered the watermelon rind in the otherwise spotless area littered at a significantly lower rate (3.6%). The finding that the completely litter-free environment actually yielded higher littering rates than the environment containing the lone rind is especially noteworthy because the data cannot be accounted for by other perspectives, such as social learning theory (e.g., Bandura, 1977). That is, if this were simply a modeling effect, participants who observed the discarded rind would have been more likely, not less, to litter than participants in the completely unadulterated environment.

Researchers have also demonstrated the importance of focus when the injunctive and descriptive norms of a setting are not in line with one another. For example, in an experiment conducted by Reno and colleagues (1993, Study 1), library-goers returning to their parked cars passed by a confederate who either littered a piece of trash, picked up a piece of trash, or simply walked by. To manipulate the descriptive norm for littering in that setting, the environment was altered to be either completely devoid or completely full of litter. Much like the presence of the rind in the previously described experiment, the littering of the rubbish by the confederate was meant to *focus* participants on that descriptive norm. The picking up of the litter, on the other hand, was meant to focus participants on the widely held injunctive norm—that is, people, and society at large, roundly

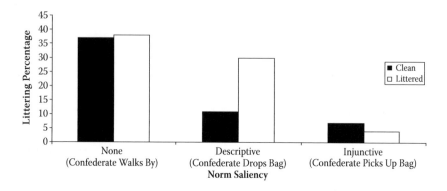

FIGURE 4.1
Littering rates as a function of norm saliency and condition of the environment. (From R. R. Reno, R. B. Cialdini, & C. A. Kallgren, *Journal of Personality and Social Psychology,* 64, 1993, p. 106. With permission.)

disapprove of people who litter. The researchers found that compared with those in the control conditions the library-goers in the descriptive-norm focus condition littered less only when the environment was litter free (Figure 4.1). However, those in the injunctive-norm condition littered less than their control counterparts regardless of the state of the surrounding environment, demonstrating that by focusing the participants' attention on the injunctive norm the information conveyed by the descriptive norm was rendered uninfluential.

The evidence from the normative literature makes it clear that one's behaviors seem to be relatively unaffected by normative information— even one's own—unless the information is in focus (Cialdini & Goldstein, 2004). Given that relevant norms must be salient to trigger the appropriate norm-congruent behavior, those attempting to persuade others to engage in a particular behavior face the dual challenge of making the norm focal not only immediately following message reception but also in the future. Cialdini et al. (2010) argue that the long-term effectiveness of persuasive communications such as public service announcements is threatened because normative information becomes less accessible over time. They hypothesized that linking an injunctive normative message to a functional mnemonic cue (see Tulving, 1983) would increase norm accessibility at later times when the norm would not have been focal otherwise. Consistent with their predictions, they found that participants who viewed a PSA in which the wording of an injunctive norm ("You

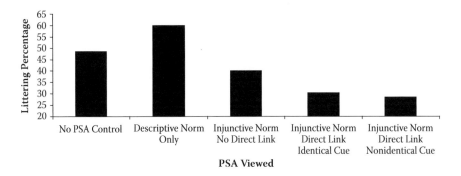

FIGURE 4.2
Littering rates as a function of public service announcement viewed. (From R. B. Cialdini, D. W. Barrett, R. Bator, L. Demaine, B. J. Sagarin, K. v. L. Rhoads, et al., manuscript submitted for publication, 2009. With permission.)

know, people who litter are real jerks") was superimposed directly over a piece of litter (retrieval cue) were significantly less likely to litter a paper towel in a stairwell several hours later than were those who saw the same wording placed elsewhere on the screen (Figure 4.2). This was the case regardless of whether the retrieval cue featured in the PSA was a paper towel or a newspaper, suggesting that linking social disapproval to the basic category of litter was enough to elicit the desired change (Cialdini et al., 2010). Moreover, participants who saw the phrase, "Americans will produce more litter than ever," superimposed on the litter were most likely to litter, demonstrating once again the potential harm caused by characterizing a behavior as regrettably common.

What this all suggests is that, whereas top-level managers in organizations might assume that employees are fully aware of organizational norms (and abiding by them), it is imperative for organizations to take steps to ensure that such norms are salient in the contexts and time periods in which they are most relevant.

THE CONSTRUCTIVE, DESTRUCTIVE, AND RECONSTRUCTIVE POWER OF SOCIAL NORMS

Communicators who are attempting to create maximally effective normative messages must decide whether to activate injunctive norms, descriptive norms, or both. Recall two central postulates of Focus Theory: (1) that norms direct behavior only when they are salient (Kallgren, Reno, & Cialdini, 2000); and (2) that the activation of the injunctive norm or the descriptive norm may elicit considerably different behavioral responses (Reno et al., 1993). Unfortunately, many communicators fail to be mindful that they must focus the target audience on the type of norm that is aligned with the end objective. For example, officials attempting to combat detrimental behavior (and raise public awareness of this behavior) often make the mistake of characterizing it as regrettably prevalent, which unintentionally focuses their audience on the unfavorable descriptive norm.

One notable example of a subtle misalignment of injunctive and descriptive norms comes from a commercial produced in the early 1970s by the Keep America Beautiful organization. Designed to reduce littering nationwide, the spot begins with a stately and serious-looking Native American dressed in traditional garb canoeing across a river. As he paddles through the waterway, the river is clearly effluent filled and debris ridden, and the air is replete with industrial pollutants spewing from smokestacks. After pulling his craft along a soiled shore, a driver zooming down an adjacent street tosses a bag of trash out of his car, splattering its contents across the Native American's feet. As a lone teardrop tracks slowly down his previously stoic countenance, a voiceover intones, "People start pollution. People can stop it."

Several years ago, the Keep America Beautiful organization brought the teary-eyed Native American back in another antilittering commercial that in our view retains, if not amplifies, the potentially problematic feature of the original ad. The camera features several people waiting at a bus stop, engaging in everyday activities such as drinking coffee, reading the newspaper, and smoking cigarettes. After the bus arrives and they all climb aboard, the camera cuts to the empty bus stop waiting area, now completely covered with cups, newspapers, and cigarette butts that are strewn about. The camera slowly zooms in to a poster of the Native American overlooking the garbage, still with a tear in his eye. As the screen fades to black, the text of the spot's take-home message appears: "Back by *popular neglect*" (emphasis added).

What sort of message is conveyed by this phrase and by the litter-filled environments featured in both of these ads? Although the injunctive norm against littering is obvious and powerful, both of the ads present a descriptive norm for littering that indicates that, despite strong disapproval of the behavior, many people do in fact engage in that behavior. Thus, it is possible that the descriptive norm depicting the prevalence of littering behavior may have actually undermined the potency of the antilittering injunctive norm.

Other examples are abundant. In a long-running print ad titled "Gross National Product," Woodsy Owl proclaims, "This year Americans will produce more litter and pollution than ever before." As another example, visitors at Arizona's Petrified Forest National Park quickly learn from prominent signage that the park's existence is threatened because so many past visitors have been taking pieces of petrified wood from the grounds: "Your heritage is being vandalized every day by theft losses of petrified wood of 14 tons a year, mostly a small piece at a time." Furthermore, a commercial intended to discourage minors from using marijuana depicts a lone middle school student resisting the pressures of a whole busload of her peers. Similarly, to call attention to the need for government intervention against cigarette smoking among children, U.S. Federal Drug Administration commissioner David Kessler publicized the fact that "more than 3 million youths in the U.S. smoke and that 3,000 become regular smokers each day" (Scott, 1995).

Although these communications may in fact reflect reality and are clearly motivated by good intentions, the influence agents behind these campaigns may fail to realize that, by using a negative descriptive norm as part of a rallying cry, they might be inadvertently focusing the message recipients on the prevalence, rather than the undesirability, of that behavior. To test this hypothesis, Cialdini and colleagues (Cialdini, 2003; Cialdini, Demaine, Sagarin, Barrett, Rhoads, & Winter, 2006) created two signs designed to deter wood theft at Petrified Forest National Park: one was injunctive in nature, and the other was descriptive in nature. The researchers secretly placed marked pieces of petrified wood along visitor pathways and alternated which of the two signs were posted at the entrance of each pathway. The injunctive normative sign stated, "Please don't remove the petrified wood from the park, in order to preserve the natural state of the Petrified Forest," and was accompanied by a picture of a visitor stealing a piece of wood, with a red circle-and-bar (i.e., the universal "no" symbol) superimposed over his hand. The descriptive normative sign emphasizing the prevalence of theft informed visitors, "Many past visitors have removed the petrified wood from the park, changing the natural state of the Petrified Forest," and was accompanied by a picture of several park visitors taking pieces of wood.

Compared with a no-sign control condition in which 2.92% of the pieces were stolen, the descriptive norm message resulted in significantly more theft (7.92%). The injunctive norm message, in contrast, resulted in marginally less theft (1.67%) than the control condition. These results are in line with the suggestion that, when a descriptive norm for a situation indicates that an undesirable behavior occurs with great frequency, managers might indeed cause unintentional damage by publicizing this information.

The aforementioned research shows that norms can influence behaviors in ways that are constructive or destructive depending on the context. But social norms can also influence behaviors in ways that are reconstructive as well. Consider a type of descriptive norm that we have not discussed to this point—the mean. Whether it is the average number of days that employees arrive late to work, the average amount in sales made by each member of the sales force, or the average number of hours worked within an organization, measures of central tendency such as the mean can potentially result in constructive influence for some workers and destructive influence for others.

As we have already discussed, descriptive norms provide a standard that people are motivated to follow. Because workers tend to measure the appropriateness of their behavior by how far away they are from the norm or average, being deviant is being above *or* below the norm. This means that the average information may serve as sort of a "magnetic middle" that draws workers from or toward the norm regardless of whether they are above or below the norm. For example, if a company memo communicates that employees come late to work 2.7 days per month on average, those who are late to work 5 days per month on average are likely to start coming in on time more often. However, the norm that might have a constructive influence on perpetually tardy workers might prove to have a destructive influence on perpetually on-time workers.

This analysis raises an important question: If descriptive normative information can elicit such an undesirable and inadvertent backfire effect, is there a way to eliminate this problematic effect? As we discussed earlier, according to Focus Theory, if only one of the two types of norms is prominent in consciousness for individuals, it will direct their behavior accordingly (for a review, see Cialdini & Goldstein, 2004). Therefore, in situations in which descriptive normative information might normally produce an undesirable backfire effect, it is possible that adding an explicit injunctive element to the message—in this case, one explicitly reminding on-time workers how much their behavior is approved and appreciated—might prevent the occurrence of the backfire effect.

Schultz, Nolan, Cialdini, Goldstein, and Griskevicius (2007) conducted a field experiment to investigate these hypotheses in the context of household residential energy consumption and conservation. In that study, the authors obtained permission from participating residents to read their energy meters at various times before, during, and after the intervention took place. After obtaining baseline energy usage measures, households were divided by examining whether their energy consumption level was either above or below that of the average household in the community at baseline. Next, all households received feedback about how much energy they had consumed in the prior week. However, half of the households were randomly assigned to receive information about the energy consumption of the average household in their neighborhood over the same period (the descriptive norm). In contrast, the other half of the households received both the same descriptive normative information and an injunctive message conveying that their energy consumption level behavior was either approved or disapproved. Specifically, households that were consuming less than the average received a positively valenced emoticon (☺), whereas those that were consuming more than the average received a negatively valenced emoticon (☹). The dependent measure was residents' actual household energy consumption after the intervention.

The researchers had three major predictions, all of which were confirmed. First, for households consuming *more* energy than their neighborhood average, descriptive normative information alone *decreased* energy consumption—a result indicative of the constructive power of social norms, whereby descriptive normative information facilitated conservation rather than consumption behavior. Second, for households consuming *less* energy than their neighborhood average, descriptive normative information *increased* energy consumption—that is, actually produced an undesirable backfire effect. This result is indicative of the destructive power of social norms, whereby a well-intended application of normative information actually served to decrease conservation behaviors and increase consumption behaviors. Third, for the households consuming *less* energy than their neighborhood average, providing both descriptive normative information and an injunctive message that others approve of this low consumption behavior prevented the undesirable backfire effect from occurring; these households continued to consume energy at low rates. Such a result is indicative of the reconstructive power of the injunctive message to eliminate the untoward effects of the descriptive norm.

The results of this study demonstrate not only the power of the social norm to bring people's behaviors toward it like a powerful magnet but also how managers can reduce the likelihood of their message backfiring for half of the population that receives it: They should convey their approval for, and appreciation of, those already acting in a socially desirable way.

In sum, norm-based persuasive approaches are likely to be most effective when the descriptive and injunctive norms are presented in concert and aligned with one another (Cialdini & Goldstein, 2004). To examine the influence of an information campaign that combined the motivational prowess of injunctive and descriptive norms, Cialdini and colleagues (Cialdini, 2003; Cialdini et al., 2010) created a set of three PSAs designed to increase recycling activity in Arizona. Each PSA featured a scene in which the majority of individuals in the ad engaged in recycling, spoke approvingly of it, and spoke disapprovingly of a single person in the scene who did not recycle. Thus, the act of recycling material was linked to images indicating that recycling activity is both widely performed and almost unanimously approved. The PSAs also included humorous dialogue, information about how to recycle, and the benefits of doing so. In a field test, this PSA and two others like it were played on local TV and radio stations of four Arizona communities. The results revealed a 25.35% net advantage in recycling tonnage over a pair of control communities not exposed to the PSAs.

REFERENCE GROUPS AND NORMATIVE INFLUENCE

To this point, we have focused our attention on the *what, when, where, why,* and *how* of social normative influence, but we have not yet addressed another important factor: *who.* Although it should be clear to this point that people tend to "follow the herd," what seems less obvious is which particular herd managers should point to when they want employees to engage in a given behavior. That is, within any organization, different groups of individuals may have vastly different norms associated them. What predicts which reference group's norms are most likely to be influential?

The Role of Social Identification in Normative Influence

One important consideration in understanding the answer to this question is that people have a strong drive to maintain positive views of themselves, and they often achieve this goal by identifying with and conforming to valued groups (Brewer & Roccas, 2001; Cialdini & Goldstein, 2004; Pool, Wood, & Leck, 1998). The majority of the research conducted in this area over the past two decades has come from the perspective of social identity (Tajfel, 1978; Tajfel & Turner, 1979; see also Hogg & Abrams, 1988) and self-categorization theories (Turner, 1987, 1999).

The concept of social identity has taken on a variety of different meanings in various disciplines within social psychology (Brewer, 2001). However, social identity is often defined broadly as an expansion of the self-concept involving a shift in the level of self-conception from the individual self to the collective self, typically based on perceived membership in a social category (Brewer, 2003; Hogg, 2003). Categorization can occur at different levels of abstraction, from a concrete group of people (e.g., my department) to broader concepts (e.g., worker, manager, subordinate, colleague) (Turner, 1991). Self-categorization theory is the successor of social identity that stresses the more cognitive processes involved in intergroup relations (Terry, Hogg, & White, 2000; Turner, Hogg, Oakes, Reicher, & Wetherell, 1987), but the two are usually discussed together because of their shared theoretical underpinnings and the similar predictions that are derived from their common perspective.

The social identity and self-categorization perspective contends that behavioral outcomes are influenced by reference group norms, but only for those who consider group membership to be a salient basis for self-representation (e.g., Ellemers, Spears, & Doosje, 2002; Hogg, 2003; White, Hogg, & Terry, 2002). Notably, one of the primary factors appearing to influence whether group membership is seen as a salient basis for self-conceptualization is the meaningfulness and level of identification that one has for the group (e.g., Terry, Hogg, & White, 1999). For instance, researchers have found that the perceived norms of participants' reference group of peers and friends was a significant predictor of the participants' intentions to engage in healthy behaviors (Terry & Hogg, 1996) and household recycling (Terry et al., 1999) only for those who strongly identified with the group. Thus, workers are more likely to follow the norms of their organizations to the extent that they identify strongly with their organizations (for a review, see Ashforth & Mael, 1989).

The Role of Contextual Similarity in Normative Influence

The aforementioned literature makes it clear that individuals are most likely to conform to the norms of a reference group when they see themselves as similar in identity to the reference group. However, comparatively little research exists that examines the role *contextual* similarity plays in adherence to reference group norms. Goldstein, Cialdini, and Griskevicius (2008) investigated this topic when they studied how to optimally motivate people to engage in energy and environmental conservation behaviors. Nearly all guests who have stayed in a hotel in the last few years have seen signs in their hotel rooms urging them to reuse their towels to help conserve environmental resources by saving energy and reducing the amount of detergent-related pollutants released into the environment. According to the company that supplies such cards to hoteliers, most guests will recycle at least one towel sometime during their stay, provided that they are asked to do so.

An informal survey of the messages conveyed by dozens of request cards from a wide variety of hotels revealed that the cards most frequently attempt to boost recycling efforts by focusing guests on either form of basic environmental protection (Cialdini & Goldstein, 2002). That is, guests are almost invariably informed that reusing one's towels will conserve energy and help save the environment. However, considering the finding that the majority of hotel guests who are asked to participate in these programs do in fact reuse their towels at least once during their stay, it was notable that none of these programs communicated these descriptive norms to guests. Thus, Goldstein and colleagues (2008) set out to test whether simply informing guests that the majority of their counterparts participate in these programs might enhance compliance rates. However, beyond that, they also sought to learn what kinds of reference groups are most powerful when communicating descriptive norms.

A close inspection of the normative social identity literature and of the body of research examining the role of similarity on norm adherence reveals that both research areas have focused almost exclusively on the importance of commonalities between personal, rather than contextual, characteristics of individuals and the groups whose behaviors they observe. That is, these literatures examine how personal similarities (e.g., in attitudes, gender, ethnicity, age, values) between a target individual and a group of people influence the target's adherence to the group's social norms. However, researchers have largely failed to address the role of *contextual* similarities in norm adherence.

Adhering to provincial norms—the norms of one's local setting and circumstances—is typically both logical and effective. For example, what may be effective and norm-consistent behavior at one's fraternity party is certainly not going to be adaptive in other settings and situations, especially those with powerful and well-established norms, such as how to behave in a library during finals week (Aarts & Dijksterhuis, 2003). After all, the old adage tells us that we should do as the Romans do *when we are in Rome*—not when we are in Egypt. In contrast, much of the current social norms literature, which focuses on the importance of personal similarities, would emphasize that Romans should do what other Romans do—especially if they highly identify with other Romans—while saying little about the role of their surroundings. Therefore, individuals may be more likely to be influenced by the norms of their immediate surroundings than those of their less immediate surroundings.

Consistent with this line of thinking, Goldstein and colleagues (2008) examined whether the towel reuse norm of hotel guests' immediate surroundings (i.e., the provincial norm for their particular room) motivates participation in the conservation program to a greater extent than the norm of guests' less immediate surroundings (i.e., the global norm for the whole hotel) despite the fact that, in this context, the provincial norm is rationally no more diagnostic of effective or appropriate behavior than the global norm. They also sought to investigate whether individuals might be more likely to follow the norms of a personally unimportant reference group than those of a more important one when the personally unimportant reference group is provincial in nature.

The researchers created five towel-reuse signs soliciting the participation of guests. One sign was a standard environmental sign, which focused on the importance of environmental protection but provided no explicit descriptive norm. All four of the other messages, which communicated the descriptive norm, informed guests that most of the people who are asked to participate in these programs did so. However, the reference group identity varied in those four normative messages. One of the signs conveyed that these norms were characteristic of other hotel guests (global norm), whereas another conveyed that these norms were characteristic of a rationally meaningless and relatively nondiagnostic group—other hotel guests who had stayed in the guests' particular rooms (provincial norm). The other two signs conveyed norms of reference groups that are considered to be important and personally meaningful to people's social identities. Specifically, a third sign paired the descriptive norm with the reference group identity of *citizen* (see Madrigal, 2001), whereas a fourth sign paired it with a meaningful social category commonly used in reference group and social identity research—gender (Bardach & Park, 1996; Maccoby, 1988; Meyers-Levy, 1988; Skitka & Maslach, 1996).

Based on the premise that it is generally beneficial to follow the norms that most closely match one's environment, situation, or circumstances, the authors hypothesized that the appeal conveying the descriptive norm of that particular room's previous occupants—the identity that should be the least meaningful but most relevant to guests' local circumstances—would result in higher towel-reuse rates than the other descriptive norm appeals. Several findings from that experiment are noteworthy. First, the social identity salience data suggested that the social categories highlighted in each of the messages focused the participants on the intended social identity and that the messages did so equally. Second, the data confirmed expectations regarding the large disparities in the extent to which the various social categories were considered by participants to be important to their own identities. Specifically, the categories of both hotel guest and guest in a particular room were significantly less important to participants' identities than were those associated with gender, citizenship, and environmentalism. Third, the researchers found that the towel-reuse rates of the four descriptive normative message identities did not map onto to the extent to which individuals would consider those identities personally meaningful and important to them. These data are particularly interesting in light of the research suggesting that the more important a social category is to an individual's social identity, the more likely he or she will be to follow the norms of that category. That is, much of the extant literature suggests that participants' conservation behaviors should map onto the importance ratings. According to the importance ratings, participants should have been most likely to follow the norms of citizens or males/females and least likely to conform to the norms of hotel guests for the particular room in which the participants are staying. Yet the data indicate that the appeal conveying the descriptive norm of those who had previously stayed in the guests' room yielded not the lowest compliance rate, as predicted by the importance ratings, but in fact the highest compliance rate.

These findings are not entirely consistent with a key prediction of social identity and self-categorization theories—that people should be more likely to follow group norms when the reference group is personally meaningful to them. These results also suggest that researchers going forward should consider focusing greater attention on the role that *contextual* similarities (e.g., the same immediate environment), rather than *personal* similarities (e.g., belonging to the same social category), play in influencing adherence to social norms. A close inspection of the normative social identity literature and of the body of research examining the role of similarity on norm adherence reveals that both research areas have focused almost exclusively on the importance of commonalities between personal, rather than contextual, characteristics of individuals and the groups whose behaviors they observe (Goldstein et al., 2008). That is, these literatures examine how personal similarities (e.g., in attitudes, gender, ethnicity, age, values) between a target individual and a group of people influence the target's adherence to the group's social norms. Future research further investigating the largely ignored role of *contextual* similarities in norm adherence would be welcome.

The results from the hotel experiment suggest that mangers implementing a descriptive normative component to their persuasive appeals should ensure that the norms of the reference group are as situationally similar to the intended audience's circumstances or environment as possible. For example, assuming the norms do not differ by location, a manager at a large, multinational corporation would optimize her persuasive prowess by communicating to the employees at her branch the norms of their particular branch rather than either the norms at the organizational level or the norms of another branch.

CONCLUSION

Managing behavior in an organization is as much about managing the norms within the organization as managing individual workers. However, to manage those norms, it is very imperative to know what factors will lead social norms to operate in ways that are constructive, destructive, or even reconstructive. We feel that a better understanding of the *who, what, when, where, why,* and *how* of social norms helps elucidate important aspects of organizational behavior and provides guidelines for how to best manage it.

REFERENCES

Aarts, H., & Dijksterhuis, A. (2003). The silence of the library: Environment, situational norm and social behavior. *Journal of Personality and Social Psychology, 84*, 18–28.

Abrams, D., & Hogg, M. A. (1990). Social identification, self-categorization, and social influence. *European Review of Social Psychology, 1*, 195–228.

Ashforth, B. E., & Mael, F. (1989). Social identity theory and the organization. *Academy of Management Review, 14*, 20–39.

Bandura, A. (1977). *Social learning theory.* Englewood Cliffs, NJ: Prentice Hall.

Bardach, L., & Park, B. (1996). The effect of in-group/out-group status on memory for consistent and inconsistent behavior of an individual. *Personality and Social Psychology Bulletin, 22*, 169–178.

Berkowitz, L. (1972). Social norms, feelings, and other factors affecting helping and altruism. In L. Berkowitz (Ed.), *Advances in experimental social psychology* (Vol. 6, 63–108). New York: Academic Press.

Bettenhausen, K., & Murnighan, J. K. (1985). The emergence of norms in competitive decision-making groups. *Administrative Science Quarterly, 30*, 350–372.

Brewer, M. (2003). Optimal distinctiveness, social identity, and the self. In M. R. Leary & J. P. Tangney (Eds.), *Handbook of self and identity* (pp. 480–491). New York: Guilford Press.

Brewer, M. B. (2001). The many faces of social identity: Implications for political psychology: *Political Psychology, 22*, 115–125.

Brewer, M. B., & Roccas, S. (2001). Individual values, social identity, and optimal distinctiveness. In C. Sedikides & M. Brewer (Eds.), *Individual self, relational self, collective self* (pp. 219–237). Philadelphia: Psychology Press.

Cialdini, R. B. (2003). Crafting normative messages to protect the environment. *Current Directions in Psychological Science, 12*, 105–109.

Cialdini, R. B. (2008). *Influence: Science and practice* (5th ed.). Needham Heights, MA: Allyn & Bacon.

Cialdini, R. B., Barrett, D. W., Bator, R., Demaine, L., Sagarin, B. J., Rhoads, K. v. L., et al. (2010). *Activating and aligning social norms for persuasive impact.* Manuscript in preparation.

Cialdini, R. B., Demaine, L. J., Sagarin, B. J., Barrett, D. W., Rhoads, K. v. L., & Winter, P. L. (2006). Managing social norms for persuasive impact. *Social Influence, 1*, 3–15.

Cialdini, R. B., & Goldstein, N. J. (2002). The science and practice of persuasion. *Cornell Hotel and Restaurant Administration Quarterly, 43*, 40–50.

Cialdini, R. B., & Goldstein, N. J. (2004). Social influence: Compliance and conformity. *Annual Review of Psychology, 55*, 591–622.

Cialdini, R. B., Kallgren, C. A., & Reno, R. R. (1991). A focus theory of normative conduct: A theoretical refinement and reevaluation of the role of norms in human behavior. In L. Berkowitz (Ed.), *Advances in experimental social psychology* (Vol. 24, pp. 201–234). San Diego, CA: Academic Press.

Cialdini, R. B., Reno, R. R., & Kallgren, C. A. (1990). A focus theory of normative conduct: Recycling the concept of norms to reduce littering in public places. *Journal of Personality and Social Psychology, 58,* 1015–1026.

Cialdini, R. B., & Trost, M. R. (1998). Social influence: Social norms, conformity, and compliance. In D. T. Gilbert, S. T. Fiske, & G. Lindzey (Eds.), *The handbook of social psychology* (Vol. 2, pp. 151–192). Boston: McGraw-Hill.

Darley, J. M., & Latané, B. (1970). Norms and normative behavior: Field studies of social interdependence. In J. Macaulay & L. Berkowitz (Eds.), *Altruism and helping behavior* (pp. 83–102). New York: Academic Press.

Deutsch, M., & Gerard, H. B. (1955). A study of normative and informational social influences upon individual judgment. *Journal of Abnormal and Social Psychology, 51,* 629–636.

Ellemers, N., Spears, R., & Doosje, B. (2002). Self and social identity. *Annual Review of Psychology, 53,* 161–186.

Feldman, D. C. (1984). The development and enforcement of group norms. *Academy of Management Review, 9,* 47–53.

Fishbein, M., & Ajzen, I. (1975). *Belief, attitude, intention, and behavior.* Reading, MA: Addison-Wesley.

Goldstein, N. J., Cialdini, R. B., & Griskevicius, V. (2008). A room with a viewpoint: Using social norms to motivate environmental conservation in hotels. *Journal of Consumer Research, 35,* 472–482.

Goodman, P. S., Ravlin, E., & Schminke, M. (1987). Understanding groups in organizations. In L. L. Cummings & B. M. Staw (Eds.), *Research in organizational behavior, Vol. 9.* Greenwich, CT: JAI Press.

Hogg, M. A. (2003). Social identity. In M. R. Leary & J. P. Tangney (Eds.), *Handbook of self and identity* (pp. 462–479). New York: Guilford Press

Hogg, M. A., & Abrams, D. (1988). *Social identifications. A social psychology of intergroup relations and group processes.* London: Routledge.

Kallgren, C. A., Reno, R. R., & Cialdini, R. B. (2000). A focus theory of normative conduct: When norms do and do not affect behavior. *Personality and Social Psychology Bulletin, 26,* 1002–1012.

Kerr, N. L. (1995). Norms in social dilemmas. In D. Schroeder (Ed.), *Social dilemmas: Perspectives on individuals and groups* (pp. 31–48). Westport, CT: Praeger.

Maccoby, E. E. (1988). Gender as a social category. *Developmental Psychology, 24,* 755–765.

Madrigal, R. (2001). Social identity effects in a belief-attitudes-intentions hierarchy: Implications for corporate sponsorship. *Psychology and Marketing, 18,* 145–165.

Meyers-Levy, J. (1988). The influence of sex roles on judgment. *Journal of Consumer Research, 14,* 522–530.

Pool, G. J., Wood, W., & Leck, K. (1998). The self-esteem motive in social influence: Agreement with valued majorities and disagreement with derogated minorities. *Journal of Personality and Social Psychology, 75,* 967–975.

Reno, R. R., Cialdini, R. B., & Kallgren, C. A. (1993). The transsituational influence of social norms. *Journal of Personality and Social Psychology, 64,* 104–112.

Schultz, P. W. (1999). Changing behavior with normative feedback interventions: A field experiment on curbside recycling. *Basic and Applied Social Psychology, 21*, 25–36.

Schultz, P. W., Nolan, J. M., Cialdini, R. B., Goldstein, N. J., & Griskevicius, V. (2007). The constructive, destructive, and reconstructive power of social norms. *Psychological Science, 18*, 429–434.

Scott, W. (1995, December 24). Personality parade. *Parade Magazine*, p. 2.

Shaffer, L. S. (1983). Toward Pepitone's vision of a normative social psychology: What is a social norm? *Journal of Mind and Behavior, 4*, 275–294.

Sherif, M. (1936). *The psychology of social norms*. New York: Harper.

Skitka, L. J., & Maslach, C. (1996). Gender as schematic category: A role construct approach. *Social Behavior and Personality, 24*, 53–73.

Tajfel H. (1978). *Differentiation between social groups: Studies in the social psychology of intergroup relations*. New York: Academic.

Tajfel, H., & Turner, J. (1979). An integrative theory of intergroup conflict. In W. G. Austin & S. Worchel (Eds.), *The social psychology of intergroup relations* (pp. 33–48). Monterey, CA: Brooks-Cole.

Terry, D. J., & Hogg, M. A. (1996). Group norms and the attitude-behavior relationship: A role for group identification. *Personality and Social Psychology Bulletin, 22*, 776–793.

Terry, D. J., & Hogg, M. A. (2000). *Attitudes, behavior, and social context: The role of norms and group membership*. Mahwah, NJ: Lawrence Erlbaum Associates.

Terry, D. J., Hogg, M. A., & White, K. M. (1999). The theory of planned behaviour: Self-identity, social identity, and group norms. *British Journal of Social Psychology, 38*, 225–244.

Terry, D. J., Hogg, M. A., & White, K. M. (2000). Attitude-behavior relations: Social identity and group membership. In D. J. Terry & M. A. Hogg (Eds.), *Attitudes, behavior, and social context: The role of norms and group membership* (pp. 67–93). Mahwah, NJ: Erlbaum.

Tulving, E. (1983). *Elements of episodic memory*. New York: Oxford University Press.

Turner, J. C. (1987). A self-categorization theory. In J. C. Turner, M. A. Hogg, P. J. Oakes, S. D. Reicher, & M. S. Wetherell (Eds.), *Rediscovering the social group: A self-categorization theory* (pp. 42–67). Oxford: Blackwell.

Turner, J. C. (1991). *Social influence*. Milton Keynes, UK: Open University Press.

Turner, J. C. (1999). Some current issues in research on social identity and self-categorization theories. In N. Ellemers, R. Spears, & B. Doosje (Eds.), *Social identity: Context, commitment, content* (pp. 6–34). Oxford, UK: Blackwell.

Turner, J. C., Hogg, M. A., Oakes, P. J., Reicher, S. D., & Wetherell, M. S. (Eds.) (1987). *Rediscovering the social group: A self-categorization theory*. Oxford: Blackwell.

White, K. M., Hogg, M. A., & Terry, D. J. (2002). Improving attitude-behavior correspondence through exposure to normative support from a salient ingroup. *Basic and Applied Social Psychology, 24*, 91–103.

5

*Entrepreneurial Actions: An Action Theory Approach**

Michael Frese
National University of Singapore and University of Lüneburg

This chapter attempts to contribute to the psychology of organization and management by discussing a theory of entrepreneurship, its empirical base, and its implications. First, it argues that a psychology of organization is incomplete if we do not understand how organizations get started—which is usually the doing of one entrepreneur or of a group of entrepreneurs. Second, it argues that any theory of entrepreneurship should use active actions as a starting point—entrepreneurship is the epitome of an active agent in the market (rather than a reactive agent). Third, it discusses an action regulation theory to better understand the psychology of entrepreneurship. Fourth, it provides empirical work based on this theory that is supposed to help understand entrepreneurial success. Finally, a theoretically derived intervention is suggested to help entrepreneurs to be successful at growing an organization.

Entrepreneurship is defined by the actions of the entrepreneur—either as starting an organization (Gartner, 1989) or by the more elaborate definition that entrepreneurship involves discovery, evaluation, and exploitation of opportunities (Shane & Venkataraman, 2000). Entrepreneurship often comes about not just by "detecting" opportunities but also by establishing them (as Schumpeter, 1935, has emphasized). These opportunities exist only within a certain context. Nearly all definitions emphasize that the entrepreneur is an active actor in the market. Some entrepreneurship researchers reserve the concept of entrepreneur for those who are particularly successful with their firms (Carland, Hoy, Boulton, & Carland, 1984). However, this chapter, instead of including the functionality of a behavior

---

* A prior version of this chapter appeared in *Foundations and Trends in Entrepreneurship* (Hanover, MA: NOW Publishers, 2009).

in the definition, offers a more descriptive definition of the entrepreneur: someone who develops and detects opportunities and who is organizing production or services that represent these potential opportunities. It should also be emphasized that entrepreneurship does not necessarily imply the start-up of business organizations but can also refer to social entrepreneurs; thus, founders of religious organizations (e.g., Mohamed) or founders of social service organizations (e.g., Greenpeace) should be studied under the umbrella of entrepreneurship as well.

There is a paradox in organizational behavior research and in organizational psychology. On one hand, there exists some consensus that organizations are constituted by the actions of actors and are therefore social constructions—the organization can exist only if social actors continue to keep up the organization (Berger & Luckmann, 1966; Katz & Kahn, 1978). On the other hand, most organizational psychologists take organizations as given. In methodological terms, organizations are seen as exogenous variables in most introductory textbooks on organizational psychology or organizational behavior. Even in organizational development, the organization is assumed to be already present in order to be developed (French & Bell, 1995). Entrepreneurship is integrated into very few textbooks, even though the original development of an organization is always an act of entrepreneurship.

A second paradox is that (organizational) psychology, although once at the forefront of developing entrepreneurship research (McClelland, 1961; McClelland & Winter, 1971), had for some time given up research on entrepreneurship; only recently has it again become part of organizational psychology (Baum, Frese, & Baron, 2007). It is of utmost importance to organizational psychology to have an understanding of the process of starting and growing an organization. The founders of an organization have an enormous role in shaping the structure and culture of the organization (Katz & Kahn, 1978; Schein, 1987); in addition, the dynamics of starting, growing, and keeping a certain organizational size or overseeing the death of an organization needs to be a centerpiece of any organizational psychology (Katz & Kahn, 1978).

ACTIVE ENTREPRENEURIAL ACTIONS

Entrepreneurs' actions need to be the starting point for theorizing in entrepreneurship. As will be shown in this chapter, entrepreneurs are most frequently the most active participants in the market—more so than rank-and-file employees and managers (Utsch, Rauch, Rothfuss, & Frese, 1999). This chapter's theory of entrepreneurial actions is therefore based on the so-called action theory or action regulation theory (Frese & Sabini, 1985; Frese & Zapf, 1994; Hacker, 1998; Miller, Galanter, & Pribram, 1960).

Scientists have been interested in the issue of being active ever since they have shed the constraints of behaviorism and psychoanalysis. White (1959) pointed out that, phylogenetically, organisms have developed into being more and more mastery oriented. The same theme has been addressed in the theory of internal control (Rotter, 1972), the helplessness theory (which, of course, taught people not to be helpless; Seligman, 1975), the achievement motive theory (McClelland, 1987), and self-efficacy (Bandura, 1982). This chapter differs in that it takes an action theory approach to understand the phenomenon of being active and then applies the phenomenon to the area of entrepreneurship. Entrepreneurship requires a high degree of active behavior because it starts and develops organizations; entrepreneurship cannot be explained except by recourse to the active nature of human activities.

I have been interested in an active approach to work by using the concept of personal initiative (Frese & Fay, 2001). I started to work on this issue because I was originally interested in cross-cultural differences of personal initiative in East Germany (Frese, Kring, Soose, & Zempel, 1996). It soon occurred to me that entrepreneurs actually have to be more active than normal employees and even managers (Utsch et al., 1999), which led me to begin researching entrepreneurship, with a focus on changing economies, such as in East Germany and in developing countries like in Africa and Asia. Changing economies was of more interest to me because of the greater opportunities for entrepreneurship and the possibility for business owners to be of more practical importance for the development of wealth. Entrepreneurship has been argued to be an important factor for economic development in transitional economies (Mead & Liedholm, 1998; Reynolds, Bygrave, & Autio, 2004).

What does it mean to be active? Being active implies three aspects: self-starting, long-term proactivity, and persistence in the face of obstacles (Frese & Fay, 2001). *Self-starting* implies that a person does something without being told, without getting an explicit instruction, or without an explicit role requirement. This is in contrast to assigned tasks. Unlike entrepreneurs, employees usually work within some organizational hierarchy; there is usually some superior present who tells the employee what to do, or at the very least, such as in the case of managers, there tend to be explicit, descriptive role requirements (sometimes formalized explicitly). This rarely exists for entrepreneurs; they must be self-starters. *Reactive* can be considered the opposite of self-starting; this would imply that entrepreneurs do everything only because the environment (e.g., important people) demands a certain action.

Second, proactivity means having a focus on the long-term and not waiting for explicit demands. A long-term focus can be related to future opportunities and stressors; preparing now for opportunities suggests a need to collect resources for quick employment when future opportunities arise. Similarly, preparing now for future problems and stressors is consistent with being active—preparation facilitates action when confronted with such stressors. The opposite, again, is to be reactive, which implies that entrepreneurs do only what the situation demands of them.

Persistence in the face of obstacles implies two self-regulatory processes: protecting and overcoming. *Protecting* implies consciously taking care of goals, plans, and feedback seeking when competing goals, plans, and feedback appear or when goals, plans, and feedback seeking are frustrated or taxed by difficult situations. Overcoming external barriers is necessary in the face of difficulty, which is inevitable. This continues to connect with being active, that is, difficulties in an effective and persistent manner. The reactive approach is again the opposite: A reactive approach backs away from problems when they occur and stumbles when difficulties appear insurmountable.

The proposition then follows that the more entrepreneurs are self-starting, proactive, and persistent, the higher is the likelihood of a successful start of an organization and the more successful is the organization after having been started by the entrepreneur.

Action theory is a particularly useful tool for analyzing active behavior. The following sections briefly describe action theory and how this theory uses active actions; action theory is also used to present empirical data that illuminate the phenomenon of being active.

ACTION THEORY: BUILDING BLOCKS

Action is goal-oriented behavior (Frese & Sabini, 1985), with three aspects that are important for humans who regulate their actions: (1) sequence refers to how actions unfold; (2) structure involves levels of regulation; and (3) the focus of a task can be the task, the social context in which the task is done, or the self. This chapter presents the argument that every action can be decomposed into these three components of actions.

Sequence

The steps described in Table 5.1 can be minimally differentiated in the action sequence: goal and intention; processing of information relevant to the environment; planning; monitoring of the execution; and feedback processing (Dörner & Schaub, 1994; Frese & Zapf, 1994; Gollwitzer, 1993; Heckhausen & Gollwitzer, 1985; Norman, 1986). (The term sequence does not mean that there is an immutable sequence and that each of these action steps has to be traversed to be able to reach the next).

The facets of this sequence are active if the goals and plans are self-starting and if the information collection and feedback seeking are based on an active search. The aspects of the sequence are proactive if future problems and opportunities are converted into goals, if some knowledge on alternative routes to action is developed, if there are back-up plans in case something goes wrong, and if one actively develops unusual feedback signals. Persistence exists if goals and plans are protected against diversions and competing ideas. In addition, barriers need to be overcome on the way to reaching active goals.

Action Structure

The action structure is concerned with the hierarchical cognitive regulation of behavior (Hacker, 1998). The notion of hierarchy is needed to understand well-organized behaviors that achieve higher-level goals (e.g., launching a new product) by using lower-level behaviors (e.g., uttering a sentence, typing a word, using the appropriate muscles to strike a key; cf. Carver & Scheier, 1982; Miller et al., 1960). The higher levels of the hierarchy of action regulation are conscious, thought oriented, and general;

TABLE 5.1

Facets of Active Performance of Entrepreneurs

Action Sequence	Self-Starting	Proactive	Overcome Barriers
Goals/redefinition of tasks	Active goal, not just goals that are taken over from others Setting higher goals (growth goals)	Anticipate future opportunities and problems and convert into goals	Protect goals when frustrated or taxed by difficult environment or complex goals structure
Information collection and prognosis	Active search (i.e., exploration, active scanning)	Search for potential problem areas and opportunities before they occur Develop knowledge on alternatives routes of action	Maintain search in spite of lack of resources, problems, complexity, and negative emotions
Plan and execution	Active plan High degree of self-developing a plan Don't imitate; don't just follow advisors	Back-up plans Have action plans for opportunities ready Being proactive with planning and detail	Overcome barriers Return to plan quickly when disturbed
Monitoring and feedback	Self-developed feedback and active search for feedback	Develop presignals for potential problems and opportunities	Protect feedback search

Source: Based on Frese, M., & Fay, D., *Research in Organizational Behavior, 23,* 144, 2001. With permission.

the lower levels consist of specific routines that frequently involve muscle movements. This hierarchy is not neatly organized but allows for potential reversals. This chapter differentiates among three task-oriented levels of regulation and one metacognitive level (Frese & Zapf, 1994; Hacker, 1998).

The Skill Level of Regulation

The lowest level of regulation, called skill level (Rasmussen, 1982), sensorimotor level of regulation (Hacker, 1998), psychomotor (Ackerman,

1988), automatized (Schneider & Shiffrin, 1977), or procedural knowledge (Anderson, 1983), regulates situationally specific automatized or routinized skills. Information on this level is parallel, rapid, effortless, and without apparent limitations. However, it is difficult to substantially modify action programs at this level. To change them, they have to be lifted to a higher level of regulation, so that some conscious form of (effortful) processing can be applied. The skill level of regulation is the preferred level of regulation (March & Simon, 1958), particularly when there is high load (Kahneman, 2003).

Level of Flexible Action Patterns

Well-trained schematic action patterns (Norman, 1981) dominate here. These ready-made action programs are available in memory but must be flexibly adjusted to situationally defined parameters. This makes those perceptual processes that are connected to action signals important here (Ackerman, 1988; Hacker, 1998). Whenever possible, lower levels of regulation (skill level or flexible action patterns) are preferred because processing is less effortful and the action is smoother.

Conscious Level

On this level, the concern is with conscious regulation of goal-oriented behavior, also referred to by various scholars as "knowledge-based reasoning" (Rasmussen, 1982), "declarative knowledge" (Anderson, 1983), "controlled reasoning" (Schneider & Shiffrin, 1977), "cognitive reasoning" (Ackerman, 1992), "intellectual-level reasoning" (Frese & Zapf, 1994; Hacker, 1998), or "system 2 reasoning" (Kahneman, 2003). While the term *consciousness* has had a checkered history in psychology, it seems to be a good umbrella term for being aware of one's actions. Consciousness or awareness does not imply that everything can be verbalized; people can hold an image in awareness—in the sense of a vivid mental simulation of a certain action (Shepard & Metzler, 1971). Conscious processing implies effort (Kahneman, 1973); it is slow, constrained by limited resources of the central (conscious working memory) processor (Baddeley, 1986), and works in a serial mode. These are the task-oriented levels of regulation.

Level of Metacognitive Heuristics

To deal with the world, we have not only conscious strategies but also knowledge about how we use these strategies (knowledge about our cognitive regulation; cf. Brown, 1987). Moreover, people self-reflect about how they go about their actions (Brown, 1987). People often know how much they will be able to learn (Metcalfe, 1993), what they do not know (Kruger & Dunning, 1999), and what kind of strategies they use (Gleitman, 1985; Weinert & Kluwe, 1987). Metacognitive heuristics are also related to the steps of the previously discussed action sequence; people have general heuristics about how they set goals, get information, plan, monitor, and process feedback (Frese, Stewart, & Hannover, 1987). These general heuristics can be processed either consciously or automatically (Brown, 1987; Flavell, 1987), and they may be highly generalized or specific. Generalized and automatic heuristics with regard to action regulation are called action styles and function as equivalents to personality traits (Frese et al., 1987). They directly affect how one consciously regulates actions.

The highest level—the metalevel—is usually not activated when we receive routine tasks with known solutions. Since routine tasks dominate many of our working lives, people are usually not thinking on this metalevel. Since life goals, moral issues, or general procedures of how we deal with things are regulated on this level, we are usually not aware of it in our everyday activities.

Active Actions and the Levels of Regulation

Active actions may be conceptualized in two ways: (1) as stronger motivation to act, which implies a high degree of vigor in actions; or (2) as active actions defined by being self-starting, proactive, and persistent (as previously described). Being highly motivated and vigorous is more strongly related to being active on the lower levels of regulation (skill level or flexible action pattern); actions regulated on this level are done with vigor and frequently (which may include longer working hours). In contrast, active actions in the sense of the present chapter's definition require the conscious level of regulation; this is particularly so for self-starting (one has to think of ways to do it that may be new to the environment) and being proactive (which implies anticipating future opportunities and problems and some degree of conscious planning for them). With practice, routinization is achieved (an overlearning process), and experts have more routines than novices. This carries the interesting implication that experts who regulate more actions on the lower levels may show less active actions with regard to tasks that are central to their expertise. A certain degree of nonexpertise may thus help people to be more active (and more innovative) because they are required to think through the actions on a conscious level.

On the other hand, using lower levels of regulation frees up the higher levels of regulation. These high levels of regulation can then be used to find *other* tasks that may either increase our enjoyment (e.g., when we have an interesting conversation with a friend while driving a car) or allow us to think more deeply about issues that are not currently in the foreground of our task performance. Thus, freeing up higher levels of regulation makes it possible to show active performance in three ways. First, it increases the chances to think creatively about tasks and to develop new ideas and to start to implement them (the self-starting component of active performance). Second, it makes it possible to think of future problems and opportunities and to prepare for them now (the proactive component of active performance). Third, we may develop better strategies to protect our goals, information search, plans, monitoring, and feedback processing, which guide our actions and thereby overcome barriers on the way to achieving a goal.

Freeing up the higher levels of regulation increases the chance to be creative and active for experts (Ohly, Sonnentag, & Pluntke, 2006). Routinization, work characteristics, and their relationships with creative and proactive behaviors (*Journal of Organizational Behavior, 27,* 257–279). However, entrepreneurs usually do not think about the actions that they are performing right now because they often use heuristics to deal with their everyday behavior (Markman, 2007). However, they should do more planning for potential future actions—this leads to higher performance (Frese et al., 2007; Brinckmann, Grichnik, & Kapsa, 2010). However, thinking about longer term actions does not come automatic but needs to be motivated. In contrast, non-experts have to regulate everyday activities consciously. Therefore, they are automatically motivated to think things through to a higher extent. Therefore, they may sometimes develop more innovative ways of doing things than experts— thus, nonexpertise may have positive implications for innovation.

Thus, experts who have many routines available have to be motivated to become ready and interested to switch routines to a conscious level to show a high degree of active and innovative actions. The more entrepreneurs are motivated to switch to conscious level thinking, the better they can think of future opportunities in certain action contexts and are able to come with new and self-starting ideas. Need for cognition may play an important role here to influence entrepreneurs to develop more conscious approaches to their actions (Cacioppo, Petty, Kao, & Rodriguez, 1986).

Routines have a double-edged function. On one hand, in keeping with the concept of cognitive misery, people tend to keep routines. On the other hand, routines help to increase the motivation to go beyond routines. People have a tendency to stick to their routines even against a certain amount of environmental pressure. This goes for thought routines (e.g., using a certain theory and keeping this theory even when better alternatives are available) as well as for sensorimotor routines (e.g., entrepreneurs are likely to use an old approach to selling even though better alternatives are available). Entrepreneurs who have done well in the past and who are wedded to their routines may have problems when the environment changes, when continuous improvement is necessary, when innovations have to be speedily implemented (e.g., "not-invented-here syndrome"), or when team composition changes quickly (e.g., in project work; Audia, Locke, & Smith, 2000).

In contrast, if a person is driven only by routine (thus, the higher levels of regulation are underoccupied), boredom ensues. Boredom, however, does not necessarily lead to higher-level processing on a particular task. Instead, the higher levels may then be searching for other tasks. This may lead to daydreaming or to radical and innovative changes (e.g., starting a new company).

The Focus: Task, Social, and Self

All the concepts developed so far are applicable to regulating actions with the three foci of performance: task, social context, and self. This also implies that active actions can be done with regard to these foci.

The Task as Focus of Regulation

The task at hand is the major focus of regulation—the task may be social (e.g., persuading a customer to buy a product), creative (thinking of alternative marketing approaches), or specific (returning the correct change).

Task focus is of obvious importance: any diversion from the task probably reduces success. An interesting finding relevant for our topic exists in the expertise literature showing that experts and nonexperts alike may get diverted from the task, but experts are quicker to return to task orientation than nonexperts (Sonnentag, 1998). This relates to persistence. In general, as described in Table 5.1, entrepreneurs need to set themselves to the task and be long-term oriented (proactive), self-starting, and persistent vis-à-vis task regulation.

The Social Context as Focus of Regulation

Most tasks are done within a social setting (even if done alone, a social entity may still be the focus); this is particularly true of entrepreneurship, as it is oriented toward the market. Therefore, next to the task, the social environment is critical. If the social context is the only focus and becomes more important than the task, people cannot finish their tasks and will therefore be ineffective. However, if there is no social focus at all, tasks become insular, and people become ineffective in their social environment. Thus, there needs to be a healthy balance between these two foci. Entrepreneurship is a social endeavor: Starting an organization is a social endeavor because other people are involved. Therefore, to be successful, entrepreneurs must actively regulate the social contexts of their task performance; they can accomplish this by being active toward the social environment.

The Self as the Focus of Regulation

High performance requires effective regulation: self-management (including personality management), self-efficacy, and a switch from self to task. Whenever attention moves to a higher level of regulation, the self-system may be potentially implicated (Carver & Scheier, 1982). This is particularly so after failure (Mikulincer, 1989).

Self-management implies that people manage and regulate themselves. This implies that people know their weaknesses and work consciously (and over time automatically) against them and know their strengths and capitalize on them. Self-management also implies some metacognitive questions: Which long-range goals do entrepreneurs pursue? What approaches might they typically take? What has gone wrong and why, and what has gone right and why? Of particular importance of the self as focus is to improve one's skills and expertise. Deliberate practice is one particular aspect of improving task performance by turning to aspects that still need improvement. A certain level of self-focus is necessary in such situations.

The self system is regulated on the metalevel. However, attending to the self implies that people consciously think about whether they are doing well. Reflection on the self is therefore an additional load on the working memory. Thus, attention to the self may lead to improved performance on easy tasks but, at least in the short term, to a reduction of achievement in difficult tasks (Mikulincer, Glaubman, Ben-Artzi, & Grossman, 1991). This implies that persistence is necessary.

CHARACTERISTICS OF ACTIVE ACTION; CHARACTERISTICS AND ENTREPRENEURIAL SUCCESS

Figure 5.1 describes characteristics of active actions and asks how they are related to success (and whether personality may play an additional role).

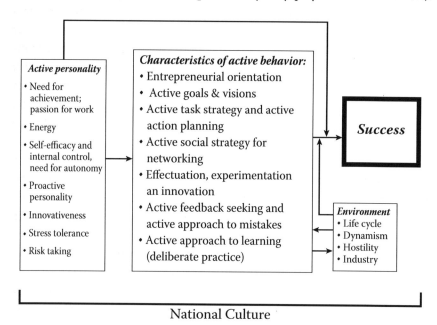

FIGURE 5.1

Characteristics of active behavior and entrepreneurial success.

Also, it is assumed that active actions may influence the environment and are in turn influenced by the environment. In addition, personality and the environment are suggested to have moderator effects on the relationship between active behavior characteristics and success.

Entrepreneurial Orientation

Entrepreneurial orientation is a central predictor for becoming an entrepreneur and for being successful (Lumpkin & Dess, 1996). In contrast to other constructs it uses the firm as the referent and not the individual (thus, questions are related to whether the firm is entrepreneurially oriented). Nevertheless, this is thought of as a psychological concept for two reasons. First, in most of the studies only one high manager (e.g., the chief executive officer) of the firm is asked about entrepreneurial orientation. Thus, entrepreneurial orientation is about managers' perceptions. Second, entrepreneurial orientation relates to the culture or climate of the organization. Perceptions of entrepreneurial orientation and climate are clearly psychological concepts.

Entrepreneurial orientation is an omnibus variable as it includes a number of different constructs—most of its facets are strongly related to our concept of active behavior. Lumpkin and Dess (1996) summarized the literature and differentiated five dimensions: autonomy, innovativeness, risk taking, competitive aggressiveness, and proactivity. Autonomy implies being self-directed when pursuing opportunities. An autonomous person acts independently and makes decisions in spite of constraints—this is a concept clearly related to two factors of active behavior (*independently* refers to self-starting; *in spite of constraints* refers to being persistent). Innovativeness refers to developing new ideas (on products, services, and processes). New ideas are an important aspect of being self-starting, because to be self-starting is the opposite of imitating what others are doing. Risk taking implies venturing into the unknown to commit one's assets to the business and to borrow money. Whenever self-starting behavior involves something unknown and investing in the unknown, certain risks are taken. Competitive aggressiveness implies making it difficult for competitors to enter the same market and to attempt to outperform one's competitors. This is the only dimension that does not directly refer to the active behavior dimensions but seems to be a consequence of it; a proactive person takes the initiative to actively exploit market opportunities and may therefore be seen as aggressive. The final subconstruct of entrepreneurial orientation is proactivity, which is directly related to one facet of this chapter's active behavior concept.

Entrepreneurial orientation is highly and relatively consistently related to organizational success (Rauch, Wiklund, Lumpkin, & Frese, 2009). For example, the meta-analytic correlation is .273 for microbusinesses. There have been attempts to make the concept more psychological in the sense of an individual action orientation (with the individual as the referent), and this has also been associated with firm success in two cross sectional studies (Koop, De Reu, & Frese, 2000; Krauss, Frese, Friedrich, & Unger, 2005) and one unpublished longitudinal study (Krauss, Frese, & Friedrich, 2009a). In addition, entrepreneurial orientation and the environment interact. Entrepreneurial orientation is more directly related to firm success in difficult rather than nondifficult environments (Frese, Brantjes, & Hoorn, 2002).

Active Goals and Visions

Active performance was defined previously as being self-started, proactive, and persistent. This implies that goals and visions will be called active if they are self-set (instead of assigned or expected), if they are long-term (in the sense of proactivity), and if they imply that one should not give up a goal in case of problems (persistent).

To my knowledge, no studies directly examine all of these factors. However, there are some approximations. First, a growth goal should be more long-term and more proactive than a nongrowth goal because growth visions have been shown to be related to organizational performance (Baum, Locke, & Kirkpatrick, 1998). Growth goals were interacting with moderators to impact longitudinally on employment and sales growth of small companies in Germany. Growth goals have an impact only when an entrepreneur's goals are characterized by high goal specificity, which follows from goal-setting theory by Locke and Latham (2002) and when they are long-term rather than short-term (Krebber, Frese, & Rauch, 2009). These findings are consistent with an active goal setting concept.

Active Task Strategy and Active Action Planning

Action theory views plans as the bridge between goals (intention) and actions (Miller et al., 1960). Plans can be conscious or nonconscious (automatized or routinized). I focus on conscious plans because they refer to new and important situations. These plans are steps toward important goals to be reached within a few months or a year. They might include, for example, buying or building a new, relatively expensive machine (or in Africa, building a roof for an open-air auto repair shop). From an action theory perspective, the time perspective requires conscious plans to control action; plans make it possible to anticipate the action environment and action parameters and planning analysis of the situation and decisions on how to proceed to achieve a goal (Hacker, 1992). Experimental research has demonstrated that specific plans on the when and where of actions convert goals into actions (Gollwitzer, 1996).

Plans can be differentiated according to their detail and proactivity (Frese & Zapf, 1994). Detail may vary from an elaborate, detailed, and specific plan to one that is very general and does not specify steps to achieve the goals. Detailed planning tends to be accompanied by consideration of contingencies or a plan B if plan A does not work out. The proactivity dimension of planning may go from reactive to proactive (Hacker, 1992). A reactive plan implies that owners react to environmental signals that tell them what needs to be done (e.g., paying when the supply arrives). Thus, for a reactive approach to tasks, a kind of stimulus-response model is adequate—once there is a stimulus, the response follows. These stimuli may be objective facts (e.g., receiving a bill; the breaking down of a machine) or may lie in the social environment, such as if competitors do things in a different way (e.g., adding a product or changing the way they produce their products). In contrast, proactive planning implies that owners influence their environment by anticipating future demands and preparing to meet them. This also goes for opportunities—a proactive approach implies that one anticipates potential opportunities and is prepared to take advantage of them when they appear. Both preparatory as well as preventive activities are stimulated by a proactive planning process (Hacker, 1998). Therefore, the proactivity dimension and the time dimension are highly related— the longer that owners' mental simulations reach into the future (within reason), the more proactive is their approach. People who are focused on the long term also tend to develop more elaborate plans because there are more potential issues and signals to be considered. Therefore, the scope of anticipation increases both the detail and proactivity of planning. Action theory has argued and shows that very good employees (from blue-collar workers to software developers) perform better when they produce proactive and elaborate plans (Hacker, 1992).

Elaborate and proactive plans are based on broad and deep mental models of the work to be done, including a large inventory of potential signals (Hacker, 1992), which tell entrepreneurs whether it is useful to implement a plan. Once something is planned out, one also knows the signals that indicate future difficulties and opportunities, such as when an owner anticipates potential errors and therefore develops backup plans in case something goes wrong. Elaborate planning does *not* mean, however, that *all* important parameters are planned out in detail; rather, it implies that several important parameters of reaching the goal are, at least briefly, considered. The advantages of elaborate and proactive planning are that these plans structure the situation, lead to good knowledge of important environmental signals and feedback, help to interpret the situation adequately, and show that the owner is well prepared when unexpected problems arise. However, elaborate planning also entails costs. Planning takes time, and psychological investments in planning may increase the tendency to stick to plans developed earlier even if they are no longer adequate.

Action theory suggests and experimental research has shown that elaborate and proactive planning helps people to be successful, increases the likelihood that people get started by translating their goals into actions and mobilizing extra effort (Gollwitzer, 1996), amplifies persistence, decreases distraction (Diefendorff & Lord, 2003), reduces load during actions because some parts of the actions have been planned beforehand (actions will therefore run more smoothly), motivates the people to deal with additional problems, and prepares them to have a ready-made answer if something goes wrong. Elaborate and proactive planning allows a person to cope with the inherent insecurities of being a business owner by making good use of scarce resources. Planning helps a person to stay on track and ensures that the goal is not lost or forgotten (Locke & Latham, 2002) and makes the premature triggering of an action less likely (Kuhl & Kazén, 1999). In addition, the proactivity of a plan increases exploration and allows the person to learn better (Bruner, 1966), which improves the mental model of the situation and one's action opportunities. A proactive plan produces better knowledge on contingency conditions and time allocation to tasks and leads to a clearer focus on priorities (Tripoli, 1998), and it also allows people to explore new strategies and to quickly pull back if things do not work; consequently, knowledge of the boundary conditions of one's explanatory concepts is enhanced.

The opposite side of proactive planning implies that actions are regulated on the spot during the course of acting; this leads to a higher reliance on external conditions and signals that determine the action to a much higher extent than when there is a well-developed plan of action—thus, people react to rather than act upon the situation. Therefore, this end of the dimension is called "reactive." Owners with reactive approaches are driven by immediate situational demands. They are dependent on others, which may mean that owners copy their competitors' products, follow a consultant's advice word by word, or wait for their suppliers, customers, or distributors to tell them what to do next. If people are reactive and nonplanning, they do not change conditions. Empirically, some studies showed that a reactive approach contributes negatively to success (Frese et al., 2002; van Gelderen, Frese, & Thurik, 2000). Reactive companies reach the market late (Lieberman & Montgomery, 1998).

In the following I describe one empirical study in a bit more detail (Frese et al., 2007). Action theory and resource allocation theory argue that resources of energy and motivation and of knowledge and working memory are needed to develop elaborate and proactive plans (Kanfer & Ackerman, 1989). Thus, motivational and cognitive resources are related to success with proactive and elaborate plans as mediators. On the cognitive side, *cognitive ability* is related to working memory (Kyllonen & Christal, 1990). Elaborate and proactive conscious planning is complex, and complexity increases the need for cognitive resources (Kanfer & Ackerman, 1989). Given high complexity, high cognitive resources contribute to better planning, including thinking about more relevant issues and about the relationships between these issues. The opposite of elaborate and proactive planning—a reactive approach—does not require manipulating many concepts in the working memory because the relevant action cues are taken directly from the environment. The same arguments as for cognitive ability also hold for *human capital* (skills and knowledge). A high degree of skill implies that a person has ready-made available and routinized responses (Frese & Zapf, 1994) and therefore needs less processing capacity (Kahneman, 1973). This frees up cognitive resources that are then available to develop elaborate and proactive plans to achieve goals.

On the motivational side, elaborate and proactive planning requires energy and direction, which are related to feasibility and desirability.

People have to know that they are able to achieve something and that they want to achieve something before they invest in elaborate and proactive planning. Studies on entrepreneurial success have shown that the following motivational traits are related to entrepreneurial success: internal locus of control, self-efficacy, achievement motivation, and proactive personality (Rauch & Frese, 2000, 2007). Outcome and competency expectancies make it feasible to develop plans and to implement them actively. *Internal locus of control* (Rotter, 1972) implies that people think of themselves as masters of their own fate and that they are able to achieve desired outcomes. An internal locus of control should lead to more elaborate and proactive planning because it makes sense to be proactive and to plan one's actions if one is the master of one's fate (Skinner, 1997). An internal locus of control should lead to better entrepreneurial performance because entrepreneurship requires self-motivation and not waiting for others to indicate what needs doing. *Self-efficacy* refers to the belief that one is able to competently perform actions (Bandura, 1997). A feeling of competence makes it more useful to develop elaborate and proactive plans (lack of competence leads to less elaborate and proactive planning, because one does not have control over one's own actions). Self-efficacy contributes to performance in various domains (Stajkovic & Luthans, 1998). Achievement motivation and proactive personality relate to the desire to develop proactive plans not suggested by others and to change the environment. *Achievement motivation* implies that people want to have an impact and that they do not give up easily (McClelland, 1961); they therefore develop proactive plans. It is a resource that guards a person from switching tasks. *Proactive personality* makes proactive and elaborate planning desirable; moreover, proactive personality is related to entrepreneurial success (Crant, 1995).

Figure 5.2 illustrates that results have supported the theory in three African samples (Frese et al., 2007) and various others studies (Frese, van Gelderen, & Ombach, 2000; Keyser, De Kruif, & Frese, 2000; van Steekelenburg, Lauw, & Frese, 2000). Three studies have examined the issues in a longitudinal design (Escher et al., 2002; Krauss, Frese, & Friedrich, 2009b; van Gelderen et al., 2000). The overall results conclusively showed that active planning is related to success. This is true of Western countries, such as Germany (Utsch & Rauch, 2000; Zempel, 1999) and the Netherlands (van Gelderen et al., 2000) as well as in various African countries (Frese et al., 2007). Moreover, active planning is a mediator between cognitive capacity and human capital on one hand and success on the

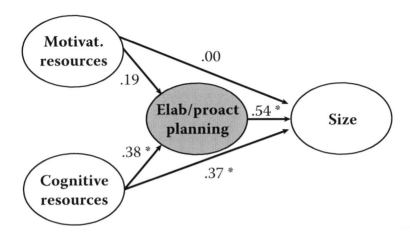

FIGURE 5.2
Elaborate and proactive planning as mediator: Results from Namibia, South Africa, and Zimbabwe. (From Frese, M., Krauss, S., Keith, N., Escher, S., Grabarkiewicz, R., Luneng, S. T., et al., *Journal of Applied Psychology*, 92, 1481–1498, 2007. With permission.)

other (Frese et al., 2007). Motivational resources seem to just barely fail to reach a significant relationship with firm success via active planning (Frese et al., 2007), but other studies tend to emphasize and find significant results for the motivational components (Baum & Locke, 2004).

Active Social Strategy for Networking

The reasoning behind using active action planning also applies to active social strategies for networking. In this case, the focus is not on the task per se but on the social environment. There is a large literature suggesting that entrepreneurial success is increased by better and larger social networks (Hoang & Antoncic, 2003; Johannisson, 2002). Social networks can mean many things, such as network quality and network structure. One of the more robust indicators of networks is network size, that is, the number of people whom the business owners know. Entrepreneurs, as active agents, will also develop their networks if they find the networks to be useful in their endeavors (Batjargal, 2006; Johannisson, 2002).

Zhao, Frese, and Giardini (in press) recently developed a central concept called comprehensive social competency that consists of social skills, the employment of approaches to actively enhance and broaden networks and manipulate the social environment in one's interests (proactive and elaborate social strategies) and to overcome difficulties when there are problems to achieve social goals (relational perseverance). This construct was then related to network size and to entrepreneurial success. This study was conducted in China because social relations are of particular importance in China, as is suggested by the concept of *guanxi* (a special relationship between people in China). Social relations are important in collectivistic societies, and China is high in collectivism (Gelfand, Bhawuk, Nishii, & Bechtold, 2004); they are also important in societies in which institutions are not yet well developed (Xin & Pearce, 1996).

The empirical results show that, indeed, *guanxi* (network size) is an effective mediator between comprehensive social competency, which includes an active approach to broadening social relationships, and entrepreneurial success. However, the effects are related to *guanxi* only toward government officials; in addition, the effects of *guanxi* toward government officials are more important in a smaller rural area than in metropolitan Beijing. The most important finding for the context of the present theory is the relationship between an active approach to developing networks (proactive and elaborate social strategies and relational perseverance) with the success of the owners' firms. The relationships are between $r = .24$ and $r = .36$ in Beijing and between $r = .25$ and $r = .65$ in rural areas. These relationships are reproduced in regression analyses as well, in which a number of control variables are added. Thus, active task performance and active social approaches are both useful for entrepreneurs in the quest for success.

Effectuation, Improvisation, and Experimentation

In entrepreneurship research, being active is often equated with experimentation (i.e., the attempt to try things out and keep what works); this is often contrasted with structured processes, particularly planning. An alternative to having a clear goal and planning for this goal was suggested in Sarasvathy's (2001) concept of effectuation. Effectuation implies that would-be entrepreneurs attempt to achieve the best combination of what they have available (skills, money, material, access to market, and other resources). Once they perceive some success in a market, they take further steps to accomplish further market success. In many ways, this is an active process of "shaping" in contrast to the behaviorist (Skinner, 1953) concept of shaping; it is not the active environment that shapes the behavior but the person who actively explores to find better ways to access markets for potential new products and services that are within the realm of an entrepreneur's possibilities. This concept is a highly useful addition to the more traditional concept of having a goal in mind and planning things out well. Clearly, it is also an active process; entrepreneurs need ideas about what they want to achieve and standards and goals by which they determine that they are achieving something. Thus, the nomenclature of action theory also applies here.

A somewhat similar concept is bricolage (Baker, Miner, & Eesley, 2003, p. 256): "a construct frequently used to describe the resource set invoked by improvisation." Bricolage implies that there are happy circumstances—a certain degree of wanting to change jobs and opportunities appearing—that lead to starting a company (Baker et al., 2003). Thus, the start-up process is greatly opportunistic; a quick change of jobs in which the environment (e.g., customers, old company) seems to suggest that founding something new may be the best option. Empirically, founding was usually done within a few weeks rather than in an extended period of time. There was no long-range planning for the complete start-up phase, but that does not mean that the behavior was accidental or by trial and error. Rather, the founders already had a well-developed and active strategy although the timing for this strategy measured in periods of weeks rather than months. All of the activities described in the study by Baker et al. (2003) fit the present perspective of active behavior: They were self-starting, proactive, persistent.

The debate on whether planning is useful also ranges in strategy research (Bhide, 1994; Mintzberg, 1991). This may be surprising given the fact that meta-analytic evidence is strongly in favor of business planning to be related to success (Miller & Cardinal, 1994). However, unlike the small entrepreneurship studies that usually examine informal planning done by the entrepreneurs themselves, strategic planning is usually done by departments in larger firms. Here formal and well-developed business plans can be described as antidotes to trying things out and experimenting.

Small-scale business owners also create well-developed business plans, which are needed to get financing from banks and business angels (and in this way, producing one leads to more success than not producing any) but may not be directly related to success (Honig, 2004). A business plan may even be outsourced, and consultants may write it for the business owner. It is one of the many concepts developed in economics, where it pays off to look at the detailed behavior of the actors involved rather than assuming that a product is already good enough in and by itself. A detailed behavioral analysis of planning by business owners and high managers may provide better understanding of its functionality. Planning behavior may be of particular importance for business owners, but a good formal business plan may be of much less importance for producing long-term success of the firm. When it comes to real behavior, behavioral planning is necessary for success and, more often, for experimenting.

Obviously, behavioral planning does not mean that owners should spend a lot of time before they can start to act. For example, owners who use elaborate and proactive plans do not need a complete blueprint mapped out in their heads (or on paper) before they act. The process is much less structured than that (cf. Frese & Zapf, 1994): People often redevelop their plans when some actions did not work out; they often develop plans on the spot and change their well-developed plans as a result of feedback. Planning helps owners prepare their actions, quickly realize whether they are on the wrong track, have alternative ideas on hand (plan B) when things do not work out, and finally interpret feedback better because they have a notion of what feedback to expect.

Elaboration of a plan is often complementary to experimenting (Benner & Tushman, 2003; Peters, 1987) or improvising (Baker et al., 2003). It is useful to develop somewhat sketchy plans and then to improvise the rest—that is, a moderate form of action planning (van Gelderen et al., 2000). Elaborate and proactive planning can and should be combined with improvisation and experimentation. Planning helps to develop explicit mental models of how to achieve goals (via mental simulation). This allows entrepreneurs to develop explicit hypotheses and to think of their relevant parameters of how the action should proceed and how the environment should react—the number of relevant signals and potential feedbacks increases (Hacker, 1992). Thus, owners can recognize more quickly whether they are "on track" than if there had been no planning. Moreover, planning helps interpret feedback at the end of a long action cycle—a situation that occurs quite frequently for owners, for example, when they recognize after a long drive to get a big contract that they will not be awarded the contract for which they strove. Then they can mentally simulate the action process retrospectively and develop better hypotheses on where they failed. Planning is also important because it helps owners concentrate and stay focused (Armor & Taylor, 2003). A final reason for combining planning with an action orientation and experimentation is that pure planning without a strong action orientation may lead to procrastination (van Eerde, 2000).

Active Feedback Seeking and Active Approach to Mistakes

Active goal setting, active approach to understanding the situation, active planning, and active feedback seeking are parts of an active action sequence (Table 5.1). Active feedback seeking is important for performance in various domains (Ashford & Black, 1996), and active feedback seeking of managers has also been shown to be related to organizational performance (Daft, Sormunen, & Parks, 1988).

In my research, I have been interested in one type of feedback, namely, errors and error feedback. Errors are the results of nonintended actions that contribute to not achieving a goal. Thus, error feedback is negative feedback par excellence. Errors appear more frequently in complex environments; entrepreneurship emerges in complex environments, partly because there is no complete preparation for entrepreneurship and partly because entrepreneurship deals with new products and services. A person cannot completely prepare for entrepreneurship; errors are inevitable. Thus, error learning should be important for entrepreneurs.

Indeed, evidence indicates that how entrepreneurs perceive errors and how they deal with them is related to their firms' performance. An individual learning orientation (learning from errors, being competent to deal with errors, action orientation when confronted with errors) was related to entrepreneurial success in a German study (Goebel, 1998). Mid-sized companies in Germany and in the Netherlands that had a culture of error management clearly showed a higher degree of organizational performance (van Dyck, Frese, Baer, & Sonnentag, 2005), and a relationship between an error management culture and organizational innovativeness was shown (Frese et al., 2009).

Why is error management orientation thought of as an active form of dealing with feedback? One set of studies examined how people learn from errors. One factor that appears consistently is that people must be encouraged to learn actively from their errors (Keith & Frese, 2008). Thus, error management training produces more metacognition, allowing people to develop hypotheses about how they can deal with errors and learn from testing ideas (Keith & Frese, 2005; van der Linden, Sonnentag, Frese, &

van Dyck, 2001). This is an active form of dealing with errors rather than attempting a trial-and-error procedure or by acting helpless.

Active Approach to Learning (Deliberate Practice)

An active approach to learning from errors has already been discussed. Generalizing from these remarks, we can ask how an active approach to learning is structured and whether it has a positive effect on entrepreneurial success. The concept of deliberate practice can help here. Deliberate practice consists of individualized, self-regulated, effortful activities aimed at improving one's current performance level, implying that there is a high degree of effort and that a person attempts to deeply think and practice those skills that are particularly useful (Ericsson, Krampe, & Tesch-Römer, 1993; Unger, Keith, Rauch, König, & Frese, 2009). Because self-regulation is so important for entrepreneurs, there is a certain focus on the self. The self-focus should not last too long but may enhance the meta-cognitive approach of deliberate practice. Empirical work on entrepreneurs in South Africa and Germany has shown that deliberate practice is, indeed, predictive of entrepreneurial success (Unger, Keith, Hilling, Gielnik, & Frese, 2009; Unger, Keith, Rauch, et al., 2009).

Active Approach in Personality

Figure 5.1 includes several personality factors. The personality approach to entrepreneurship has been criticized in several ways (Aldrich & Widenmayer, 1993; Gartner, 1989): Entrepreneurship requires too many varied behaviors to be related to specific personality traits; personality traits are not strongly enough related to entrepreneurship to warrant further studies; and alternative views, such as ecological approaches, concentrate on environmental forces. These arguments have been quite effective and have led to a dominant position in entrepreneurship research in the 1990s that work on personality traits should be discontinued (Low & MacMillan, 1988).

A meta-analysis on personality factors in entrepreneurship research (Rauch & Frese, 2007) showed that there was a clear and relatively solid relationship between personality factors and entrepreneurship. However, these relationships were much higher for the active personality factors displayed in Figure 5.1. Rauch and Frese (2007) also found that those factors that were most frequently mentioned were also the most active (e.g., self-efficacy, proactive personality, tenacity, need for achievement). The highest correlations with starting an organization and organizational success were the personality factors of self-efficacy, proactive personality, innovativeness, need for achievement, and internal locus of control (the latter to some extent). Risk taking was less highly correlated with starting an organization or with entrepreneurial success than other personality factors. Of course, some personality factors had not been studied often enough to include them in the meta-analysis. Some studies suggest that these newer active personality concepts may play an important role as well (Baum & Locke, 2004).

TRAINING

The arguments presented herein have been based on descriptive studies; most of them were cross sectional, although there were also a few longitudinal studies. It would be useful to test the theory by actually changing entrepreneurs' performance and examining long-term effects on firms' success. Active performance is one form of personal initiative; therefore, an intervention (personal initiative training) was developed for business owners. Evidence of change in personal initiative (active performance) in the entrepreneurs, which leads to changes in success, provides better proof for the active approach.

Glaub, Fischer, Klemm, and Frese (2010) developed a broadband training that changed a number of dimensions. It was successful in increasing success in the entrepreneurs but not necessarily due to personal initiative (i.e., personal initiative changes were not the mediator of the positive effect of the trainings on success). Moreover, a number of methodological problems limited the internal validity of these studies. Therefore, Glaub, Fischer, Klemm, and Frese (2010) conducted a study on the effectiveness of a true personal initiative training in which aspects of personal initiative were changed. Thus, broadband training was abandoned in favor of a small-band approach that zeroed in on personal initiative. Moreover, Glaub et al. chose a randomized control-group field study that truly allows a test of the long-term effect of this chapter's theory based on real-life intervention. This research showed the best results to date: A three-day training course changed the personal initiative of the African entrepreneurs significantly, which in turn changed the positive effect of the training on success (Glaub et al., 2010).

CONCLUSION

Active action is central for entrepreneurship. Active actions can be described well with action theory—an active approach may have as focus the task, the social situation, or the self (cf. action theory above).

An attempt was made here to think through the concept of active actions as being central to entrepreneurship theoretically and to empirically show that active actions play a role in all of the determinants of success. In addition, an effort was given to understanding whether a change in the active action approach can actually accomplish enhanced success—at least the training intervention presented here seems to have this effect.

Up to this point, the empirical results seem to support what we are doing. The empirical answer is that active actions are important for entrepreneurial success. They are also important as an intervention procedure. But in a multifaceted field, such as entrepreneurship, the relative importance of this theoretical approach is yet unknown in comparison with alternative approaches. Thus, what still needs to be determined is to differentiate this theory of entrepreneurship from other theories of entrepreneurship and to empirically test the add-on value of active actions in comparison with other broad-based entrepreneurship theories. It is predicted that other approaches have something to offer. Therefore, it would be interesting to empirically examine, for example, the two approaches: the psychological approach presented here and the ecological approach. Although preliminary data seem to support the former (Frese, 2000), an added question would be to determine which circumstances (moderators) are responsible for the functionality of the psychological theory versus the functionality of the ecological approach.

REFERENCES

Ackerman, P. L. (1988). Determinants of individual differences during skill acquisition: Cognitive abilities and information processing. *Journal of Experimental Psychology: General, 117*(3), 288–318.

Ackerman, P. L. (1992). Predicting individual differences in complex skill acquisitions: Dynamics of ability determinants. *Journal of Applied Psychology, 77,* 598–614.

Aldrich, H. E., & Widenmayer, G. (1993). From traits to rates: An ecological perspective on organizational foundings. In J. A. Katz & R. H. Brockhaus (Eds.), *Advances in entrepreneurship, firm emergence, and growth* (Vol. 1, pp. 145–195). Greenwich, CT: JAI Press.

Anderson, J. R. (1983). *The architecture of cognition.* Cambridge, MA: Harvard University Press.

Armor, D. A., & Taylor, S. E. (2003). The effects of mindset on behavior: Self-regulation in deliberative and implemental frames of mind. *Personality & Social Psychology Bulletin, 29*, 86–95.

Ashford, S. J., & Black, J. S. (1996). Proactivity during organizational entry: The role of desire for control. *Journal of Applied Psychology, 81*, 199–214.

Audia, P. G., Locke, E. A., & Smith, K. G. (2000). The paradox of success: An archival and a laboratory study of strategic persistence following radical environmental change. *Academy of Management Journal, 43*, 837–853.

Baddeley, A. D. (1986). *Working memory*. Oxford: Oxford University Press.

Baker, T., Miner, A., & Eesley, D. (2003). Improvising firms: Bricolage, account giving, and improvisational competencies in the founding process. *Research Policy, 32*, 255–276.

Bandura, A. (1982). Self-efficacy mechanism in human agency. *American Psychologist, 37*, 122–147.

Bandura, A. (1997). *Self-efficacy: The exercise of control*. New York: Freeman and Co.

Batjargal, B. (2006). The dynamics of entrepreneurs' networks in a transitioning economy: The case of Russia. *Entrepreneurship & Regional Development, 18*, 305–320.

Baum, J. R., Frese, M., & Baron, R. A. (Eds.). (2007). *The psychology of entrepreneurship*. Mahwah, NJ: Lawrence Erlbaum Publishers.

Baum, J. R., & Locke, E. A. (2004). The relation of entrepreneurial traits, skill, and motivation to subsequent venture growth. *Journal of Applied Psychology, 89*, 587–598.

Baum, J. R., Locke, E. A., & Kirkpatrick, S. A. (1998). A longitudinal study of the relation of vision and vision communication to venture growth in entrepreneurial firms. *Journal of Applied Psychology, 83*, 43–54.

Benner, M. J., & Tushman, M. L. (2003). Exploitation, exploration, and process management: The productivity dilemma revisited. *Academy of Management Review, 28*, 238–256.

Berger, P. L., & Luckmann, T. (1966). *The social construction of reality*. Garden City, NY: Doubleday.

Bhide, A. (1994). How entrepreneurs craft strategies that work. *Harvard Business Review, 72*(2), 150–161.

Brown, A. L. (1987). Metacognition, executive control, self-regulation, and other more mysterious mechanisms. In F. W. Weinert & R. H. Kluwe (Eds.), *Metacognition, motivation, and understanding* (pp. 65–116). Hillsdale, NJ: Lawrence Erlbaum Associates.

Bruner, J. S. (1966). *Toward a theory of instruction*. Cambridge, MA: Harvard University Press.

Cacioppo, J. T., Petty, R. E., Kao, C. F., & Rodriguez, R. (1986). Central and peripheral routes to persuasion: An individual difference perspective. *Journal of Personality & Social Psychology, 51*, 1032–1043.

Carland, J. W., Hoy, F., Boulton, W. R., & Carland, J. C. (1984). Differentiating entrepreneurs from small business owners: A conceptualization. *Academy of Management Review, 9*, 354–359.

Carver, C. S., & Scheier, M. F. (1982). Control theory: A useful conceptual framework for personality-social, clinical, and health psychology. *Psychological Bulletin, 92*, 111–135.

Crant, J. M. (1995). The proactive personality scale and objective job performance among real estate agents. *Journal of Applied Psychology, 80*, 532–537.

Daft, R. L., Sormunen, J., & Parks, D. (1988). Chief executive scanning, environmental characteristics, and company performance: An empirical study. *Strategic Management Journal, 9*, 123–139.

Diefendorff, J. M., & Lord, R. G. (2003). The volitional and strategic effects of planning on task performance and goal commitment. *Human Performance, 16*, 365–387.

Dörner, D., & Schaub, H. (1994). Errors in planning and decision-making and the nature of human information processing. *Applied Psychology: An International Review, 43*, 433–453.

Ericsson, K. A., Krampe, R. T., & Tesch-Römer, C. (1993). The role of deliberate practice in the acquisition of expert performance. *Psychological Review, 100*, 363–406.

Escher, S., Grabarkiewicz, R., Frese, M., van Steekelenburg, G., Lauw, M., & Friedrich, C. (2002). The moderator effect of cognitive ability on the relation between planning strategies and business success of small scale business owners in South Africa: A longitudinal study. *Journal of Developmental Entrepreneurship, 7*, 305–318.

Flavell, J. H. (1987). Speculations about the nature and development of metacognition. In F. E. Weinert & R. H. Kluwe (Eds.), *Metacognition, motivation, and understanding* (pp. 21–29). Hillsdale, NJ: Erlbaum.

French, W. L., & Bell, C. H., Jr. (1995). *Organization development* (5th ed.). Englewood Cliffs, NJ: Prentice-Hall.

Frese, M. (2000). Executive summary, conclusions, and policy implications. In M. Frese (Ed.), *Success and failure of microbusiness owners in Africa: A psychological approach* (pp. 161–190). Westport, CT: Greenwood.

Frese, M., Brantjes, A., & Hoorn, R. (2002). Psychological success factors of small scale businesses in Namibia: The roles of strategy process, entrepreneurial orientation and the environment. *Journal of Developmental Entrepreneurship, 7*, 259–282.

Frese, M., & Fay, D. (2001). Personal Initiative (PI): A concept for work in the 21st century. *Research in Organizational Behavior, 23*, 133–188.

Frese, M., Glaub, M., Gramberg, K., Hass, L., Friedrich, C., & Solomon, G. (2009). *Training business owners in personal initiative: Two evaluation studies in South Africa and Germany.* Technical report, University of Giessen, manuscript in preparation.

Frese, M., Krauss, S., Keith, N., Escher, S., Grabarkiewicz, R., Luneng, S. T., et al. (2007). Business owners' action planning and its relationship to business success in three African countries. *Journal of Applied Psychology, 92*, 1481–1498.

Frese, M., Kring, W., Soose, A., & Zempel, J. (1996). Personal initiative at work: Differences between East and West Germany. *Academy of Management Journal, 39*(1), 37–63.

Frese, M., Mertins, J. C., Hardt, J. V., Fischer, S., Flock, T., Schauder, J., et al. (2009). Innovativeness of firms and organizational culture: The role of error management culture and pro-initiative climate. Manuscript submitted for publication.

Frese, M., & Sabini, J. (Eds.). (1985). *Goal directed behavior: The concept of action in psychology.* Hillsdale, NJ: Erlbaum.

Frese, M., Stewart, J., & Hannover, B. (1987). Goal orientation and planfulness: Action styles as personality concepts. *Journal of Personality and Social Psychology, 52*, 1182–1194.

Frese, M., van Gelderen, M., & Ombach, M. (2000). How to plan as a small scale business owner: Psychological process characteristics of action strategies and success. *Journal of Small Business Management, 38*(2), 1–18.

Frese, M., & Zapf, D. (1994). Action as the core of work psychology: A German approach. In H. C. Triandis, M. D. Dunnette, & L. Hough (Eds.), *Handbook of industrial and organizational psychology* (Vol. 4, pp. 271–340). Palo Alto, CA: Consulting Psychologists Press.

Gartner, W. B. (1989). "Who is an entrepreneur?" is the wrong question. *Entrepreneurship Theory and Practice, 13*(4), 47–68.

Gelfand, M. J., Bhawuk, D. P. S., Nishii, L. H., & Bechtold, D. J. (2004). Individualism and collectivism. In R. J. House, P. J. Hanges, M. Javidan, P. W. Dorfman, & V. Gupta (Eds.), *Culture, leadership, and organizations: The GLOBE study of 62 societies* (pp. 437–512). Thousand Oaks, CA: Sage.

Glaub, M., Fischer, S., Klemm, M., & Frese, M. (2010). Training personal initiative to business owners. Manuscript submitted for publication.

Gleitman, H. (1985). Some trends in the study of cognition. In S. Koch & D. E. Leary (Eds.), *A century of psychology as science: Retrospections and assessments* (pp. 420–436). New York: McGraw-Hill.

Goebel, S. (1998). Persoenlichkeit, Handlungsstrategien und Erfolg [Personality, action strategies, and success]. In M. Frese (Ed.), *Erfolgreiche Unternehmensgruender [Successful start-ups]* (pp. 99–122). Goettingen, Germany: Verlag fuer Angewandte Psychologie.

Gollwitzer, P. M. (1993). Goal achievement: The role of intentions. In W. Stroebe & M. Hewstone (Eds.), *European review of social psychology* (Vol. 4, pp. 141–185). London: Wiley.

Gollwitzer, P. M. (1996). The volitional benefits of planning. In P. M. Gollwitzer & J. A. Bargh (Eds.), *The psychology of action* (pp. 287–312). New York: Guilford Press.

Hacker, W. (1992). *Expertenkönnen. Erkennen und Vermitteln [Detection and communication of expert mastery]*. Göttingen: Hogrefe.

Hacker, W. (1998). *Allgemeine Arbeitspsychologie [General work psychology]*. Bern: Huber.

Hass, L., & Friedrich, C. (2010, in prep). Training business owners in personal initiative: Two evaluation studies in South Africa and Germany. Lueneburg: Leuphana. Technical report.

Heckhausen, H., & Gollwitzer, P. (1985). Information processing before and after the formation of an intent. In F. Klix & H. Hagendorf (Eds.), *In memoriam Hermann Ebbinghaus: Symposium on the structure and function of human memory* (pp. 1071–1082). Amsterdam: Elsevier.

Hoang, H., & Antoncic, B. (2003). Network-based research in entrepreneurship: A critical review. *Journal of Business Venturing, 18,* 165–187.

Honig, B. (2004). Entrepreneurship education: Toward a model of contingency-based business planning. *Academy of Management Learning and Education, 3,* 258–273.

Johannisson, B. (2002). Networking and entrepreneurial growth. In D. L. Sexton & H. Landström (Eds.), *The Blackwell handbook of entrepreneurship* (pp. 368–386). Oxford, UK: Blackwell.

Kahneman, D. (1973). *Attention and effort*. Englewood Cliffs, NJ: Prentice Hall.

Kahneman, D. (2003). A perspective on judgment and choice: Mapping bounded rationality. *American Psychologist, 58,* 697–720.

Kanfer, R., & Ackerman, P. L. (1989). Motivation and cognitive abilities: An integrative/aptitude-treatment interaction approach to skill acquisition. *Journal of Applied Psychology, 74,* 657–690.

Kanfer, R., & Heggestad, E. D. (1997). Motivational traits and skills: A person-centered approach to work motivation. *Research in Organizational Behavior, 19,* 1–56.

Katz, D., & Kahn, R. L. (1978). *Social psychology of organizations* (2nd ed.). New York: Wiley.

Keith, N., & Frese, M. (2005). Self-regulation in error management training: Emotion control and metacognition as mediators of performance effects. *Journal of Applied Psychology, 90,* 677–691.

Keith, N., & Frese, M. (2008). Performance effects of error management training: A meta-analysis. *Journal of Applied Psychology, 93,* 59–69.

Keyser, M., De Kruif, M., & Frese, M. (2000). The psychological strategy process and socio-demographic variables as predictors of success in micro- and small-scale business owners in Zambia. In M. Frese (Ed.), *Success and failure of microbusiness owners in Africa: A psychological approach* (pp. 31–53). Westport, CT: Greenwood.

Koop, S., De Reu, T., & Frese, M. (2000). Sociodemographic factors, entrepreneurial orientation, personal initiative, and environmental problems in Uganda. In M. Frese (Ed.), *Success and failure of microbusiness owners in Africa: A psychological approach* (pp. 55–76). Westport, CT: Greenwood.

Krauss, S. I., Frese, M., & Friedrich, C. (2010, in preparation). Longitudinal effects of planning and entrepreneurial orientation on performance and vice versa: The case of performance cycles. National University of Singapore: Manuscript.

Krebber, M., Frese, M., & Rauch, A. (2009). The effects of growth goals on business success: Moderating effects of environmental dynamics, cognitive resources, and goal setting characteristics. University of Giessen, in preparation.

Kruger, J., & Dunning, D. (1999). Unskilled and unaware of it: How difficulties in recognizing one's own incompetence lead to inflated self-assessments. *Journal of Personality and Social Psychology, 77,* 1121–1134.

Kuhl, J., & Kazén, M. (1999). Volitional facilitation of difficult intentions: Joint activation of intention memory and positive affect removes Stroop interference. *Journal of Experimental Psychology: General, 128,* 382–399.

Kyllonen, P. C., & Christal, R. E. (1990). Reasoning ability is (little more than) working-memory capacity?! *Intelligence, 14,* 389–433.

Lieberman, M. B., & Montgomery, D. B. (1998). First mover (dis-)advantages: Retrospective and link with the resource-based view. *Strategic Management Journal, 19,* 1111–1125.

Locke, E. A., & Latham, G. P. (2002). Building a practically useful theory of goal setting and task motivation. *American Psychologist, 57,* 705–717.

Low, M. B., & MacMillan, I. C. (1988). Entrepreneurship: Past research and future challenges. *Journal of Management, 14,* 139–161.

Lumpkin, G. T., & Dess, G. G. (1996). Clarifying the entrepreneurial orientation construct and linking it to performance. *Academy of Management Review, 21,* 135–172.

March, J., & Simon, H. A. (1958). *Organizations.* New York: Wiley.

McClelland, D. C. (1961). *The achieving society.* New York: Free Press.

McClelland, D. C. (1987). *Human motivation.* Cambridge, UK: Cambridge University Press.

McClelland, D. C., & Winter, D. G. (1971). *Motivating economic achievement.* New York: Free Press.

Mead, D. C., & Liedholm, C. (1998). The dynamics of micro and small enterprises in developing countries. *World Development, 26,* 61–74.

Metcalfe, J. (1993). Novelty monitoring, metacognition, and control in a holographic associative recall model: Implications for Korsakoff amnesia. *Psychological Review, 100,* 3–22.

Mikulincer, M. (1989). Cognitive interference and learned helplessness: The effects of off-task cognitions on performance following unsolvable problems. *Journal of Personality and Social Psychology, 57,* 129–135.

Mikulincer, M., Glaubman, H., Ben-Artzi, E., & Grossman, S. (1991). The cognitive specificity of learned helplessness and depression deficits: The role of self-focused cognitions. *Anxiety Research, 3,* 273–290.

Miller, C. C., & Cardinal, L. B. (1994). Strategic planning and firm performance: A synthesis of more than two decades of research. *Academy of Management Journal, 37,* 1649–1665.

Miller, G. A., Galanter, E., & Pribram, K. H. (1960). *Plans and the structure of behavior.* London: Holt.

Mintzberg, H. (1991). Learning I. Planning 1: A reply to Igor Ansoff. *Strategic Management Journal, 12,* 463–466.

Norman, D. A. (1981). Categorization of action slips. *Psychological Review, 88,* 1–15.

Norman, D. A. (1986). Cognitive engineering. In D. A. Norman & S. W. Draper (Eds.), *User centered system design* (pp. 31–61). Hillsdale, NJ: Lawrence Erlbaum.

Rasmussen, J. (1982). Human errors. A taxonomy for describing human malfunction in industrial installations. *Journal of Occupational Accidents, 4,* 311–333.

Rauch, A., & Frese, M. (2000). Psychological approaches to entrepreneurial success: A general model and an overview of findings. In C. L. Cooper & I. T. Robertson (Eds.), *International Review of Industrial and Organizational Psychology,* (Vol. 15, pp. 101–142).

Rauch, A., & Frese, M. (2007). Let's put the person back into entrepreneurship research: A meta-analysis on the relationship between business owners' personality traits, business creation and success. *European Journal of Work and Organizational Psychology, 16,* 353–385.

Rauch, A., Wiklund, J., Lumpkin, G. T., & Frese, M. (2009). Entrepreneurial orientation and business performance: Cumulative empirical evidence. *Entrepreneurship Theory and Practice, 33,* 761–787.

Reynolds, P. D., Bygrave, W. D., & Autio, E. (2004). *Global entrepreneurship monitor 2003 executive report.* London: London Business School.

Rotter, J. B. (1972). Generalized expectancies for internal versus external control of reinforcement. In J. B. Rotter, J. E. Chance, & E. J. Phares (Eds.), *Applications of a social learning theory of personality* (pp. 260–294). New York: Holt.

Sarasvathy, S. D. (2001). Causation and effectuation: Toward a theoretical shift from economic inevitability to entrepreneurial contingency. *Academy of Management Review, 26,* 243–263.

Schein, E. H. (1987). *Organizational culture and leadership.* San Francisco, CA: Jossey-Bass.

Schneider, W., & Shiffrin, R. M. (1977). Controlled and automatic human information processing: I. detection, search, and attention. *Psychological Review, 84,* 1–66.

Schumpeter, J. (1935). *Theorie der wirtschaftlichen Entwicklung* [*Theory of economic development*], 4th ed. Munich, Germany: Von Duncker & Humblot.

Seligman, M. (1975). *Helplessness: On depression, development and death.* San Francisco, CA: Freeman.

Shane, S., & Venkataraman, S. (2000). The promise of entrepreneurship as a field of research. *Academy of Management Review, 25,* 217–226.

Shepard, R. N., & Metzler, J. (1971). Mental rotation of three-dimensional objects. *Science, 171,* 701–703.

Skinner, B. F. (1953). *Science and human behavior.* New York: Free Press.

Skinner, E. A. (1997). Planning and perceived control. In S. L. Friedman & E. K. Scholnick (Eds.), *The developmental psychology of planning: Why, how, and when do we plan?* (pp. 263–284). Mahwah, NJ: Lawrence Erlbaum.

Sonnentag, S. (1998). Expertise in professional software design: A process study. *Journal of Applied Psychology, 83,* 703–715.

Stajkovic, A. D., & Luthans, F. (1998). Self-efficacy and work-related performance: A meta-analysis. *Psychological Bulletin, 124*, 240–261.

Tripoli, A. M. (1998). Planning and allocating: Strategies for managing priorities in complex jobs. *European Journal of Work and Organizational Psychology, 7*, 455–475.

Unger, J. M., Keith, N., Hilling, C., Gielnik, M., & Frese, M. (2009). Deliberate practice among South African small business owners: Relationships with education, cognitive ability, knowledge, and success. *Journal of Occupational and Organizational Psychology, 82*, 21–44.

Unger, J. M., Keith, N., Rauch, A., König, C., & Frese, M. (2009). Deliberate practice and entrepreneurial success: A longitudinal analysis among German small business owners. University of Giessen, in preparation.

Utsch, A., & Rauch, A. (2000). Innovativeness and initiative as mediators between achievement orientation and venture performance. *European Journal of Work and Organizational Psychology, 9*, 45–62.

Utsch, A., Rauch, A., Rothfuss, R., & Frese, M. (1999). Who becomes a small scale entrepreneur in a post-socialist environment: On the differences between entrepreneurs and managers in East Germany. *Journal of Small Business Management, 37*(3), 31–42.

van der Linden, D., Sonnentag, S., Frese, M., & van Dyck, C. (2001). Exploration strategies, performance, and error consequences when learning a complex computer task. *Behaviour and Information Technology, 20*, 189–198.

van Dyck, C., Frese, M., Baer, M., & Sonnentag, S. (2005). Organizational error management culture and its impact on performance: A two-study replication. *Journal of Applied Psychology, 90*, 1228–1240.

van Eerde, W. (2000). Procrastination: Self-regulation in initiating aversive goals. *Applied Psychology: An International Review, 49*, 372–389.

van Gelderen, M., Frese, M., & Thurik, R. (2000). Strategies, uncertainty and performance of small business startups. *Small Business Economics, 15*, 165–181.

van Steekelenburg, W., Lauw, A. M., & Frese, M. (2000). Problems and coping, strategies and initiative in microbusiness owners in South Africa. In M. Frese (Ed.), *Success and failure of microbusiness owners in Africa* (pp. 77–102). Westport, CT: Greenwood.

Weinert, F. E., & Kluwe, R. H. (1987). *Metacognition, motivation, an understanding*. Hillsdale, NJ: Erlbaum.

White, R. (1959). Motivation reconsidered: The concept of competence. *Psychological Review, 66*, 297–333.

Xin, K. R., & Pearce, J. L. (1996). Guanxi: Connections as substitues for formal institutional support. *Academy of Management Journal, 39*, 1641–1658.

Zempel, J. (1999). Selbstaendigkeit in den neuen Bundeslaendern: Praediktoren, Erfolgsfaktoren und Folgen - Ergebnisse einer Laengsschnittuntersuchung. In K. Moser, B. Batinic, & J. Zempel (Eds.), *Unternehmerisch erfolgreiches Handeln* (pp. 69–91). Goettingen, Germany: Verlag fuer Angewandte Psychologie.

Zhao, X.-Y., Frese, M., & Giardini, A. (in press). Business owners' network size and business growth in China: The role of comprehensive social competency. *Entrepreneurship & Regional Development*.

Section III

Conflict, Cooperation, and Decision Making

6

Responsive Leaders: Cognitive and Behavioral Reactions to Identity Threats

Roderick M. Kramer
Stanford University

In recent months, following the almost daily revelations of corporate fraud and abuse by the heads of some of the country's largest corporations, the American people have been witness to a parade of leaders earnestly denying any wrongdoing. And they've seen these same leaders, contritely arrayed at long tables facing angry and accusing Congressional committees, declaring they hadn't seen it coming and it wasn't their fault.

Such events remind us that it isn't easy being at the top. They also remind us that leaders are expected not only to make sensible and prudent decisions as they manage their organizations but also to be adept at explaining and justifying those decisions. Yet, given the intense scrutiny directed at current leaders, successfully maintaining a positive image can be truly problematic (Sutton & Galunic, 1996). Both a skeptical and vigilant media and the various stakeholders of an organization have greater access to information and feel empowered to challenge leaders' judgments and actions. As a consequence, leaders find their decisions endlessly dissected and debated by television pundits, watchdog groups, and bloggers. As Pfeffer (1992) succinctly noted, "To be in power is to be watched more closely, and this surveillance affords one the luxury of few mistakes" (p. 302).

When leaders do make mistakes—or are perceived to have made mistakes—they are likely to find their intentions, motives, attentiveness, or competence called into question. Questions about their integrity, credibility, or competence present them with severe identity-threatening predicaments. When accusations challenge cherished, central aspects of a leader's own sense of identity, they constitute a particularly serious, personal threat.

The research that I summarize in this chapter explores the array of cognitive responses leaders experience when they face these identity-threatening predicaments. My primary aim in the chapter is to systematically explore two central questions. First, how do leaders construe identity-threatening predicaments? In other words, what cognitive tactics do they use to make sense of (and potentially attenuate or mitigate) these threats to their identity and sense of self? And, second, how do they adjust their cognitions to preserve their sense of self and justify their actions? Stated in slightly different terms, I explore the cognitive strategies leaders use when they try to make sense of identity-threatening predicaments and the cognitive tactics they use when they try to repair their threatened or tarnished identities.

In pursuing these two issues, I should note that my analysis differs somewhat from prior approaches. For the most part, previous research has focused on decision makers' explanatory accounts, including tactics such as apologies, excuses, and justifications (e.g., Elsbach, 1994; Elsbach & Sutton, 1992; Ginzel, Kramer, & Sutton, 1993; Salancik & Meindl, 1984). In the present research, I investigate the role of *strategic categorization* (and also recategorization) processes. In particular, I present the results of three studies that explored leaders' responsive construals of identity-threatening predicaments and the tactics they chose in their attempts to repair their tarnished identities.

My research also takes a different methodological approach to these phenomena. The traditional, preferred method in social psychological research has been the laboratory experiment (Runkel & McGrath, 1974); it has many well-known advantages for investigating the efficacy of self-presentational strategies (e.g., Leary, 1989, 1995; Schlenker, 2003). My research, in contrast, has taken a qualitative, archival approach, investigating the self-presentational strategies and tactics real-world leaders use when responding to real-world predicaments. Thus, I have focused on analyzing the thoughts and responses of experienced, skillful leaders, possibly assisted by their advisors, to actual predicaments.

To begin, I provide a brief conceptual summary of the meaning of a leader's psychological identity or sense of self. I then describe how organizational events, external and beyond a leader's control, as well as those resulting from a leader's own decisions can threaten these identities. I discuss how I analyzed leaders' responses and then present findings from three different domains. I conclude the chapter by discussing some theoretical and practical implications.

LEADER IDENTITY AND IDENTITY-THREATENING PREDICAMENTS

For the present analysis, I define *psychological identity* in terms of the attributes individuals use to describe themselves (Hoyle, Kernis, Leary, & Baldwin, 1999). Thus, leaders' identities constitute the set of self-perceived attributes they use to characterize themselves or their leadership, including unique or distinctive personal qualities leaders associate with themselves. Leaders might, for example, consider themselves intelligent, competent, trustworthy, competitive, visionary, or resilient. These self-ascriptions also include references to various social and political categories they might use to label themselves. Thus, a leader might also describe herself as a feminist, a centrist Democrat, a neoconservative, or a radical environmentalist.

As with other forms of psychological identity, leader identities are highly differentiated and include multiple identity components (Brewer & Hewstone, 2004). Thus, when asked to describe themselves, most leaders will experience little difficulty invoking a variety of different attributes and categories. To be sure, some may describe themselves in terms of a very few, closely related attributes, and others may list many attributes, some of which may seem inconsistent with, and not easily integrated into, a single, coherent sense of self. They may also vary in their comfort or ambivalence toward their attributes. Martin Luther King Jr., for example, was acutely sensitive to what he perceived as his personal moral weaknesses, especially those related to "womanizing." Nonetheless, he understood and accepted these critical self-perceptions to sharpen his thinking regarding his role in the leadership of the civil rights movement (Branch, 2006).

Identity attributes also vary in their importance and centrality. For example, some leaders might define themselves first and foremost in terms of their ability to manifest grace under pressure (an attribute President John F. Kennedy highly valued). In contrast, Ronald Reagan valued optimism, a deep faith in himself, and the wisdom of his judgment. Other leaders view their ability to bounce back from personal or political crises as central; for example, Bill Clinton famously referred to himself as "the Comeback Kid." Similarly, Richard Nixon perceived himself as a scrappy, street-tough fighter whom the Harvard-trained intellectuals and media critics underestimated, with other attributes taking a secondary, more peripheral place.

I characterize those attributes and categories leaders view as particularly important, fundamental, and central to their self-conceptions as *core identity* attributes or categories. From a functional perspective, all of the self-ascriptions and self-categorizations leaders employ when describing themselves can be viewed as helping them define who they are and how they should interpret and act in those situations (March, 1994). Threats to core identity attributes should then be particularly salient.

A few other preliminary points merit mention. As with other forms of identity, leader identities are to some extent socially constructed and socially validated. Leaders attempt to project desired identities through their actions, but a diverse organizational audience—allies, constituents, shareholders, employees, board members, pundits, and critics—*interprets* their actions. Leaders face a constant social challenge in sustaining their desired identity. Because of this interdependence, leaders' success or failure at constructing and maintaining a valued identity depends on others' reactions to their identity affirmations and claims. In this sense, leaders' identities emerge and are sustained through their interactions with other people, especially audiences to whom they feel particularly accountable. Stated differently, identity management is a reciprocal, dynamic influence process between leaders and their audiences (Ginzel et al., 1993).

Because leaders' identities are socially constructed and negotiated, the success or failure of leaders' attempts to restore or repair a damaged identity is likely to depend on a perceptive reading of their organizational audience and a deft negotiation of that audience's concerns, interpretations, and beliefs. This obviously brings leaders' self-presentation and impression management skills to the fore. Thus, the results of any identity repair process critically depend upon leaders' persuasion, influence, and negotiation skills.

These ideas and assumptions provide the backdrop for my investigation of leaders' approaches to the problem of identity threat and repair. The term *identity-threatening predicament* refers to any event that calls into question or challenges a leader's cherished or valued identity attributes (Tedeschi, 1981). For example, if a leader considers herself to be a moral and trustworthy leader and highly values those attributes, then an event that calls into question her morality or trustworthiness is likely to constitute an identity threat, especially if it creates an expectation of some sort of response or reaction from her. In other words, both leaders and their various stakeholders understand when an important identity-threatening predicament emerges; they are public, recognizable events that require a response.

STUDYING LEADER IDENTITY THREAT AND REPAIR PROCESSES

A number of approaches have been used to study how individuals respond to identity threats. As noted, most social psychologists have employed experimental methods to investigate antecedents and consequences of identity threats. Steele's (1988) programmatic studies on self-affirmation are an excellent illustration: His experiments demonstrate that when individuals experience a threat to one aspect of their social identities, they can sometimes mitigate the severity of that threat by affirming other positive social identities. Thus, if a student's competence in mathematics is challenged, the student might affirm other compensatory attributes, including his writing ability or knowledge of art.

Although these studies involve inexperienced undergraduate students responding to abstract and artificial social stimuli, they are quite valuable in exploring the basic psychological processes associated with social identity threat and repair processes. They are less useful, however, for building an understanding of the likely reactions of organizational or political leaders. It's hard to bring presidents, senators, or corporate chief executive officers into the laboratory to measure their response to a hypothetical, transient threat. For these kinds of cases, experimental investigations can be only suggestive.

A different approach, represented here in three studies, is to use qualitative data to inductively investigate how leaders respond to identity threats. The first study explored how business school leaders respond to threats to their leadership and the second and third examined Lyndon Johnson's and Reagan's different responses to threats to their presidential performance.

STUDY 1: COUNTERING THE *BUSINESS WEEK* RANKINGS—SELECTIVE CATEGORIZATION AND STRATEGIC SOCIAL COMPARISONS

Business Week (*BW*) magazine began ranking U.S. business schools in 1988. It used a survey to evaluate business schools on two primary criteria: (1) master of business administration (MBA) graduates' satisfaction with their school, including the quality of the educational experience and support for career placement; and (2) recruiters' satisfaction with recent graduates of the school. It constructed a composite score from these two dimensions to rank business schools, with a special focus on its idea of the "Top Twenty" schools in the country. It is important to note that competition among business schools for the best students is fierce, and a school's rankings in surveys like *BW*'s are viewed as important drivers of prospective MBA students' selections of schools. Thus, these rankings constituted a new, serious threat to business schools and their administrative leaders.

The *BW* rankings also represented a serious threat to business schools because they essentially changed "the name of the game" for many schools. Prior to the rankings, many top schools had created distinct reputational niches for themselves. Harvard, for example, was renowned for producing top-flight, management-oriented leaders. Northwestern was considered the most prominent marketing program. The University of Pennsylvania's Wharton School of Business was famous for its finance program. Stanford was known as the premier "basic research-oriented" business school, and Massachusetts Institute of Technology (MIT) and University of California (UC)–Berkeley were known for their high-tech, entrepreneurial orientation. Other schools enjoyed regional reputations that helped them attract students; one school, for example, was known as the "Harvard of the South."

Because of these distinctive niches, it was possible for many schools to consider themselves quite outstanding, claiming high status even as they avoided invidious comparisons. By suggesting a single, common, and purportedly objective metric, the *BW* ranking forced schools to respond to its criteria. Because of the obvious threat posed by students selecting schools primarily on the basis of their absolute ranking, the "live and let live" feeling among schools prior to the rankings was replaced by more a universally competitive mindset.

This was the context that Kim Elsbach and I used to explore business school deans' responses to organizational identity threats; our central focus was on their identity construal and repair tactics (Elsbach & Kramer, 1996). We collected a variety of different kinds of evidence. First, we collected and content analyzed school documents, including press releases and published interviews. We also collected articles from campus, regional, and national newspapers. Finally, we conducted extensive interviews ourselves with business school deans, associate deans, and administrators involved in media relations.

Content analyses of the interview and archival materials revealed strong evidence that the *BW* rankings were a serious threat to many business schools in at least two distinct ways. First, the rankings often devalued or ignored altogether the schools' core identity dimensions and, by implication, their leadership. For example, by emphasizing MBA students' satisfaction with teaching as a primary evaluative criterion, *BW* implicitly questioned the value of a research orientation: UC–Berkeley, MIT, and Stanford's basic missions.

Second, by ranking the schools, *BW* questioned many schools' claims of status, both nationally and regionally. As John Byrne, the creator and editor of the survey, noted, "For years and years there were probably 50 business schools that claimed that they were in the top 20 and probably hundreds that claimed they were in the top 40.... The Business Week survey eliminated the ability of some schools to claim that they [were] in a top group" (Elsbach & Kramer, 1996, p. 445).

Business school leaders are naturally motivated to protect the status and prestige of their schools and their leadership. Students also want their schools to be highly ranked because job placement and starting salaries are tied to a school's prestige and reputation. Alumni pressure deans to keep rankings high to preserve the value of their degree and the status it confers. As one dean from an Ivy League school put it, when asked why he couldn't just ignore the rankings if their validity was so suspect, "Regardless of my personal views, I wouldn't be dean of this institution for very long if I did nothing to respond to even the *perception* that our school was slipping in its national standing" (p. 446).

The rankings clearly created a severe threat for business school leaders. How did they respond? To answer this question, we again analyzed press releases and interviews from campus, regional, and national newspapers. We coded every statement made by any administrative leader in response to the threats posed by the *BW* rankings. We also interviewed leaders from each of the schools in our sample. Our research identified several common tactics. First, leaders frequently used *strategic recategorization tactics* to challenge *BW*'s implicit characterization of their core identity or their positional status. Leaders used these tactics to affirm positive aspects of their school's identity that the rankings had neglected or minimized and to make sense of the threat and explain to important constituents why their schools had achieved a disappointing ranking.

An administrator from Berkeley, for instance, categorized his school as a "public management, entrepreneurial-oriented" program, implying that it was different from and should not be compared with other general purpose, private business schools. In noting the importance of this identity attribute, he emphasized to us, "We *really value* our entrepreneurial culture around here. It's central to how we see ourselves…. If the Haas emphasis on high-tech and entrepreneurship were to change, the school would lose its identity and competitive advantage." He also noted the unique complexity of the school's identity, "As a public institution, we have numerous missions private schools don't have" (Elsbach & Kramer, 1996, p. 451).

In a similar vein, a dean at Stanford observed that its entrepreneur-oriented program catered to the career aspirations of its students, many of whom hoped to found a Silicon Valley start-up rather than work for more traditional, large corporations: "More Stanford MBAs have non-Fortune 1000 interests, choosing instead, smaller and entrepreneurial ventures." As a consequence, he noted, "Some of the things that improve rankings are part of what we don't want to change [about our school]" (p. 454).

A University of Texas administrator emphasized that his business school "catered to regional labor markets" better than other schools and that regional standing was a "more important" and salient metric for evaluating his effectiveness as a school leader, since students were seeking jobs within the region rather than on the West or East Coast: "I feel responsible for making sure our students get the jobs they want locally, so much of our focus is on that goal" (p. 455).

The second recategorization tactic focused on *favorable social comparisons* that the rankings had neglected. Hogg and Abrams (1988, p. 23) noted how effective this tactic can be: "By differentiating ingroup and outgroup on dimensions on which the ingroup is at the evaluatively positive pole, the ingroup acquires a positive distinctiveness, and thus a relatively positive social identity in comparison to the outgroup." Research has often shown that, following unfavorable social comparisons, people invoke comparisons based on other, more flattering dimensions that give them a comparative advantage (Wood & Wilson, 2003). Many business school leaders also responded to the *BW* rankings by selectively categorizing their schools to create more favorable interschool comparisons. This tactic seemed to serve the dual purpose of both affirming their perceptions of their valued core identity and their perceptions of their school's status. Thus, many leaders used categorizations that increased the salience of identity dimensions that were also held by other well-respected, highly ranked schools but were neglected or devalued by *Business Week*. For example, in categorizing her school as a regional leader, a University of Texas administrator noted, "We're in a similar situation as highly-ranked University of Michigan Business School…. [In fact] we are considered to be the best in our region … like Michigan, which is a very powerful regional school, and is also of national stature with Stanford, Harvard, and Wharton. So that's how we'd like to be seen. We'd like to be a school that totally dominates a region." Similarly, a University of Chicago dean indicated, "We're a top research institution. I think of us in the same academic league as Harvard or Stanford" (p. 458).

One UC–Berkeley administrator was particularly articulate about the unfair, illogical use of *BW*'s single metric in its rankings: "In its market, Berkeley does a better job than most schools. But *Business Week* is throwing the Fords and the Chevys and the Porsches in the same mix…. It's really not fair. It's like judging apples and oranges, and we're not the same type of school as many others" (p. 458). As these examples illustrate, business school leaders used this tactic not only to affirm positive aspects of their school's identity that the rankings had minimized or neglected but also to deflect attention away from the attributes the rankings emphasized.

They also used these tactics to help constituents make sense of or explain why their school had achieved a disappointing ranking. By directing attention away from the ranking itself, they showed how it was misleading or incomplete in its representation of the school, because it ignored aspects of the school's identity that were more important than the criteria used in the survey. These categorization tactics tried to change the perceived field of salient, available comparisons. Our study reaffirms the potency of such tactics not just for making sense of where one stands in the social order or how well one is doing on some standard but also in helping leaders repair threats to their core identity or the core identifies of the ongoing actions they represent.

Elsbach and I (Elsbach & Kramer, 1996) used the metaphor of a microscope, as it is used to view material on a slide, to visualize how these identity repair tactics work. Just as evaluators peer through the lens of a microscope, selective categorization processes can manipulate a perceiver's field of view and, by implication, the inclusiveness or exclusiveness of comparisons. Thus, the first strategy of highlighting cherished or valued identity attributes is like using a high level of magnification to concentrate only on the focal organization; moving the slide around highlights positive attributes or facets of that focal organization. By concentrating only on positive identity attributes and excluding tainted or tarnished attributes from view, leaders can help perceivers retain a more positive overall perception of the organization and its leadership.

The second strategy is akin to using a lower-powered or reduced magnification to selectively enlarge the field of view to include a set of comparison organizations that reflect favorably on the focal organization and its leadership. Highlighting alternate comparison groups in the field of view involves, metaphorically, moving the slide around to focus on different subsets of organizations and their interrelationships or similarities. Placing the organization in a broader visual field can alter its relationship to other organizations (e.g., its perceived similarity and distinctiveness). For instance, by focusing narrowly on a specific region or subset of schools, leaders can generate a social comparison group in which their organization enjoys high status.

To summarize, this study (Elsbach & Kramer, 1996) identified several cognitive tactics that organizational leaders used to make sense of and manage external threats to their organizations and to their leadership. The *Business Week* rankings were an external threat, largely beyond the control of any individual business school or its leadership.

In the next study (Kramer, 1995), I explored the results of identity-threatening predicaments that have resulted because of decisions that leaders themselves have made. Unlike external threats, leaders are responsible for these events; thus, they must find ways of making sense of and deflecting direct challenges to their own actions.

STUDY 2: LEADERS' DECISIONS AS IDENTITY-THREATENING PREDICAMENTS—A CASE STUDY OF LYNDON JOHNSON AND HIS VIETNAM DECISIONS

Not only are leaders expected to explain and make sense of their organization's performance; they are also responsible for making the decisions that influence that performance. Swift, sure, effective decisiveness may even be regarded as one of the *sine qua nons* of the true leader. In fact, this is the clear conclusion of the voluminous leadership literature that characterizes effective leaders in terms of bold decisions rendered in moments of great crisis or opportunity (e.g., Janis, 1989; Useem, 1998).

Obviously, leaders' decisions have important identity-relevant consequences. For example, Kennedy enhanced his identity (and received rave reviews from American journalists and political pundits) following his successful management of the Cuban Missile Crisis. In contrast, Kennedy's indecisive handling of the Bay of Pigs invasion created an identity-threatening predicament that threatened to undermine his desired identity. More recently, George W. Bush was widely criticized for his slow, indecisive handling of emergency relief in the wake of Hurricane Katrina.

To investigate how leaders' own decisions create identity-threatening predicaments and how they might respond to such threats, I sought a well-documented case of a leader who was widely respected for political acumen and leadership skills, especially self-presentational abilities and impression management skills, but who had also created a severe identity threat for himself. The case of Lyndon Johnson and his Vietnam decisions met all of these criteria: Few instances of leader decision making have generated so much attention from historians, political scientists, psychologists, and organizational theorists. In fact, these decisions have been the focus of enormous scholarly scrutiny—not only because of their intrinsic historical importance but also because of their perplexing character (Kramer, 1995, 1998).

Johnson's Vietnam decisions provide a stark contrast between his attributes as a decision maker and the decisions he made in this instance. Few U.S. presidents have entered the Oval Office with a clearer perception of their ultimate goals and ambitions, and few have seemed better positioned to implement those goals and achieve those ambitions. Johnson was widely regarded as one of the most capable wielders of power ever to have assumed the presidency; he was a master politician who understood better than almost anyone else in his time how Washington worked.

Johnson's performance in his first months in office, following the unexpected death of President Kennedy, only contribute to our perplexity regarding his subsequent Vietnam decisions. Shortly after assuming the presidency, Johnson performed flawlessly as the nation's leader, winning over a wary Congress and a skeptical public as he sought to enact both President Kennedy's stalled legislation and his own initiatives. After only a few months in office, he was elected to the presidency on his own in 1964 with the then-largest popular mandate in U.S. history. His priorities were clear, and he was confident in pursuing them. Indeed, on the basis of his early White House performance, it looked as if Lyndon Johnson was on his way to achieving his aim of being remembered in history as a great activist president, especially with respect to his legislative accomplishments and advances in civil rights, health care, education, and the war against poverty.

Johnson's initial assessments of the Vietnam situation also seemed remarkably prescient. He clearly understood, for example, the prospect of becoming mired in a costly, escalating conflict with little upside (Beschloss, 1997, 2001); early in his presidency, he confessed to his mentor, Richard Russell, and others that he saw no way such a war might be won. He believed that this conflict was not worth the blood of a single American soldier. He begged his advisors to exercise great caution and care, suggesting that future historians would dissect their decisions with the same critical scrutiny as the Bay of Pigs decisions.

The clarity and force of these initial, perceptive assessments seem to be in direct conflict with Johnson's subsequent decisions on Vietnam, which dramatically escalated the conflict. In the end, his policies went terribly awry, undoing his beloved domestic programs, his presidency, and ultimately his legacy.

Previous psychological research on Johnson's Vietnam decisions has taken several approaches, primarily focusing on decision quality. Groupthink remains one of the more influential social psychological interpretations (Janis, 1983), explaining Johnson's performance largely in terms of defective group dynamics. Another approach has been escalation of commitment (Staw, 1976). These accounts have emphasized leaders' experience of the psychological pressures toward private and public consistency.

In contrast, I approached the Vietnam decisions from an identity perspective (Kramer, 2003). To explicate how identity and decision collided, with devastating consequence, I first provide a brief characterization of Lyndon Johnson's "self-categorization" as president. I then analyze his cognitive responses to the identity-threatening predicament posed by his Vietnam decisions.

Johnson's Identity as a Leader

Lyndon Johnson described his aspirations and goals to many people (e.g., Henggeler, 1991; Kearns-Goodwin, 1976; Valenti, 1977). His views surfaced frequently in his public pronouncements and his private ruminations with close confidantes and aides. As his aide Jack Valenti put it, "He had one goal: to be the greatest president doing the greatest good in the history of the nation" (quoted in Kramer, 1995, p. 120). He wanted, in his own words, to be "the greatest father the country had ever had" (Grubin, 1991). He once expressed the view that he aspired—figuratively at least—to have his visage placed alongside the other great figures on Mount Rushmore.

In Johnson's eyes, presidential greatness had two cornerstones: a record of historic domestic achievement and the ability of a president to keep the nation out of harm's way. Thus, Johnson first sought, as Nicholas Lemann once aptly commented, to "set world records in politics the way a star athlete would in sports" (Dallek, 1991, p. 109). In pursuit of this goal, Johnson displayed a breathtaking legislative genius, passing more sweeping domestic legislation than any president in history. He was determined to rival Franklin Roosevelt, who knew how to throw the great machinery of government into high gear in pursuit of great if difficult aims. In this spirit, Johnson embarked on a broad set of initiatives under the umbrella of his Great Society program. He felt that this historic, domestic program would be the capstone of his presidency, the banner on which his legacy as a great democratic president would hang. Johnson recognized also that achieving greatness as a president required waging a successful war. In Johnson's eyes, Abraham Lincoln and Roosevelt were the two premier examples of great wartime presidents.

Johnson not only had entertained a clearly defined vision of the identity he sought as president; he also knew how he would achieve it. His reading of history and his intense study of the presidency led him, as Kearns-Goodwin (1976, pp. 343–344) put it, to believe that "if you had the energy and drive to work harder than everyone else you would achieve what you set out to accomplish." Johnson, she went on to note, "held before him the image of the daring cowboy, the man with the capacity to outrun the wild herd, riding at a dead run in the dark of the night" (pp. 343–344). He drew a clear distinction between leaders who were the "doers" and those he dismissed as the "thinkers" and "talkers" of the world. Thus, Johnson clearly defined both the ends and the means of his desired identity.

This is the context of his Vietnam decisions. In his view, he had inherited the dilemma of Vietnam just as he had inherited his presidency—on a tragic moment's notice on November 22, 1963. From the instant of that assumed presidency, Johnson clearly recognized the threat that Vietnam posed to his legacy (Beschloss, 1997, 2001): He felt it had little upside. In terms of furthering his ambitions, unfortunately, none of his alternatives seemed attractive or viable either. "I feel like a hound bitch in heat in the country," he poignantly complained. "If you run, they chew your tail off. And if you stand still, they slip it to you" (Berman, 1989, p. 183). The thought of "cutting and running," as he once put it, was anathema to someone who had such a keenly developed image of what great, activist presidents need to do in moments of crisis or challenge.

In Johnson's eyes, the Vietnam decisions also directly threatened his ability to implement his Great Society initiatives. In his view, the Great Society decisions would enable him to demonstrate to the American public the sweep and grandeur of his presidential vision. He envisioned a revitalized, completed America, where people would be judged by the "quality of their minds" and not merely by the "quantity of their goods" (Grubin, 1991). He described the program as being like a beautiful woman that the American people would love (Kearns-Goodwin, 1976).

The intensity of the conflict between his desired identity and his Vietnam decisions intensified as the war drained economic and attentional resources from the Great Society. The program that he had characterized as a young and beautiful woman now withered under the economic hardships imposed by the war: "She's getting thinner and thinner and uglier and uglier all the time.... Soon she'll be so ugly the American people will refuse to look at her; they'll stick her in a closet to hide her away and there she'll die. And when she dies, I, too, will die" (Kearns-Goodwin, 1976, pp. 286–287).

In Johnson's mind, the threat to his identity was intensified by the sudden disaffection of large segments of the American public—the same public that, only months before, had made him one of the most popular and beloved presidents in U.S. history. As Berman (1989, p. 183) noted, "It pained him that those he believed had been helped most by his presidency [e.g., students, Blacks, and educators] were leading the opposition to his war."

How did Johnson respond to the identity-threatening predicament he perceived in his Vietnam decisions? Initially, he responded with extremely vigilant, mindful information processing of the sort described by Janis (1989) in his classic work on high-quality decision making. Johnson studied all of the details of the decisions and vigorously pressed his secretary of defense Robert McNamara and his other advisors to consider every implication of every decision:

> What I would like to know is what has happened .... I want this discussed in full detail, from everyone around this table ... what are the compelling reasons [for this decision]? What results can we expect? Again, I ask you, what are the alternatives? I don't want us to make snap judgments. I want us to consider all our options. (Valenti, 1975, p. 259–260).

As the war escalated and continued to defy resolution, Johnson increasingly displayed two less adaptive cognitive responses. The first response was hypervigilant information processing (Janis, 1989). "A compulsive reader, viewer, and listener who took every criticism personally and to heart, he was at first intent on, and then obsessed with, answering every accusation, responding to every charge" (Herring, 1993, p. 95).

His second dysfunctional cognitive response was intense and intrusive dysphoric rumination about Vietnam. "If Johnson was unhappy thinking about Vietnam," Kearns-Goodwin (1976, p. 299) noted, "he was even less happy not thinking about it." Johnson often "consciously and deliberately decided not to think another thought about Vietnam, yet discussions that started on poverty or education invariably ended up on Vietnam.... He found himself unwilling, and soon unable, to break loose from what had become an obsession" (Kearns-Goodwin, p. 299). In particular, he tended to ruminate at length about his deteriorating image as a leader and as president. He began to imagine a vast web of conspiracy, including his many political enemies, whom he felt were lined up against him with the common aim of denying him his desired presidential legacy (e.g., Califano, 1991; Dallek, 1991; Goodwin, 1988). As he put it, even years later, "They'll get me anyhow, no matter how hard I try.... The reviews are in the hands of my enemies—the *New York Times* and my enemies—so I don't have a chance" (Kearns-Goodwin, p. 357).

In trying to repair his threatened presidential identity, two interesting cognitive responses evidenced in the archival data parallel the results of our study of business school responses to the *Business Week* rankings (Elsbach & Kramer, 1996). Both responses represent Johnson's attempts to recategorize himself. The first was his use of *selective self-categorizations* to cognitively focus on the self-enhancing facets of his identity while downplaying or minimizing his less flattering facets. For example, when the critics challenged the wisdom of his military policy, Johnson would remind them of all he had done for civil rights, poverty, education, and health-care reform (Beschloss, 2001). According to his friend, Texas governor John Connally, he had a list of all his legislative accomplishments in his pocket, ready to pull out and read off as if it were a baseball score card (Grubin, 1991). By highlighting alternative accomplishments in the domestic realm, Johnson tried to enhance his faltering identity.

A second, also frequent cognitive tactic was the sort of strategic (i.e., motivated or self-enhancing) social comparisons observed in the *Business Week* study. For instance, in characterizing his difficult choices, Johnson continually compared himself to other presidents, particularly Franklin Roosevelt and Woodrow Wilson. Thus, in justifying his persistence in Vietnam, despite evidence that the war was not progressing favorably, he argued, "You see, I deeply believe we are quarantining aggressors over there ... just like FDR [did with] [Adolf] Hitler, just like Wilson [did] with Kaiser [Wilhelm]. You've simply got to see this thing in historical perspective" (Kearns-Goodwin, 1976, p. 313).

Similarly, when friends, aides, advisors, and critics suggested that he might be perceived as a greater president if he decisively ended such an unpopular conflict, Johnson recoiled. "Everything I know about history," he asserted, "proves this absolutely wrong. It was our lack of strength and failure to show stamina, our hesitancy, vacillation, and love of peace being paraded so much that caused all our problems before World War I, World War II, and Korea" (Kearns-Goodwin, 1976, p. 313).

Johnson also drew solace in comparisons to Lincoln and his unpopular decisions: "I read all about the troubles Lincoln had in conducting the Civil War. Yet he persevered and history rewarded him for his perseverance" (Kearns-Goodwin, 1976, p. 314). "We're going to have our troubles," Johnson acknowledged, but "we're not running from nothing ... and remember old Abraham Lincoln..." (Bechloss, 2001, p. 136). As he admonished his confidantes, "They [the public] don't ever remember many of these Presidents from Jackson to Lincoln. They don't remember many from Lincoln to Roosevelt. The ones they remember are those that stood up" (Bechloss, 2001, p. 136).

To summarize, the results of this second study (Kramer, 1995) replicate and extend the findings from our study of business school leaders' responses to identity threats. The analysis suggests that leaders' own decisions can create identity-threatening predicaments in at least two ways. First, their decisions can create an internal "credibility gap" that challenges or invalidates their self-perceptions of their cherished self-categorizations. Second, their decisions can also threaten their public claims regarding their core identities. When decisions cause important constituents to question a leader's intentions, motives, actions, or competence, then they may feel like they are in a serious crisis management situation.

The data revealed that Johnson used both of the tactics observed in the *Business Week* study: selective self-categorizations to highlight alternate identity attributes; and selective social comparisons to highlight alternate comparison groups. Both of these tactical responses can be thought of as recategorization efforts in the service of identity maintenance and repair. Selective social comparison, for instance, can be viewed as a form of recategorization of one's perceived social identity group; it can succeed because "healthy [psychological] functioning may depend on the ability to exhibit flexibility in the choice of evaluative comparisons in order to maintain a sense of competence and high self-esteem" (Frey and Ruble, 1990, p. 169).

Analysis from the point of view of an individual's identity provides a somewhat novel perspective on leader decision making. Some studies, for example, have examined the role of power in decision making (Neustadt, 1990; Pfeffer, 1992); others have explored the role of a leader's advisory systems (Burke & Greenstein, 1989; George, 1980; Janis, 1983); and others have investigated the impact of accountability mechanisms and structures on judgment and choice (Allison, 1971; Tetlock, 1992). Approaching leader decision making from an identity perspective indicates that leaders' perceived core identities influence how they frame their decisions. Their decisions, in turn, have important implications for leaders' identity claims and aspirations. The ability of leaders to construct and sustain valued or desired identities clearly depends on the favorable or unfavorable consequences of their decisions. The research described here indicates how these decisions also represent important parts of leader identity construction and maintenance.

An identity perspective on leader decision making also helps illuminate some of the particular reasons leaders sometimes make the idiosyncratic decisions they do. This perspective also suggests why leaders persist even when the consequences of their decisions seem self-defeating. Thus, although intended to resolve an identity threat, leaders' responses have sometimes increased the threats to their identities, especially when their responses inadvertently invite further hostile or critical scrutiny.

STUDY 3: TRANSFORMING FAILURE TO SUCCESS— PRESIDENTIAL SELF-PRESENTATIONAL TACTICS IN THE ICELAND ARMS CONTROL TALKS

My third study investigated attempts by Ronald Reagan and his advisors to address threats to the perception of him as a competent negotiator with the Soviet Union. In this study, Robert Sutton and I analyzed the "spin control" efforts in the historic 1986 Iceland Arms Control talks between President Reagan and Soviet premier Mikhail Gorbachev (Sutton & Kramer, 1990).

Several events precipitated this incident. On September 19, 1986, Soviet Foreign Minister Eduard Shevardnadze delivered a letter from Soviet premier Mikhail Gorbachev to President Reagan proposing that they have some informal presummit discussions prior to their official summit. Reagan responded affirmatively, suggesting such a meeting could indeed be productive. Accordingly, the two leaders met in Reykjavik, Iceland, on October 11–12, 1986, discussing a wide range of issues, including their countries' nuclear policies and strategic arms postures.

Almost immediately afterward, journalists and media pundits presented a grim, negative assessment of the talks. *Newsweek* (October 27, 1986, p. 31, as cited in Sutton & Kramer, 1990) summarized the failure in a particularly scathing characterization: "The dejection in the President's carriage as he walked out of Hofdi house, the disappointment etched into every line of Secretary of State George Shultz's face as he briefed the press, had flashed an unmistakable message to TV watchers around the world: the summit meeting with Mikhail Gorbachev had ended in failure. Moreover, the blame was placed squarely at Reagan's feet." As *Newsweek* put it, "Worse, headlines were spreading the impression that Reagan had thrown away the promise of a nuclear-free world by clinging to his vision of a space-based defense—even if there might be no missiles to defend against."

These conclusions presented a serious identity threat to Reagan on several fronts. First, Reagan considered himself a masterful negotiator, competent and tough. He felt both confident and comfortable in his face-to-face meetings with Gorbachev and apparently entertained little fear or doubts about his abilities. When aides expressed concern about Reagan's ability to debate nuclear strategy with Gorbachev, Reagan dismissed their concerns by claiming that Gorbachev didn't really understand all that stuff either. His speechwriter, Peggy Noonan (1995, p. 218), said, "When he first met with Gorbachev and had to negotiate arms control, he had no great anxiety because, as he put it, he'd been president of the Screen Actor's Guild, he'd negotiated with Sam Goldwyn and Jack Warner, and Gorbachev was nothing compared to those guys."

Second, Reagan believed that our security was his responsibility: If necessary, he would stand up to communist leaders and contain the menace of communism. In his view, the leader of one of the world's most evil empires should not be appeased or allowed to expand Soviet influence. Moreover, Reagan had a sense of destiny—he had a strong view about his place in American history, and that place included helping restore America's confidence and strength. In short, Reagan considered himself America's lifeguard.

These talks being discussed as failures, plus suggesting that historic gains in arms reductions had been within grasp only to be unrealized, left Reagan and his team scrambling for a better story line. They were not long in finding one. White House communications director Patrick Buchanan suggested an alternative framing: "Basically, our story is this. The President made the most sweeping, far-reaching arms control proposal in history" (*New York Times,* October 15, 1986, A1). It was Gorbachev, he asserted, who said no. Buchanan further contended that press analyses suggesting that the talks were a failure were simply "mistaken." One White House aide put it this way: "We weren't focusing on the one yard we didn't gain.... What about the ninety-nine yards we did? We kept saying, 'Let's focus on that'" (Sutton & Kramer, 1990, p. 240).

It is important to note that the effort expended to respond to this identity-threatening predicament—including forty-four "on-the-record" briefings and interviews in the first week following the talks—was unusually extensive, even by White House standards. One reporter I interviewed said, "It was impossible to even use the restroom without some White House aide following you into the bathroom trying to tell you more about 'what really happened.'" Buchanan himself acknowledged that their efforts constituted "the most extensive and intensive communications plan I've ever been associated with in the White House" (*New York Times*, October 15, 1986, A1). Even Secretary of State Shultz acknowledged the active efforts to "reshape perceptions" of the Reykjavik meeting. Shultz, initially dispirited immediately following the talks, now characterized the discussions as a "watershed" because "for the first time the two sides agreed to dramatic reductions in nuclear and strategic arms" (Sutton & Kramer, 1990, p. 240).

In an attempt to echo Winston Churchill, the White House Communications Office released a statement characterizing the meeting as "Reagan's finest hour." President Reagan himself argued, "We prefer no agreement than to bring home a bad agreement to the United States" (*New York Times*, October 13, 1986).

Donald Regan suggested to a *New York Times* reporter only a few days later that these efforts at explaining what had really transpired had paid off handsomely:

> Look at the polls. The American people are behind us. The point was we wanted to tell people what happened inside, so the outsiders will understand the enormity of the accomplishments that the President made. It wasn't a defeat at all, but it might have been characterized that way if we had sat still…. Why not tell what happened? Why not let it all hang out? We have nothing to be ashamed of. (*New York Times*, October, 16, 1986, A1)

Data from several independent polls support Regan's assessment: Over a few months, perception of the talks changed from outright failure to a dramatic success. Indeed, as time passed and the event was reassessed, Americans reported *greater* confidence in Reagan's ability to successfully negotiate an effective arms control agreement with the Soviets. In a perceptive (if perhaps unintentionally disparaging) appraisal of their success, Regan offered a colorful image of their feat: "Some of us [in the administration] were like a shovel brigade that follows a parade down Main Street cleaning up," he noted with a laugh. "We took Reykjavik and turned what was a sour situation into something that turned out pretty well."

These events further illustrate the efficacy of cognitive repair tactics. In particular, by recategorizing the outcome in terms of American resolve and avoidance of losses, Reagan was able to suggest he had effectively avoided making undesirable concessions or retreating from a strong position. He even suggested he had avoided being lulled by Gorbachev into a public relations trap. In short, he maintained his identity as a tough, vigilant negotiator who had stood up to and faced down his opponent.

SUMMARY, IMPLICATIONS, AND CONCLUSIONS

Viewed in concert, the findings from these three studies converge on several insights regarding how leaders initially construe identity threats as well as some of the cognitive tactics they use to respond to those perceived threats.

First, these studies suggest that threats to a leader's sense of self create a psychological state we might characterize as *identity dissonance*. The magnitude of this dissonance depends on the perceived discrepancy between the leaders' desired or claimed identity and the identity they perceive is held by important or powerful members of their organizational audience. Thus, for leaders who want to be perceived as trustworthy but feel that an important set of constituents question their credibility, the result is highly dissonant.

As with other forms of cognitive dissonance, identity dissonance is an aversive psychological state that motivates individuals to reduce or eliminate it. Threats to core identity attributes should be especially aversive and, therefore, particularly motivating. Also like other forms of cognitive dissonance, identity dissonance should lead to a variety of identity repair tactics, which is just what we observed in these studies. Leaders will logically select the particular tactics that they believe will be effective, and their perceptions of their audience and the validity of the threat will influence their effectiveness estimates. As these results further suggest, identity repair becomes a dynamic, iterative process: Leaders negotiate their identities by making (and remaking) a series of claims and by responding to their stakeholders' responses to those claims.

In addition to their theoretical implications and contributions, the findings from these studies have several practical implications for organizational and political leaders. First, identity-based categorization (and recategorization) tactics are potent tools that allow leaders to help not only themselves but also other individuals—both inside and outside the organization—make sense of an organization's values, decisions, and purposes. As March (1994, p. 71) observed, "Organizations [and their leaders] shape individual action both by providing the content of identities ... and by providing appropriate cues for invoking them." Such identity cues enable leaders to focus members' attention on what they want them to be thinking about. They also provide broad cognitive frames for action. Few leader activities are more consequential to the vitality of an organization or the legitimacy of his leadership. As Pfeffer (1981, p. 26) noted, "Every organization has an interest in seeing its definition of reality accepted ... for such acceptance is an integral part of the legitimization of the organization and the development of assured resources." The same is true for organizational leaders—their authority and credibility clearly hinge, at least in part, on their ability to proffer identities that others view as legitimate, valuable, and efficacious.

The results from these studies also suggest that identity-based recategorization processes may help leaders change or reshape not only their own identities but also the identities of their organizations. Along these lines, Burgelman and Grove (1996, p. 20) proposed a model of what they termed "strategic dissonance" whereby leaders purposefully take advantage of distress related to perceived incongruities or discrepancies between an organization's avowed strategic intent and leader's strategic actions. They suggest that leaders can use the information generated by strategic dissonance "when trying to discern the true shape of the company" (p. 20). They argued, however, that "it must be a realistic picture grounded in the company's distinctive competencies—existing ones or new ones that are already being developed.... Getting through that period of immense change requires reinventing the company's identity" (p. 20).

It may be useful to close this chapter on a methodological note. Laboratory investigations have contributed many important insights into the antecedents and consequences of effective self-presentational strategies and tactics. These studies have typically evaluated the efficacy of a particular strategy and identified its limitations and its psychological underpinnings (see Leary, 1995 and Schlenker, 2003 for literature reviews). For example, researchers have investigated the efficacy of ingratiation as a strategy for increasing interpersonal liking or attraction (Jones, 1990). The important, distinctive advantage of qualitative case studies is their opportunity to explore the complexity and diverse effects of leaders' actual strategies and tactics. These same methods have been used to investigate the efficacy of the self-presentational strategies of Hollywood screenwriters trying to sell their screenplays in studio settings (Elsbach & Kramer, 2003) and of physicians trying to build rapport and trust with their patients in managed care settings (Cook et al., 2004). Thus, the broad use of multiple methodologies, each having its own advantages and disadvantages, provides an opportunity for retrospective, archival case studies, laboratory experiments, and real-time fieldwork to contribute important, multifaceted insights into the dynamics of leaders and effective leadership.

REFERENCES

Allison, G. T. (1971). *Essence of decision: Explaining the Cuban Missile Crisis*. Boston: Little, Brown.

Ambrose, S. (1991). *Nixon: Ruin and recovery, 1973–1990*. New York: Simon & Schuster.

Berman, L. (1989). *Lyndon Johnson's war*. New York: Norton.

Beschloss, M. (2001). *Reaching for glory: Lyndon Johnson's secret White House tapes, 1964–1965*. New York: Simon and Schuster.

Beschloss, M. R. (1997). *Taking charge: The Johnson White House tapes, 1963–1964*. New York: Simon & Schuster.

Branch, T. (2006). *At Canaan's edge: America in the King years, 1965–1968*. New York: Simon and Schuster.

Brewer, M. B., & Hewstone, M. (2004). *Self and social identity*. Oxford, UK: Blackwell.

Burgelman, R. A., & Grove, A. S. (1996). Strategic dissonance. *California Management Review, 38*, 8–28.

Burke, J. P., & Greenstein, F. I. (1989). *How presidents test reality: Decisions on Vietnam, 1954 and 1965*. New York: Russell Sage Foundation.

Califano, J. A. (1991). *The triumph and tragedy of Lyndon Johnson*. New York: Simon & Schuster.

Cook, K. S., Kramer, R. M., Thom, D. M., Stepanikova, I., Mollborn, S. B., & Cooper, R. M. (2004). Trust and distrust in patient-physician relationships: Perceived determinants of high- and low-trust relationships in managed care settings. In R. M. Kramer & K. S. Cook (Eds.), *Trust and distrust in organizations: Dilemmas and approaches* (pp. 65–98). New York: Russell Sage Foundation.

Dallek, R. (1991). *Lone star rising: Lyndon Johnson and his times, 1980–1960*. New York: Oxford University Press.

Elsbach, K. D. (1994). Managing organizational legitimacy in the California cattle industry: The construction and effectiveness of verbal accounts. *Administrative Science Quarterly, 39*, 57–88.

Elsbach, K. D. (2006). *Organizational perception management*. Mahwah, NJ: Erlbaum.

Elsbach, K. D., & Kramer, R. M. (1996). Members' responses to organizational identity threats: Encountering and countering the *Business Week* rankings. *Administrative Science Quarterly, 41,* 442–476.

Elsbach, K., & Kramer, R. M. (2003). Assessing creativity in Hollywood pitch meetings: Evidence for a dual process model of creativity judgment. *Academy of Management Journal, 46*(3), 283–301.

Elsbach, K. D., & Sutton, R. (1992). Acquiring organizational legitimacy through illegitimate actions: A marriage of institutional and impression management theories. *Academy of Management Journal, 35,* 699–738.

Frey, K. S., & Ruble, D. N. (1990). Strategies for comparative evaluation: Maintaining a sense of competence across the life span. In R. J. Sternberg & J. Kolligan (Eds.), *Competence considered* (pp. 167–189). New Haven, CT: Yale University Press.

George, A. (1980). *Presidential decisionmaking in foreign policy: The effective use of information and advice.* Boulder, CO: Westview.

Ginzel, L. E., Kramer, R. M., & Sutton, R. I. (1993). Organizational impression management as a reciprocal influence process: The neglected role of the organizational audience. In L. L. Cummings & B. M. Staw (Eds.), *Research in organizational behavior* (Vol. 15, pp. 227–266). Greenwich, CT: JAI Press.

Goodwin, R. N. (1988). *Remembering America: A voice from the sixties.* New York: Harper & Row.

Grubin, D. (1991). *LBJ: A biography* (video). Dallas: North Texas Public Broadcasting.

Hatch, M. J., & Schultz, M. (2004). *Organizational identity: A reader.* New York: Oxford University Press.

Henggeler, P. R. (1991). *In his steps: Lyndon Johnson and the Kennedy mystique.* Chicago: Dee.

Herring, G. C. (1993). The reluctant warrior: Lyndon Johnson as Commander in Chief. In D. L. Anderson (Ed.), *Shadow on the White House: Presidents and the Vietnam War, 1945–1975* (pp. 87–112). Lawrence: University of Kansas Press.

Hogg, M. A., & Abrams, D. (1988). *Social identifications.* London: Routledge.

Hoyle, R. H., Kernis, M. H., Leary, M. R., & Baldwin, M. W. (1999). *Selfhood: Identity, esteem, and regulation.* Boulder, CO: Westview.

Janis, I. L. (1983). *Groupthink* (2nd ed.). Boston: Houghton Mifflin.

Janis, I. L. (1989). *Crucial decisions.* New York: Free Press.

Jones, E. E. (1990). *Interpersonal perception.* San Francisco: W. H. Freeman.

Kearns-Goodwin, D. (1976). *Lyndon Johnson and the American dream.* New York: New American Library.

Kramer, R. M. (1995). In dubious battle: Heightened accountability, dysphoric cognition and self-defeating bargaining behavior. In R. M. Kramer & D. M. Messick (Eds.), *Negotiation as a social process* (pp. 95–120). Thousand Oaks, CA: Sage Publications.

Kramer, R. M. (1998). Revisiting the Bay of Pigs and Vietnam decisions 25 years later: How well has the groupthink hypothesis stood the test of time? *Organizational Behavior and Human Decision Processes, 73,* 236–271.

Kramer, R. M. (2003). The imperatives of identity: The role of identity in leader judgment and decision making. In D. van Knippenberg & M. A. Hogg (Eds.), *Leadership and power* (pp. 184–196). Thousand Oaks, CA: Sage.

Leary, M. R. (1989). Self-presentational processes in leadership emergence and effectiveness. In R. A. Giacalone & P. Rosenfeld (Eds.), *Impression management in the organization* (pp. 363–374). Mahwah, NJ: Erlbaum.

Leary, M. R. (1995). *Self-presentation: Impression management and interpersonal behavior.* Boulder, CO: Westview.

March, J. G. (1994). *A primer on decision making.* New York: Free Press.

Neustadt, R. E. (1990). *Presidential power and the modern presidents.* New York: Free Press.

Noonan, P. (1995). Ronald Reagan, 1981–1989. In R. Wilson (Ed.), *Character above all: Ten presidents from FDR to George Bush* (pp. 202–223). New York: Simon & Shuster.

Pfeffer, J. (1981). Management as symbolic action. In L. L. Cummings & B. M. Staw (Eds.), *Research in organizational behavior* (Vol. 3, pp. 1–52). Greenwich, CT: JAI Press.

Pfeffer, J. (1992). *Managing with power.* Cambridge, MA: Harvard Business School Press.

Runkel, P. J., & McGrath, J. E. (1974). *Research on human behavior: A systematic guide to method.* New York: Holt, Rinehart, & Winston.

Salancik, G. R. & Meindl, J. R. (1984). Corporate attributions as strategic illusions of management control. *Administrative Science Quarterly, 29,* 238–254.

Schlenker, B. (2003). Self-presentation. In M. R. Leary & J. P. Tangney (Eds.), *Handbook of self and identity* (pp. 492–518). New York: Guilford Press.

Staw, B. M. (1976). Knee-deep in the big muddy: A study of escalating commitment to a chosen course of action. *Organizational Behavior and Human Performance, 16,* 27–44.

Steele, C. M. (1988). The psychology of self-affirmation: Sustaining the integrity of the self. In L. Berkowitz (Ed.), *Advances in experimental social psychology* (Vol. 21, pp. 261–302). New York: Academic Press.

Sutton, R. I., & Galunic, D. C. (1996). Consequences of public scrutiny for leaders and their organizations. In B. M. Staw & L. L. Cummings (Eds.), *Research in organizational behavior* (Vol. 18, pp. 201–250). Greenwich, CT: JAI Press.

Sutton, R. I, & Kramer, R. M. (1990). Transforming failure into success: Spin control in the Iceland arms control talks. In R. L. Kahn & M. Zald (Eds.), *Organizations and nation-states: New perspectives on conflict and cooperation* (pp. 221–248). San Francisco: Jossey-Bass.

Tedeschi, J. T. (1981). *Impression management theory and social psychological research.* New York: Academic Press.

Tetlock, P. E. (1992). The impact of accountability on judgment and choice: Toward a social contingency model. In L. Berkowitz (Ed.), *Advances in experimental social psychology* (Vol. 25, pp. 331–376). New York: Academic Press.

Useem, M. (1998). *The leadership moment.* Times Business Books.

Valenti, J. (1977). A very human president. New York: W. W. Norton.

Wood, J. V., & Wilson, A. E. (2003). How important is social comparison? In M. R. Leary & J. P. Tangney (Eds.), *Handbook of self and identity* (pp. 344–366). New York: Guilford Press.

7

The Three Faces of Overconfidence in Organizations

Don A. Moore
Tepper/CMU

Samuel A. Swift
Tepper/CMU

Plous (1993) wrote that "no problem in judgment and decision making is more prevalent and more potentially catastrophic than overconfidence" (p. 217). His words ring true when we consider the role of overconfident beliefs in the events leading up to the economic crisis and stock market crash of 2008. Consumers fed a huge housing bubble by taking out larger mortgages than they could afford. Their willingness to take such risks was based on their optimism about the housing market continuing to go up. Mortgage brokers quickly came up with innovative mortgage products to serve the growing market. They made no income nor assets (NINA), and then no income, no job, and no assets (NINJA) loans, apparently confident that the big banks would keep buying these loans and packaging them into collateralized debt obligations (CDOs). Brokers realized that these loans were risky, but many believed that if the market began to unravel they would be able to get out more quickly than would others.

The banks continued to buy CDOs, behaving as if they understood how risky they were. And insurers like AIG continued to sell insurance against default by borrowers, in the form of credit default swaps. But the risk models on which the banks and insurers were basing their risk estimates were obsolete. They estimated rates of mortgage default using historical data that did not include NINJA loans. These historical data grossly underestimated the actual rate of default, yet large and sophisticated financial institutions, in setting prices for CDOs and credit default swaps, behaved as if they were very confident that these faulty risk estimates were actually correct.

147

These examples demonstrate the magnitude of the problems overconfidence can produce. But overconfidence is a phenomenon with many facets. This chapter will attempt to differentiate and elucidate them.

THREE FACES OF OVERCONFIDENCE

Overestimation

Consumers' optimism about a housing market in which values go only up represents one form of overconfidence, which we will refer to as overestimation. The majority of empirical research papers on overconfidence examine overestimation. These studies document overestimates of personal abilities, performance, chances of success, or level of control. Some findings from this literature include the following: investors overestimate the performance of their holdings (Moore, Kurtzberg, Fox, & Bazerman, 1999); students overestimate their performance on exams (Clayson, 2005); physicians overestimate the accuracy of their diagnoses (Christensen-Szalanski & Bushyhead, 1981); people overestimate how much control they have (Presson & Benassi, 1996); and people overestimate the speed with which they can get work done (Buehler, Griffin, & MacDonald, 1997). The tendency to overestimate the speed at which we can get work done has been called the planning fallacy (Buehler, Griffin, & Ross, 1994) and helps explain why nine of ten major infrastructure projects go past deadline and over budget (Flyvbjerg, Skamris Holm, & Buhl, 2002).

Overplacement

Mortgage brokers' belief that they would be more nimble than would other mortgage brokers in anticipating the market downturn would be an example of the belief that one is better than others, or what Larrick, Burson, and Soll (2007) called overplacement. Sample findings from this literature include the following. In one study, 37% of one firm's professional engineers placed themselves among the top 5% of performers at the firm (Zenger, 1992). In a survey of high school seniors, 25% rated themselves in the top 1% in their ability to get along with others (College Board, 1976–1977). People believe they are more likely to experience positive events and less likely to experience negative events than are others (Weinstein, 1980). But perhaps the most frequently cited result from this literature is that 93% of a sample of American drivers and 69% of a sample of Swedish drivers reported that they were more skillful than the median driver in their own country (Svenson, 1981).* Research on overplacement often refers to it as the "better-than-average" effect (Alicke & Govorun, 2005).

Overprecision

The third approach to the study of overconfidence examines what we will call overprecision. This research finds that people tend to be excessively certain of the precision of their private beliefs. Researchers typically assess certainty by asking people questions with quantitative answers (e.g., How tall is Mt. Everest?) and then asking them to specify a 90% confidence interval around their best guess. These 90% confidence intervals often contain the correct answer less than 50% of the time (Alpert & Raiffa, 1969/1982; Klayman, Soll, Gonzalez-Vallejo, & Barlas, 1999; Soll & Klayman, 2004). Excessively narrow confidence intervals suggest that people are inappropriately confident they have the right answer. Overprecision could have contributed to the excessive confidence among banks that they knew the risk of default among the mortgages they were buying and insuring.

Researchers often assume that the three different types of overconfidence are produced by the same underlying psychological causes (e.g., Alba & Hutchinson, 2000; Barber & Odean, 2001; Belsky & Gilovich, 2000; Daniel, Hirshleifer, & Subrahmanyam, 1998; Dunning, 2005; Juslin, Winman, & Olsson, 2000; Kirchler & Maciejovsky, 2002; Malmendier & Tate, 2005; Moore et al., 1999; Odean, 1998; Plous, 1993; Stone, 1994; Stotz & von Nitzsch, 2005). In this chapter we differentiate the three varieties of overconfidence and discuss the motives and biases that can contribute to each one. But first, we must address three problems with the overconfidence literature (see Moore & Healy, 2008). As we will see, some of these problems arise from the assumption that the three types of overconfidence are the same when they are not.

---

* While it is possible for the majority to be either above or below average (in skewed distributions), it is statistically impossible for the majority to be above (or below) the median.

THREE PROBLEMS

Problem 1: Confounding

The first problem with overconfidence research is that the most popular research paradigms confound overestimation and overprecision. These paradigms measure confidence of correctness at the level of the individual item by reporting their confidence (usually the probability) that they got a specific problem right. For instance, when participants in Fischhoff, Slovic, and Lichtenstein's (1977) study estimated at least a 99% chance they had gotten a question correct, they were actually correct only 87% of the time, on average. In this paradigm, overestimation and overprecision are one and the same, since being excessively sure you got the item right indicates both overestimation of your performance and excessive confidence in the precision of your knowledge.

One way to distinguish the two is measuring perceptions of performance over a set of items. It is easy to see how measuring beliefs about performance over a set of items can reduce the confound between overprecision and overestimation. It is possible, for instance, for someone to underestimate how well he has done yet to be excessively confident that his low estimate is correct. Estimating performance over a set of items usually entails making a frequentistic judgment (e.g., the number of items correct), whereas estimation of performance at the item level is more often elicited as a probabilistic judgment. There is a vigorous debate over frequentistic versus probabilistic judgment. A number of researchers have found that overconfidence is reduced or eliminated when people are given frequentistic judgment tasks, such as estimating performance across a set of items (Gigerenzer, 1993; Gigerenzer & Hoffrage, 1995; Gigerenzer, Hoffrage, & Kleinbölting, 1991; Juslin, Olsson, & Björkman, 1997; Sniezek & Buckley, 1991). While other researchers argue that frequentistic judgments are not necessarily more accurate than probabilistic judgments (Griffin & Buehler, 1999), there is consensus that frequency judgments across a set of items are less prone to overconfidence than are judgments of correctness at the item level.

Some have suggested that the difference between frequentistic and probabilistic judgments may be due to the human mind being better adapted to reason frequentistically (Cosmides & Tooby, 1996; Gigerenzer & Hoffrage, 1995). While that may be so, another possibility is simply that overconfidence in item-confidence judgments is attributable to overprecision. Item-level (probabilistic) confidence judgments will be biased upward by both overestimation and overprecision, whereas set-level (frequentistic) judgments will not necessarily be biased upward by overprecision.

The fact that most of the evidence for the existence of overconfidence confounds overestimation and overprecision raises important questions about which effect is responsible for the pervasiveness of apparent overconfidence in the results. It is possible that both causes share equally in the observed results, but it may be that one alone is primarily responsible. Prior data from item-confidence judgments cannot answer this question. We must ask it using different paradigms.

Problem 2: Underconfidence

The second problem with overconfidence is that in some contexts the opposite is observed. Sometimes, people underestimate themselves, and sometimes they underplace themselves. We consider the evidence on each type of underconfidence in turn.

Underestimation

Underestimation of performance is most likely to occur on easy tasks, on easy items, when success is likely, or when the individual making the estimate is especially skilled (Fu, Koutstaal, Fu, Poon, & Cleare, 2005; Griffin & Tversky, 1992; Kirchler & Maciejovsky, 2002; Koriat, Sheffer, & Ma'ayan, 2002; Lichtenstein & Fischhoff, 1977; Lichtenstein, Fischhoff, & Phillips, 1982; Sniezek, 1990; Stankov & Crawford, 1997). It is those individuals with the best performances on any given task who are most likely to underestimate their actual performances (Klayman et al., 1999; Krueger & Mueller, 2002; Kruger & Dunning, 2002; Larrick et al., 2007).

Erev, Wallsten, and Budescu (1994) offered what has been called a Thurstonian explanation for the so-called hard/easy effect: the fact that overestimation occurs on hard tasks but underestimation occurs for easy tasks. Their theory, following in the tradition of Thurstone (1927), takes into account that any judgment is likely to include some error component. When people have imperfect knowledge of their own performances, the error in their estimates will make those estimates regressive (Burson, Larrick, & Klayman, 2006; Krueger & Mueller, 2002). It is, after all, easier to underestimate than overestimate your score on a test when you get everything right. As a result, people underestimate their performance when it is high.

Underestimation has also been documented in domains other than beliefs about one's own prior performance, including the illusion of control, the planning fallacy, and optimism about future events.

The Illusion of Control

Research on the illusion of control has generally shown that when people have no control over some event, they frequently act as if they have some sort of control (for reviews see Presson & Benassi, 1996; Thompson, Armstrong, & Thomas, 1998). While these results make it appear that people overestimate their control, the research paradigms have generally focused on situations in which people have very little control. Just as overestimation of performance is most likely to occur when performance is low, overestimation of control is most likely to occur when control is low. It is, after all, difficult to underestimate one's control if one has none. Studies find that people actually tend to underestimate their control when it is high (Alloy & Abramson, 1979; Gino, Sharek, & Moore, 2009; Jenkins & Ward, 1965).

The Planning Fallacy

The planning fallacy documents the tendency for people to underestimate how long it takes to get things done or to overestimate their own productivity (Buehler et al., 1994). Again, it is easiest to underestimate how long it will take to get something done when the task will be time consuming. When the task doesn't take long to complete (i.e., it's easy), people are more likely to overestimate completion times—thereby underestimating their future performance (Boltz, Kupperman, & Dunne, 1998; Burt & Kemp, 1994).

Pessimism About the Future

While people prefer to imagine bright futures for themselves (Markus & Nurius, 1986), they sometimes evince pessimism. For instance, shortly after September 11, 2001, a sample of Americans estimated they had a 20%

chance of being injured in a terrorist attack in the coming year (Lerner, Gonzalez, Small, & Fischhoff, 2003). This is clearly a radical overestimate. In another study, smokers estimated their risk of dying of lung cancer at about 33%, when in fact the actual base rate among smokers is below 10% (Viscusi, 1990). Women estimate their chances of falling ill with breast cancer by as much as eight times the actual risk (Woloshin, Schwartz, Black, & Welch, 1999). Chinese people overestimated their actual chances of falling ill with severe acute respiratory syndrome (SARS) during the disease's outbreak in China (Ji, Zhang, Usborne, & Guan, 2004). People overestimate their risk of dying in the coming year (Fischhoff, Bruine de Bruin, Parker, Milstein, & Halpern-Felsher, 2006). Carnegie Mellon undergraduates estimated their chances of being struck by lightning at about 20%, when the actual chance is closer to .009% (Moore & Small, 2008). It is notable that all these overestimates of risk occur in domains where the outcome has a low probability. All of these are also "easy" tasks, in the sense that the positive outcomes (*not* being the victim of a terrorist attack or *not* contracting cancer) is by far the most likely outcome. Again, when success is likely, people tend to underestimate it.

Underplacement

It is also common to find situations in which people underplace their performances, reporting that they are worse than others (Kruger, 1999). As a rule, this underplacement tends to occur on difficult tasks where success is rare (Blanton, Axsom, McClive, & Price, 2001; Chambers & Windschitl, 2004; Krizan & Windschitl, 2007b; Moore, 2007a; Radzevick & Moore, 2008).

Comparative Pessimism

Weinstein's (1980) findings are the most frequently cited evidence of comparative optimism. Comparative optimism is the belief that one is more likely to experience positive events than are others, and that one is less likely to experience negative events than are others. However, it just so happens that Weinstein asked his participants about positive common events (e.g., owning your own house) and rare negative events (e.g., attempting suicide). When event commonness and valence are unconfounded, results reveal that, while both influence judgments of comparative likelihood, the effect of event commonness is roughly four times the size of valence (Kruger & Burrus, 2004). That is, people believe that common events (even undesirable ones) are more likely to happen to them than to others and they believe that rare events (even desirable ones) are less likely to happen to them than to others (Chambers, Windschitl, & Suls, 2003).

Underprecision

Results showing underprecision are rarer than results showing underestimation or underplacement. Since Alpert and Raiffa's (1969/1982) original demonstration, numerous studies have examined the tendency for people's judgments to reflect excessive confidence that their beliefs are true and accurate. As described earlier, participants asked to create 90% confidence intervals around their point estimates typically err by creating intervals so narrow that the true answer is included only 30% to 50% of the time (Teigen & Jorgensen, 2005). Soll and Klayman (2004) note that the standard paradigm tends to overstate the true size of the overprecision effect somewhat but they find that overprecision is nevertheless robust. Some research has found that overprecision is sensitive to exactly how the question is asked of participants, with some methods producing less overprecision than others (Budescu & Du, 2007; Juslin, Wennerholm, & Olsson, 1999; Winman, Hansson, & Juslin, 2004), and overprecision tends to be stronger for unfamiliar tasks (Block & Harper, 1991). Despite the work on these moderating factors, overprecision lacks a demonstration of its underprecision counterpart the way that underestimation and underplacement have been shown to mirror their positive counterparts.

Problem 3: Apparent Inconsistency

The third problem with overconfidence is one that should be obvious after the preceding review: Overestimation and overplacement are seemingly inconsistent with one another. Easy tasks produce *under*estimation and *over*placement. Hard tasks produce *over*estimation and *under*placement (Larrick et al., 2007; Moore & Small, 2007). Evidence of overestimation tends to come from difficult domains (Campbell, Goodie, & Foster, 2004; Fischhoff et al., 1977; Hoffrage, 2004). Overplacement is most likely to arise in easier domains (College Board, 1976–1977; Svenson, 1981).

These apparent inconsistencies have produced some serious disputes. For instance, Viscusi (1990) asked smokers to estimate their chances of contracting lung cancer and found that they overestimated this small risk. On the other hand, when Weinstein (1998) asked smokers whether they were more or less likely than other smokers to get lung cancer, they told him they were less likely than others to fall ill. Slovic (2000) and Viscusi (2000) have argued bitterly on the question of whether smokers are overconfident or not.

In this chapter, we review a theory that can help address the three previously identified problems. Our work builds on that of Larrick et al. (2007), who presented an insightful analysis of the statistical relationships among overestimation, overplacement, and actual performance. Our theory goes beyond theirs by considering the underlying beliefs regarding one's own and others' performance that produce these relationships and by considering overprecision. Furthermore, we explore some implications and open questions that arise from the theory, which focuses on differences in the quality of information people have about themselves versus others.

DIFFERENTIAL INFORMATION THEORY

Moore and Healy (2008) present a theory that can help resolve these three problems in the overconfidence literature. Put simply, their differential information theory is this: People often have imperfect information about their own performances, abilities, or chances of success but even worse information about those of others. Consequently, people's estimates of themselves are regressive, and their estimates of others are even more regressive. Both estimates are regressive in the sense that, because they are known to be imperfect, they will tend to regress toward baseline expectations (i.e., a Bayesian prior). It follows that when performance is exceptionally high, people will underestimate their own performances, will underestimate others even more so, and thus will believe that they are better than others. When performance is low, people will overestimate themselves, will overestimate others even more so, and will believe that they are worse than others. The theory's predictions are illustrated in Figure 7.1.

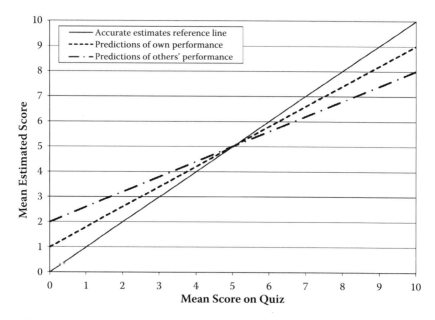

FIGURE 7.1

An example of the theory's prediction of beliefs about performance by self and others on a 10-item trivia quiz as a function of the actual score of the person doing the predicting, assuming the person expected a score of 5 prior to taking the quiz.

The theory makes some clear predictions regarding overestimation and overplacement:

> *Estimation*: People will overestimate their performances on hard tasks but will underestimate their performances on easy tasks.
>
> *Placement*: People will overplace their performance on easy tasks but will underplace their performances on hard tasks.

The theory is agnostic with respect to the origins of overprecision. None of the previous hypotheses described depend on the accuracy in people's estimations of performance. However, the theory implies that the precision with which people are able to estimate performance should moderate the effects of task difficulty on both estimation and placement. In particular, individuals who are least confident in their estimations of their own performances should make estimates that are most regressive toward the prior and will also show the least precision (i.e., the greatest variance). If this effect holds, then the hard/easy effect will be associated with greater precision in estimates of one's own performance.

Likewise, the theory implies that accuracy in beliefs about others will result in both more precision of estimates and also in less overplacement on easy tasks and underplacement on hard tasks. On the other hand, individuals who are least confident in their estimations of others' performance will make the most regressive estimates of others. If this effect holds, then greater precision in the estimates of others will be associated with less overplacement on easy tasks and underplacement on hard tasks.

EXPERIMENTAL EVIDENCE

Moore and Healy (2008) devised an experiment to test the differential information theory. They gave 82 participants in their experiment a series of 18 10-item trivia quizzes covering six topics, each topic with a quiz that was easy, medium, and hard. Quiz difficulty was manipulated within subjects by using quizzes of varying difficulty. However, quizzes were not explicitly labeled with respect to ease. Participants estimated their scores and the scores of another randomly selected previous participant (RSPP) at two phases: (1) before they took the test; and (2) again immediately after they took it. These are the prior and interim measures, respectively. In addition, participants estimated the RSPP's score a third time (the posterior measure) after they had graded their own quizzes. Participants were rewarded for scoring well on the quiz, and received other (smaller) payments for accurately estimating their own scores and the scores of an RSPP.

The results of the experiment were consistent with the predictions of the theory. On easy quizzes, people underestimated their scores but believed that they were better than others. On hard quizzes, people overestimated their scores but believed they were worse than others. For the quizzes of medium difficulty, people were fairly accurate in estimating both self and others. As it happened, there were not main effects for overestimation or overplacement. That is to say that, on average, people did not overestimate (or underestimate) their own scores or believe that they were better (or worse) than others. The results are shown in Figure 7.2.

Overprecision

Moore and Healy (2008) employed a novel method for eliciting beliefs. Instead of just asking people to make point estimates of the quiz scores,

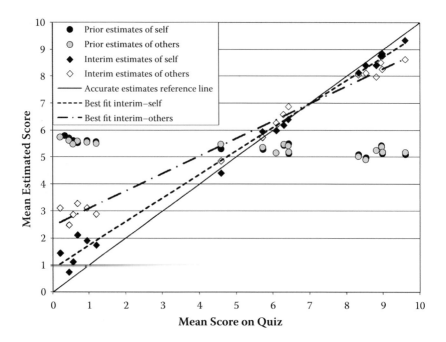

FIGURE 7.2
Estimated scores for self and other on the 18 different quizzes.

they asked participants to report their full subjective probability distributions across the range of scores. Participants estimated the likelihood of each of the 11 possible outcomes, from getting zero quiz items correct to getting all 10 correct. Participant's responses were constrained such that their probability estimates of the 11 possible outcomes always summed to 100%. This belief elicitation allowed Moore and Healy to also assess not only the overestimation and overplacement effects already discussed but also the precision in people's beliefs. It also represents a methodological advance over previous methods used to assess overprecision, avoiding some of the problems identified by Soll and Klayman (2004). Unlike overestimation and overplacement, participants' judgments *do* appear to show systematic overprecision. Indeed, as we discuss next, the evidence of overprecision in the data is quite strong. These results are particularly interesting for three reasons: (1) overprecision emerges clearly as the most robust form of overconfidence in the Moore and Healy data; (2) overprecision is likewise more robust (in the sense it shows few reversals with underprecision) than either overestimation or overplacement; and (3) overprecision is the most poorly understood of the three varieties of overconfidence, since we still lack a good theory to account for it that is consistent with the key empirical results. We will analyze the overprecision results in more depth than were possible in Moore and Healy's paper.

The overprecision in participants' judgments begins at the prior stage. The entire sample of 1,476 quiz scores has variance of 16.97. But participants' prior judgments have a smaller variance, suggesting they were inappropriately sure they knew what their scores would be. The variance of participants' estimates of themselves is 6.37, and the variance of the RSPP is 6.51, both of which are significantly smaller than 16.97 (p's < .001). But that could just be because the distribution of actual quizzes was more strongly bimodal than they were expecting, as the quizzes included so many surprisingly easy and surprisingly difficult quizzes, which drove up the variance on actual quiz scores.

More interestingly, their estimates of the RSPP show lower variance (and imply greater precision) than the actual set of scores on each specific quiz, both at the interim and the posterior phase. Across the 18 quizzes, the average variance in scores is 5.19. However, at the interim phase, the variance in the average participant's estimate of the RSPP's score is only 2.86, and this shrinks to 2.67 at the posterior phase. Both of these represent significant underestimation of the actual variance (p's < .001). Note that it does not make sense to perform this analysis on participants' estimates of their own scores because they observe useful private signals that ought to produce more precise estimates of their own scores.

The tendency toward overprecision in estimation of the RSPP's score is moderated by test difficulty. We computed an index of interim overprecision* by subtracting the variance of each participant's estimate of the RSPP from the actual variance on that quiz. When this measure is subject to a 6 (test block) × 3 (difficulty) within-subjects analysis of variance (ANOVA), the result reveals a significant main effect for difficulty (F (2, 162) = 1,647, p < .001, η^2 = .95). Participants' judgments reveal greater overprecision for

---

* Note that we observe the same results if we compare the variance of posterior (rather than interim) estimations of the RSPP with actual quiz variances. We think these analyses are less interesting, however, if performed on prior estimates because these priors are based on so little information and we do not know what that information is. Also, the comparison of variances between beliefs and the actual distribution of scores does not make sense for the self at either the interim or posterior phase, because then people have excellent knowledge about their own particular quiz performances, so the variance in each person's estimate ought to be smaller than the variance across all participants.

medium quizzes (*mean variance difference* = 6.63) than for easy quizzes (*mean variance difference* = 2.17) and underprecision for difficult quizzes (*mean variance difference* = –1.78). Neither the main effect for block (F (5, 405) = 1.56, p = .17) nor its interaction with difficulty (F (10, 810) < 1, p = .96) attains significance.

The reason for the significant difference across quiz difficulties is that the precision implied by participants' estimates of performance is not sufficiently responsive to changes in the variance of actual quiz scores. Because the variance in medium quizzes is quite large (*mean variance* = 9.87), participants' estimates (*mean variance* = 3.12) appear too precise. Because variance in the difficult quizzes is so small (*mean variance* = 1.48), participants' estimates (*mean variance* = 3.05) appear insufficiently precise.

The differential information theory offers a hint regarding why we might be most likely to observe underprecision in participants' estimates of others' scores on difficult quizzes. We have argued that overestimation occurs on difficult tests in part because when performance is low it is easier to overestimate it than undererstimate it. Just so, when variance on a quiz is exceptionally low, it is easier to overestimate it than to underestimate it. As with estimations of performance, the precision of those estimates is insufficiently sensitive to reality (see Budescu & Du, 2007).

An Additional Measure of Overprecision

We should admit that the comparison of variances is an incomplete measure of overprecision because it fails to take actual accuracy into account. Not all precision is overprecision. There is, in fact, a positive correlation between precision and accuracy. The smaller the variance in people's interim estimates of their own scores, the smaller the error in their estimates (r = .55, p < .001). The same is true for people's estimates of the RSPP: the smaller the variance in their interim estimates, the smaller the error in those estimates (r = .25, p < .001). Consider, for instance, a quiz on which no one gets anything right. An individual who reports that he is sure (100% confidence) that the RSPP has score of 0 would not be overestimating the precision of his beliefs. An alternative approach is to examine the one score an individual estimates is most likely. When takers of a difficult quiz report that a score of 2 is most likely, how often did they, in fact, get just two correct?

At the interim phase, participants report being, on average, 73% confident that they know their own scores but are correct only 59% of the time (t (1,476) = 18.84, $p < .001$). They report being 43% sure they knew what the RSPP had scored but are correct only 31% of the time (t (1,476) = 17.86, $p < .001$). When averaged across all rounds and all belief elicitations for both self and the RSPP, participants reported, on average, being 44% confident that they had correctly identified the score. In actuality, they were correct only 29% of the time, and participants' 44% estimate is significantly greater than this figure (t (81) = 8.64, $p < .001$). Overprecision measured this way is greater than zero for all five belief elicitations (all p's < .001), all quizzes (all p's < .005), all levels of difficulty (all p's < .001), and all blocks (all p's < .001).

Does difficulty moderate the degree of overprecision shown by this measure, as previously observed? To answer this question, we computed the difference between confidence and accuracy for each participant at each level of difficulty.* We then subjected this measure to a three-level within-subjects ANOVA. The results do indeed reveal a within-subjects effect of quiz difficulty (F (2, 162) = 13.55, $p < .001$, $\eta^2 = .14$). However, the effect runs in the opposite direction as previously. Instead of finding the greatest underprecision for the hard quiz, we observe that the difference between confidence and hit rates is greater for the hard (M = 22%) and medium (M = 23%) quizzes than for the easy quizzes (M = 16%). While this appears to be a contradiction, its explanation is straightforward.

The explanation is twofold. First, because participants' estimates of hard quiz scores were so much more regressive than easy quiz scores, their estimates are systematically off, pushing down their hit rates. In other words, they overestimate hard quiz scores more than they underestimate easy quiz scores. The second reason has to do with floor effects. The variance in scores on the hard quizzes is so small that floor effects (variances don't go below zero) made it difficult for people to exhibit underprecision by underestimating the variance.

---

* To be specific, we computed the percentage confidence accorded to the score rated as most likely and subtracted from this the actual hit rate. We averaged this across all five elicitations in each round and all six blocks for each level of difficulty.

The Relationship Among Overprecision, Overestimation, and Overplacement

As expected, the precision of participants' judgments is related in interesting ways to overestimation and overplacement. These associations are most fruitfully examined at the interim phase, where participants have some information about performance on that quiz and we have measures of beliefs for both self and others.

We predicted that precision in estimates of one's own score would be associated with less underestimation on easy quizzes and also with less overestimation on hard quizzes. Indeed, this was the case. On the easy quizzes, the correlation between variance (i.e., lack of precision) and *under*estimation is positive ($r = .45$, $p < .001$). Participants' tendency to underestimate their scores on easy quizzes was smaller among those who reported narrow belief distributions. On the hard quizzes, the correlation between variance and *over*estimation is also positive ($r = .46$, $p < .001$), because the more precise the estimate, the less the overestimation. The tendency to overestimate one's score on the hard quiz was associated with narrower belief distributions.

We also predicted that greater precision in estimates of the RSPP's score would be associated with less overplacement on easy quizzes and also with less underplacement on hard quizzes. Indeed, this was the case. On easy quizzes, the correlation between variance (i.e., lack of precision) and *over*placement is positive ($r = .34$, $p < .001$). The broader the confidence interval in estimating others, the more the overplacement. On hard tests, the correlation between variance and *under*placement is also positive ($r = .26$, $p < .001$) because the broader the confidence interval in estimating the RSPP, the less the overplacement. In other words, precise estimates decrease the tendency to underplace one's own performance on hard quizzes.

Individual Differences

There have been some attempts to examine individual differences in the propensity to be overconfident. While not every study that looks has found a relationship (Jonsson & Allwood, 2003), there are some that claim to have identified the traits that predict overconfidence. It is particularly interesting to examine the influence of individual differences in the Moore and Healy (2008) data, given that their study is the first to have examined all three varieties of overconfidence simultaneously.

For this reason, Moore and Healy (2008) collected some measures that prior research has found to be related to overconfidence: gender (Niederle & Vesterlund, 2007; Pulford & Colman, 1997; Soll & Klayman, 2004), narcissism (Ames & Kammrath, 2004; Campbell et al., 2004), cognitive abilities (Kleitman & Stankov, 2007; Stankov & Crawford, 1996); and the "big five" dimensions of personality: conscientiousness, agreeableness, neuroticism, openness, and extraversion (Schaefer, Williams, Goodie, & Campbell, 2004). In addition, there were three measures related to self-enhancement: overclaiming (Paulhus, Harms, Bruce, & Lysy, 2003), self-esteem (Rosenberg, 1965), and the generalized sense of power (Anderson, John, & Keltner, 2005). Because they could be related to individuals' willingness and ability to understand others, there were the empathy and perspective-taking subscales of the Interpersonal Reactivity Index (Davis, 1983) and social comparison orientation (Gibbons & Buunk, 1999). Finally, because it might be related to confidence in one's judgments and willingness to endure uncertainty there were measures of political conservatism (Jost, Glaser, Kruglanski, & Sulloway, 2003). This last measure included two questions: *How liberal or conservative do you tend to be when it comes to social issues?* and *How liberal or conservative do you tend to be when it comes to economic issues?* Participants were provided with a seven-point scale on which to respond, with endpoints labeled "very liberal" and "very conservative." Space constraints did not allow analyses of the individual-differences data in Moore and Healy's paper, so we present these analyses here.

These seventeen measures allow us to test whether individual differences between participants are correlated with any of the overconfidence measures. But first, it makes sense to ask whether any of the three types of overconfidence are consistent within-individual. If measures of overconfidence do not vary consistently between people, then the search for individual-difference correlates of overconfidence is likely to prove fruitless. We have multiple measures of overconfidence for each person. What is the test–retest reliability of these different measures?

The alpha reliability for the 18 measures of overestimation is .21. Clearly this falls short of satisfactory reliability. The situation is much the same with overplacement: Its alpha reliability is only .29. Overprecision is different, however. The average overprecision measure yields an alpha reliability of .95. We were concerned that this last result was the consequence of some lazy participants simplifying their jobs by reporting 100% confidence of a single score for each quiz and so moving more quickly through the experimental task. So we examined the length of time it took participants to complete the experiment and found that it was not significantly correlated ($r = .06$) with the degree of overprecision.

Correlations between the measures of overconfidence and a variety of individual difference measures appear in Table 7.1. While three correlations in this table are significant at the .05 level, that criterion is not sufficiently stringent given that we're casting about for possible associations between our 17 individual-difference variables and our three overconfidence measures. After the Bonferroni adjustment to our significance criterion for these 51 tests, none of the correlations is significant.

TABLE 7.1

Correlations Across the 82 Individuals Between Measures of Overconfidence and Measures of Individual Difference

	Overestimation	Overplacement	Overprecision
Overestimation	$\alpha = .21$		
Overplacement	0.06	$\alpha = .29$	
Overprecision	0.24	−0.03	$\alpha = .95$
Extraversion	−0.15	−0.02	−0.08
Agreeableness	0.13	0.01	0.12
Conscientiousness	−0.02	−0.09	0.11
Neuroticism	−0.08	−0.15	0.04
Openness	−0.11	−0.26	−0.08
Social comparison orientation	0.03	0.14	0.05
Narcissism	−0.01	0.09	−0.19
Self-esteem	−0.13	0.03	−0.10
Overclaiming	0.21	0.07	−0.12
Generalized sense of power	−0.16	0.01	−0.12
Perspective taking	0.12	−0.11	−0.07
Empathy	0.13	0.00	−0.13
Cognitive reflection	−0.19	0.08	−0.19
Social conservatism	−0.10	−0.01	0.17
Economic conservatism	−0.10	−0.01	0.20
Male	0.18	0.13	0.02
Age	0.18	−0.08	0.10

The failure of the individual differences we measured to account for differences between people in their tendency to display overconfidence is noteworthy. We do not have a good explanation for the failure to replicate findings from prior studies. It is probably not because participants became fatigued filling out the many surveys and started responding without much thought. If that had been the case we would expect the different measures to show poor reliability. In fact, interitem alpha reliability measures are satisfactory (above .8) for all the multi-item scales. We can speculate only that the failure to replicate prior findings has to do with differences between the experimental procedures Moore and Healy (2008) used and those used in prior studies.

What differences in procedures led to our failure to replicate prior results? It is hard to know without varying each systematically and comparing the results with prior findings. But our failure to replicate does make us wonder how sensitive prior findings are to the exact experimental paradigms those studies employed. At the very least, our failure to replicate those results makes us more skeptical about the robustness of earlier findings of individual difference. We are forced to consider the example of gender, which experimenters routinely test for, but report only when they find an effect. If the presence of gender effects is taken as evidence for real gender differences and the absence of gender effects is ignored, we run the risk of overestimating the importance of gender differences that arise due to chance or idiosyncratic features of particular research designs.

STRENGTHS OF THE DIFFERENTIAL INFORMATION THEORY

The differential information theory has a number of virtues. First, it posits a parsimonious explanation for the negative relationship between overestimation and overplacement across tasks. Second, it is consistent with most of the evidence on overestimation and overplacement, including the complex results of Moore and Healy's (2008) experiment. Third, it can help explain a number of otherwise incongruous research findings. Fourth, the theory can accommodate moderators of overconfidence previously documented in the literature.

Reconciling Incongruous Results

For instance, the theory may be able to reconcile the Slovic–Viscusi debate about whether smokers are overconfident. Smokers do indeed overestimate the probability of contracting lung cancer, as Viscusi (1990) shows. But they also believe that others are more likely than they are to experience this rare event, as Weinstein (1998) shows. The theory can accommodate these findings if people have imperfect information about their own risky behavior and its consequences but have better information about their own behavior than that of others. Likewise, when it comes to predicting whether they are going to die in the coming year, people tend to overestimate this small probability. Nevertheless, because people have better information for themselves than for others, they overestimate others more than self and consequently believe they are at less risk than others.

False Consensus and False Uniqueness

Our results reveal the simultaneous co-occurrence of both false consensus (thinking that others are more like you than they are; Ross, Greene, & House, 1977) and false uniqueness (believing that others are more different from you than they are; Perloff & Brickman, 1982) on the same dependent measures (see also Moore & Kim, 2003; Moore & Small, 2007). Participants' judgments reveal false uniqueness because participants reported believing that their scores were more exceptional than they actually were—0.48 points higher than those of others on the easy quiz and 1.36 points lower on the hard quiz. At the same time, participants' judgments reveal false consensus because people believed that others would perform more like them than they actually did. Performance by participants and their RSPPs were uncorrelated within quiz ($r = -.05$). However, participants believed that others were like them—estimations of performance by self and other are strongly correlated within quiz ($r = .48$).

As Dawes (1989) pointed out, there is a rational basis for the so-called false consensus effect. If the only source of information participants had about quiz difficulty was their own performance, then they would do well to assume others would perform as they did (Krueger, 2003; Krueger, Acevedo, & Robbins, 2005). Indeed, people who assume others are like them will, on average, make more accurate estimates of others than will people who ignore the information they have about themselves and do not update their prior beliefs (Dawes & Mulford, 1996). And false uniqueness effects arise quite naturally from the fact that people possess better information about themselves than about others, as Fiedler (1996) has shown. Differential information theory accounts for the co-occurrence of these seemingly contradictory findings by explaining both phenomena as functions of the information available about the reference population.

MODERATORS OF OVERCONFIDENCE

The Moore and Healy (2008) theory is consistent with empirical results demonstrating a number of key moderators of overconfidence. We mention a few of them here.

Controllability

Research suggests that the tendency to believe that one's performance will be better than that of others is stronger for outcomes under personal control than for chance outcomes (for reviews see Harris, 1996; Klein & Helweg-Larsen, 2002). This result makes perfect sense since, when performance is entirely determined by chance, it is not possible for people to have better information about their own future performances than about others'.

Observability

People believe they are more likely than others to be honest (difficult to observe). They are less likely to believe they are friendlier than others (friendliness is easier to observe) (Alicke, 1985; Allison, Messick, & Goethals, 1989; Paunonen, 1989). As differential information theory would predict, this effect reverses itself for rare behaviors (Kruger & Savitsky, 2006). These results follow from the fact that people have better information about others for observable behaviors.

Personal Experience

Personal familiarity with some event or outcome seems to increase comparative optimism (Weinstein, 1980). This contrasts with the effects of observability, which increases information about performance or outcomes, particularly for others. Personal familiarity with one's own chances of experiencing an event, on the other hand, is likely to increase the disparity between the quality of information about self versus others.

Absent/Exempt

When people have exposed themselves to some risk but haven't experienced a negative outcome, they sometimes conclude that they are immune to that risk. For instance, young women who have unprotected sex and do not get pregnant may incorrectly conclude that they are infertile (Downs, Bruine de Bruin, Murray, & Fischhoff, 2004), or sexually active college students who have had unprotected sex but who haven't contracted AIDS may come to believe think they're less vulnerable to getting AIDS than are others (Weinstein, 1982). Basically, their personal experience with (the absence of) a rare negative event leads them to reduce their estimates of their own personal risk, and they wind up believing that they are less likely than others to experience it (see Hertwig, Barron, Weber, & Erev, 2004). People remain quite clueless about the low actual risk of contracting AIDS (roughly 1 in 500 chance of becoming infected from a single act of unprotected coitus with an infected partner; Hearst & Hulley, 1988) and so overestimate this small probability. This result is obviously consistent with our theory.

Debiasing

Metcalfe's (1998) review discusses debiasing methods that work to reduce or eliminate overestimation where it does occur. These are all strikingly consistent with our differential information theory. Most of Metcalfe's recommendations involve giving people better information about themselves or others. Indeed, Metcalfe argues that what evidence exists for overestimation is more consistent with poor information about one's own performance (and the causes of it) than with self-deception.

LIMITATIONS OF THE DIFFERENTIAL INFORMATION THEORY

We cannot claim that the patterns we observe here and elsewhere (Klar & Giladi, 1997; Kruger, 1999; Moore, 2005; Moore & Cain, 2007; Moore & Healy, 2008; Moore & Kim, 2003; Moore & Klein, 2008; Moore, Oesch, & Zietsma, 2007; Moore & Small, 2007, 2008; Windschitl, Kruger, & Simms, 2003) would hold regardless of context, task domain, or subject population, although the differential information theory does not suggest that these factors should matter. The theory is, however, not meant to account for all overconfidence effects. Here, we specify four key limitations to what the differential information theory can explain.

What Constitutes Performance?

We have implicitly assumed that it is easy to specify what constitutes performance. Sometimes, there is little ambiguity about how many items each participant answered correctly on each trivia quiz. However, a substantial proportion of the evidence showing overplacement employs tasks on which performance is largely subjective. Svenson (1981), for instance, did not tell his participants exactly what constituted driving skill—he asked them how their driving skills compared with those of other drivers and left it up to them to determine how to assess driving skill. Indeed, Dunning, Meyerowitz, and Holzberg (1989) showed that the more subjective the domain, the more latitude people have to claim that they are better than others. This may be because the motivation to claim undeserved distinctiveness is unleashed in domains where people know that nobody can expose their exaggerations. It could also be the consequence of varied and idiosyncratic definitions of what constitutes performance (Santos-Pinto & Sobel, 2005; van den Steen, 2004).

We should note that when the performance criterion is vague, it becomes difficult to assess the accuracy of estimations of performance. Consequently, it is not easy to measure the relationship between overestimation and overplacement in vague domains. This is why these vague performance domains did not provide a useful context in which to test our theory.

Direct Versus Indirect Measures

Indirect comparative judgments are computed using the implicit comparison between individual judgments of self and other. For example, a direct measure of overplacement would be asking people to give themselves a percentile ranking relative to all other test-takers. An indirect measure of overplacement would be to compute the difference between people's estimates of their own scores and their estimates of the scores of others. The Moore and Healy (2008) data rely exclusively on indirect comparisons.

The leading explanation for above- and below-average effects is differential weighting: When making comparative judgments, people overweight self-knowledge and underweight knowledge about others (Chambers & Windschitl, 2004; Giladi & Klar, 2002). Research has generally found that both overplacement on easy tasks and underplacement on difficult tasks are stronger when comparisons are elicited directly rather than indirectly (Chambers & Windschitl). The Moore and Healy (2008) theory cannot account for this difference in elicitation formats.

However, some research suggests that discrepancies between direct and indirect elicitation methods are an artifact of question format and that parallel question formats can eliminate the discrepancy (Burson & Klayman, 2005; Moore, 2007b; Radzevick & Moore, 2009b). And while the differential weighting explanation is useful for accounting for some important results in direct comparative judgments (Kruger, Windschitl, Burrus, Fessel, & Chambers, 2008), it cannot account for the presence of overplacement or underplacement effects in indirect comparative judgments, such as those we present.

The Self-Selection Problem

Even if, as our theory implies, people believe just as easily in their own inferiority as in their superiority, it does not follow that we should expect to see unbiased judgment most of the time. In life, people are not randomly assigned to the universe of all possible tasks. Instead, people self-select based, in part, on where they believe they can distinguish themselves from others (Tesser, 1988). This fact has two important consequences. First, easy tasks, on which more people feel competent, will attract too many competitors (Moore & Cain, 2007; Moore et al., 2007). It is, after all, industries such as restaurants, bars, and hobby shops that see the highest rates of entry, most intense competition, and, consequently, the highest rates of failure (Geroski, 1995; U.S. Small Business Administration, 2003). Second, we should expect overplacement to be the rule if we sample the beliefs of only those who have chosen to enter or compete (Cain, Moore, & Chen, 2009).

Motivational Effects

Moore and Healy's (2008) theory is clearly a cognitive one. It explains over- and underconfidence not as the product of bravado or humility but as the natural consequence of rational judgments with imperfect information. We have emphasized the virtues of the theory and the many things it can parsimoniously explain. However, we would be remiss if we did not note the fact that most theories invoked to explain overconfidence (and under-confidence) in the past have invoked motivation as a key cause, and there is some support for these theories that our theory cannot explain. Some have found that overestimation increases with the personal importance of the task domain (Ross, McFarland, & Fletcher, 1981; Sanbonmatsu, Shavitt, Sherman, & Roskos-Ewoldsen, 1987; Sanitioso, Kunda, & Fong, 1990). Other research has found that people are more likely to believe that they are better than others with whom they expect to compete ver-sus cooperate (Klein & Kunda, 1992). Then there is evidence showing that estimations of future performance are reduced when the moment of truth draws near (Carroll, Sweeny, & Shepperd, 2006; Gilovich, Kerr, & Medvec, 1993; Nussbaum, Liberman, & Trope, 2006). The differential information theory cannot account for these effects.

It is easy to imagine that there are many circumstances in which over-confidence can be adaptive. Self-confidence can increase your chances of success (Stajkovic & Luthans, 1998), self-perceived abilities predict actual performance over and above actual abilities (Greven, Harlaar, Kovas, Chamorro-Premuzic, & Plomin, 2009), optimism is correlated with positive health outcomes (Scheier & Carver, 1993), and high confidence makes you more persuasive to others (Anderson & Brion, 2008; Zarnoth & Sniezek, 1997). However, it is not the case that overconfidence is always adaptive. There are, of course, situations in which increased motivation can lead to defensive pessimism (Norem & Cantor, 1986; Norem & Illingworth, 1993) or even choking (Ariely, Gneezy, Loewenstein, & Mazar, 2005; Beilock & Carr, 2001; Benoît, Dubra, & Moore, 2009; Markman & Maddox, 2006). A number of researchers have examined the effect of event desirability on optimism and found no effects (Helweg-Larsen & Shepperd, 2001). As Krizan and Windschitl's (2007a) review of the literature shows, the evidence for wishful thinking, in which optimism is influenced by event desirability, is not strong.

FUTURE RESEARCH

Overprecision

We think that the greater robustness of overprecision is interesting, but we are reluctant to conclude that overprecision is a universal tendency. Research clearly shows that overprecision is sensitive to the situational context (Block & Harper, 1991) and the elicitation method (Budescu & Du, 2007; Juslin & Persson, 2002; Juslin et al., 1999). Furthermore, important questions remain about the causes for overprecision. Some research has suggested that anchoring and insufficient adjustment might be at work in causing overprecision (Block & Harper, 1991; Juslin et al., 1999). If people anchor on an initial answer and adjust insufficiently from it when building a confidence interval around it, that would produce apparent overprecision. Other researchers have suggested that confirmation bias or biased information retrieval may be at work (Hoch, 1985; Klayman et al., 1999; Koriat, Lichtenstein, & Fischhoff, 1980). Some research suggests the same memory processes that give rise to confirmation bias may lead to anchoring (Mussweiler & Strack, 1999; Strack & Mussweiler, 1997) and maybe also to overprecision. Some of the most promising evidence highlights the role of faulty statistical intuitions surrounding the construction of confidence intervals (Juslin, Winman, & Hansson, 2007).

Despite the many studies that have shown overprecision, it has been examined primarily in just two ways: (1) using interval estimates of numerical answers to trivia questions; and (2) using the item-confidence paradigm, which confounds it with overestimation. Overprecision deserves to be studied with a greater variety of methods and in a greater variety of contexts than it has been in the past. Mamassian (2008) developed a promising new research approach that could be used to infer precision in judgment without forcing people to state it explicitly. Mamassian's approach could even be used for studying overprecision in animals, children, or other populations who have difficulty understanding confidence intervals and probabilities.

The Benefits of Overconfidence

There are a number of interesting open questions surrounding the issue of when it might be in the individual's interest to be overconfident. If believing in your own self-efficacy can increase motivation, effort, and performance, then it might be in your interest to fool yourself into being overconfident (Benabou & Tirole, 2002). Believing that you can succeed does, at least sometimes, increase work performance (Pajares, 1996; Stajkovic & Luthans, 1998). Indeed, merely visualizing success can even contribute to future performance (Taylor, Pham, Rivkin, & Armor, 1998). And Scheier and Carver (1993, 2003) documented some positive health correlates of optimism. However, Baumeister, Campbell, Krueger, and Vohs (2003) argued that high self-confidence is more a consequence than a cause of success. It is also the case that believing in your own success can undermine that very success, such as when the student who is sure she will ace the test fails to study (Goodhart, 1986; Stone, 1994). And as explanations for the high rate of teenage deaths in auto accidents have often noted, belief in one's invincibility leads to actions that increase the risk of injury and death (Johnson, McCaul, & Klein, 2002; Williams, 2003).

If overconfidence isn't always good for individual performance, maybe its effects on well-being are more salutary. Many have argued that "positive illusions" of our own superiority over others are individually beneficial, in the sense that they increase well-being and psychological adjustment (Taylor & Brown, 1988). Certainly, belief in a positive future allows one to savor anticipated pleasures (Loewenstein & Thaler, 1997). But excessively optimistic forecasts undermine satisfaction when reality intervenes on our pleasant illusions (McGraw, Mellers, & Ritov, 2004). Indeed, the salient upward counterfactual provided by an unfulfilled expectation is likely to contribute to disappointment, frustration, and attempts to change one's behavior (Roese, 1999; Roese & Olson, 1995).

Then maybe the benefits of overconfidence accrue in social situations where people who are most overconfident are those most likely to attain status and influence in social settings (Anderson & Brion, 2008; Radzevick & Moore, 2009a). Indeed, high degrees of confidence increase your persuasiveness to others (Sah, Moore, & MacCoun, 2009; Zarnoth

& Sniezek, 1997), but arrogance can also alienate others. Individuals who overestimate their status within groups are prone to ostracism (Anderson, Srivastava, Beer, Spataro, & Chatman, 2006). And those who claim the greatest confidence are at the greatest risk of undermining their credibility when they turn out to be wrong (Tenney, MacCoun, Spellman, & Hastie, 2007; Tenney, Spellman, & MacCoun, 2008).

CONCLUSION

There are clearly many adaptive benefits of having accurate information about yourself—your ability to jump across the crevasse, your probability of winning the promotion, your probability of getting the grant over other contestants, your chance of seducing the attractive stranger, or the accuracy of your estimate regarding the value of the stock you are thinking about buying. When individuals, groups, companies, and markets display overconfidence, they will make some predictable mistakes. The research discussed in this chapter helps advance our understanding of what causes overconfidence, and in this way it should help us predict when we will observe the different sorts of overconfidence and in what contexts.

What can it tell us about the role of overconfidence in the growth and subsequent collapse of the subprime mortgage market? Our work suggests that banks' excessive confidence that they knew how to price collateralized debt obligations and credit default swaps was likely to have been the real culprit. That is where overprecision came into play. Without that overprecision, there would have been little supply of capital for subprime mortgages. Banks' willingness to buy and insure these speculative investments created the opportunity for markets to select those home buyers who were either so optimistic or so risk seeking that they were willing to take out mortgages they could not afford. It would be nice to think that the implosion in the subprime mortgage market might have corrected the overprecision in banks' valuations, but the data suggest otherwise. There can be little doubt that the financial crisis has led to more pessimistic valuations of subprime mortgages. But market prices and trading volumes suggest that individuals and institutions are still behaving as if they were excessively confident that these newly pessimistic beliefs are accurate and that the mortgages that were once so valuable are now worthless.

REFERENCES

Alba, J. W., & Hutchinson, J. W. (2000). Knowledge calibration: What consumers know and what they think they know. *Journal of Consumer Research, 27*, 123–156.

Alicke, M. D. (1985). Global self-evaluation as determined by the desirability and controllability of trait adjectives. *Journal of Personality and Social Psychology, 49*(6), 1621–1630.

Alicke, M. D., & Govorun, O. (2005). The better-than-average effect. In M. D. Alicke, D. Dunning, & J. Krueger (Eds.), *The self in social judgment* (pp. 85–106). New York: Psychology Press.

Allison, S. T., Messick, D. M., & Goethals, G. R. (1989). On being better but not smarter than others: The Muhammad Ali effect. *Social Cognition, 7*(3), 275–295.

Alloy, L. B., & Abramson, L. Y. (1979). Judgment of contingency in depressed and nondepressed students: Sadder but wiser? *Journal of Experimental Psychology: General, 108*, 441–485.

Alpert, M., & Raiffa, H. (1969/1982). A progress report on the training of probability assessors. In D. Kahneman, P. Slovic, & A. Tversky (Eds.), *Judgment under uncertainty: Heuristics and biases* (pp. 294–305). Cambridge, UK: Cambridge University Press.

Ames, D. R., & Kammrath, L. (2004). Mind-reading and metacognition: Narcissism, not actual competence, predicts self-estimated ability. *Journal of Nonverbal Behavior, 28*, 187–209.

Anderson, C., & Brion, S. (2008). Overconfidence and the attainment of social status. Unpublished manuscript. Berkeley, CA: University of California at Berkeley.

Anderson, C., John, O. P., & Keltner, D. (2005). *The subjective sense of power: Structure and antecedents.*

Anderson, C., Srivastava, S., Beer, J. S., Spataro, S. E., & Chatman, J. A. (2006). Knowing your place: Self-perceptions of status in face-to-face groups. *Journal of Personality and Social Psychology, 91*(6), 1094–1110.

Ariely, D., Gneezy, U., Loewenstein, G., & Mazar, N. (2005). *Large stakes and big mistakes.* Available at SSRN: http://papers.ssrn.com/sol3/papers.cfm?abstract_id=774986

Barber, B., & Odean, T. (2001). Boys will be boys: Gender, overconfidence, and common stock investment. *Quarterly Journal of Economics, 116*(1), 261–293.

Baumeister, R. F., Campbell, J. D., Krueger, J. I., & Vohs, K. D. (2003). Does high self-esteem cause better performance, interpersonal success, happiness, or healthier lifestyles? *Psychological Science in the Public Interest, 4*, 1–44.

Beilock, S. L., & Carr, T. H. (2001). On the fragility of skilled performance: What governs choking under pressure? *Journal of Experimental Psychology: General, 130*(4), 701–725.

Belsky, G., & Gilovich, T. (2000). *Why smart people make big money mistakes—and how to correct them: Lessons from the new science of behavioral economics* (1st Fireside ed.). New York: Simon & Schuster.

Benabou, R., & Tirole, J. (2002). Self-confidence and personal motivation. *Quarterly Journal of Economics, 117*(3), 871–915.

Benoît, J.-P., Dubra, J., & Moore, D. A. (2009). Does the better-than-average effect show that people are overconfident?: An experiment. Unpublished manuscript. University of London. Available at http://ssrn.com/abstract=1337733.

Blanton, H., Axsom, D., McClive, K. P., & Price, S. (2001). Pessimistic bias in comparative evaluations: A case of perceived vulnerability to the effects of negative life events. *Personality and Social Psychology Bulletin, 27*(12), 1627–1636.

Block, R. A., & Harper, D. R. (1991). Overconfidence in estimation: Testing the anchoring-and-adjustment hypothesis. *Organizational Behavior and Human Decision Processes, 49*(2), 188–207.

Boltz, M. G., Kupperman, C., & Dunne, J. (1998). The role of learning in remembered duration. *Memory & Cognition, 26*(5), 903–921.

Budescu, D. V., & Du, N. (2007). The coherence and consistency of investors' probability judgments. *Management Science, 53*(11), 1731–1744.

Buehler, R., Griffin, D., & MacDonald, H. (1997). The role of motivated reasoning in optimistic time predictions. *Personality and Social Psychology Bulletin, 23*(3), 238–247.

Buehler, R., Griffin, D., & Ross, M. (1994). Exploring the "planning fallacy": Why people underestimate their task completion times. *Journal of Personality and Social Psychology, 67*(3), 366–381.

Burson, K. A., & Klayman, J. (2005). *Judgments of performance: The relative, the absolute, and the in-between.* Unpublished manuscript, Ann Arbor, MI. Available at SSRN: http://ssrn.com/abstract=894129

Burson, K. A., Larrick, R. P., & Klayman, J. (2006). Skilled or unskilled, but still unaware of it: How perceptions of difficulty drive miscalibration in relative comparisons. *Journal of Personality and Social Psychology, 90*(1), 60–77.

Burt, C. D. B., & Kemp, S. (1994). Construction of activity duration and time management potential. *Applied Cognitive Psychology, 8*(2), 155–168.

Cain, D. M., Moore, D. A., & Chen, M. K. (2009). Overconfidence and entry into difficult competitions: reconciling discrepant results. Unpublished manuscript. New Haven, CT: Yale University.

Campbell, W. K., Goodie, A. S., & Foster, J. D. (2004). Narcissism, confidence, and risk attitude. *Journal of Behavioral Decision Making, 17*(4), 297–311.

Carroll, P., Sweeny, K., & Shepperd, J. A. (2006). Forsaking optimism. *Review of General Psychology, 10*(1), 56–73.

Chambers, J. R., & Windschitl, P. D. (2004). Biases in social comparative judgments: The role of nonmotivational factors in above-average and comparative-optimism effects. *Psychological Bulletin, 130*(5), 813–838.

Chambers, J. R., Windschitl, P. D., & Suls, J. (2003). Egocentrism, event frequency, and comparative optimism: When what happens frequently is "more likely to happen to me." *Personality and Social Psychology Bulletin, 29*(11), 1343–1356.

Christensen-Szalanski, J. J., & Bushyhead, J. B. (1981). Physicians' use of probablistic information in a real clinical setting. *Journal of Experimental Psychology: Human Perception and Performance, 7*, 928–935.

Clayson, D. E. (2005). Performance overconfidence: Metacognitive effects or misplaced student expectations? *Journal of Marketing Education, 27*(2), 122–129.

College Board. (1976–1977). *Student descriptive questionnaire.* Princeton, NJ: Educational Testing Service.

Cosmides, L., & Tooby, J. (1996). Are humans good intuitive statisticians after all? Rethinking some conclusions from the literature on judgment under uncertainty. *Cognition, 58*(1), 1–73.

Daniel, K., Hirshleifer, D., & Subrahmanyam, A. (1998). Investor psychology and security market under- and overreactions. *Journal of Finance, 53*(6), 1839–1885.

Davis, M. H. (1983). Measuring individual differences in empathy: Evidence for a multidimensional approach. *Journal of Personality and Social Psychology, 44,* 113–126.

Dawes, R. M. (1989). Statistical criteria for establishing a truly false consensus effect. *Journal of Experimental Social Psychology, 25*(1), 1–17.

Dawes, R. M., & Mulford, M. (1996). The false consensus effect and overconfidence: Flaws in judgment or flaws in how we study judgment? *Organizational Behavior and Human Decision Processes, 65*(3), 201–211.

Downs, J., Bruine de Bruin, W., Murray, P. J., & Fischhoff, B. (2004). When "it only takes once" fails: Perceived infertility predicts condom use and STI acquisition. *Journal of Pediatric and Adolescent Gynecology, 17*(3), 224.

Dunning, D. (2005). *Self-insight: Roadblocks and detours on the path to knowing thyself.* New York: Psychology Press.

Dunning, D., Meyerowitz, J. A., & Holzberg, A. D. (1989). Ambiguity and self-evaluation: The role of idiosyncratic trait definitions in self-serving assessments of ability. *Journal of Personality and Social Psychology, 57*(6), 1082–1090.

Erev, I., Wallsten, T. S., & Budescu, D. V. (1994). Simultaneous over- and underconfidence: The role of error in judgment processes. *Psychological Review, 101*(3), 519–527.

Fiedler, K. (1996). Explaining and simulating judgment biases as an aggregation phenomenon in probabilistic, multiple-cue environments. *Psychological Review, 103*(1), 193–214.

Fischhoff, B., Bruine de Bruin, W., Parker, A. M., Milstein, S. G., & Halpern-Felsher, B. L. (2006). *Adolescents' perceived risk of dying.* Paper presented at the Center for Risk Perception and Communication Seminar Series, Carnegie Mellon University.

Fischhoff, B., Slovic, P., & Lichtenstein, S. (1977). Knowing with certainty: The appropriateness of extreme confidence. *Journal of Experimental Psychology: Human Perception and Performance, 3*(4), 552–564.

Flyvbjerg, B., Skamris Holm, M. K., & Buhl, S. L. (2002). Underestimating costs in public works projects: Error or lie? *Journal of the American Planning Association, 68*(3), 279–295.

Fu, T., Koutstaal, W., Fu, C. H. Y., Poon, L., & Cleare, A. J. (2005). Depression, confidence, and decision: Evidence against depressive realism. *Journal of Psychopathology and Behavioral Assessment, 27,* 243–252.

Geroski, P. A. (1995). What do we know about entry? *International Journal of Industrial Organization, 13*(4), 421–440.

Gibbons, F. X., & Buunk, B. P. (1999). Individual differences in social comparison: Development of a scale of social comparison orientation. *Journal of Personality and Social Psychology, 76*(1), 129–142.

Gigerenzer, G. (1993). The bounded rationality of probabilistic mental modules. In K. I. Manktelow & D. E. Over (Eds.), *Rationality* (pp. 127–171). London: Routledge.

Gigerenzer, G., & Hoffrage, U. (1995). How to improve Bayesian reasoning without instruction: Frequency formats. *Psychological Review, 102*(4), 684–704.

Gigerenzer, G., Hoffrage, U., & Kleinbölting, H. (1991). Probabilistic mental models: A Brunswikian theory of confidence. *Psychological Review, 98*(4), 506–528.

Giladi, E. E., & Klar, Y. (2002). When standards are wide of the mark: Nonselective superiority and inferiority biases in comparative judgments of objects and concepts. *Journal of Experimental Psychology: General, 131*(4), 538–551.

Gilovich, T., Kerr, M., & Medvec, V. H. (1993). Effect of temporal perspective on subjective confidence. *Journal of Personality and Social Psychology, 64*(4), 552–560.

Gino, F., Sharek, Z., & Moore, D. A. (2009). The illusion of the illusion of control. Unpublished manuscript. Pittsburgh, PA: Carnege Mellon University.

Goodhart, D. E. (1986). The effects of positive and negative thinking on performance in an achievement situation. *Journal of Personality and Social Psychology, 51*, 117–124.

Greven, C. U., Harlaar, N., Kovas, Y., Chamorro-Premuzic, T., & Plomin, R. (2009). More than just IQ: School achievement is predicted by self-perceived abilities—but for genetic rather than environmental reasons. *Psychological Science, 20*(6), 753–762.

Griffin, D. W., & Buehler, R. (1999). Frequency, probability, and prediction: Easy solutions to cognitive illusions? *Cognitive Psychology, 38*(1), 48–78.

Griffin, D. W., & Tversky, A. (1992). The weighing of evidence and the determinants of confidence. *Cognitive Psychology, 24*(3), 411–435.

Harris, P. (1996). Sufficient grounds for optimism? The relationship between perceived controllability and optimistic bias. *Journal of Social and Clinical Psychology, 15*(1), 9–52.

Hearst, N., & Hulley, S. B. (1988). Preventing the heterosexual spread of AIDS: Are we giving our patients the best advice? *Journal of the American Medical Association, 259*, 2428–2432.

Helweg-Larsen, M., & Shepperd, J. A. (2001). Do moderators of the optimistic bias affect personal or target risk estimates? A review of the literature. *Personality and Social Psychology Review, 5*(1), 74–95.

Hertwig, R., Barron, G., Weber, E. U., & Erev, I. (2004). Decisions from experience and the effect of rare events in risky choice. *Psychological Science, 15*(8), 534–539.

Hoch, S. J. (1985). Counterfactual reasoning and accuracy in predicting personal events. *Journal of Experimental Psychology: Learning, Memory, and Cognition, 11*(4), 719–731.

Hoffrage, U. (2004). Overconfidence. In R. F. Pohl (Ed.), *Cognitive illusions: A handbook on fallacies and biases in thinking, judgment, and memory* (pp. 235–254). Hove, UK: Psychology Press.

Jenkins, H. M., & Ward, W. C. (1965). Judgment of contingency between responses and outcomes. *Psychological Monographs, 79*(1), 1–17.

Ji, L.-J., Zhang, Z., Usborne, E., & Guan, Y. (2004). Optimism across cultures: In response to the severe acute respiratory syndrome outbreak. *Asian Journal of Social Psychology, 7*, 25–34.

Johnson, R. J., McCaul, K. D., & Klein, W. M. P. (2002). Risk involvement and risk perception among adolescents and young adults. *Journal of Behavioral Medicine, 25*(1), 67–82.

Jonsson, A., & Allwood, C. M. (2003). Stability and variability in the realism of confidence judgments over time, content domain, and gender. *Personality & Individual Differences, 34*, 559–574.

Jost, J. T., Glaser, J., Kruglanski, A. W., & Sulloway, F. J. (2003). Political conservatism as motivated social cognition. *Psychological Bulletin, 129*(3), 339–375.

Juslin, P., Olsson, H., & Björkman, M. (1997). Brunswikian and Thurstonian origins of bias in probability assessment: On the interpretation of stochastic components of judgment. *Journal of Behavioral Decision Making, 10*(3), 189–209.

Juslin, P., & Persson, M. (2002). PROBabilities from EXemplars (PROBEX): A "lazy" algorithm for probabilistic inference from generic knowledge. *Cognitive Science, 26*(5), 563–607.

Juslin, P., Wennerholm, P., & Olsson, H. (1999). Format dependence in subjective probability calibration. *Journal of Experimental Psychology: Learning, Memory, and Cognition, 25*(4), 1038–1052.

Juslin, P., Winman, A., & Hansson, P. (2007). The naïve intuitive statistician: A naïve sampling model of intuitive confidence intervals. *Psychological Review, 114*(3), 678–703.

Juslin, P., Winman, A., & Olsson, H. (2000). Naive empiricism and dogmatism in confidence research: A critical examination of the hard-easy effect. *Psychological Review, 107*(2), 384–396.

Kirchler, E., & Maciejovsky, B. (2002). Simultaneous over- and underconfidence: Evidence from experimental asset markets. *Journal of Risk and Uncertainty, 25*(1), 65–85.

Klar, Y., & Giladi, E. E. (1997). No one in my group can be below the group's average: A robust positivity bias in favor of anonymous peers. *Journal of Personality and Social Psychology, 73*(5), 885–901.

Klayman, J., Soll, J. B., Gonzalez-Vallejo, C., & Barlas, S. (1999). Overconfidence: It depends on how, what, and whom you ask. *Organizational Behavior and Human Decision Processes, 79*(3), 216–247.

Klein, C. T. F., & Helweg-Larsen, M. (2002). Perceived control and the optimistic bias: A meta-analytic review. *Psychology and Health, 17*(4), 437–446.

Klein, W. M., & Kunda, Z. (1992). Motivated person perception: Constructing justifications for desired beliefs. *Journal of Experimental Social Psychology, 28*(2), 145–168.

Kleitman, S., & Stankov, L. (2007). Self-confidence and metacognitive processes. *Learning and Individual Differences, 17*(2), 161–173.

Koriat, A., Lichtenstein, S., & Fischhoff, B. (1980). Reasons for confidence. *Journal of Experimental Psychology: Human Learning and Memory, 6*(2), 107–118.

Koriat, A., Sheffer, L., & Ma'ayan, H. (2002). Comparing objective and subjective learning curves: Judgments of learning exhibit increased underconfidence with practice. *Journal of Experimental Psychology: General, 131*(2), 147–162.

Krizan, Z., & Windschitl, P. D. (2007a). The influence of outcome desirability on optimism. *Psychological Bulletin, 133*(1), 95–121.

Krizan, Z., & Windschitl, P. D. (2007b). Team allegiance can lead to both optimistic and pessimistic predictions. *Journal of Experimental Social Psychology, 43*(2), 327–333.

Krueger, J. I. (2003). Return of the ego—Self-referent information as a filter for social prediction: Comment on Karniol (2003). *Psychological Review, 110*(3), 585–590.

Krueger, J. I., Acevedo, M., & Robbins, J. M. (2005). Self as sample. In K. Fiedler & P. Juslin (Eds.), *Information sampling and adaptive cognition* (pp. 353–377). New York: Cambridge University Press.

Krueger, J. I., & Mueller, R. A. (2002). Unskilled, unaware, or both? The better-than-average heuristic and statistical regression predict errors in estimates of own performance. *Journal of Personality and Social Psychology, 82*(2), 180–188.

Kruger, J. (1999). Lake Wobegon be gone! The "below-average effect" and the egocentric nature of comparative ability judgments. *Journal of Personality and Social Psychology, 77*(2), 221–232.

Kruger, J., & Burrus, J. (2004). Egocentrism and focalism in unrealistic optimism (and pessimism). *Journal of Experimental Social Psychology, 40*(3), 332–340.

Kruger, J., & Dunning, D. (2002). Unskilled and unaware—but why? A reply to Krueger and Mueller (2002). *Journal of Personality and Social Psychology, 82*(2), 189–192.

Kruger, J., & Savitsky, K. (2006). On the genesis of inflated (and deflated) judgments of responsibility: Egocentrism revisited. Available at SSRN: http://ssrn.com/abstract=946245

Kruger, J., Windschitl, P. D., Burrus, J., Fessel, F., & Chambers, J. R. (2008). The rational side of egocentrism in social comparisons. *Journal of Experimental Social Psychology, 44*(2), 220–232.

Larrick, R. P., Burson, K. A., & Soll, J. B. (2007). Social comparison and confidence: When thinking you're better than average predicts overconfidence (and when it does not). *Organizational Behavior & Human Decision Processes, 102*(1), 76–94.

Lerner, J. S., Gonzalez, R. M., Small, D. A., & Fischhoff, B. (2003). Effects of fear and anger on perceived risks of terrorism: A national field experiment. *Psychological Science, 14*(2), 144–150.

Lichtenstein, S., & Fischhoff, B. (1977). Do those who know more also know more about how much they know? *Organizational Behavior and Human Decision Processes, 20*(2), 159–183.

Lichtenstein, S., Fischhoff, B., & Phillips, L. D. (1982). Calibration of probabilities: The state of the art in 1980. In D. Kahneman, P. Slovic, & A. Tversky (Eds.), *Judgment under uncertainty. Heuristics and biases* (pp. 306–333). Cambridge, UK: Cambridge University Press.

Loewenstein, G., & Thaler, R. H. (1997). Intertemporal choice. In W. M. Goldstein & R. M. Hogarth (Eds.), *Research on judgment and decision making: Currents, connections, and controversies. Cambridge series on judgment and decision making* (pp. 365–378). New York: Cambridge University Press.

Malmendier, U., & Tate, G. (2005). CEO overconfidence and corporate investment. *Journal of Finance, 60*(6), 2661–2700.

Mamassian, P. (2008). Overconfidence in an objective anticipatory motor task. *Psychological Science, 19*(6), 601–606.

Markman, A. B., & Maddox, W. T., & Worthy, D. A. (2006). Choking and excelling under pressure. *Psychological Science, 17*(11), 944–948.

Markus, H., & Nurius, P. (1986). Possible selves. *American Psychologist, 41*(9), 954–969.

McGraw, A. P., Mellers, B. A., & Ritov, I. (2004). The affective costs of overconfidence. *Journal of Behavioral Decision Making, 17*(4), 281–295.

Metcalfe, J. (1998). Cognitive optimism: self-deception or memory-based processing heuristics? *Personality and Social Psychology Review, 2*(2), 100–110.

Moore, D. A. (2005). Myopic biases in strategic social prediction: Why deadlines put everyone under more pressure than everyone else. *Personality and Social Psychology Bulletin, 31*(5), 668–679.

Moore, D. A. (2007a). Not so above average after all: When people believe they are worse than average and its implications for theories of bias in social comparison. *Organizational Behavior and Human Decision Processes, 102*(1), 42–58.

Moore, D. A. (2007b). When good = better than average. *Judgment and Decision Making, 2*(5), 277–291.

Moore, D. A., & Cain, D. M. (2007). Overconfidence and underconfidence: When and why people underestimate (and overestimate) the competition. *Organizational Behavior & Human Decision Processes, 103*, 197–213.

Moore, D. A., & Healy, P. J. (2008). The trouble with overconfidence. *Psychological Review, 115*(2), 502–517.

Moore, D. A., & Kim, T. G. (2003). Myopic social prediction and the solo comparison effect. *Journal of Personality and Social Psychology, 85*(6), 1121–1135.

Moore, D. A., & Klein, W. M. P. (2008). The use of absolute and comparative performance feedback in absolute and comparative judgments and decisions. *Organizational Behavior & Human Decision Processes, 107*, 60–74.

Moore, D. A., Kurtzberg, T. R., Fox, C. R., & Bazerman, M. H. (1999). Positive illusions and forecasting errors in mutual fund investment decisions. *Organizational Behavior and Human Decision Processes, 79*(2), 95–114.

Moore, D. A., Oesch, J. M., & Zietsma, C. (2007). What competition? Myopic self-focus in market entry decisions. *Organization Science, 18*(3), 440–454.

Moore, D. A., & Small, D. A. (2007). Error and bias in comparative judgment: On being both better and worse than we think we are. *Journal of Personality and Social Psychology, 92*(6), 972–989.

Moore, D. A., & Small, D. A. (2008). When it is rational for the majority to believe that they are better than average. In J. I. Krueger (Ed.), *Rationality and social responsibility: Essays in honor of Robyn Mason Dawes* (pp. 141–174). New York: Psychology Press.

Mussweiler, T., & Strack, F. (1999). Hypothesis-consistent testing and semantic priming in the anchoring paradigm: A selective accessibility model. *Journal of Experimental Social Psychology, 35*(2), 136–164.

Niederle, M., & Vesterlund, L. (2007). Do women shy away from competition? Do men compete too much? *Quarterly Journal of Economics, 122*(3), 1067–1101.

Norem, J. K., & Cantor, N. (1986). Defensive pessimism: Harnessing anxiety as motivation. *Journal of Personality and Social Psychology, 51*(6), 1208–1217.

Norem, J. K., & Illingworth, K. S. S. (1993). Strategy-dependent effects of reflecting on self and tasks: Some implications of optimism and defensive pessimism. *Journal of Personality and Social Psychology, 65*(4), 822–835.

Nussbaum, S., Liberman, N., & Trope, Y. (2006). Predicting the near and distant future. *Journal of Experimental Psychology: General, 135*(2), 152–161.

Odean, T. (1998). Volume, volatility, price, and profit when all traders are above average. *Journal of Finance, 53*(6), 1887–1934.

Pajares, F. (1996). Self-efficacy beliefs and mathematical problem-solving of gifted students. *Contemporary Educational Psychology, 21*, 325–344.

Paulhus, D. L., Harms, P. D., Bruce, M. N., & Lysy, D. C. (2003). The over-claiming technique: Measuring self-enhancement independent of ability. *Journal of Personality and Social Psychology, 84*(4), 890–904.

Paunonen, S. V. (1989). Consensus in personality judgments: Moderating effects of target–rater acquaintanceship and behavior observability. *Journal of Personality and Social Psychology, 56*(5), 823–833.

Perloff, L. S., & Brickman, P. (1982). False consensus and false uniqueness: Biases in perceptions of similarity. *Academic Psychology Bulletin, 4*(3), 475–494.

Plous, S. (1993). *The psychology of judgment and decision making.* New York: McGraw-Hill.

Presson, P. K., & Benassi, V. A. (1996). Illusion of control: A meta-analytic review. *Journal of Social Behavior & Personality, 11*(3), 493–510.

Pulford, B. D., & Colman, A. M. (1997). Overconfidence: Feedback and item difficulty effects. *Personality and Individual Differences, 23*(1), 125–133.

Radzevick, J. R., & Moore, D. A. (2008). Myopic biases in competitions. *Organizational Behavior & Human Decision Processes, 107*(2), 206–218.

Radzevick, J. R., & Moore, D. A. (2009a). Competing to be certain (but wrong): Social pressure and overprecision in judgment. Unpublished manuscript. Pittsburgh, PA: Carnege Mellon University.

Radzevick, J. R., & Moore, D. A. (2009b). Psychological processes in comparative judgment. Unpublished manuscript. Pittsburgh, PA: Carnege Mellon University.

Roese, N. J. (1999). Counterfactual thinking and decision making. *Psychonomic Bulletin & Review, 6*(4), 570–578.

Roese, N. J., & Olson, J. M. (1995). Counterfactual thinking: A critical overview. In N. J. Roese & J. M. Olson (Eds.), *What might have been: The social psychology of counterfactual thinking* (pp. 1–55). Mahwah, NJ: Lawrence Erlbaum.

Rosenberg, M. (1965). *Society and the adolescent self-image.* Princeton, NJ: Princeton University Press.

Ross, L., Greene, D., & House, P. (1977). The false consensus effect: An egocentric bias in social perception and attribution processes. *Journal of Experimental Social Psychology, 13*(3), 279–301.

Ross, M., McFarland, C., & Fletcher, G. J. (1981). The effect of attitude on the recall of personal histories. *Journal of Personality and Social Psychology, 40*(4), 627–634.

Sah, S., Moore, D. A., & MacCoun, R. J. (2009). Expertise, confidence, and persuasion. Unpublished manuscript. Pittsburgh, PA: Carnege Mellon University.

Sanbonmatsu, D. M., Shavitt, S., Sherman, S. J., & Roskos-Ewoldsen, D. R. (1987). Illusory correlation in the perception of performance by self or a salient other. *Journal of Experimental Social Psychology, 23*(6), 518–543.

Sanitioso, R., Kunda, Z., & Fong, G. T. (1990). Motivated recruitment of autobiographical memories. *Journal of Personality and Social Psychology, 59*(2), 229–241.

Santos-Pinto, L., & Sobel, J. (2005). A model of positive self-image in subjective assessments. *American Economic Review, 95*(5), 1386–1402.

Schaefer, P. S., Williams, C. C., Goodie, A. S., & Campbell, W. K. (2004). Overconfidence and the big five. *Journal of Research in Personality, 38*(5), 473–480.

Scheier, M. F., & Carver, C. S. (1993). On the power of positive thinking: The benefits of being optimistic. *Current Directions in Psychological Science, 2*(1), 26–30.

Scheier, M. F., & Carver, C. S. (2003). Self-regulatory processes and responses to health threats: Effects of optimism on well-being. In J. Suls & K. Wallston (Eds.), *Social psychological foundations of health and illness* (pp. 395–428). Oxford, UK: Blackwell.

Slovic, P. (2000). Rejoinder: The perils of Viscusi's analyses of smoking risk perceptions. *Journal of Behavioral Decision Making, 13*(2), 273–276.

Sniezek, J. A. (1990). A comparison of techniques for judgmental forecasting by groups with common information. *Group & Organizational Studies, 15*(1), 5–19.

Sniezek, J. A., & Buckley, T. (1991). Confidence depends on level of aggregation. *Journal of Behavioral Decision Making, 4*, 263–272.

Soll, J. B., & Klayman, J. (2004). Overconfidence in interval estimates. *Journal of Experimental Psychology: Learning, Memory, and Cognition, 30*(2), 299–314.

Stajkovic, A. D., & Luthans, F. (1998). Self-efficacy and work-related performance: A meta-analysis. *Psychological Bulletin, 124*(2), 240–261.

Stankov, L., & Crawford, J. D. (1996). Confidence judgments in studies of individual differences. *Personality and Individual Differences, 21*(6), 971–986.

Stankov, L., & Crawford, J. D. (1997). Self-confidence and performance on tests of cognitive abilities. *Intelligence, 25*(2), 93–109.

Stone, D. N. (1994). Overconfidence in initial self-efficacy judgments: Effects on decision processes and performance. *Organizational Behavior and Human Decision Processes, 59*(3), 452–474.

Stotz, O., & von Nitzsch, R. (2005). The perception of control and the level of overconfidence: Evidence from analyst earnings estimates and price targets. *Journal of Behavioral Finance, 6*(3), 121–128.

Strack, F., & Mussweiler, T. (1997). Explaining the enigmatic anchoring effect: Mechanisms of selective accessibility. *Journal of Personality and Social Psychology, 73*(3), 437–446.

Svenson, O. (1981). Are we all less risky and more skillful than our fellow drivers? *Acta Psychologica, 47*, 143–148.

Taylor, S. E., & Brown, J. D. (1988). Illusion and well-being: A social psychological perspective on mental health. *Psychological Bulletin, 103*(2), 193–210.

Taylor, S. E., Pham, L. B., Rivkin, I. D., & Armor, D. A. (1998). Harnessing the imagination: Mental simulation, self-regulation, and coping. *American Psychologist, 53*, 429–439.

Teigen, K. H., & Jorgensen, M. (2005). When 90% confidence intervals are 50% certain: On the credibility of credible intervals. *Applied Cognitive Psychology, 19*(4), 455–475.

Tenney, E. R., MacCoun, R. J., Spellman, B. A., & Hastie, R. (2007). Calibration trumps confidence as a basis for witness credibility. *Psychological Science, 18*(1), 46–50.

Tenney, E. R., Spellman, B. A., & MacCoun, R. J. (2008). The benefits of knowing what you know (and what you don't): How calibration affects credibility. *Journal of Experimental Social Psychology, 44*, 1368–1375.

Tesser, A. (1988). Toward a self-evaluation maintenance model of social behavior. In L. Berkowitz (Ed.), *Advances in experimental social psychology* (Vol. 21, pp. 181–227). New York: Guilford.

Thompson, S. C., Armstrong, W., & Thomas, C. (1998). Illusions of control, underestimations, and accuracy: A control heuristic explanation. *Psychological Bulletin, 123*(2), 143–161.

Thurstone, L. L. (1927). A law of comparative judgment. *Psychological Review, 34*, 273–286.

U.S. Small Business Administration. (2003). *Longitudinal Establishment and Enterprise Microdata*. Washington, DC: Office of Advocacy.

van den Steen, E. (2004). Rational overoptimism (and other biases). *American Economic Review, 94*(4), 1141–1151.

Viscusi, W. K. (1990). Do smokers underestimate risks? *Journal of Political Economy, 98*(6), 1253–1269.

Viscusi, W. K. (2000). Comment: The perils of qualitative smoking risk measures. *Journal of Behavioral Decision Making, 13*, 267–271.

Weinstein, N. D. (1980). Unrealistic optimism about future life events. *Journal of Personality and Social Psychology, 39*(5), 806–820.

Weinstein, N. D. (1982). Unrealistic optimism about susceptibility to health problems. *Journal of Behavioral Medicine, 5*(4), 441–460.

Weinstein, N. D. (1998). Accuracy of smokers' risk perceptions. *Annals of Behavioral Medicine, 20*(2), 135–140.

Williams, A. F. (2003). Teenage drivers: Patterns of risk. *Journal of Safety Research, 34*(1), 5–15.

Windschitl, P. D., Kruger, J., & Simms, E. (2003). The influence of egocentrism and focalism on people's optimism in competitions: When what affects us equally affects me more. *Journal of Personality and Social Psychology, 85*(3), 389–408.

Winman, A., Hansson, P., & Juslin, P. (2004). Subjective probability intervals: How to reduce overconfidence by interval evaluation. *Journal of Experimental Psychology: Learning, Memory, and Cognition, 30*(6), 1167–1175.

Woloshin, S., Schwartz, L. M., Black, W. C., & Welch, H. G. (1999). Women's perceptions of breast cancer risk: How you ask matters. *Medical Decision Making, 19*(3), 221–229.

Zarnoth, P., & Sniezek, J. A. (1997). The social influence of confidence in group decision making. *Journal of Experimental Social Psychology, 33*(4), 345–366.

Zenger, T. R. (1992). Why do employers only reward extreme performance? Examining the relationships among performance, pay, and turnover. *Administrative Science Quarterly, 37*, 198–219.

8

Conflict in Workgroups: Constructive, Destructive, and Asymmetric Conflict

Sonja Rispens
Eindhoven University of Technology

Karen A. Jehn
Melbourne Business School

THE CONFLICT DEBATE: PAST CONFLICT RESEARCH

When the concept of conflict emerged in the organizational literature, the general belief was that conflict could have only detrimental effects. This belief is apparent in the early definitions of conflict. For example, March and Simon (1958) defined conflict as a malfunction of standard working procedures. According to Rapoport (1960), conflict referred to nonrational fights fueled by aggressive feelings among individuals. Researchers suggested that organizational conflict leads to an imbalance in the cooperative system (e.g., Pondy, 1967). In the organizational decision-making literature, for example, researchers proposed that conflicts inhibited information search (e.g., Argyris, 1976). Empirical research supported this early negative outlook on conflict. Carnevale and Probst's (1998) study showed that conflicts interfere with group members' information processing because their cognitive load increases when group members are in conflict, and consequently members are performing worse than in situations without conflict. During conflicts, group members are likely to spend (or waste) time on ignoring, resolving, or fighting the conflict rather than focusing on the task. The research on intragroup conflict documents negative effects for effective group processes (e.g., Amason, 1996; Evan,

1965; Jehn, 1995), group performance (e.g., De Dreu & Weingart, 2003; Jehn, 1995; Li & Hambrick, 2005; Nibler & Harris, 2003; Pelled, 1997; Rau, 2005), and innovation (e.g., Matsuo, 2006). Furthermore, conflict leads to distrust (Deutsch, 1973; Pruitt & Rubin, 1986) and decreased satisfaction with the job and the workgroup (e.g., Amason, 1996; Jehn, 1995; Tjosvold, 1991). Similarly, Richter, West, van Dick, and Dawson (2006) examined intergroup collaborations and found that conflict between teams can be a source of lower productivity.

Despite the abundance of evidence and logical theoretical reasoning about the negative effects of conflict, extensive support exists for circumstances in which conflict can be a positive force in organizational workgroups. Coser (1956) theorized that conflict may contribute to establishing and maintaining individuals' identity and the relational boundaries of the involved parties In intergroup conflicts, the in-group cohesion is likely to increase. Furthermore, power balances are established and maintained, and allies or coalitions are created. Another potentially positive result of conflict is creativity (Deutsch, 1973). More recently, De Dreu (2006) suggested that moderate levels of conflict are positively related to innovation in teams. In the context of decision making, Amason's (1996) study showed that the quality of decisions made by top-management teams may benefit from conflict. Pelz and Andrews' (1966) findings from a survey among scientists indicated that high-performing scientists were those who had conflicts with colleagues about how to approach their task.

We define conflict as perceived incompatibilities by the involved parties (Boulding, 1963). Another way to solve the debate about whether conflict can be constructive is the typology in conflict type (task and relationship conflict; Jehn, 1995). Task conflicts are disagreements in workgroups regarding ideas and opinions about the task, for example, differing opinions regarding what information to include in a report (cf. Jehn & Rispens, 2008). Relationship conflicts, on the other hand, refer to disagreements and incompatibilities among group members about personal issues that are not related to the task, such as social events, gossip, and world news (cf. Jehn & Rispens, 2008).

In an attempt to solve this ongoing debate in the workgroup conflict literature, several meta-analyses have been conducted. De Dreu and Weingart (2003) conducted a meta-analysis on 30 studies and found that conflict was disruptive for team performance and team member satisfaction, irrespective of the type of conflict (i.e., task conflict vs. relationship conflict). More recently De Wit, Greer, and Jehn (2008) showed however that in about 40% of the studies investigating the conflict–performance relationship, a nonnegative relationship was found between task conflict and performance. Additional moderator analyses revealed that task conflict was less negatively related to performance in the case of more complex tasks and, in line with previous findings of De Dreu and Weingart (2003), when task conflict and relationship conflict were weakly, rather than strongly, correlated. Since these meta-analyses did not end the debate as to whether conflicts can be beneficial for workgroup functioning, we argue that we need to rethink the concept of workgroup conflict. In the following section we introduce the concept of conflict asymmetry—the dispersion of conflict perceptions in groups that, as recent empirical results suggest, seem to be a more plausible description of conflict on the group level of analysis.

ADDRESSING THE CONFLICT DEBATE: CONFLICT ASYMMETRY

Most group research in organizations assumes that groups possess *shared* team properties or that experiences and perceptions are commonly held by team members (Klein & Kozlowski, 2000; Mason, 2006) rather than by *configural* team properties, or properties that reflect the differences or dispersion in attitudes and perceptions among team members (Chan, 1998; Colquitt, Noe, & Jackson, 2002; Dineen, Noe, Shaw, Duffy, & Wiethoff, 2007; Klein & Kozlowski, 2000). Group research tends to assume that groups possess shared emotions (e.g., George, 1990; cf. Mason, 2006; Totterdell, Kellett, Teuchmann, & Briner, 1998), attitudes (e.g., Mason & Griffin, 2003), and perceptions (e.g., Cannon-Bowers, Salas, & Converse, 1993; Klimoski & Mohammed, 1994). This is surprising given the amount of research indicating that asymmetries of perceptions and experiences exist in groups. The view that there are different perceptions of the same reality has been the basis for much social cognition research (Bruner, 1957; Searle, 1997), social cognitive theory (cf. Bandura, 2001), as well as the social information processing approach (Salancik & Pfeffer, 1978) to explain the different experiences of individuals in organizations. For example, research on varying motivations in negotiations and experimental games shows that individuals attach different interpretations to the same situation (Liebrand, Jansen, Rijken, & Suhre, 1986; Sattler & Kerr, 1991; van Lange & Kuhlman, 1994). The literature on power suggests that individuals with different levels of power will have different experiences within a group during task performance (e.g., Galinsky, Magee, Inesi, & Gruenfeld, 2006; Guinote, Judd, & Brauer, 2002; Smith & Trope, 2006; for a review see Keltner, Gruenfeld, & Anderson, 2003), and the social network research investigates cognitive inconsistencies and dyadic asymmetries in relationships (Carley & Krackhardt, 1996; Casciaro, Carley, & Krackhardt, 1999). Thus, we suggest that conflict asymmetry, as a configural team property, has often been ignored in past conflict research (e.g., Amason, 1996; De Dreu & Weingart, 2003; Jehn, 1995; cf. Jehn & Rispens, 2008) and can substantially influence group and individual outcomes such as satisfaction with the team, absenteeism, and individual and group performance. We define conflict asymmetry as the degree to which group members differ in their perception of how much conflict there is in the group (Jehn, Rispens, & Thatcher, in press).

Group and Individual Conflict Asymmetry

Past research (e.g., Amason, 1996; De Dreu & Weingart, 2003; Jehn, 1995) has focused mainly on the *level* of conflict within a group—that is, how much conflict is experienced in the group, in general. In this chapter, we consider the general level of conflict within the group (e.g., task conflict, relationship conflict) but claim that perceptual asymmetry is equally if not more important, especially in solving the aspects of conflict that can lead to constructive or destructive outcomes. We propose two components of asymmetry: group conflict asymmetry and individual conflict asymmetry (Jehn et al., in press). In contrast to the general conflict level (or the aggregate level of conflict within the group), *group conflict asymmetry* is the degree to which group members differ in their perception of how much conflict there is in the group. This is the *dispersion*, or variation (Chan, 1998; Colquitt et al., 2002; Dineen et al., 2007; Klein & Kozlowski, 2000), of members' perceptions regarding conflict within the group. For example, while some members may not perceive any conflict within the group, others may perceive that there is a high level of conflict occurring within the group. *Individual conflict asymmetry* is an aspect of conflict asymmetry that refers to the direction

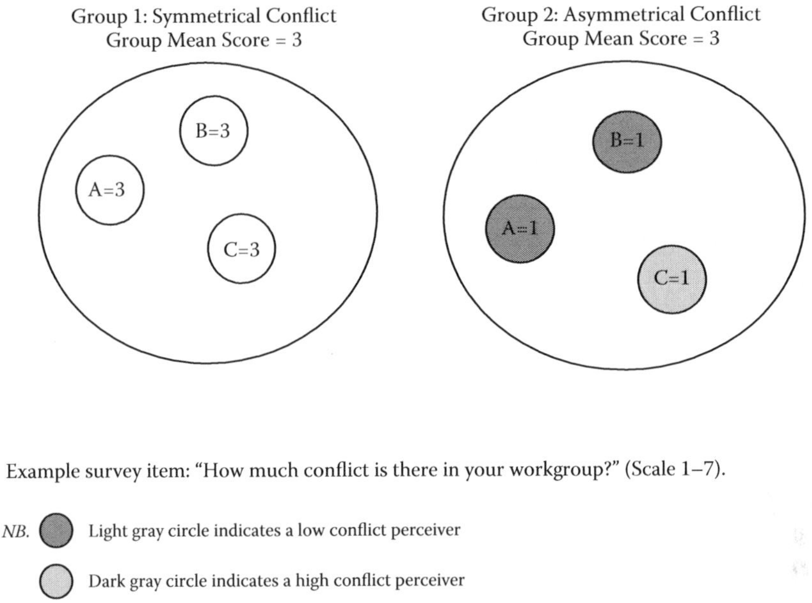

Group 1: Symmetrical Conflict
Group Mean Score = 3

Group 2: Asymmetrical Conflict
Group Mean Score = 3

B=3

A=3

C=3

B=1

A=1

C=1

Example survey item: "How much conflict is there in your workgroup?" (Scale 1–7).

NB. Light gray circle indicates a low conflict perceiver

Dark gray circle indicates a high conflict perceiver

FIGURE 8.1
Examples of conflict asymmetry. (Adapted from Jehn, K. A. & Rispens, S., in C. I. Cooper & J. Barlings (Eds.), *Handbook of organizational behavior, volume 1: Micro approaches.* Thousand Oaks, CA, Sage Publications Inc., 2008, p. 268. With permission.)

of the effect—that is, whether a member perceives more (or less) conflict than other group members. We call these members in the team high or low conflict perceivers (Figure 8.1).

We discuss how group and individual conflict asymmetry affect various group processes and group and individual outcomes. We will present the ultimate dependent variables, and then we go on discussing the mediating mechanisms (Figure 8.2). We chose to discuss specific group and individual outcomes such as performance, creativity, satisfaction with the team, and future behavioral intentions since these variables are important organizational outcomes (Balkundi & Harrison 2006; Barrick, Stewart, Neubert, & Mount, 1998; Hackman, 1987; Hackman & Wageman, 2005). In addition, the satisfaction of the individual members with the team and the members' intentions to continue working in the team are important in reducing absenteeism and turnover, which can be costly consequences with regard to lost productivity and increased training costs if new workgroup members need to be hired (Kacmar, Andrews, van Rooy, Steilberg, & Cerrone, 2006; Kozlowski & Ilgen, 2006; Mueller & Price, 1989; Sagie,

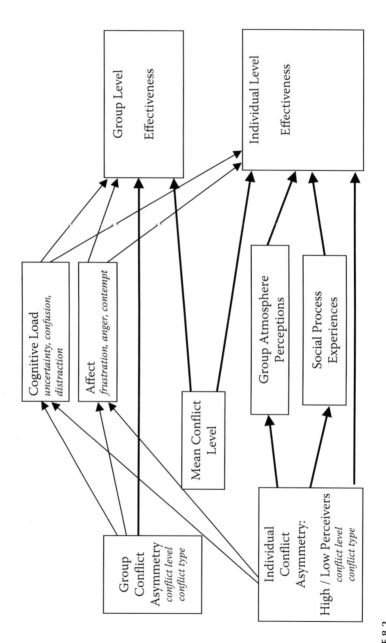

FIGURE 8.2
Research framework.

Birati, & Tziner, 2002; Staw, 1980). Researchers should ideally compare the results of the asymmetry studies we present with past studies that consider conflict a shared team property (cf. De Dreu & Weingart, 2003). As reflected in the results of past studies, conflict affects performance and satisfaction with the team via both relational and cognitive processes (De Dreu, 2008; De Dreu & Weingart, 2003; Jehn & Bendersky, 2003; Roseman, Wiest, & Swartz, 1994; Staw, Sandelands, & Dutton, 1981). In addition, research should also include dependent variables that have been understudied in conflict research yet are relevant for organizations. For instance, creativity in groups (the production of novel and useful ideas within a workgroup; see also Chapter 13 in this volume; Amabile, 1988; Pirola-Merlo & Mann, 2004) and future intentions may be important outcomes influenced by conflict and interpersonal tensions (e.g., Beersma & De Dreu, 2002; DeFillippi, Grabher, & Jones, 2007; Nemeth, Personnaz, Personnaz, & Goncalo, 2004; van Dyne, Jehn, & Cummings, 2002); however, they are not thoroughly studied in the conflict domain (for exceptions, see De Dreu, 2006). Similar to past outcomes examined in the conflict literature, these constructs are related to cognitive processing (creativity) and relational satisfaction (intention to remain).

Finally, we cover both group- and individual-level outcomes that we believe are specifically influenced by the asymmetric perceptions of group members. Therefore, based on theories regarding shared mental models and within-group agreement, we discuss how group performance and creativity will be influenced by the dispersion of conflict perceptions within the group (group conflict asymmetry) that interfere with cognitive processing and process gains (Amabile, 1988; Choi & Thompson, 2005; Klein, Conn, Smith, & Sorra, 2001; McGlynn, McGurk, Effland, Johll, & Harding, 2004; Nemeth et al., 2004; Steiner, 1972). In addition, at the individual level, satisfaction with the team, reports of individual performance, and intentions of a member to remain with the group will be influenced by members' perceptions of conflict relative to other group members (individual conflict asymmetry).

Theoretical Framework

Based on theories regarding social cognition, positive illusions, and social comparisons, we propose that these individual outcomes are influenced by the cognitive and motivational processes that may be inhibited by an individual's perception of conflict relative to other group members (Searle, 1997; Swann, 1999; Taylor & Brown, 1988, 1994). We discuss, therefore, the effects of conflict asymmetry, both at the individual and group levels, above and beyond the general aggregate level of conflict studied by past researchers. For instance, in a study of top-management teams and lower-level workgroups, Jehn and Chatman (2000) found that differences in member perceptions of conflict were detrimental to group functioning. In fact, the asymmetry of conflict perceptions was more detrimental than shared perceptions of high levels of conflict among all members. There are a number of theories that can inform us about why asymmetry is detrimental in workgroups: shared mental models, belief structures, and negotiation research. We now briefly describe each of these.

Shared mental models are cognitive structures that team members develop and share in which characteristics, duties, and needs of teammates are reflected (Mohammed, Klimoski, & Rentsch, 2000) as well as team member interactions and processes such as conflict (e.g., Cannon-Bowers et al., 1993; Thompson & Loewenstein, 2004). Groups can perform well if they share a common understanding of the information and goals of the group (Hinz, Tindale, & Vollrath, 1997) that is likely to enhance social integration (Dineen et al., 2007). Groups will then develop an organized structure of knowledge and duties that is both predictable (Mohammed et al., 2000) and accurate (Smith-Jentsch, Campbell, Milanovich, & Reynolds, 2001). If team members agree on experiences regarding group interactional processes, such as conflict, they are better able to accurately predict group interactions and therefore to cooperate more effectively toward a group goal.

The construct of collective cognition and negotiated beliefs is similar to that of shared mental models (Swaab, Postmes, van Beest, & Spears, 2007; Walsh, Henderson, & Deighton, 1988). Research in this tradition suggests that, although common perspectives or beliefs are most useful, within the same social setting individuals may differ in their experiences and views (Bandura, 1997). Klein et al. (2001), for example, show that group members indeed can differ in their perspective of the group interaction processes and how that affects the outcomes of the group. When team members hold different views of, for instance, the amount or level of conflict within the group, this is likely to decrease group performance due to ineffective discussions. Discussing a problem when some members may not even perceive that a problem might exist is difficult. Indeed, research has shown that if members of a group do not have the same perception about conflict, insurmountable communication problems inhibit the constructive resolution of the conflict (De Dreu, Kluwer, & Nauta, 2008; Kluwer & Mikula, 2002; Major, 1987). Groups perform better when members agree on the quality of their social interaction, even if the interaction is negative (Mason & Griffin, 2003).

The negotiation literature deals with differing views of conflict directly. During negotiations, parties involved often assume that they have opposing views of the conflict and desired outcome (De Dreu, Koole, & Steinel, 2000; Schelling, 1960), implying a fixed-pie bias ("If you win, I lose"; Bazerman & Neale, 1983; Thompson & Hastie, 1990). This assumption of differing views leads to suboptimal outcomes in negotiation settings due to inferior cooperation strategies (Bazerman, Curhan, Moore, & Valley, 2000; cf. De Dreu, 2008; Thompson & Hastie, 1990) and biased judgments about the accuracy of information (Carnevale & Pruitt, 1992; Thompson, 1990). When group members have differing views of the conflict (e.g., regarding motives or goals) this impedes the requisite information processing and exchange that lead to integrative and creative agreements (Neale & Bazerman, 1991). Integrative agreements are those in which *all* parties benefit without competing in a win–lose fashion (Thompson & Hastie, 1990). This is the essence of successful common-goal workgroups, our focus in this chapter—members must exchange and process information without competing to benefit the group as a whole. If groups have conflict asymmetry, this will impede the information exchange (i.e., idea generation, novel contributions; Choi & Thompson, 2005; Ford & Sullivan, 2004) necessary for high performance and group creativity (Amabile, 1988; Carnevale & Probst, 1998; Leenders, van Engelen, & Kratzer, 2003; Nemeth et al., 2004). Thus, by incorporating the information gleaned from negotiation dyadic-level research to the level of common-goal workgroups, we predict that asymmetry of conflict perceptions will lead to decreased information exchange and process loss that inhibits performance and creative outcomes for the group (Figure 8.2).

Research Framework

Studies on parties involved in conflict mediation have shown that symmetry leads to better dyadic outcomes than asymmetry (Jehn, Rupert, & Nauta, 2006; Jehn, Rupert, Nauta, & van den Bossche, 2008). To be more precise, these studies found that, when individuals perceive that they and their opponents experience different levels of conflict, the mediation experience was less likely to be successful. In addition, Jehn et al. (2006) suggest that individuals who perceived the mediator to be in favor of one party over the other were less satisfied and more often absent, indicating a second type of asymmetrical perceptions within the conflict mediation domain. In addition, laboratory studies have also shown that individuals who perceive conflict symmetry show more commitment, invest more effort, and perform higher than those who perceive conflict asymmetry (Jehn, De Wit, Barreto, & Rink, 2008).

Most of the current, but limited, literature on differences of conflict perceptions within groups (Jehn & Chatman, 2000; Jehn et al., 2006), to date, has focused mainly on general group asymmetry (dispersion of members' perceptions regarding conflict) and not on the individual directional effects (high vs. low perceivers) of conflict asymmetry. Recently, the concept of individual direction, or individual-level asymmetry, has also been added to the study of conflict asymmetry. This framework builds on cognitive psychology and argues that individuals have very different attitudes, reactions, and behaviors if they perceive *less* conflict than others in their group or if they perceive *more* (Jehn et al., in press). These results are consistent with arguments from self-verification theory (Swann, Milton, & Polzer, 2000; Swann, Polzer, Seyle, & Ko, 2004; Swann, Rentfrow, & Guinn, 2002) and the concept of positive illusions (Felson, 1984; Isen & Daubman, 1984; Taylor & Brown, 1988, 1994). The findings show that a member who perceives more conflict than the other group members is less satisfied, is less likely to believe he or she performs well, and is less likely to want to work in the group again. Attempting to resolve nonexistent conflicts (nonexistent, that is, to other group members) may lead to high levels of frustration and withdrawal consistent with self-verification predications (Swann, 1999), hence decreasing the individual's effort and satisfaction with the team. Self-verification theory even suggests that individuals would prefer to have *negative* views confirmed than to have others hold a more positive view (Giesler, Josephs, & Swann, 1996; Wiesenfeld, Swann, Brockner, & Bartel, 2007). While self-verification research has typically focused on verification of identities, characteristics, and beliefs about oneself, our research extends this to verification of a member's beliefs about the situation or experience one is having in the group and expectations that one's view will be verified.

Studies have also been conducted within other settings such as conflict asymmetry in marital relationships (Kluwer & Mikula, 2002) and negotiation settings (De Dreu et al., 2008). These studies focus on the asymmetrical *structure* of the conflict, which exists when one disputant wants to change the status quo whereas the other wants the situation to stay the same. These studies also point out that how conflicting parties perceive the conflict influences their conflict responses.

Asymmetrical conflict perceptions are also studied in dual-career couples and couples who commute to work (Jehn & Rispens, 2009). The results indicate that partners in intimate or romantic relationships may differ in their perceptions of the level of conflict. Moreover, spouses may even have asymmetrical perceptions of the *type* of conflict—for instance, when one partner perceives the conflict with her spouse to be related to the commute whereas the other thinks it regards the division of household tasks.

Mediators of Conflict Asymmetry and Group Outcomes

Why is it that asymmetric conflict workgroups perform less well than symmetric workgroups, regardless of the level of conflict? We suggest two categories of mediators that influence effects related to group functioning: group atmosphere and social processes. We then present two categories related to individual thinking and feeling that may explain the relationship between conflict asymmetry and outcomes.

Especially relevant, according to group researchers (e.g., Barrick, Bradley, Kristof-Brown, & Colbert, 2007; Jehn & Mannix, 2001; Marks, Mathieu, & Zaccaro, 2001), is the role that member attitudes and cognitions about the team (e.g., trust, commitment, respect) have on outcomes. Jehn and Mannix (2001), in their study of conflict in groups, examined the group atmosphere (attitudes members have about their workgroup environment) as distinct from social processes within groups (e.g., communication and cooperation). The concept of a group atmosphere was introduced earlier by Konar-Goldband, Rice, and Monkarsh (1979) to assess individuals' positive team attitudes. Group atmosphere is similar to the construct of group states, which was introduced by Marks et al. (2001) with the intent of clarifying how perceptions of the group environment (Mannix & Jehn, 2004; Nemeth et al., 2004; Tidd, McIntyre, & Friedman, 2004), in addition to social processes, influence group outputs. A group atmosphere can be assessed at any moment in the group's life (e.g., Jehn & Mannix, 2001; Konar-Golband et al., 1979) to predict individual-level outcomes. Jehn et al. (in press) argued that low-conflict perceivers feel more commitment toward the group and show higher levels of identification, increasing their satisfaction and reaching for group goals. Group members perceiving more conflict than others, on the other hand, may feel disrespected because their concerns are not validated by fellow group members, which is likely to increase negative affect and to decrease positive views of one's group and performance.

Social processes such as cooperation and communication among group members is the second set of mediators that we propose to mediate the effect of conflict asymmetry on group functioning (Figure 8.2). Perceiving more conflict than other group members inhibits involvement in effective group processes (Jehn et al., in press). Those who hold more negative views about the level of conflict will have a hard time perceiving others as cooperative and to respond effectively. Members who perceive more conflict than other group members are less likely to believe in the cooperation and communication of their fellow group members, which decreases their satisfaction with the team as well as their performance.

An empirical study by Jehn et al. (in press) investigated the effects of conflict asymmetry on group functioning on a sample of 51 workgroups in a controlled task environment. Jehn and colleagues examined the effects of conflict asymmetry on both group- and individual-level outcomes. The results show that conflict asymmetry negatively affects creativity, satisfaction, and performance. In addition, they find proof for mediation by social processes and a positive group atmosphere. In this study, social processes reflected interactions among members (i.e., communication and cooperation), whereas the group atmosphere reflected the attitudes of members about the environment within the group (i.e., trust, respect, and commitment).

Adding members' views of the group atmosphere (Figure 8.2) as a mediator of the relationship between asymmetrical conflict perceptions and outcomes in groups in addition to the social process experiences that are part of the traditional process-to-outcome (P-O) relationship within groups (Barrick et al., 2007; Gladstein, 1984; McGrath, 1964) allows researchers to provide a more thorough explanatory model of the effects of workgroup conflict on individuals in groups than past research (Lindenberg, 2006)—that is, examination of individual cognitions and motivations to specify and explain the mechanisms by which conflict asymmetry affects group functioning.

Another set of mediators focuses on individual psychological and affective states in asymmetric conflict situations and how they influence performance. Jehn and coauthors (in press) make a distinction between intraindividual cognitions (uncertainty, distraction, and confusion) and affective states (anger, frustration, and contempt). Regarding individuals' cognitions, when group members differ in their perception of the conflict, it is likely that this inhibits their accurate information processing and an integrative agreement will hardly be reached (Neale & Bazerman, 1991). Asymmetrical conflicts in workgroups are likely to influence individuals' feelings of uncertainty, level of distraction, as well as the level of confusion. Conflict asymmetry triggers uncertainty because individual group members are not able to predict the (conflict) situation accurately (Milliken, 1987). Conflict asymmetry in workgroups is a complex and highly cognitively demanding situation. When group members focus on the conflict about conflict, they are distracted from the task. Furthermore, it is likely that workgroup members when experiencing conflict asymmetry will feel confused. They are less able to think with their usual speed or clarity and have a hard time focusing their attention. Past research suggests that feelings of confusion interfere with the ability to make decisions and to increase individual attempts to disassociate from the group and the group task (Barinaga, 2007). Thus, group members may feel disassociated from their group and the group task.

In addition, conflict asymmetry is likely to be associated to affective states. When an individual experiences conflict but other group members act as if there is none, this can be a very frustrating experience. Specifically, when the individual experiencing conflict tries to explain his or her view to other group members and others do not verify the problem, frustration and angriness are expected to emerge. Over time, these feelings of anger may change into disgust (Fischer & Roseman, 2007) leading not just to a greater perceptual distance but also to a social distance between the conflict experiencer and the rest of the group.

CONTINGENCIES AND DIRECTIONS FOR FUTURE RESEARCH

Asymmetrical Perceptions and Recognition

One very fruitful area for future research is to investigate the extent to which conflict asymmetry is recognized by team members—that is, whether members are actually aware that they differ in their perceptions. In a recent study (Jehn et al., in press) the reported level of conflict was different for each member in a group. Thus, in further research, Jehn, Sanchez-Burks, and Peterson (2009) asked participants directly whether they believed others viewed more conflict than they did and found that individuals believe others to see the same level of conflict; hence, they do not recognize asymmetry in conflict perceptions. Differences of perceptions about conflict were enough to influence social processes, group atmosphere perceptions, and outcomes (Jehn et al., in press); however, research should examine if the effects increase or change when members are actually aware of the extent to which their views of conflict differ. If group members are aware of conflict perception differences, a discussion about their different views could allow them to reach agreement on the level of conflict and how to proceed. This could be very constructive for their group process and performance. However, if group members are not aware of differences in conflict perceptions they may feel more frustration, confusion, and a lack of verification that would lead to negative outcomes. Future research should investigate how the distinction between the basic presence of different perceptions and the awareness of difference perceptions influence members' behavior.

A different interesting direction for future research in line with the asymmetry perspective is how conflict transfers among group members (Felps, Mitchell, & Byington, 2006; Greer, 2008), and how status and power may affect this. For example, the power of one dissenter may influence the perceptions of other members regarding conflict. In Smith's (1989) discussion of the movement of conflict in organizations, he states that an individual involved in a conflict might actively recruit members to join in supporting his or her point of view regarding a conflict issue. This may be especially relevant when group members, trying to make sense of the conflict perceptions in a group, tend to gravitate toward the point of view espoused by a powerful member (Keltner et al., 2003). In this way, coalitions surrounding the level and perceptions of conflict may occur and activate dormant demographic faultlines within a group. Although researchers on faultlines have argued that conflict results from demographic subgroups (Lau & Murnighan, 1998; Thatcher, Jehn, & Zanutto, 2003), it is feasible that differing perceptions of conflict within a group may further exacerbate divisiveness among existing faultline subgroups (Bezrukova, Jehn, Zanutto, & Thatcher, 2009). If coalitions exist, members may experience conflict across the coalition-based subgroups but may not experience conflict within their subgroup. Furthermore, members who span subgroups may have very different perceptions, as would a solo member against a coalition. These specific forms of asymmetry of conflict perceptions in groups with faultlines and coalitions should be given further attention.

Physiological Explanations: Threat Versus Challenge

Another solution to the debate of whether conflict is constructive or destructive is to take into account the biopsychosocial model to consider whether people feel threatened or challenged by different types of conflict. A recent study by De Wit and Jehn (2009) builds upon the biopsychosocial model proposed by Blascovich and colleagues (e.g., Blascovich & Tomaka, 1996; Tomaka, Blascovich, Kelsey, & Leitten, 1993) and suggests that conflict has positive effects on team performance when the conflict is perceived and physiologically experienced as a challenge. Team members who perceive and feel conflict as a challenge feel motivated to discuss ideas and opinions as well as to consider different perspectives more comprehensively, which is likely to result in better team decisions and performance. In contrast, when conflict is perceived and experienced as a threat, team performance declines. Based on the empirical findings of the consequences of external threats (e.g., Rempel & Fisher, 1997; Staw et al., 1981), conflict may "freeze" team members, which means they avoid expressing their opinions and will not consider those of others (e.g., Janis, 1972). Thus, conflicts that induce threats fail to grasp the potential benefits of constructive discussions and are unlikely to improve a team's performance. Therefore, we suggest that a new avenue for research is to consider human physiology as a direction that can help solve the debate about whether conflict can ever be constructive for group and individual outcomes.

Conflict Perceptions: Power and Status

Extending the idea of asymmetric conflict perceptions, recent research tries to unravel how third parties perceive conflict situations. When people experience conflicts at work, they often consult a third party, either for advice or actual conflict intervention (Giebels & Janssen, 2005; Volkema, Farquhar, & Bergman, 1996). Given the results of recent studies that people seem to rarely agree on how much they fight (cf. Jehn & Rispens, 2008; Jehn et al., in press) or what their fights are about (Rispens, 2009; Simons & Peterson, 2000; Xin & Pelled, 2003), it is important to examine how third parties perceive conflict since they occupy a crucial role in the resolution or escalation of the conflict. Since third parties at work usually are either those in power positions (i.e., the boss, manager, or supervisor) or those equal in power (i.e., coworker or colleague), Rispens and Giebels (2009) examined whether these differences in power can predict how third parties perceive a mixed conflict situation and how they, consequently, intend to manage the conflict. Manipulating power by randomly assigning participants to a manager or a coworker role, the results of two experimental studies suggest that high-power third parties report significantly more socioemotional or relationship aspects of the conflict situation than third parties who were equal in power to those in conflict. In addition, high-power third parties are more likely to adopt a supportive conflict management style than equal-power third parties. Furthermore, these results are likely to be explained by differences between high- and equal-power third-parties' motivation to perform and motivation to think. Although preliminary, these results imply that perceptions and interpretations of the conflict, and consequent behavioral intentions (i.e., conflict management style), are dependent upon the structural position a third party occupies within the organization. Thus, we emphasize that one of the interesting avenues for future research on conflict in organizations is to unravel how conflict perceptions emerge, from the perspective of third parties as well as from the conflicting parties' perspectives. What roles play other situational variables as well as individual (e.g., dispositional) differences in forming conflict perceptions?

Moving Beyond Conflict

We stress that the concept of asymmetrical perceptions can be extended beyond the conflict realm. An early attempt is the study by Rispens

(2006) in which she investigated the effect of perceiving different levels of functional connectedness on individual and group performance in a small sample. Functional connectedness refers to the degree to which group members feel actively involved in their group regarding the work-flow among them (Rispens, Greer, & Jehn, 2007). The results suggest that a high deviation from the average perception of functional connectedness is associated with a decrease in performance and in-role behavior. In addition, Rispens and Kuipers (2006) examined how differences among members of self-managing teams regarding their perceptions of the team's autonomy affected team members' effectiveness. Their results suggest that when team members differ from the general opinion in the group, individuals' satisfaction with the team as well as their commitment to the team decreased. In sum, we urge researchers to investigate the important role of differences in perceptions that work group members may have regarding multiple aspects of teams, such as the within-group processes as well as regarding, for instance, the composition of the group (e.g., Homan & Humphrey, 2009).

CONCLUSION

We hope that we have shown how useful social and cognitive psychology are for organizational research, especially regarding asymmetric perceptions within workgroups. By introducing a perceptual view of conflict that takes into account the asymmetries of conflict perceptions within the group by considering multiple aspects of asymmetry (group and individual conflict asymmetry) to predict individual- and group-level outcomes, we extended previous research on intragroup conflict. Second, we provided an elaborate model of the effects of conflict by discussing group atmosphere perceptions and social processes as mediators of the relationship between asymmetrical conflict direction and outcomes. Furthermore, we argued that individual psychological and affective states are two other important mediating factors in explaining the effects of asymmetric conflict situations. Drawing on diverse literatures, we developed a multilevel model to explain the negative effect of conflict asymmetries on performance, creativity, member satisfaction with the team, and future intentions.

Regarding the negative effect of conflict asymmetries, we would like to stress that the research summarized in this chapter shows that it is better to *agree* that there are high levels of conflict—to have symmetry regarding the level of conflict in the group compared with disagreeing about the level of conflict (i.e., conflict asymmetry). Only when group members agree on the level of conflict is it possible to move on and try to resolve the conflict effectively (Jehn & Chatman, 2000; Jehn et al., in press). It is possible to prevent the emergence of conflict asymmetries within groups as research suggests that groups can be trained to correctly interpret the different types of conflict and how to deal with them, resulting in higher levels of performance (Rispens, Jehn, & Thatcher, 2005).

We hope to inspire future research to investigate asymmetric perceptions in groups regarding a variety of group processes and phenomena. While in different literatures (i.e., communication research, intergroup relations, social psychology, cognitive psychology) it is acknowledged that people may differ in their perception of a same situation, in group (conflict) research this has been largely ignored. Some researchers have indeed paid attention to this idea of dispersion in groups (e.g., Dineen et al., 2007; Klein & Kozlowski, 2000); however, these studies remain largely methodological. We think that group researchers should invest in creating new theories regarding asymmetrical perceptions in groups.

REFERENCES

Amabile, T. (1988). A model of creativity and innovation in organizations. In B. M. Staw & L. L. Cummings (Eds.), *Research in Organization Behavior* (Volume 10, pp. 123–167). Greenwich, CT: JAI Press.

Amason, A. (1996). Distinguishing the effects of functional and dysfunctional conflict on strategic decision making: Resolving a paradox for top management teams. *Academy of Management Journal, 39*, 123–148.

Argyris, C. (1976). Single loop and double loop models in research on decision making. *Administrative Science Quarterly, 21*, 363–375.

Balkundi, P., & Harrison, D.A. (2006). Ties, leaders, and time in teams: Strong inference about network structure's effects on team viability and performance. *Academy of Management Journal, 49,* 49–68.

Bandura, A. (1997). *Self-efficacy: The exercise of control.* New York: Freeman.

Bandura, A. (2001). Social cognitive theory: An agentic perspective. *Annual Review of Psychology, 52,* 1–26.

Barinaga, E. (2007). "Cultural diversity" at work: "National culture" as a discourse organizing an international project group. *Human Relations, 60,* 315–340.

Barrick, M. R., Bradley B. H., Kristof-Brown, A. L., & Colbert, A. E. (2007). The moderating role of top management team interdependence: Implications for real teams and working groups. *Academy of Management Journal, 50,* 544–557.

Barrick, M. R., Stewart, G. L., Neubert, M. J., & Mount, M. K. (1998). Relating member ability and personality to work–team processes and team effectiveness. *Journal of Applied Psychology, 83,* 377–391.

Bazerman, M. H., Curhan, J. R., Moore, D. A., & Valley, K. L. (2000). Negotiation. *Annual Review of Psychology, 51,* 279–314.

Bazerman, M. H., & Neale, M. (1983). Heuristics in negotiation: Limitations to effective dispute resolution. In M. H. Bazerman & R. Lewicki (Eds.), *Negotiating in organizations* (pp. 51–67). Beverly Hills, CA: Sage.

Beersma, B., & De Dreu, C. K. W. (2002). Integrative and distributive negotiation in small groups: Effects of task structure, decision rule, and social motive. *Organizational Behavior and Human Decision Processes, 87,* 227–252.

Bezrukova, K., Jehn, K. A., Zanutto, E. & Thatcher, S. M. B. (2009). Do workgroup faultlines help or hurt? A moderated model of faultlines, team identification, and group performance. *Organization Science, 20,* 35–50.

Blascovich, J., & Tomaka, J. (1996). The biopsychosocial model of arousal regulation. In M. P. Zanna (Ed.), *Advances in experimental social psychology* (Vol. 28, pp. 1–51). San Diego, CA: Academic Press.

Boulding, K. (1963). *Conflict and defense.* New York: Harper & Row.

Bruner, J. S. (1957). On perceptual readiness. *Psychological Review, 64,* 123–152.

Cannon-Bowers, J. A., Salas, E., & Converse, S. (1993). Shared mental models in expert team decision making. In N. J. Castellan, Jr. (Ed.), *Individual and group decision making: Current issues* (pp. 221–246). Hillsdale, NJ: Lawrence Erlbaum Associates Inc.

Carley, K. M., & Krackhardt, D. (1996). Cognitive inconsistencies and non-symmetric friendship. *Social Networks, 18,* 1–27.

Carnevale, P. J., & Probst, T. M. (1998). Social values and social conflict in creative problem solving and categorization. *Journal of Personality and Social Psychology, 74,* 1300–1309.

Carnevale, P. J., & Pruitt, D. G. (1992). Negotiation and mediation. *Annual Review of Psychology, 43,* 531–582.

Casciaro, T., Carley, K. M., & Krackhardt, D. (1999). Positive affectivity and accuracy in social network perception. *Motivation and Emotion, 23,* 285–306.

Chan, D. (1998). Functional relations among constructs in the same content domain at different levels of analysis: A typology of composition models. *Journal of Applied Psychology, 83,* 234–246.

Choi, H. S., & Thompson, L. (2005). Old wine in a new bottle: Impact of membership change on group creativity. *Organizational Behavior and Human Decision Processes, 98,* 121–132.

Colquitt, J. A., Noe, R. A., & Jackson, C. L. (2002). Justice in teams: Antecedents and consequences of procedural justice climate. *Personnel Psychology, 55,* 83–109.

Coser, L. (1956). *The functions of social conflict.* Glencoe, IL: Free Press.

De Dreu, C. K. W. (2006). When too little or too much hurts: Evidence for a curvilinear relationship between task conflict and innovation in teams. *Journal of Management, 32,* 83–107.

De Dreu, C. K. W. (2008). The virtue and vice of workplace conflict: Food for (pessimistic) thought. *Journal of Organizational Behavior, 29,* 5–18.

De Dreu, C. K. W., Kluwer, E., & Nauta, A. (2008). The structure and management of conflict: Fighting or defending the status quo. *Group Processes & Intergroup Relations, 11*, 331–353.

De Dreu, C. K. W., Koole, S. L., & Steinel, W. (2000). Unfixing the fixed pie: A motivated information-processing approach to integrative negotiation. *Journal of Personality and Social Psychology, 79*, 975–987.

De Dreu, C. K. W., & Weingart, L. R. (2003). Task versus relationship conflict, team performance, and team member satisfaction: A meta-analysis. *Journal of Applied Psychology, 88*, 741–749.

DeFillippi, R., Grabher, G., & Jones, C. (2007). Introduction to paradoxes of creativity: Managerial and organizational challenges in the cultural economy. *Journal of Organizational Behavior, 28*, 511–521.

Deutsch, M. (1973). *The resolution of conflict*. New Haven, CT: Yale University Press.

De Wit, F., Greer, L. L., & Jehn, K. A. (2008). The effects of team member diversity and conflict on team performance: A meta-analysis. Paper presented at the Association of Researchers in Work and Organizational Psychology, Heerlen, the Netherlands.

De Wit, F., & Jehn, K. A. (2009). Asymmetries in perceptions of conflict: The role of human physiology. Paper presented at the Academy of Management Conference, August, Chicago, IL.

Dineen, B.R., Noe, R. A., Shaw, J. D., Duffy, M. K., & Wiethoff, C. (2007). Level and dispersion of satisfaction in teams: Using foci and social context to explain the satisfaction–absenteeism relationship. *Academy of Management Journal, 50*, 623–643.

Evan, W. (1965). Conflict and performance in R&D organizations. *Industrial Management Review, 7*, 37–46.

Felps, W., Mitchell, T. R., & Byington, E. (2006). How, when, and why bad apples spoil the barrel: Negative group members and dysfunctional groups. *Research in Organizational Behavior, 27*, 175–222.

Felson, R. B. (1984). The effects of self-appraisals of ability on academic performance. *Journal of Personality and Social Psychology, 47*, 944–952.

Fischer, A. H., & Roseman, I. J. (2007). Beat them or ban them: The characteristics and social functions of anger and contempt. *Journal of Personality and Social Psychology, 93*, 103–115.

Ford, C., & Sullivan, D. M. (2004). A time for everything: How the timing of novel contributions influences project team outcomes. *Journal of Organizational Behavior, 25*, 279–292.

Galinsky, A. D., Magee, J. C., Inesi, M. E., & Gruenfeld, D. H. (2006). Power and perspectives not taken. *Psychological Science, 17*, 1068–1074.

George, J. M. (1990). Personality affect and behavior in groups. *Journal of Applied Psychology, 75*, 107–116.

Giebels, E., & Janssen, O. (2005). Conflict stress and reduced wellbeing at work: The buffering effect of third-party help. *European Journal of Work and Organizational Psychology, 14*, 137–155.

Giesler, R. B., Josephs, R. A., & Swann, W. B. (1996). Self-verification in clinical depression. *Journal of Abnormal Psychology, 105*, 358–368.

Gladstein, D. L. (1984). Groups in context: A model of task group effectiveness. *Administrative Science Quarterly, 29*, 499–517.

Greer, L. L. (2008). *Team composition and conflict: The role of the individual in small group research*. Unpublished doctoral dissertation, Leiden University, the Netherlands.

Guinote, A., Judd, C. M., & Brauer, M. (2002). Effects of power on perceived and objective group variability: Evidence that more powerful groups are more variable. *Journal of Personality and Social Psychology, 82*, 708–721.

Hackman, J. R. (1987). The design of work teams. In J. W. Lorsch (Ed.), *Handbook of organizational behavior* (pp. 315–342). Englewood Cliffs, NJ: Prentice-Hall.

Hackman, J. R., & Wageman, R. (2005). A theory of team coaching. *Academy of Management Review, 30*, 269–287.

Hinz, V. B., Tindale, R. S., & Vollrath, D. A. (1997). The emerging conception of groups as information processors. *Psychological Bulletin, 121*, 43–64.

Homan, A. C., & Humphrey, S. E. (2009). The role of one's position in diverse teams on perceptions of anticipated action. Paper presented at the Academy of Management Conference, August, Chicago, IL.

Isen, A., & Daubman, K. (1984). The influence of affect on categorization. *Journal of Personality and Social Psychology, 47*, 1206–1217.

Janis, I. (1972). *Victims of groupthink*. Boston: Houghton-Mifflin.

Jehn, K. A. (1995). A multimethod examination of the benefits and detriments of intragroup conflict. *Administrative Science Quarterly, 40*, 256–282.

Jehn, K. A., & Bendersky, C. (2003). Intragroup conflict in organizations: A contingency perspective on the conflict-outcome relationship. *Research in Organizational Behavior, 25*, 187–242.

Jehn, K. A., & Chatman, J. A. (2000). The influence of proportional and perceptual conflict composition on team performance. *International Journal of Conflict Management, 11*, 56–73.

Jehn, K. A., De Wit, F. R. C., Barreto, M., & Rink, F. (2008). Conflict asymmetries: Effects on motivation, attitudes, and performance. Paper presented at the International Association for Conflict Management, Chicago, IL.

Jehn, K. A., & Mannix, E. (2001). The dynamic nature of conflict: A longitudinal study of intragroup conflict and group performance. *Academy of Management Journal, 44*, 238–251.

Jehn, K. A., & Rispens, S. (2008). Conflict in workgroups. In C. L. Cooper & J. Barlings (Eds.), *The Sage Handbook of organizational behavior, volume 1: Micro approaches* (pp. 262–276). Thousand Oaks, CA: Sage Publications Inc.

Jehn, K. A., & Rispens, S. (2009). Conflict asymmetry in commuting couples. Paper presented at FACE 2 Conference, December 2009 (London, UK).

Jehn, K. A., Rispens, S., & Thatcher, S. M. B. (in press). The effects of conflict asymmetry on workgroup and individual outcomes. *Academy of Management Journal*.

Jehn, K. A., Rupert, J., & Nauta, A. (2006). The effects of conflict asymmetry on mediation outcomes: Satisfaction, work motivation and absenteeism. *International Journal of Conflict Management, 17*, 96–109.

Jehn, K. A., Rupert, J., Nauta, A., & van den Bossche, S. (2008). Crooked conflicts: The effects of conflict asymmetry in mediation. Paper submitted for publication.

Jehn, K. A., Sanchez-Burks, J., & Peterson, R. S. (2009). Conflict asymmetry reactions in workgroups. Working paper. Melbourne Business School.

Kacmar, K. M., Andrews, M. C., van Rooy, D. L., Steilberg, R. C., & Cerrone, S. (2006). Sure everyone can be replaced ... but at what cost? Turnover as a predictor of unit-level performance. *Academy of Management Journal, 49*, 133–144.

Keltner, D., Gruenfeld, D. H., & Anderson, C. (2003). Power, approach, and inhibition. *Psychological Review, 110*, 265–284.

Klein, K. J., Conn, A. B., Smith, D. B., & Sorra, J. S. (2001). Is everyone in agreement? An exploration of within-group agreement in employee perceptions of the work environment. *Journal of Applied Psychology, 86,* 3–16.

Klein, K., & Kozlowski, S. (2000). *Multilevel theory, research and methods in organizations.* San Francisco: Jossey-Bass.

Klimoski, R. J., & Mohammed, S. (1994). Team mental model: Construct or metaphor? *Journal of Management, 20,* 403–437.

Kluwer, E. S., & Mikula, G. (2002). Gender-related inequalities in the division of family work in close relationships: A social psychological perspective. *European Review of Social Psychology, 13,* 185–216.

Konar-Goldband, E., Rice, R. W., & Monkarsh, W. (1979). Time-phased interrelationships of group atmosphere, group performance, and leader style. *Journal of Applied Psychology, 64,* 401–409.

Kozlowski, S. W. J., & Ilgen, D. R. (2006). Enhancing the effectiveness of work groups and teams. *Psychological Science in the Public Interest,* 777–124.

Lau, D., & Murnighan, J. K. (1998). Demographic diversity and fautlines: The compositional dynamics of organizational groups. *Academy of Management Review, 23,* 325–310.

Leenders, R. T., van Engelen, J., & Kratzer, J. (2003). Virtuality, communication, and new product team creativity: A social network perspective. *Journal of Engineering and Technology Management, 20,* 69–92.

Li, J., & Hambrick, D. C. (2005). Factional groups: A new vantage on demographic faultlines, conflict, and disintegration in work teams. *Academy of Management Journal, 48,* 794–813.

Liebrand, W. B. G., Jansen, R. W. T. L., Rijken, V. M., & Suhre, C. J. M. (1986). Might over morality: Social values and the perception of other players in experimental games. *Journal of Experimental Social Psychology, 22,* 203–215.

Lindenberg, S. (2006). How social psychology can build bridges to the social sciences by considering motivation, cognition, and constraints simultaneously. In P. A. M. van Lange (Ed.), *Bridging social psychology: Benefits of transdisciplinary approaches* (pp.151–157). Hillsdale, NJ: Erlbaum.

Major, B. (1987). Gender, justice, and the psychology of entitlement. In P. Shaver & C. Hendricks (Eds.), *Review of personality and social psychology* (Vol. 7, pp. 124–148). Newbury Park, CA: Sage.

Mannix, E., & Jehn, K. A. (2004). Let's storm and norm but not right now: Integrating models of group development and performance. In E. Mannix, M. Neale, & S. Blount (Eds.), *Research on managing groups and teams: Temporal issues* (Vol. 6, pp. 11–38). New York: Elsevier.

March, J., & Simon, H. (1958). *Organizations.* New York: Wiley.

Marks, M. A., Mathieu, J. E., & Zaccaro, S. J. (2001). A temporally based framework and taxonomy of team processes. *Academy of Management Review, 26,* 356–376.

Mason, C. M. (2006). Exploring the processes underlying within-group homogeneity. *Small Group Research, 37,* 233–270.

Mason, C. M., & Griffin, M. A. (2003). Identifying group task satisfaction at work. *Small Group Research, 34,* 413–442.

Matsuo, M. (2006). Customer orientation, conflict, and innovativeness in Japanese sales departments. *Journal of Business Research, 59,* 242–250.

McGlynn, R. P., McGurk, D., Effland, V. S., Johll, N. L., & Harding, D. J. (2004). Brainstorming and task performance in groups constrained by evidence. *Organizational Behavior and Human Decision Processes, 93,* 75–87.

McGrath, J. E. (1964). *Social psychology: A brief introduction.* New York: Holt Rinehart & Winston.

Milliken, F. J. (1987). Three types of perceived uncertainty about the environment: State, effect, and response uncertainty. *Academy of Management Review, 12,* 133–143.

Mohammed, S., Klimoski, R., & Rentsch, J. R. (2000). The measurement of team mental models: We have no shared schema. *Organizational Research Methods, 3,* 123–165.

Mueller, C. W., & Price, J. L. (1989). Some consequences of turnover: A work unit analysis. *Human Relations, 42,* 389–402.

Neale, M. A., & Bazerman, M. H. (1991). *Cognition and rationality in negotiation.* New York: Free Press.

Nemeth, C. J., Personnaz, B., Personnaz, M., & Goncalo, J. A. (2004). The liberating role of conflict in group creativity: A study in two countries. *European Journal of Social Psychology, 34,* 365–374.

Nibler, R., & Harris, K. L. (2003). The effects of culture and cohesiveness on intragroup conflict and effectiveness. *Journal of Social Psychology, 143,* 613–631.

Pelled, L. H. (1997). Relational demography and perceptions of group conflict and performance: A field investigation. *International Journal of Conflict Resolution, 22*(1), 54–67.

Pelz, D. C., & Andrews, F. M. (1966). *Scientists in organizations: Productive climates for research and development.* New York: Wiley.

Pirola-Merlo, A., & Mann, L. (2004). The relationship between individual creativity and team creativity: Aggregating across people and time. *Journal of Organizational Behavior, 25,* 235–257.

Pondy, L. R. (1967). Organizational conflict: Concepts and models. *Administrative Science Quarterly, 12,* 296–320.

Pruitt, D., & Rubin, J. (1986). *Social conflict: Escalation, stalemate and settlement.* New York: Random House.

Rapoport, A. (1960). *Fights, games, and debates.* Ann Arbor: University of Michigan Press.

Rau, D. (2005). The influence of relationship conflict and trust on the transactive memory. *Small Group Research, 36*(6), 746–771.

Rempel, M. W., & Fisher, R. J. (1997). Perceived threat, cohesion, and group problem solving in intergroup conflict. *International Journal of Conflict Management, 8,* 216–234.

Richter, A. W., West, M. A., van Dick, R., & Dawson, J. F. (2006). Boundary spanners' identification, intergroup contact, and effective intergroup relations. *Academy of Management Journal, 49,* 1252–1269.

Rispens, S. (2006). *Multiple interdependencies and workgroup effectiveness.* Unpublished doctoral dissertation, Leiden University, the Netherlands.

Rispens, S. (2009). When conflicts don't escalate: The influence of conflict characteristics on the co-occurence of task and relationship conflict in teams. Manuscript submitted for publication.

Rispens, S., & Giebels, E. (2009). Making sense of he said she said: The influence of power on 3rd parties' conflict perceptions. Paper presented at the Academy of Management Conference, August, Chicago, IL.

Rispens, S., Greer, L. L., & Jehn, K. A. (2007). It could be worse: A study on the alleviating roles of trust and connectedness in intragroup conflict. *International Journal of Conflict Management, 18,* 325–344.

Rispens, S., Jehn, K. A., & Thatcher, S. M. B. (2005). Creating constructive task conflict: Reward structures and group process training. Paper presented at the International Association for Conflict Management, Seville, Spain.

Rispens, S., & Kuipers, B. S. (2006). The dark side of different autonomy perceptions in SMWTs. Paper presented at the 10th International Workshop on Teamworking, September, Groningen, the Netherlands.

Roseman, I. J., Wiest, C., & Swartz, T. S. (1994). Phenomenology, behaviors, and goals differentiate discrete emotions. *Journal of Personality & Social Psychology, 67*, 206–221.

Sagie, A., Birati, A., & Tziner, A. (2002). Assessing the costs of behaviorial and psychological withdrawal: A new model and an empirical illustration. *Applied Psychology: An International Review, 51*, 67–89.

Salancik, G. R., & Pfeffer, J. (1978). A social information processing approach to job attitudes and task design. *Administrative Science Quarterly, 23*, 224–253.

Sattler, D. N., & Kerr, N. L. (1991). Might versus morality explored: Motivational and cognitive bases for social motives. *Journal of Personality and Social Psychology, 60*, 756–765.

Schelling, T. C. (1960). *The strategy of conflict.* Boston: Harvard University Press.

Searle, J. R. (1997). Précis of the construction of social reality. *Philosophy and Phenomenological Research, 57*, 427–428.

Simons, T. L., & Peterson, R. S. (2000). Task conflict and relationship conflict in top management teams: The pivotal role of intragroup trust. *Journal of Applied Psychology, 85*, 102–111.

Smith, K. K. (1989). The movement of conflict in organizations: The joint dynamics of splitting and triangulation. *Administrative Science Quarterly, 34*, 1–20.

Smith, P. K., & Trope, Y. (2006). You focus on the forest when you're in charge of the trees: Power priming and abstract information processing. *Journal of Personality and Social Psychology, 90*, 578–596.

Smith-Jentsch, K. A., Campbell, G. E., Milanovich, D. M., & Reynolds, A. M. (2001). Measuring teamwork mental models to support training needs assessment, development, and evaluation: Two empirical studies. *Journal of Organizational Behavior, 22*, 179–194.

Staw, B. M. (1980). The consequences of turnover. *Journal of Occupational Behavior, 1*, 253–273.

Staw, B. M., Sandelands, L. E., & Dutton, J. E. (1981). Threat-rigidity effects in organizational behavior: A multilevel analysis. *Administrative Science Quarterly, 26*, 501–524.

Steiner, I. D. (1972). *Group process and productivity.* New York: Academic Press.

Swaab, R., Postmes, T., van Beest, I., & Spears, R. (2007). Shared cognition as a product of, and precursor to, shared identity in negotiations. *Personality and Social Psychology Bulletin, 33*, 187–199.

Swann, W. B., Jr. (1999). *Resilient identities: Self, relationships, and the construction of social reality.* New York: Basic Books.

Swann, W. B., Jr., Milton, L. P., & Polzer, J. T. (2000). Should we create a niche or fall in line? Identity negotiation and small group effectiveness. *Journal of Personality and Social Psychology, 79*, 238–250.

Swann, W. B., Jr., Polzer, J. T., Seyle, D. C., & Ko, S. J. (2004). Finding value in diversity: Verification of personal and social self-views in diverse groups. *Academy of Management Review, 29*, 9–27.

Swann, W. B., Jr., Rentfrow, P. J., & Guinn, J. (2002). Self-verification: The search for coherence. In M. Leary & J. Tanney (Eds.), *Handbook of self and identity* (pp. 367–383). New York: Guilford.

Taylor, S. E., & Brown, J. D. (1988). Illusion and well-being: A social psychological perspective on mental health. *Psychological Bulletin, 103*, 193–210.

Taylor, S. E., & Brown, J. D. (1994). Positive illusions and well-being revisited separating fact from fiction. *Psychological Bulletin, 116*, 21–27.

Thatcher, S. M. B., Jehn, K. A., & Zanutto, E. (2003). Cracks in diversity research: The effects of diversity faultlines on conflict and performance. *Group Decision and Negotiation, 12*, 217–241.

Thompson, L. (1990). Negotiation behavior and outcomes: Empirical evidence and theoretical issues. *Psychological Bulletin, 108*, 515–532.

Thompson, L., & Hastie, R. (1990). Social perception in negotiation. *Organizational Behavior and Human Decision Processes, 47*, 98–123.

Thompson, L., & Loewenstein, J. (2004). Mental models of negotiations. In M. A. Hogg & J. Cooper (Eds.), *Sage handbook of social psychology* (pp. 494–511). Thousand Oaks, CA: Sage.

Tidd, S. T., McIntyre, H. H., & Friedman, R. A. (2004). The importance of role ambiguity and trust in conflict perception: Unpacking the task conflict to relationship conflict linkage. *International Journal of Conflict Management, 15*, 364–380.

Tjosvold, D. (1991). *The conflict-positive organization: Stimulate diversity and create unity.* Reading, MA: Addison-Wesley.

Tomaka, J., Blascovich, J., Kelsey, R. M., & Leitten, C. L. (1993). Subjective, physiological, and behavioral effects of threat and challenge appraisal. *Journal of Personality and Social Psychology, 65*, 248–260.

Totterdell, P., Kellett, S., Teuchmann, K., & Briner, R. (1998). Evidence of mood linkage in work groups. *Journal of Personality and Social Psychology, 74*, 1504–1515.

van Dyne, L., Jehn, K. A., & Cummings, A. (2002). Pink collar stress: Employee performance, creativity, and satisfaction in hair salons. *Journal of Organizational Behavior, 23*, 57–74.

van Lange, P. A. M., & Kuhlman, D. M. (1994). Social value orientations and impressions of partner's honesty and intelligence: A test of the might versus morality effect. *Journal of Personality and Social Psychology, 67*, 126–141.

Volkema, R. J., Farquhar, K., & Bergman, T. J. (1996). Third-party sensemaking in interpersonal conflicts at work: A theoretical framework. *Human Relations, 49*, 1437–1454.

Walsh, J. P., Henderson, C. M., & Deighton, J. (1988). Negotiated belief structures and decision performance: An empirical investigation. *Organizational Behavior and Human Decision Processes, 42*, 194–216.

Wiesenfeld, B. M., Swann, W. B., Brockner, J., & Bartel, C. A. (2007). Is more fairness always preferred? Self-esteem moderates reactions to procedural justice. *Academy of Management Journal, 50*, 1235–1253.

Xin, K. R., & Pelled, L. H. (2003). Supervisor–subordinate conflict and perceptions of leadership behavior: A field study. *Leadership Quarterly, 14*, 25–40.

9

The Repair of Trust: Insights From Organizational Behavior and Social Psychology

Kurt T. Dirks
Olin Business School, Washington University in St. Louis

David De Cremer
Rotterdam School of Management

Trust has become one of the central concepts of interest within organizational behavior. Kramer (1999) noted the dramatic surge of interest in the concept of trust from organizational behavior scholars, observing that it moved "from bit player to center stage in contemporary organizational theory and research" (p. 594). One decade later this interest appears to be unabated, although the questions being asked have changed to reflect the growth in theoretical knowledge and new problems in business and society.

Within this time period, organizational scholars have examined an array of questions about the concept of trust, including its nature, how it affects the functioning of groups and organizations, and how it develops. Given its central role in many behavioral phenomena it has been discussed in multiple literatures including economics, sociology, and psychology, to name a few. As we discuss in this chapter, social psychology has played a particularly critical role in the development of knowledge about trust. In particular, we focus on how it is informing a new and important question in the literature: how trust is repaired once broken. Before turning to this issue, however, we review research that has discussed the role that trust plays in facilitating effectiveness of individuals and groups. This work helps to understand not only why the literature on trust has been of significant interest but also why the topic of trust repair is important. The chapter summarizes our own perspectives and research on these issues, but we also draw liberally from work of other scholars.

WHY TRUST MATTERS

A fundamental problem in organizational behavior is that individuals often benefit by or are forced to rely on and cooperate with others, such as coworkers, group members, and leaders. However, uncertainty about the motives and behavior of these parties often hinders their willingness to do so. Trust—a psychological state regarding the confidence one has in the relationship with the party or character of that party—is believed to be one of the factors that can help address this issue (Rousseau, Sitkin, Burt, & Camerer, 1998). It is because it resolves this fundamental problem that trust has been of such great interest.

Empirical research has revealed that the benefits are real for groups and individuals. Dirks and Ferrin (2002) conducted a meta-analysis that summarizes the research over the past four decades on the implications of trusting one's leader. They report that trust in leadership had a significant relationship with individual outcomes including job performance ($r = .16$), organizational citizenship behavior (altruism, $r = .19$), turnover intentions ($r = -.40$), job satisfaction ($r = .51$), organizational commitment ($r = .49$), and a commitment to the leader's decisions ($r = .24$). Data from the samples were drawn from a variety of contexts ranging from financial institutions to manufacturing firms to military units to public institutions.

Recent experimental social psychology research has further demonstrated that trusting others promotes cooperation in mixed-motive situations such as social dilemmas (De Cremer, Snyder, & Dewitte, 2001). These authors showed that trusting others promotes cooperation in social dilemmas because it indicates that one believes that the others do not have to be monitored in their behavior. In other words, high trust promotes cooperation because it reduces fear to be exploited. Other research also showed that trust in leaders can be promoted by enacting fair procedures (De Cremer, 2004) and, even more so, that decision-making procedures such as giving voice to followers can promote cooperation directly if these followers trust the enacting leader to take care of their interests (De Cremer

& Tyler, 2007). Thus, trusting others reveals positive consequences for group processes such as cooperation and procedural decision making.

Not only is being able to trust others important, but the benefits may be even greater for individuals when they are trusted. For example, Dirks and Skarlicki (2009) proposed that to the extent that individuals were seen as trustworthy in terms of both competence and integrity (i.e., both are necessary), the more likely they were to be sought after as exchange partners (e.g., individuals whom to share valuable information and resources with) and hence the better they would perform. Data from a field study and an experiment provided support for these ideas and controlled for the effects of trusting others (the previously described effort).

While trust has important consequences for individuals, it may be equally or more important for groups as illustrated in Dirks's (2000) study of NCAA basketball teams. Using survey data from players collected early in the season, and statistically adjusting for other potential determinants of team performance (i.e., player talent and tenure, coach experience and record, preseason performance, performance in prior years, and trust between team members), trust in head coach (team leader) accounted for almost 7% of the variance in winning percentage. Trust in team members can also be important. For example, Dirks (1999) found that when team members trusted each other, they channeled their efforts toward group goals as opposed to individual goals. As a result, trust among team members facilitated performance of the team (also see De Jong & Elfring, in press).

In sum, although trust can have downsides (Langfred, 2004) there is ample evidence that trust often brings benefits for the trustors, trustees, and the groups of which they are members.

THE REPAIR OF TRUST

These benefits will quickly disappear, however, when trust is broken by a transgression by a party. In other words, individuals may engage in negative actions that call into question their trustworthiness. When this happens, not only are trustors hurt by the violation, but trustees are also likely to forego benefits associated with future exchanges that would require trust.

Unfortunately, the damage to trust is not an uncommon situation. Over the past few years, the news has been replete with examples of business leaders who engaged in acts that call into question their integrity or their competence. Indeed, one recent poll found that when it came to dealing with the economy business leaders were less trusted than politicians (CNN/Opinion Research Corporation, 2009). Although the phenomenon may be particularly acute at present, evidence suggests that the problem has been long-standing. For example, a 2002 poll revealed that only 39% of employees reported trusting senior leaders of their firms (Watson Wyatt, 2007). In earlier research, Robinson and Rousseau (1994) found that 55% of employees reported that their employers violated their psychological contract with the firm, resulting in a drop in trust. There is some evidence that this extends to relationships between employees, as Conway and Briner (2002) reported frequent perceived violations between employees.

This issue might be less alarming if trust were easy to repair. Unfortunately, once broken, trust is notoriously difficult to repair (Lount, Zhong, Sivanathan, & Murnighan, 2008; Schweitzer, Hershey, & Bradlow, 2006), as epitomized by Publius's adage that "trust, like the soul, never returns once it is gone."

The importance of trust, the fact that is not uncommon for it to be broken, and the apparent challenge of trying to repair it once it is broken present an intriguing and important challenge for organizational behavior researchers. For example, in their reflections on the literature on trust, Schoorman, Mayer, and Davis (2007) asserted that the topic of repair was one of the most important but understudied problems. Revealing this interest, the *Academy of Management Review* devoted a special topics forum to the topic of relationship repair to help establish a conceptual foundation for this work (Dirks, Lewicki, & Zaheer, 2009). Trust repair was one of the fundamental aspects of relationship repair on which this issue focused, along with restoring positive exchange and managing negative affect.

A small, but growing, body of literature focused on this topic has emerged in recent years. As we describe in this chapter, social psychology has contributed much to this line of work. In particular, there are three different theoretical processes being advanced for the trust repair that derive from social psychology: attributional, social equilibrium, and the negotiation of trustworthiness. The three perspectives on trust repair are summarized and compared in Table 9.1. We discuss each one in turn.

TABLE 9.1

Perspectives on Trust Repair

	Attributional	**Social Equilibrium**	**Negotiation of Trustworthiness**
Perspective	Transgression leads to loss of trust through attribution process. Repair involves cognitive processes by which trust is restored.	Transgression leads to disequilibrium in relationship and social context. Repair involves social processes by which equilibrium in relationship is restored.	Loss of trust due to transgression is important concern for both trustor and trustee. Repair involves both parties engaging in actions to arrive at attribution.
Assumption	Individual differences of actor (trustworthiness) are primary determinant of behavior. Therefore, perceivers are motivated to draw attributions and targets are motivated to shape those attributions.	Individuals desire to have equilibrium in norms and social relationships.	Following a violation, (a) trustees want to be considered trustworthy, (b) trustors are predisposed to believe that greater trust is not deserved, and (c) trustors and trustees attempt to resolve discrepant beliefs through dynamic process.
Implications for repair strategies and tactics	Targets will try to shape perceivers' attributions about whether they committed transgression, whether it reflects on their true nature, or whether they experienced redemption.	Target will engage in appropriate social rituals to restore equilibrium in standing and norms.	Trustees will take actions to establish trustworthiness, and trustors will resist.
Examples of articles	Kim et al. (2004, 2006) Schweitzer et al. (2006) Tomlinson and Mayer (2009)	Bottom et al. (2002) Desmet et al. (2008)	Kim et al. (2009)

Attributions and Trust Repair

Perhaps the most commonly used perspective focuses on the attributional processes that occur when the trustor perceives another to have committed a transgression. Specifically, this perspective suggests that a transgression provides negative information, which the perceiver uses to draw a negative inference about the traits and intentions of the trustee (e.g., the trustee is untrustworthy) and is thus unwilling to be vulnerable in the future. This perspective operates on the assumption that individual factors of trustworthiness—such as competence, integrity, or benevolence (Mayer, Davis, & Schoorman, 1995)—are key determinants of trustworthy behavior. Thus, according to this idea repair must involve revising upward the negative attribution made by the trustor.

A straightforward prediction from this perspective would be that, to offset negative attribution, trustees should provide positive information about themselves on the relevant dimension. However, a review of the research literature, and observations in practice, indicated that trustees actually used a variety of strategies involving positive and negative information and that they each could be successful. For example, some discussions suggest that trust may be repaired more successfully if mistrusted parties provide positive information about their future intentions by acknowledging and assuming some "ownership" for the transgressions (Lewicki & Bunker, 1996). Likewise, research on social dilemmas demonstrates that, at least in short-term interactions, apology and penance can be more effective for reestablishing cooperation after an opportunistic act than denial (Bottom, Gibson, Daniels, & Murnighan, 2002). And Schweitzer et al. (2006) showed that a promise may help to speed the process of trust repair.

In contrast, other research observes that providing an apology may fail to ameliorate the negative consequences of perceived trust violation, in part because it involves an acknowledgement of guilt. As one example, Siga, Hsu, Foodim, and Betman (1988) asked participants to watch a videotape of a simulated debate in which one political candidate was accused of sexual or financial misconduct by the other. Sigal et al. (1988) found that the accused party received more votes and was considered to be more honest, ethical, and trustworthy when that party denied culpability, rather than apologized, for the behavior. Likewise, Riordan, Marlin, and Kellogg (1983) set up an experiment involving a senator having taken a bribe and

found that subsequent character evaluations of the senator were less negative when the senator denied, rather than admitted, responsibility for the
transgression. Thus, this set of ideas leads to the conclusion that it is more
successful to manage negative information than provide positive information. How does one reconcile this apparent contradiction?

Kim, Ferrin, Cooper, and Dirks (2004) proposed that the resolution to
this apparent contradiction is provided by understanding how attributions
differ when it comes to matters of competence versus matters of integrity. As noted already, these are two factors of trustworthiness that play
a critical role in predicting the willingness to be vulnerable. In addition,
research from social psychology suggests that there are important inherent differences in the way people assess positive versus negative information about competence versus integrity.

Specifically, Reeder and Brewer (1979) developed a schematic model of
dispositional attribution that outlined the psychological bases of these differences. They proposed that people intuitively believe that individuals with
high competence are capable of exhibiting many levels of performance,
depending on their motivation and task demands, whereas those with low
competence can perform at levels that are only commensurate with or
lower than their competence level. As a result, a single success may be considered to offer a reliable signal of competence, but a single failure may be
discounted as a signal of incompetence. In contrast, this model contends
that people intuitively believe that those with high integrity would refrain
from dishonest behavior regardless of the situation, whereas those with
low integrity may exhibit either dishonest or honest behaviors depending
on their specific incentives and opportunities. Consequently, a single honest act may be discounted as a signal of honesty, but a single dishonest act
is generally considered to offer a reliable signal of low integrity.

Extending this idea to the problem of trust repair would suggest that for
a transgression associated with competence, repair efforts may be more
successful at providing positive information to offset the negative information, as the former is going to be more diagnostic, all other things being
equal (Kim et al., 2004). In contrast, for a transgression perceived to be
associated with integrity, managing the negative information would be
more effective, as it is seen as more diagnostic than positive information
that could be brought to bear, all other things being equal.

Several papers have examined the implications of this idea. For example,
Kim et al. (2004) examined the implications for the potential effectiveness

of apologies versus denials, which are two commonly used strategies that rely on opposite mechanisms. Drawing on the ideas described above, they proposed that when the violation concerns matters of competence, the negative effect on trust from an apology's admission of guilt may be outweighed by its positive effects on trust from signaling the intent to prevent future violations, because people may be willing to believe that the incident was an anomaly and that the mistrusted party would demonstrate competence in the future (i.e., people would weigh positive information about competence more heavily than negative information about competence). However, when the violation concerns matters of integrity, confirming one's guilt with an apology should offer a reliable signal that one lacks integrity outweighing any positive effects on trust from the apology's signals of redemption. This is because people tend to believe that a lack of integrity would be exhibited only by those who do not possess it, and this belief, once established, would be difficult to disconfirm (i.e., people would weigh negative information about integrity more heavily than positive information about integrity). These predictions were supported by two experimental studies.

Kim, Dirks, Cooper, and Ferrin (2006) extended these ideas by examining the implications for different forms of apologies. Specifically, they investigated differences in apologies that included a deflection of blame to situational factors (e.g., provide an excuse) as opposed to an acceptance of full blame. Again, these are two commonly observed responses that are observed in practice and the merits of which are debated in research (e.g., Shaw, Wild, & Colquitt, 2003). Kim et al. argued that, if the distinction between how individuals view information about competence versus integrity holds, trust should be repaired more successfully when the trustee apologizes with an internal, rather than external, attribution when the trust violation was seen as being due to a lapse of competence but apologizes with an external, rather than internal, attribution when the trust violation was attributed to a lapse of integrity. The researchers used a 2 (type of violation: competence vs. integrity) × 2 (response: apology – internal vs. apology – external) experimental design and found support for this prediction.

A number of other studies examined derivations of attribution theories to repair trust. For example, Ferrin, Kim, Cooper, and Dirks (2007) explored the role of belief formation to understand the implications of "reticence" (i.e., the commonly used tactic of trustees of avoiding providing a response to an allegation) by integrating the schematic model of dispositional attribution with research on belief formation. More specifically, they built on research that examined how beliefs are formed and updated and the importance of the mind "unaccepting" a belief (e.g., Gilbert, 1991), such as a belief that one is untrustworthy. This perspective provided insight into why reticence is a suboptimal response to an integrity violation because, like apology, it fails to address guilt and why it is a suboptimal response to a competence violation because, similar to a denial, it fails to signal repentance. Two empirical studies provided support for the ideas.

Recently, Tomlinson and Mayer (2009) drew on Weiner's (1986) causal attribution theory to develop a conceptual model of trust repair. Specifically, they analyzed the implications of causal attributions along three dimensions: locus of causality, controllability, and stability. They suggested that trustors will evaluate the different factors of trustworthiness along these dimensions, which in turn has implications for trust repair. For example, seeing one of these factors (e.g., integrity, aptitude) as highly stable will make it difficult to repair trust. They also explore how different social accounts by the trustee could mitigate or shape the views of trustors regarding the aptitude dimensions.

In sum, there is a growing body of theory and data suggesting that aspects of attribution theory can provide insight into the repair of trust.

Social Equilibrium

Although the attributional process is helpful for understanding the cognitive intraperson components of relationship repair, it provides limited insight into the social or interpersonal aspects of a relationship that are damaged following a transgression. In other words, transgressions call into question not only the characteristics of the trustee but also the relative standing of the parties as well as the conventions or norms that govern the relationship, thus creating "social disequilibrium" (Dirks et al., 2009). This situation results in negative emotions and a drop in trust. Thus, to repair the relationship (and trust) it is important to reestablish the equilibrium by restoring the relative standing of the parties and to reaffirm the norms that govern them through various social rituals (see, e.g., Goffman, 1967). This would typically involve some sort of social ritual to settle the accounts—rituals include apologies, penance, and punishment (Bottom et al., 2002; Ren & Gray, 2009).

One example of this is a paper by Desmet, De Cremer, and van Dijk (2008). These authors used a dictator game in which one party (the allocator) divides a sum of money or chips (20 chips in this study) between oneself and another party (the recipient). The recipient has to accept the offer that the allocator makes. In their study, all participants (who were placed in the recipient's role) received less than an equal share from the allocator (i.e., 5 of 20 chips). In some conditions the recipient was not aware of this inequality (i.e., the allocator either explicitly mentioned that 10 chips had to be distributed or implicitly gave the impression that 10 chips had to be divided) but in another condition was aware of it (the allocator explicitly mentioned that 20 chips had to be divided). Subsequently, all parties were then informed that 20 chips were divided, as such installing strong perceptions of unfairness and distrust. In a latter phase of the study, the allocator then supposedly offered a financial compensation that varied in size. This situation thus exemplifies a situation in which an accepted norm (i.e., violation of the equality rule) is violated, resulting in one party (the allocator) being in a better financial position than the other party (i.e., the recipient). Moreover, it examines how social rituals (i.e., the use of financial compensations) can undo the negative effects of this social disequilibrium. The important finding as observed by Desmet et al. was that a financial overcompensation (i.e., the recipient's final outcomes were higher than those of the allocator) was able to promote trust more than an exact financial compensation (i.e., both parties ended up with the same final outcomes). However, this effect emerged only when the allocator did not mention anything about the exact sum to be divided (i.e., implicitly gave the impression that it would be 10 chips). When the allocator explicitly mentioned that it would either be 10 or 20 chips to be divided then overcompensation did not reveal any additional benefits relative to an exact financial compensation. These findings thus reveal that sometimes giving the victim of the trust violation a final higher relative standing may increase trust again as well.

In an earlier study, Bottom et al. (2002) combined both the attribution perspective and the social equilibrium perspective. Specifically, they studied whether providing an apology and reparation following a transgression would restore cooperation, based on the idea that these responses would demonstrate remorse for the behavior and a commitment to avoid similar transgressions in the future. In addition to the signal related to attributions regarding the nature of the defecting party, the substantive reparation would presumably help to restore the loss—both real and symbolic—created by defecting party. Data from their study demonstrated that this response helped restore cooperation (trust was not directly assessed, but it was presumed to be a key mediator).

Negotiation of Trustworthiness

Research using the previous perspectives has emphasized the actions that the mistrusted party (i.e., the trustee) might take to repair trust. In doing so, the trustor is placed in the role of a passive observer. For example, the studies discussed in prior sections have explored a number of trust repair tactics trustees might initiate while portraying trustors as recipients who evaluate these trust repair efforts and form a judgment. These studies, as well as the others, have largely failed to recognize that the trustor often plays an active role in the trust repair process. Not only is the trustor's willingness to accept the mistrusted party's efforts of great importance for determining the likelihood of trust repair, but so too are the actions trustors themselves undertake to influence this outcome (Lewicki & Bunker, 1996). In both an experimental and field study, De Cremer and Schouten (2008) recently showed that apologies by the mistrusted party were indeed effective only in revealing positive impressions when the trustor in an earlier phase of the interaction felt respected by the trustee. When the trustor did not feel respected apologies given by the trustee were considered meaningless and therefore did not reveal an effect. These results clearly show that both the trustor and the trustee determine whether trust can be promoted again.

To provide deeper insight into the role of the trustee as well as to attempt to provide an integrative account of the various trustor tactics, Kim et al. (2009) proposed a bilateral model of trust repair (BTR).

The BTR model (shown in Figure 9.1) assumes that trustees would want to be considered trustworthy and, hence, advocate the belief, following a violation, that they should be trusted. This assumption is based on the fact that they may want to be trusted due to instrumental concerns (that being trusted can bring them benefits) or that they are indeed trustworthy (e.g., due to self-serving attributions). Trustors, in contrast, are assumed to be predisposed to believe that greater trust in their trustees is not deserved, at least in part due to concerns about being subject to future violations. Hence, these assumptions highlight the competing forces that tend to be

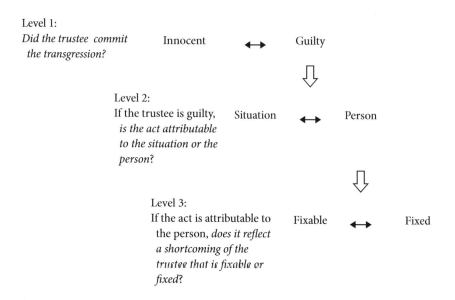

FIGURE 9.1

Bilateral model of trust repair. (From Kim, P. H., Dirks, K. T., & Cooper, C. D., *Academy of Management Review, 34,* 401–422. With permission.)

brought to the situation by trustors and trustees. The final assumption therefore is that these competing stances and efforts will create a dynamic through which trustees and trustors attempt to resolve their discrepant beliefs about the trustee's trustworthiness. This notion builds on the identity negotiation literature, which provides insight into individuals' attempts to resolve discrepancies between how they are viewed by others and how they view themselves (Swann, 1987).

Kim and colleagues propose that trustors' and trustees' disagreements about whether the trustees should be trusted can be resolved on multiple levels. These levels represent a logically derived sequence of questions about whether the trustee can be trusted following a violation: (1) Is the trustee innocent or guilty of committing the transgression? (2) If the trustee is guilty of the transgression, should this be attributed to the situation or to the person? (3) If the transgression is attributed at least in part to the person, is the personal shortcoming fixable, or is it an enduring characteristic of the trustee?

Kim and colleagues observed that these levels roughly correspond to different segments of the literature, which have explored particular strategies for repairing relationships following a transgression. For example, the second level encompasses research that has examined trustees' attempts to deflect blame (e.g., through excuses and justifications) versus accept blame (e.g., Shaw et al., 2003). As another example, Level 3 captures research that has examined the research on violations that are attributes to integrity versus competence, as these tend to be seen as fixed or fixable qualities.

This model also allows for a broader range of outcomes than the repair of trust, depending on the relative success of efforts by the trustor and trustee in advancing their respective positions. For example, trust repair would result if the trustee is able to successfully convince the trustor that he or she is indeed trustworthy. In contrast, the trustee may come to believe that he or she is indeed untrustworthy, and hence "mistrust confirmation" may result. (An intriguing question here is whether individuals hold the same assumptions about integrity violations for their own behavior and thus come to see themselves as untrustworthy following integrity violations.) A third alternative is that neither side "wins" and the parties end up maintaining their views—this would likely eventually result in a highly constrained relationship or one that dissolves.

In short, this model attempts to provide a comprehensive view of trust repair by capturing the different ways the trustor and the trustee may each act following a violation. Empirical research is needed to explore some of the ideas implied by this model.

NEW QUESTIONS FOR THEORY AND PRACTICE

The prior section discussed the different perspectives on trust repair with examples of existing research. As noted already, however, currently only a handful of studies have focused on this topic. As such, there are many opportunities for future research. In this section, we briefly consider three questions important for theory and practice. We consider how the three previously identified perspectives may provide avenues for addressing these questions.

How Can Trust in an Organization Be Repaired?

Although much of the research on trust repair has been focused on trust in people, one of the pressing questions involves how to repair trust in an organization or institution. Recent years have shown an unusually high number of organizations and institutions, many of which were once venerated, involved in situations that cause constituents to question their trust. As examples of the manifestation of these problems, between 2005 and 2008 the confidence in the business sector dropped 22%, confidence in the executive branch of government dropped 29%, and the confidence in religious institutions dropped 19% (National Leadership Index, 2008). This problem presents important questions for organizations that are hit by trust concerns. As one example, following the financial crisis, how can a financial institution restore consumer trust so that investors will invest their money, have confidence in the advice of their brokers, and so on?

Currently, there appears to be little research on this topic (for an exception, see the excellent conceptual paper by Gillespie & Dietz, 2009), and it provides an exceptional opportunity for research. Can one of the previous perspectives provide insight into this issue?

Attribution theory offers one possibility. However, attribution theory is focused on individuals as the target. This is an important caveat because, unlike organizations, individuals are seen as a coherent and unitary entity. This is a potentially important problem given that the latter is an important premise of attribution theory.

Fortunately, Hamilton and Sherman (1996) provide some insight into this issue by discussing similarities and differences in attributions related to persons versus groups. They note that perceivers typically do not expect the same degree of coherence within a group as they expect in the personality of an individual, and as a consequence the attribution principles may not always apply. There may, however, be cases in which, appropriately or inappropriately, groups are seen to represent a coherent entity on at least some dimensions (e.g., they note that stereotypes represent a potential manifestation of this fact). The more coherence or "entitativity" a group is perceived to have, the more attributional principles are applicable. This raises several considerations for understanding how and when current research might be similar to, or vary from, repair of organizations.

For example, one of the key ideas at the individual level involved the implications between integrity and competence. This distinction was important because individuals view information about these concepts differently and view them as more or less fixable. Are these concepts transferable to the organizational level of analysis? Do individuals make judgments about the "integrity" and "competence" of institutions that are separate from the individuals who lead them? If so, how? Or are there similar concepts for the organizational level?

As another example, at the individual level there appears to be some evidence that trust may be more effectively repaired by addressing the dispositional forces that may promote untrustworthy behavior as opposed to by engineering the situational forces, such as structures and systems (Dirks, Kim, Ferrin, & Cooper, 2009). Is the dispositional concept meaningful when it comes to an institution, and, if so, how? For an organization this might refer to the senior leadership team or the structures and culture of the organization.

In sum, the repair of trust in organizations and institutions is an excellent opportunity for future research. How and whether these perspectives might apply is an open question.

How Does Power Affect Trust Repair Process?

Although the relationship between power and trust has long been recognized (Luhmann, 1979) there has been little or no research on it. This is particularly surprising given that both topics have received a great deal of attention in recent years (e.g., see Galinsky's Chapter 2 in this volume). The relationship is, however, highly relevant in that being lower in power tends to make one vulnerable to the other party, which thus invokes concerns about trust.

The negotiation perspective has some potential to address this issue. Kim, Dirks, and Cooper (2009) built on their BTR model to speculate on some implications for how power might influence the repair of trust. They offer several examples. First, they observe that individuals tend to assign greater control and responsibility for outcomes when actors are in positions of power than when they are not. In particular, perceivers tend to place greater blame on individuals, rather than the situation, when the actor's power is high rather than low (Overbeck, Tiedens, & Brion, 2006). Obviously, this tendency will make it more difficult for trustees to shift blame to situations in their attempts to repair trust. Second, they propose that, as trustees' power increases, their transgressions may increasingly be seen by trustors to arise from a lack of integrity rather than a lack of competence. This may be because high-power trustors see acts by trustors as being volitional, which may increase the probability of being seen as related to integrity. Furthermore, to the extent that high-power trust-ees tend to treat their low-power counterparts as means, this perception would also be increased. This tendency may make it more difficult to repair trust or may require greater effort on the part of the trustee to offset this concern. Finally, Kim et al. propose that, to the extent that high-power actors control resources which are valued by the trustor, the latter may be more motivated to trust again in the future. This notion is related to the argument made by Weber, Malhotra, and Murnighan (2005) in their motivated attribution model of trust.

Recent research by De Cremer (2009) has started to pay closer attention to this relationship between power and trust repair. In the context of a bargaining game (in which two parties divide a certain sum of money), all participants were placed in the role of the recipient and received an unfair allocation (i.e., received less than half the amount that had to be distrib-uted). The recipient was either high in power (i.e., he or she had the power to reject the offer, which would mean that both parties would get noth-ing) or low in power (i.e., he or she had to accept the offer the other party allocated). It turned out that those recipients high in power preferred a third party (i.e., an authority) to reward cooperative and fair behavior by the allocator, whereas those low in power preferred a third party to punish competitive and unfair behavior by the allocator. Moreover, results fur-ther showed that trust was promoted (as measured by behavior in a trust game) among those high in power when a reward strategy was used by this authority and among those low in power when a punishment strategy was employed. The reason for this effect seemed to be that recipients high in power felt less inhibited to interact and for that reason preferred soft strategies such as rewarding cooperative behavior. Those low in power felt more avoidant and as a result had a stronger preference for hard tactics such as punishment. These results thus show that power dynamics influ-ence the tactics (i.e., punishment–rewards) that have to be used to promote trust successfully.

Can Trust Be Fully Repaired?

As noted already, trust is notoriously difficult to repair for various reasons. We might go further to raise the question of whether trust can ever really be fully repaired. Indeed, our unscientific observation is that even when trust has presumably been repaired, it remains fragile and can be easily called into question again in the future (e.g., the voice in the back of one's mind that whispers a cautionary note when one is interacting with that person in the future).

There may be some psychological basis for this observation that is related to attribution theory and recent advances in that area. Traditionally, trust has been seen as a cognition that is updated and changed over time as new information is received. This would mean that, following positive information, the level of trust would increase similar to an anchoring and adjust model in the attitude literature.

However, recent work on attitude change has called that model into question. For example, Petty, Tormala, Brinol, and Jarvis (2006) proposed a PAST (Past Attitudes are Still There) model of attitudes, which offers an intriguing notion. Specifically, Petty et al. suggest that old attitudes (e.g., distrust) do not necessarily disappear from memory when new information is received. Instead, the attitude may be tagged as false. When the individual needs to use the relevant attitude, it is constructed based on existing information in memory. Under certain conditions, however, the tag of "false" may not be retrieved, and the old attitude may emerge to impact the construction of the relevant attitude and consequently behavior.

For example, consider the situation in which a trustor perceives another person as untrustworthy following a transgression but at a later point in the relationship the trustee provides reason to revise that attribution. The PAST model would suggest that the new information would not revise the original attitude per se but would tag it as "false."

On one hand, this could be seen as a repair of trust. On the other hand, however, the PAST model would suggest that this repair may be ephemeral, or not robust, in that, under certain circumstances (e.g., perhaps a situation similar to the one in which the original violation occurred), the false tag will not be retrieved from memory, and trust will come into question. If this model is true, it raises the potential that trust, once violated, cannot ever be fully repaired in the way that we currently think about it. Of course, the validity of this idea, as well as the limits of it, remains a question for further research.

CONCLUSION

The objective of this chapter was to examine the research on the problem of the repair of trust, which is a fundamental but surprisingly understudied topic in organizational behavior, and related areas. As we suggested, however, the combination of social psychology and organizational behavior has begun to develop insight into this topic. We hope that our chapter has inspired other research to extend this work.

REFERENCES

Bottom, W. P., Gibson, K., Daniels, S., & Murnighan, J. K. (2002). When talk is not cheap. Substantive penance and expressions of intent in rebuilding cooperation. *Organization Science, 13*, 497–513.

CNN/Opinion Research Corporation (2009). Poll: Politicians trusted more than business leaders on economy. CNNPolitics.com. February 23.

Conway, N., & Briner, R.B. (2002). A daily diary study of affective responses to psychological contract breach and exceeded promises. *Journal of Organizational Behavior, 23*, 287–302.

De Cremer, D. (2004). The influence of accuracy as a function of leader's bias: The role of trustworthiness in the psychology of procedural justice. *Personality and Social Psychology Bulletin, 30*, 293–304.

De Cremer, D. (2009). *Trust repair and power dynamics in bargaining: When punishment versus rewards promote trust.* Unpublished paper, Rotterdam School of Management, Erasmus University, the Netherlands.

De Cremer, D., & Schouten, B. (2008). When apologies for injustice matter: The role of respect. *European Psychologist, 13*, 239–247.

De Cremer, D., Snyder, M., & Dewitte, S. (2001). The less I trust, the less I contribute (or not)? The effects of trust, accountability and self-monitoring in social dilemmas. *European Journal of Social Psychology, 31*, 93–107.

De Cremer, D., & Tyler, T. R. (2007). The effects of trust in authority and procedural fairness on cooperation. *Journal of Applied Psychology, 92*, 639–649.

De Jong, B. A., & Elfring, T. (in press). How does trust affect the performance of ongoing work teams? The mediating role of reflexivity, monitoring and effort. *Academy of Management Journal.*

Desmet, P. T. M., De Cremer, D., & van Dijk, E. (2008). *In money we trust? When financial compensations matter in repairing trust perceptions.* Working paper, Rotterdam School of Management, the Netherlands.

Dirks, K. T. (1999). The effects of interpersonal trust on work group performance. *Journal of Applied Psychology, 84*, 445–455.

Dirks, K. T. (2000). Trust in leadership and team performance: Evidence from NCAA basketball. *Journal of Applied Psychology, 85*, 1004–1012.

Dirks, K. T., & Ferrin, D. L. (2002). Trust in leadership: Meta-analytic findings and implications for research and practice. *Journal of Applied Psychology, 87*, 611–628.

Dirks, K. T., Kim, P. H., Ferrin, D. L., & Cooper, C. D. (2009). *Understanding the effects of substantive responses on trust following a transgression.* Working paper. Washington University, St. Louis, MO.

Dirks, K. T., Lewicki, R. J., & Zaheer, A. (2009). Repairing relationships within and between organizations: Building a conceptual foundation. *Academy of Management Review, 34*, 68–84.

Dirks, K. T., & Skarlicki, D. P. (2009). The relationship between being perceived as trustworthy by coworkers and individual performance. *Journal of Management, 35*, 136–157.

Ferrin, D. L., Kim, P. H., Cooper, C. D., & Dirks, K. T. (2007). Silence speaks volumes: The effectiveness of reticence in comparison to apology and denial for responding to integrity- and competence-based trust violations. *Journal of Applied Psychology, 92*, 893–908.

Gilbert, D. T. (1991). How mental systems believe. *American Psychologist, 46*, 107–119.

Gillespie, N., & Dietz, G. (2009). Trust repair after organization-level failure. *Academy of Management Review, 34*, 127–145.

Goffman, E. (1967). *Interaction ritual: Essays on face-to-face behavior.* Garden City, NY: Anchor Books.

Hamilton, D. L., & Sherman, S. J. (1996). Perceiving persons and groups. *Psychological Review, 103*, 336–355.

Kim, P. H., Dirks, K. T., & Cooper, C. D. (2009). The repair of trust: A dynamic bi-lateral perspective and multi-level conceptualization. *Academy of Management Review, 34*, 401–422.

Kim, P. H., Dirks, K. T., Cooper, C. D., & Ferrin, D. L. (2006). When more blame is better than less: The implications of internal vs. external attributions for the repair of trust after a competence- vs. integrity-based trust violation. *Organizational Behavior and Human Decision Processes, 99*, 49–65.

Kim, P. H., Ferrin, D. L., Cooper, C. D., & Dirks, K. T. (2004). Removing the shadow of suspicion: The effects of apology vs. denial for repairing competence- vs. integrity-based trust violations. *Journal of Applied Psychology, 89*, 104–118.

Kramer, R. (1999). Trust and distrust in organizations: Emerging perspectives, enduring questions. *Annual Review of Psychology, 50*, 569–598.

Langfred, C. W. (2004). Too much of a good thing? Negative effects of high trust and individual autonomy in self-managing teams. *Academy of Management Journal, 47*, 385–399.

Lewicki, R., & Bunker, B. (1996). Developing and maintaining trust in work relationships. In R. Kramer & T. Tyler (Eds.), *Trust in organizations* (pp. 114–139). Thousand Oaks, CA: Sage.

Lount, R. B., Jr., Zhong, C. B., Sivanathan, N., & Murnighan, J. K. (2008). Getting off on the wrong foot: The timing of a breach and the restoration of trust. *Personality and Social Psychology Bulletin, 34*, 1601–1612.

Luhmann, N. (1979). *Trust and power.* Chichester, UK: Wiley.

Mayer, R. C., Davis, J. H., & Schoorman, F. D. (1995). An integrative model of organizational trust. *Academy of Management Review, 20*, 709–734.

National Leadership Index. (2008). Harvard Kennedy School. Center for Public Leadership. Cambridge, MA.

Overbeck, J. R., Tiedens, L. Z., & Brion, S. (2006). The powerful want to, the powerless have to: Perceived constraint moderates causal attributions. *European Journal of Social Psychology, 36,* 479–496.

Petty, R. E., Tormala, Z. L., Brinol, P., & Jarvis, W. B. (2006). Implicit ambivalence from attitude change: An exploration of the PAST model. *Journal of Personality and Social Psychology, 90,* 21–41.

Reeder, G. D., & Brewer, M. B. (1979). A schematic model of dispositional attribution in interpersonal perception. *Psychological Review, 86,* 61–79.

Ren, H., & Gray, B. (2009). Repairing relationship conflict: How violation types and culture influence the effectiveness of restoration rituals. *Academy o f Management Review, 34,* 105–126.

Riordan, C. A., Marlin, N. A., & Kellogg, R. T. (1983). The effectiveness of accounts following transgression. *Social Psychology Quarterly, 46,* 213–219.

Robinson, S. L., & Rousseau, D. M. (1994). Violating the psychological contract: Not the exception but the norm. *Journal of Organizational Behavior, 15,* 245–259.

Rousseau, D. M., Sitkin, S. B., Burt, R. S., & Camerer, C. (1998). Not so different after all: A cross-discipline view of trust. *Academy of Management Review, 23,* 393–404

Schoorman, F. D., Mayer, R. C., & Davis, J. H. (2007). An integrative model of organizational trust: Past, present, and future. *Academy of Management Review, 32,* 344–354.

Schweitzer, M. E., Hershey, J. C., & Bradlow, E. (2006). Promises and lies: Restoring violated trust. *Organizational Behavior and Human Decision Processes, 101,* 1–19.

Shaw, J. C., Wild, E., & Colquitt, J. A. (2003). To justify or excuse? A meta-analytic review of the effects of explanations. *Journal of Applied Psychology, 88,* 444–458.

Sigal, J., Hsu, L., Foodim, S., & Betman, J. (1988). Factors affecting perceptions of political candidates accused of sexual and financial misconduct. *Political Psychology, 9,* 273–280.

Swann, W. B. (1987). Identity negotiation: Where two roads meet. *Journal of Personality and Social Psychology, 53,* 1038–1051.

Tomlinson, E., & Mayer, R. C. (2009). The role of causal attribution dimensions in trust repair. *Academy of Management Review, 34,* 85–104.

Watson, Wyatt (2007). *WorkUSA 2006/2007.* Research report, Arlington, VA.

Weber, J. M., Malhotra, D., & Murnighan, J. K. (2005). Normal acts of irrational trust: Motivated attributions and the trust development process. In B. Staw & R. Kramer (Eds.), *Research in organizational behavior* (Vol. 26, 75–101). San Diego, CA: Elsevier.

Weiner, B. (1986). *An attributional theory of motivation and emotion.* New York: Springer-Verlag.

10

Give and Take:
Psychological Mindsets in Conflict

Francis J. Flynn
Stanford University

Organizations require cooperation. Except in rare cases, individual employees must share valuable resources with one another (e.g., information, goods, services) for a firm to achieve its objectives. But what leads employees to help their colleagues or to ask for help when they are in need? To answer this question, scholars have suggested sources of interpersonal cooperation that seem intuitive. A lack of identification with an organization can discourage cooperation, while the presence of a "shared fate" can encourage it (Sherif, Harvey, White, Hood, & Sherif, 1961). Not surprisingly, trust in the firm and its leadership team often elicits more cooperative behavior from employees (Dirks & Ferrin, 2002), while the presence of negative individual traits, such as narcissism, envy, and Machiavellianism, can reduce the number of prosocial acts (cf. Darley & Batson, 1973).

In the present chapter, I argue that the problem of interpersonal cooperation begins with the basic elements of giving and receiving. Every member of an organization has to occupy the roles of giver and receiver at some point or another. Indeed, people "slip in and out of these roles every day and, in some cases, multiple times in the course of the same day" (Flynn & Adams, 2009, p. 404). But despite the fact that giving and receiving assistance are relatively mundane experiences, the differences between the two psychological mindsets are anything but mundane. Givers and receivers attend to, and respond to, similar information in social exchange in highly dissimilar ways, which can lead their exchange relations to fracture or fail to take root.

In the sections that follow, I describe the psychological mindsets of givers and receivers and review research that highlights these differences and their important consequences. In particular, I present evidence (drawn from carefully controlled laboratory environments as well as naturally occurring field settings) that givers and receivers often fail to develop healthy patterns of exchange primarily because they fail to account for each other's motives—what drives individuals to give help or to ask for help when they need it. Further, I argue that this failure costs both parties dearly in terms of building interpersonal rapport and obtaining instrumental rewards. Along the way, I highlight some directions for future research and opportunities for meaningful interventions.

THE TROUBLE WITH GIVING AND RECEIVING

Giving and receiving seem like simple, everyday social acts. We all know what it's like to benefit from another person's kindness or to provide help to someone in need. Nevertheless, there are dilemmas involved in the giving and receiving of help that can prevent people from giving valuable help when they know they should or prevent them from asking for help when they wrongly assume they won't get it. In this section, I describe a series of studies on giver–receiver perspective differences that have been shown in previous research to predict maladaptive outcomes in exchange relations, namely, a lower incidence of helping or poorer quality of help given.

The Underestimation of Help Giving

For many of us, the thought of asking someone else for help or a favor— be it a colleague or a stranger—is fraught with feelings of discomfort and unease. We generally avoid imposing on others unnecessarily or asking them to go to great lengths for us because doing so would be considered impolite or socially inappropriate. Further, we worry that our requests will not be met, and being refused could leave us embarrassed or humiliated. If we think there is even a chance that we may be rejected, we are likely to seek out other potential helpers. Together, these points suggest that people are highly motivated to be accurate in estimating whether others will say yes when they ask them for help because they want to maximize the instrumental benefits of receiving help and minimize the social costs of being rejected.

But, are people accurate in estimating others' willingness to provide help? In fact, they are not. In research conducted with my colleague Vanessa Bohns, I have found that people underestimate givers' willingness to comply in responding to requests for help because they fail to account for the social pressures that givers face (Flynn & Lake, 2008). When asked to make a prediction about whether someone will agree to provide help, people pay less attention to the social cost of saying no (i.e., the potential embarrassment one might feel for rejecting a request) than potential helpers do. What do the requesters focus on instead? Rather than account for the costs of saying no, people who need help attend to the instrumental costs of saying yes (i.e., how much time, effort, and resources are required to comply with the request) in predicting compliance.

We found support for this idea in a series of studies. First, we instructed people to randomly approach strangers on campus and ask them for help with a specific request. But, before doing so, the participants estimated how many people they thought would comply. These requests varied: Some participants asked to borrow strangers' cell phones to make a call, some solicited people to fill out brief questionnaires, and some asked passersby to escort them to the campus gym—a significant distance of three city blocks. In each of these cases, we found that participants overestimated by at least 50% the number of people they'd have to ask to get someone to agree with each request. As it turned out, people were far more likely to say yes than participants expected.

We replicated these results in a naturally occurring field setting, involving volunteers for Team in Training, a division of the Leukemia and Lymphoma Society. These individuals receive training for marathons and triathlons in exchange for raising a few thousand dollars for cancer research. Participants in our study were asked to estimate the number of people they would have to solicit for donations to reach their fundraising goal and how much they expected the average person would donate. As in our previous studies, volunteers overestimated by about 50% the number of people they would have to approach to achieve their goal. In addition, participants underestimated the amount of each donation by around $17, on average. Thus, we find evidence that receivers cannot predict whether people are willing to give or how much they are willing to give, even in a case like this where they have volunteered for the exercise and are mainly soliciting donations from family and friends.

Why do people consistently fail to appreciate others' willingness to give? In large part, the explanation lies in what both parties attend to in deciding whether to give or whether someone else is likely to give. What receivers fail to realize is that those who are asked for assistance are attending to the social costs of saying no—how awkward it might be to refuse help. For example, in another study, when participants were asked to read a hypothetical scenario from the perspective of a potential giver or a potential receiver, they made different predictions about the likelihood of compliance depending on whether they were in the role of a potential helper or the one who needed the help. Potential receivers thought they were more likely to be turned down than did potential givers because receivers thought it would be less discomforting for givers to refuse their requests than did givers.

While receivers do not adequately attend to the social costs that givers face, they do account for the instrumental costs that givers incur—perhaps too much. In a final field study, we asked participants to estimate how many people they would need to approach to get one person to fill out a questionnaire, but the social and instrumental costs involved varied across conditions. In one condition, participants were instructed to simply hand passersby a flyer with the request (low social costs of rejection), and in another condition participants asked them outright (high social costs of rejection). We also varied the length of the questionnaire, so that half of the participants asked people to fill out short, one-page questionnaires, and the other half presented more burdensome, 10-page questionnaires. What we found is that participants' estimates of compliance varied depending on the length of the questionnaire but not on the mode of the request (face-to-face vs. flyer). The opposite was true for potential givers, who were much more susceptible to the directness of the request than its magnitude.

The Overestimation of Help Seeking

Receivers are not alone in their struggles with perspective taking. Givers struggle to account for receivers' motives as well, as we have demonstrated in a series of follow-up studies that focus on estimates of help seeking rather than help giving (Bohns & Flynn, 2010). We start with the simple assumption that people hate asking for help. It makes them embarrassed, guilty, and fearful that they will look incompetent. However, we propose that potential givers do not take this into account in predicting whether someone will ask them for help and advice. In short, just as receivers fail to appreciate givers' motivation to avoid discomfort in deciding to provide help, givers fail to appreciate receivers' motivation to avoid discomfort in deciding to ask for help.

To test this idea, we recruited two samples of potential helpers: teaching assistants for undergraduate college courses, and second-year MBA students who had volunteered to serve as peer advisors to first-year students (Bohns & Flynn, 2010). At the beginning of the semester, we asked participants in both samples to predict how many students would seek their help over the course of the semester. We found that the MBA students overestimated by a whopping 66% the number of students who would come to them for help, and the teaching assistants overestimated this figure by more than 20%. This is especially noteworthy given that peer advisors had been advisees a year before, and the overwhelming majority of teaching assistants had worked as teaching assistants in the past, many of them for the same class. Yet their previous experience as givers and receivers in the same context did not lead them to make more accurate predictions of others' help-seeking behavior.

The difference between givers' and receivers' perspectives once again centered on feelings of discomfort. To demonstrate this point, we conducted a follow-up study in which we randomly assigned people to assume the role of a supervisor or an employee and asked them how likely an employee would be to seek help from her boss as well as how discomforting this might seem. Those randomly assigned to the role of supervisor in this hypothetical scenario grossly overestimated how likely it would be for employees to seek their assistance and how comfortable employees would feel about asking for help. Again, potential givers were inaccurate judges of how likely people would be to approach them and ask them for help and advice simply because they cannot recognize the awkwardness that people feel being in the position of help seeker. As a result, many managers probably feel strongly about the benefits of having an "open-door policy," not recognizing that it may take more than that for many people to get past the social barriers to requesting help.

What interventions might be best suited to address this problem? One way to encourage employees to seek help when they need it is to reassure them that they won't be judged harshly for making such requests. With this in mind, we designed an experiment in which participants were randomly assigned to the role of a new hire or a mentor in an organization. Both parties were asked to read a memo that introduced the mentorship program to new hires and encouraged them to seek help from their mentors when they needed it. In one condition, the memo emphasized the instrumental benefits of seeking help (e.g., "it will help your career") or downplayed the social costs (e.g., "no need to feel awkward about it"). As expected, participants assigned to the new-hire role said they were more inclined to approach their mentor for help when they read the memo that downplayed the social costs of mentorship rather than the memo that promoted the instrumental benefits. Nevertheless, participants assigned to the "mentor" role predicted that the opposite would be true. These individuals wrongly assumed that the key to encouraging help-seeking was to emphasize the instrumental gains rather than deemphasizing the social costs of approaching a mentor.

Taken together with the previous findings, the results of these studies are puzzling. How can people be so bad at predicting someone else's willingness to provide help or ask for it, given that they have been in that other role countless times before? Clearly they have the motivation to be accurate, and they have personal experience to draw upon for guidance. But, for some reason, these two factors cannot combine to generate accurate predictions. We suggest that the explanation for this misjudgment lies in the individual's attention focus. The underestimation of giving help and the overestimation of seeking help is rooted in an egocentric perspective, whereby people pay less attention to, or fail to fully appreciate, the social pressure that often leads people to give help or put oneself in a position to receive it.

It's the Thought That Counts

Beyond estimating the likelihood of giving and requesting help, individuals sometimes experience poor outcomes in social exchange because they make the wrong decisions in providing help. What should I give this person, and how much is too much? These are difficult questions to answer because the expectations people hold about what and how much to give often tend to be unspoken. As a result, the experience of gift giving can engender ambivalent feelings in givers. Many relish the opportunity to buy gifts to demonstrate how much they care about their intended recipients. But others dread the gift-giving process; they worry that their gifts will fail to elicit a strong feeling of appreciation and may even elicit some feeling of disappointment.

According to anthropologists who study gift exchange, the primary goal of gift giving is to elicit feelings of appreciation from the receiver, which, in turn, help to build stronger social bonds (e.g., Boas, 1895; Mauss, 1925/1967). But how can givers elicit such feelings of appreciation? Givers may believe that the key is purchasing a more expensive gift. Indeed, my colleague Gabrielle Adams and I proposed that the goal of gift giving and the purchase decision become conflated in the minds of givers, in that they equate how much they spend with how much recipients will appreciate the gift (Flynn & Adams, 2009). Although this link between gift price and feelings of appreciation might seem intuitive to givers, we doubt this link actually exists in the minds of receivers. Instead, we suggest that receivers will be less likely to calibrate their feelings of appreciation according to gift price than givers assume.

In a recent test of this idea, we examined one case of gift giving that elicits strong feelings of anxiety from givers about purchase price and expectations of appreciation: the engagement ring (Flynn & Adams, 2009). We surveyed a sample of recently engaged couples who were members of a wedding planning Web site and asked them to report the price of their engagement rings and how much they (or their fiancées) appreciated the ring. According to our results, men consistently thought their rings were more appreciated by their fiancées the more expensive they were. But fiancées did not rate themselves as any more appreciative if the rings were more costly. Thus, it seems that the biggest gift purchase that most American men ever make is a strong example of overspending and a failure of perspective taking.

In a second study, we sought more representative data to test our hypothesis that givers wrongly assume the key to eliciting feelings of appreciation is purchasing more expensive gifts (Flynn & Adams, 2009). To this end, we instructed a nationwide sample of participants to think about a recent birthday gift they had either given or received (participants were randomly assigned to the giver and receiver roles). The gifts that participants recalled varied widely, from T-shirts and CDs to jewelry and home décor. We asked participants for the price that was paid for the gift and an evaluation of how much they (or the other party) appreciated the gift. Once again, givers expected that a more costly gift would elicit higher levels of appreciation from receivers, but receivers did not feel more appreciative of more expensive gifts.

Finally, in a third study (Flynn & Adams, 2009), we turned our attention to a more tightly controlled set of experimental conditions and a direct test of the psychological explanation for our results. In this case, participants were randomly assigned to conditions in which they were asked to think about giving or receiving either a CD or an iPod as a present. But, in this case, we also asked both parties about the "signal" that gift price can send. Do more expensive gifts convey higher levels of thoughtfulness or consideration on the part of the giver? Those who were randomly assigned to be givers thought that the more expensive iPod would be seen as a more thoughtful present, and this accounted for why they thought the iPod would be more appreciated than the CD. In contrast, receivers saw no difference in perceived thoughtfulness and consideration and reported no difference in appreciation levels, regardless of which item they were given.

In sum, these results highlight a critical problem in gift exchange: Whereas givers believe that spending more money is the key to eliciting feelings of appreciation, receivers disagree. Givers would be better off buying a thoughtful gift, yet they appear to be convinced that thoughtfulness is expressed through a price tag rather than a carefully selected present—one that suits the recipient's idiosyncratic tastes. As with our previous studies givers struggle to put themselves in the shoes of receivers, and this is surprising given that people often play the role of gift giver and gift recipient. However, what is learned in one role (e.g., receiver) does not seem to inform judgments made in another (e.g., giver). In the next section, we turn from the context of giving gifts and making momentary monetary decisions to the context of favor exchange and making long-term commitment decisions.

How You Give Matters More Than What You Give

Aside from appreciation, givers and receivers may develop more or less positive feelings of commitment toward one another, according to their different role-based views. In a pair of field studies conducted with my colleague Joel Brockner (Flynn & Brockner, 2003), I found that givers' and receivers' feelings of commitment toward one another were influenced by different aspects of justice. Givers' commitment toward receivers was more influenced by how much they felt the receiver had benefited from the giver's help (outcome favorability), whereas receivers' commitment toward givers was more influenced by their judgments of how well they were treated by the giver—whether the giver treated the receiver with dignity or made them feel guilty about imposing (interactional justice). The logic for this prediction is again rooted in an egocentric focus—the most salient factor for the giver is what was given, but the most salient factor for the receiver is the process by which it is given, how uncomfortable he or she feels in receiving assistance.

The first field study involved a sample of U.S. government officials who were asked to recall either a favor they had recently performed for a colleague or a favor that they had recently received (participants were randomly assigned to roles). The favors they recalled were quite diverse, spanning both personal and professional domains and reflecting both high and low levels of outcome favorability. Aside from assessing how much the favor benefited the recipient, participants also reported the level of interactional justice involved (the extent to which the giver went out of his or her way to make the recipient feel less awkward about receiving help) and their level of commitment to the other party (how much they were interested in interacting with that person in the future). For givers and receivers, the source of commitment differed. Givers reported a strong positive association between how much the favor benefited the recipient and how committed they felt to that person whereas their treatment of the receiver had a significantly less positive association. Receivers had the opposite reaction. Their commitment to the giver increased dramatically when they were treated kindly, but not necessarily when they were treated generously.

One could look at these results and say that they are the product of selective recall bias, in the sense that givers and receivers are motivated to remember different kinds of favors: those that make them feel more altruistic (givers) or more loved (receivers). To address this concern, we collected data on a single type of favor giving, one in which the same favor—agreeing to cover someone else's eight-hour work shift—was given in every case. Participants were randomly assigned to conditions in which they were asked to recall either a time when they agreed to cover someone else's shift (giver) or someone else agreed to cover theirs (receiver). In addition, the participants filled out the same previously described questions. Once again, their feelings of commitment depended on their role in the exchange. Givers felt more committed to receivers when they had "done more" for them, but receivers felt more committed when they had been treated well by the giver.

One intriguing implication of this finding is that givers may reduce the potential goodwill engendered by performing favors if they do not pay sufficient attention to *how* they go about rendering such generous acts. It is not sufficient for givers to provide favors that are perceived as being generous. Instead, they may wish to focus more attention on how they communicate their willingness to help—that it is volitional rather than begrudging. By the same token, receivers can also take action that strengthens their relationships with givers. Specifically, they can make salient for the giver (by expressing their appreciation for) the extent to which the giver has gone out of his or her way to provide assistance. In the next section, we consider how the tendency for givers and receivers to anchor on different aspects of an exchange can also affect their evaluations of favor worth (i.e., how much did I benefit from this) and their expectations of reciprocity.

HOW MUCH IS IT WORTH TO YOU?

Much of the research I have described identifies how evaluations of prosocial behavior are affected by giver–receiver roles. Another source of these differences between givers' and receivers' subjective evaluations is rooted in the norms of politeness that govern their interactions with each other. Whereas the receiver's primary role in an episode of favor exchange is to express gratitude to the giver for not taking offense at a favor request (e.g., "Thank you so much"), the giver's role is to downplay his generosity (e.g., "Don't worry about it. It's no big deal."). Adherence to these norms of expressing generosity (for givers) and gratitude (for receivers) may lead givers to value favors less than receivers do, through a self-perception process, and thereby lead to the somewhat counterintuitive finding that givers will derive *less* influence from their helpful acts (i.e., they will expect less in return than receivers believe givers are entitled to).

I found support for this idea in a pair of studies (Flynn, 2003a, 2003b): a laboratory experiment involving undergraduates and a sample of employees who agreed to cover eight-hour work shifts for each other (previously mentioned). In each case, immediately after the favor was exchanged, the same favor was valued less by the giver than by the receiver. That is, givers expected less in return for their helpful actions than receivers were willing to provide. In fact, in the undergraduate sample the receiver was willing to offer *more than twice as much* in return for the favor than the giver expected. Although the favors being evaluated were identical, the participants' evaluation of its "worth" varied dramatically, depending on their role in the exchange. By the same token, the amount of influence that could be derived from this helpful act (i.e., in the form of reciprocation) varied accordingly.

Evidence of the impact of politeness norms emanates from another aspect of the results. The influence of role obligations on evaluations of cooperation should dissipate over time as the need to maintain role-specific norms of politeness fade. In line with this assumption, the difference between givers' and receivers' evaluations decreased after only a few weeks had passed. Receivers asked to make retrospective evaluations were willing to offer less in return than they were initially whereas givers who made retrospective evaluations expected significantly more, presumably because the role-based need to maintain an image of gratitude or generosity, respectively, had diminished. When combined, these findings set up an intriguing possibility about requesting reciprocation—one may be more likely to receive reciprocation, and a greater amount of reciprocation, the sooner it is requested.

This work suggests that helpful acts are not fixed currencies and helping behavior may be subject to a general discounting effect over time. According to Gouldner (1960, p. 171), the universal moral norm of reciprocity requires that people "help those who have helped them." But how much is one entitled to receive in return for giving help? Givers and receivers may have different expectations of precisely how much givers can rightfully request in return for their acts of kindness. The studies described here suggest that people can construe helping behavior in different ways depending on their perspective: What seems like a valuable gesture to one person might seem worthless to another. Many researchers assume that the way to resolve conflict is to increase the incidence of cooperation. However, making people cooperate more frequently might accelerate, rather than mitigate, interpersonal conflict if givers are continually taken for granted by receivers.

WHERE DO WE GO FROM HERE?

To this point in the chapter, I have reviewed several past research studies that suggest the biggest roadblock to achieving healthy patterns of give-and-take may be the roles that we occupy when we participate in social exchange. Givers and receivers simply cannot predict how one another will think, how they will act, or how they will react when they are engaged in a cooperative interaction. In this section, I will describe three current projects that help flesh out some of the directions that future research on the giver–receiver mindset can take. The first examines the problem of predicting whether past episodes of noncompliance are a good predictor of future compliance. The second considers whether offering help or asking for help is a better strategy for resolving conflict. And the third investigates the different impact that giving and receiving can have on an individual's self-concept.

Getting Past "No"

Imagine that you had to request help from someone who had previously refused to help you. Do you think this person would be more or less likely to help you given that he or she had said no in the past? Now, imagine that someone whom you had previously refused to help asked you again for help. Do you think that you would be more or less likely to help given that you had already said no? When asked the first question, people generally believe that prior refusals decrease the likelihood of future compliance. When asked the second, they believe that prior refusals will *increase* their willingness to comply. The only thing that has changed in these two cases is their perspective as either a giver or a receiver. But, this alone can make all the difference in attempting to reconcile their conflicting responses.

Along with my colleague Daniel Newark (Flynn & Newark, 2009), I have been examining the effect of noncompliance on the future likelihood of compliance. This is a topic that has been studied in the past, but never in the context of equivalent help requests. Instead, many studies of sequential-compliance tactics focus on the so-called door-in-the-face or reject-and-reduce approach to noncompliance (Cialdini et al., 1975). The basic idea here is that requests are more likely to be agreed to when they are preceded by a refusal to a much larger request. The underlying logic is that people may agree to the smaller request because it seems much smaller in comparison with the larger request and they feel obligated to reciprocate the requester's willingness to reduce the magnitude of his or her request (i.e., they comply to reciprocate the concession made by the requester).

We predict that people are more likely to increase their willingness to comply with a future request following a previous refusal, regardless of whether the previous refusal was for a larger or equivalent request. However, we also note that givers and receivers do not agree on this point. Rather, in our research, givers appear to be oblivious to the discomfort involved in refusing requests for help. Using a hypothetical scenario, we asked half of the participants to imagine being on vacation and then calling into the office in need of assistance. A colleague answers the phone, and in one condition participants read that this person refused to help with a similar request the previous week but in the other condition there is no information about their prior interaction. The other half of the participants read one version of the scenario or the other written from the colleague's perspective. In rating the likelihood of compliance in this situation, people in the receiver role felt that the colleague would be much less likely to help when they were told that they had previously refused a similar request. But participants in the giver role felt that they would be *more* likely to comply when they previously refused.

What's going on here? The answer is surprisingly simple. People find it hard to say no to a request for help because we all see ourselves as helpful individuals. And if it is hard for us to say no once, then it is even harder for us to say no twice. However, when we are in the role of a potential receiver, we don't see this situation the same way, perhaps because we are too concerned with our own discomfort to recognize someone else's (Flynn & Lake, 2008). Like the studies about underestimating compliance with direct requests for help described previously, potential receivers may be too quick to write off the willingness of others to give their help and support if they have refused to do so in the past. Ironically, these individuals may be even more willing to be helpful than someone who has never refused to provide assistance.

The Cooperation–Conflict Connection

Helping behavior can be an effective means of reducing interpersonal conflict (e.g., Sherif et al., 1961). But what kind of behavior is the more effective means of conflict resolution—asking for help or offering it instead? The answer may depend on the type of conflict involved: one driven by perceived selfishness versus one driven by perceived condescension. Help giving will likely be effective in reducing conflict when the helper has been viewed as behaving selfishly in the past, but a person who has been viewed as behaving in a "condescending" manner may cause more damage when offering help because his or her helpfulness is interpreted as further condescension. As for help seeking, the reverse may be true—a conflict stemming from perceived selfishness might be inflamed by an additional request for help. On the other hand, if the help seeker was thought to be condescending in the past, asking for assistance may help them come across as less self-aggrandizing.

In a series of studies conducted with my colleague Caitlin Hogan (Flynn & Hogan, 2009), I found strong support for these predictions. People involved in a conflict based on perceived selfishness reacted more positively when the other party offered help than when they themselves asked for it. However, in a conflict based on perceived condescension, the results completely changed—people reacted more positively when they were asked for help rather than being offered help. To be clear, this is not intuitive. In fact, in a separate study, when we asked people to estimate how effective offering and asking for help would be in either a selfishness-based conflict or a condescension-based conflict, participants thought that offering help would be significantly more effective in resolving both types of conflict. So, once again, givers and receivers fail to appreciate how the other party will react to their behavior. In this case, they fail to consider the type of conflict they are involved in when attempting to choose an effective conflict resolution strategy.

Thanks, but No Thanks

Business scholars and practitioners often attribute a lack of employee cooperation to selfishness; for one reason or another, individual employees are unwilling to make personal sacrifices on behalf of their coworkers. But cooperation is a two-way street in the sense that there must be an act of receipt for any act of giving to occur. According to Mauss (1925/1967), the obligation to receive encourages recipients to accept help graciously, regardless of their true feelings. The need for such a norm may seem unclear given that many acts of help are directly requested. However, helpful acts can also be unsolicited, and in these cases people may feel pressure to accept others' generosity, even if they are not in need of such assistance (e.g., Cialdini, 1988). A refusal may lead those who offer help to experience a loss of "face" (e.g., Goffman, 1955) or feelings of embarrassment (Brown & Levinson, 1987; Grice, 1975). Refusing help might imply that the gesture was inappropriate, inadequate, or perhaps offensive to the target (e.g., Goffman, 1971).

Given this pressure to receive gifts graciously, people often feel most threatened when they are the receiver rather than the giver. In a study of toy designers, my colleague Kim Elsbach and I (Elsbach & Flynn, 2009) found that the most commonly reported problems that arose from collaboration had to do with idea taking, not idea giving. Although most artists are viewed as selfish and unwilling to cooperate, these individuals were, in fact, happy to give helpful suggestions to their colleagues. However, they shuddered at the prospect of accepting others' advice. Instead, most designers resisted taking ideas from their peers and often pretended to accept them. While many organizational experts (e.g., consultants, scholars, pundits) will argue that the key to increasing cooperation is inspiring generosity, this work suggests that such advice may be misguided. The key to increasing cooperation is inspiring graciousness in accepting help. To instill such graciousness may require providing employees with a sense of perspective so that they recognize the value of give and take, rather than just the value of giving (see also Flynn, Reagans, Amanatullah, & Ames, 2006).

BEYOND ATTENTION FOCUS

The research reviewed here focuses on how givers and receivers attend to different things in an episode of exchange. Beyond attention focus, though, it is important to explore how givers and receivers interpret each other's actions. For example, my colleagues Dan Ames, Elke Weber, and I (Ames, Flynn, & Weber, 2004) argued that help recipients are sensitive to different bases from which helpers appear to make their decisions, such as affect (e.g., "I like you") or cost–benefit analysis (e.g., "It's worth it"). In three studies, we found that when the helping decision was based on affect (i.e., positive feelings about the recipient), receivers developed more positive impressions of, and were more willing to interact with, the giver than if a cost–benefit analysis was judged to underlie the same helpful act. However, for large favors, receivers expected givers to decide to help based on cost–benefit analysis; indeed, when they thought the giver did a "big favor" based on their warm feelings toward the focal party, they appreciated the act and liked the helper very much but also thought that individual was significantly less intelligent.

Some differences between givers and receivers go beyond their respective cognitions and affect their social reputations. In a study with my colleagues Ray Reagans, Emily Amanatullah, and Ames (Flynn et al., 2006), I found that the extent to which one is viewed as being a "giver" affects the level of influence they have in a social group. Those who are seen as givers are awarded higher levels of respect and esteem, while those who are seen as receivers are regarded with lower levels of respect and esteem. Indeed, people who *refrained from asking others for help* increased others' perceptions of their generosity and, in turn, elicited conferrals of social status. This suggests that help seekers may be right in feeling awkward about asking for help because receivers sacrifice their reputation when they decide to accept someone else's assistance. More generally, it implies that there may be a causal link between giving and social status—those who give more help more often are conferred higher levels of status by their peers (see Flynn, 2003a).

Aside from reputational effects, giver–receiver roles can also affect the experience of social identity in different ways, depending on whether the exchange was direct or indirect. Direct exchange includes direct, reciprocal prosocial actions, and indirect exchange refers to the indirect giving and receiving of benefits among three or more people who belong to the same social group or network (i.e., generalized exchange). Along with my colleagues Robb Willer and Sonya Ouzdin (Willer, Flynn, & Ouzdin, 2009), I investigated the implications of exchange structure for givers' and receivers' sense of identification with other exchange partners. In particular, we surveyed members of Craigslist and Freecycle, two online exchange communities that are two of the largest known systems of direct and generalized exchange, respectively.

In our field study (Willer et al., 2009), we surveyed people and tracked their patterns of giving and receiving over a period of time. Based on these data, we found evidence that generalized exchange creates stronger feelings of solidarity than direct exchange for both givers and receivers (see Molm, Collett, & Schaefer, 2007). Further, this effect was mediated by group identification—generalized exchange led to greater solidarity because it generated a stronger sense of "groupness" among participants. What is perhaps most interesting about these results is that they are stronger for "receivers" than for "givers." One could imagine that repeated giving behavior would lead people to conclude that they must identify strongly with the group in an effort to reduce their sense of cognitive dissonance (Festinger, 1957). But we find that the repeated experience of *receiving* generates group identification, specifically in Freecycle, most likely because the receipt of unilateral gifts in this generalized exchange community leads to positive feelings that are then attributed to the group as a whole (see Lawler, 2001, for a similar argument).

Finally, research on cooperation suggests that, although receivers may not be aware of the social pressure that givers face, they often benefit from such social pressure (Cialdini, 1988). For example, Bohns and Flynn (2009) demonstrated how the use of commitment-inducing scripts effectively elicits compliance by committing potential givers to a helpful course of action. In a field study at New York City's Penn Station, targets were approached and asked to complete a survey. In one condition, they were given a straightforward request: "Would you fill out a questionnaire?" In a second condition, they were asked, "Can you do me a favor?" before hearing the same request (to fill out a two-page questionnaire). A total of 57% of the targets in the former condition complied, whereas 84% of those in the second condition complied. Indeed, for those subjects in the second condition who offered an immediate affirmative response to the "Can you do me a favor" script (e.g., "Yeah sure, what is it?"), the compliance rate was near 100%. In short, targets acted as if they felt "trapped"—they had offered some precommitment to comply with the request before hearing the details and found it difficult to go back on this commitment, perhaps to avoid losing face.

The findings from this study go beyond prior research in clarifying the costs that receivers incur when using commitment-inducing tactics. Most social psychologists have attempted to identify tactics that can be used to influence others immediately—that is, to increase compliance (for a review, see Cialdini, 1988). In this study, use of the commitment-inducing script was effective in increasing compliance. However, we also asked targets, at the end of the questionnaire, to report how much they expected in return for their cooperation (i.e., how large a gift they should be given for their trouble). When asked this question, targets reported *higher* expectations of reciprocation when they heard the commitment-inducing script than when they heard only the direct request for help (more than twice as much). In other words, whereas using the script made others more inclined to help, it also made them inclined to request more in return for their help. Thus, managers' success in acquiring influence through the use of compliance tactics can entail trade-offs—they may get what they want in the short-term but perhaps at a higher price in the long-term.

CONCLUSION

My research highlights many opportunities for cooperation in organizations as well as some obstacles. In the past, employee cooperation has been conceptualized as a "social dilemma," or a situation in which generosity exposes employees to others' opportunistic behavior. Maybe, though, the real problem with cooperation in organizations isn't the social dilemma—it's the social cognition. To a large extent, the frustrating outcomes that result from social exchange are driven by the roles that people adopt in an episode of exchange and the unique perspectives, motives, and social pressures that accompany these roles. Practitioners should therefore take heed: Any attempts to inspire, increase, or improve patterns of cooperation must account for the psychology that underlies these giver–receiver differences to be successful.

More broadly, this research program provides valuable insight on the link between social influence and interpersonal cooperation. Episodes of helping are shaped by social roles that lead people to believe others have been more or less cooperative in the past, that they will be more or less cooperative in the future, or that they would be unlikely to cooperate in the first place. By outlining how role requirements affect subjective evaluations of help given and received, this approach becomes useful in understanding how influence can be derived from developing healthy patterns of social exchange. Future research will hopefully work toward developing a comprehensive model of influence and exchange in organizations: one that accounts for the unique aspects of give and take.

REFERENCES

Ames, D., Flynn, F. J., & Weber, E. (2004). It's the thought that counts: On perceiving how helpers decide to lend a hand. *Personality and Social Psychology Bulletin, 30*(4): 461–474.

Boas, F. (1895). The social organization and the secret societies of the Kwakiutl Indians. In *Annual Report of the Smithsonian Institution for 1895*. Washington, DC: Smithsonian Institution.

Bohns, V., & Flynn, F. (2009). *If you needed help, why didn't you ask? Overestimating the willingness to seek help and underestimating discomfort in help-seeking.* Manuscript under review.

Brown, P., & Levinson, S. (1987). *Politeness: Some universals in language usage.* Cambridge, UK: Cambridge University Press.

Cialdini, R. B. (1988). *Influence: Science and practice* (2d Ed.). Glenview, IL: Scott, Foresman.

Cialdini, R. B., Vincent, J. E., Lewis, S. K., Catalan, J., Wheeler, D., & Darby, B. L. (1975). Reciprocal concessions procedure for inducing compliance: The door-in-the-face technique. *Journal of Personality & Social Psychology, 31*(2), 206–215.

Darley, J., & Batson, C. D. (1973). "From Jerusalem to Jericho": A study of situational and dispositional variables in helping behavior. *Journal of Personality and Social Psychology, 27,* 100–108.

Dirks, K., & Ferrin, D. (2002). Trust in leadership: Meta-analytic findings and implications for research and practice. *Journal of Applied Psychology, 87,* 611–628.

Elsbach, K., & Flynn, F. (2009). *Identity threats to collaboration: A study of toy designers.* Working paper, University of California, Davis.

Festinger, L. (1957). *A theory of cognitive dissonance.* Evanston, IL: Row, Peterson.

Flynn, F. (2006). How much is it worth to you?: Subjective evaluations of help in organizations. *Research in Organizational Behavior, 27,* 133–174.

Flynn, F., & Adams, G. (2009). Money can't buy love: Asymmetric beliefs about gift price and feelings of appreciation. *Journal of Experimental Social Psychology, 45,* 404–409.

Flynn, F., & Newark, D. (2009). *Banking "No": Overestimating the effect of past noncompliance on future compliance.* Working paper, Stanford University.

Flynn, F., Reagans, R., Amanatullah, E., & Ames, D. (2006). Helping one's way to the top: Self-monitors achieve status by helping others and knowing who helps whom. *Journal of Personality and Social Psychology, 91,* 1123–1137.

Flynn, F. J. (2003a). How much should I give and how often? The effects of generosity and frequency of favor exchange on social status and productivity. *Academy of Management Journal, 46*(5), 539–553.

Flynn, F. J. (2003b). What have you done for me lately? Temporal adjustments to favor evaluations. *Organizational Behavior and Human Decision Processes, 91*(1), 38–50.

Flynn, F. J., & Brockner, J. (2003). It's different to give than to receive: Predictors of givers' and receivers' reactions. *Journal of Applied Psychology, 88*(6), 1034–1045.

Flynn, F. J., & Hogan, C. (2009). *Should I request or offer help? Two paths to resolving conflict.* Working paper, Stanford University.

Flynn, F. J., & Lake, V. (2008). "If you need help, just ask": Underestimating compliance with direct requests for help. *Journal of Personality and Social Psychology, 95,* 128–143.

Goffman, E. (1955). On face-work. *Psychiatry, 18,* 213–231.

Goffman, E. (1971). *Relations in public.* New York: Basic Books.

Gouldner, A. W. (1960). The norm of reciprocity: A preliminary statement. *American Sociological Review, 25,* 161–178.

Grice, H. P. (1975). Logic and conversation. In P. Cole & J. Morgan (Eds.), *Syntax and semantics* (Vol. 3, pp. 41–58). New York: Academic Press.

Lawler, E. J. (2001). An affect theory of social exchange. *American Journal of Sociology, 107*(2), 321–52.

Mauss, M. (1925/1967). *The gift: Forms and functions of exchange in archaic societies.* Translated by I. Cunnison. New York: W.W. Norton.

Molm, L. D., Collett, J. L., & Schaefer, D.R. (2007). Building solidarity through generalized exchange: A theory of reciprocity. *American Journal of Sociology, 113,* 205–42.

Schaumberg, R., & Flynn, F. (2009). Differentiating between grateful and indebted reactions to receiving help. *Advances in Group Processes, 26,* 105–132.

Sherif, M., Harvey, O., White, B., Hood, W., & Sherif, C. (1961). *Intergroup conflict and cooperation: The robbers cave experiment.* Wesleyan.

Willer, R., Flynn, F., & Ouzdin, S. (2009). *Group identification and solidarity in generalized exchange.* Working paper, University of California, Berkeley.

Section IV

Contemporary Issues

11

The Value of Diversity in Organizations: A Social Psychological Perspective

Katherine W. Phillips
Northwestern University

Sun Young Kim-Jun
Northwestern University

So-Hyeon Shim
Northwestern University

What is the value of diversity? This is a profound question that has spawned a proliferation of scholarly research, popular books, and civic dialogue. The desire to develop a compelling answer to this question is warranted. Demographic changes in the workforce, changes in the way organizations structure themselves, and changes in the competitive and global landscape of business have all contributed to diversity becoming more prevalent in the modern workplace (Toossi, 2006; Triandis, Kurowski, & Gelfand, 1994; Williams & O'Reilly, 1998). Despite its increasing pervasiveness, the ability of problem-solving groups (where the integration of unique perspectives is critical) to consistently reap measurable benefits from and avoid the negative consequences associated with diversity remains elusive (for reviews and meta-analyses see Jackson, Joshi, & Erhardt, 2003; Kochan et al., 2003; Mannix & Neale, 2005; Milliken & Martins, 1996; van Knippenberg & Schippers, 2007; Webber & Donahue, 2001; Williams & O'Reilly, 1998). In this chapter we will review relevant social psychological and organizational research on diversity and present a model of the psychological processes underlying the effects of diversity. Our goal here is to develop a better understanding of how and why diversity can be beneficial by integrating the apparently contradictory results from the literature on diversity in problem-solving teams and in organizations. The conventional wisdom that diversity is beneficial because people who are "different" will bring different perspectives to the table is challenged, and an alternative value of diversity focusing on the effects of diversity on *all* members of a group will be presented. The implications of this perspective for the changing demography of the workforce is readily apparent as the ability to effectively capture diversity's benefits will be increasingly important for organizations.

THE CONCEPT OF DIVERSITY

As a precursor, it is imperative to develop a shared definition of diversity. In 1998, Williams and O'Reilly drew from the vast literature on self-categorization and social identity theories (Tajfel, 1972, 1974; Turner, Hogg, Oakes, Reicher, & Wetherell, 1987) and defined diversity as resulting "from any attribute people use to tell themselves that another person is different" (Williams & O'Reilly, p. 81). This definition allowed researchers to encompass more under the umbrella of diversity than just the typical demographic characteristics such as race and gender. Researchers have thus examined the effects of many attributes on group functioning, including functional background, age, tenure in the organization, personality differences, and numerous naturally occurring social or minimal group distinctions (for examples, see Chen & Kenrick, 2002; Phillips, 2003; Phillips & Loyd, 2006). A more recent definition provided by van Knippenberg and Schippers (2007) in their review of the diversity literature covers an even broader spectrum: "diversity may be seen as a characteristic of a social grouping (i.e., group, organization, society) that reflects the degree to which there are objective or subjective differences between people within the group (without presuming that group members are necessarily aware of objective differences or that subjective differences are strongly related to more objective differences)" (p. 519). Although there has been a proliferation of labels to distinguish different sources of diversity (e.g., Harrison, Price, & Bell, 1998; Jackson, May, & Whitney, 1995; Jehn, Northcraft, & Neale, 1999; Pelled, 1996; Pelled, Eisenhardt, & Xin, 1999), we adopt a distinction that we believe is consistent with the definitions provided here and more broadly encompasses both social psychological and organizational traditions.

We will use the term *social category diversity* to refer to distinctions that serve as a salient basis of categorization into in-group (people who are like me) and out-group (people who are not like me). This social category diversity may come from salient demographic characteristics such as race, gender, or nationality or any characteristic that may not be immediately visible yet can be rendered salient in the context and thus be used to categorize group members. Using this definition, characteristics such as functional background, geographic location, and political affiliation can all be considered elements of social category diversity (e.g., Lount & Phillips, 2007; Phillips & Loyd, 2006). Furthermore, minimal distinctions such as ostensible preference for a type of painting or having a red shirt versus a blue shirt can also count as leading to social category diversity (e.g., Allen & Wilder, 1979). The critical feature here is that people use these social characteristics to tell themselves that some subset of the group of people is "like me" and that some of them are not (Williams & O'Reilly, 1998). Consistent with this typology, Harrison and colleagues (1998) adopted the term *surface-level diversity,* defined as salient characteristics that are more immediately apparent in groups (Harrison et al., 1998; Jackson et al., 1995; Phillips & Loyd, 2006; Riordan, 2000).

Social category diversity exists alongside informational or opinion diversity in task groups. *Informational diversity* captures the differences in information, opinions, perspectives, and modes of thought and action that are relevant for the task at hand being completed by a group. When individuals are brought together to solve problems in groups, they often possess different information and perspectives that can be used to inform the group. In fact, for many problem-solving groups, which we concentrate on in this chapter, the very reason they are brought together is to garner the diverse knowledge and perspectives that are uniquely held by different group members (e.g., Argote, Gruenfeld, & Naquin, 2000; Gruenfeld, Mannix, Williams, & Neale, 1996; Phillips, Mannix, Neale, & Gruenfeld, 2004; Stasser, Stewart, & Wittenbaum, 1995).

Much research on diversity in groups uses social category diversity, such as functional background, as a proxy for informational diversity. In our conceptualization, the actual functional background differences themselves are considered social category diversity (e.g., marketing, engineering, finance), and the information, opinions, and knowledge that these different individuals bring to the table is measured and conceptualized as informational diversity. Past organizational research on diversity has assumed that social category diversity is congruent (i.e., perfectly correlated) with informational diversity (Phillips, 2003; Phillips & Loyd, 2006). In the case of functional background differences, the level of congruence between social category and information diversity may indeed be relatively high (i.e., members of the marketing group share similar information, opinions, and perspectives and members of the engineering group possess different information, opinions, and perspectives from the marketers), but this same level of congruence may not exist for all sources of social category diversity. Hence, the definition of diversity provided by van Knippenberg and Schippers (2007) embraces an important distinction, namely, that the "objective" differences people see between themselves and others do not necessarily reflect the differences that these individuals have for the relevant task. We now turn to research examining the impact of social category diversity on teams and discuss the implications of assuming congruence with informational diversity in organizations.

THE INFLUENCE OF SOCIAL CATEGORY DIVERSITY

Much of the previous research on diversity has assumed that any benefit accrued from social category diversity comes from people who are "different" bringing different perspectives to the table. Indeed, researchers have typically interpreted their findings in ways that assume people with different characteristics are the individuals who can bring unique perspectives to the group. However, attributing these unique perspectives solely to the presence of those with different, or out-group, characteristics ignores the possible influence of those with similar, or in-group, characteristics. For example, Thomas and Ely (1996) predicted that important benefits would accrue from demographic heterogeneity in organizations because members of different groups such as women, Hispanics, Asian Americans, African Americans, and Native Americans could bring different or new perspectives and approaches. Furthermore, Cox, Lobel, and McLeod's (1991) research on the effects of ethnic diversity on a group task demonstrated that individuals approached tasks differently depending on their ethnic differences. Moreover, previous research arguing that diversity in a group is linked to higher levels of conflict presume (not measure) that increased conflict in diverse settings occurs because people who are different disagree and clash with each other (e.g., Jehn et al., 1999; Pelled, 1996; Pelled et al., 1999). Given the methodological designs of these studies, it is also possible that reports of increased conflict in diverse groups are at least partially due to members of the social majority disagreeing and clashing with one another. Past interpretations of the value of diversity have thus presumed that individuals in the social majority group will necessarily share the same information and perspectives with one another (i.e., members of the social majority could not be the source of the disagreement).

However, researchers have occasionally questioned this assumption of congruence between social category and informational diversity by proposing that differences in task perspective may come from where they are not expected (Janis, 1982; Jehn et al., 1999; Lawrence, 1997). According to Jehn et al. (1999), "Social category diversity may not always reflect other types of diversity (e.g., information diversity and value diversity)" (p. 742). More recently, Phillips and colleagues suggest that there may be fundamental psychological processes underlying the relatively widespread presumption by laypeople and researchers alike that there is congruence between social category and informational diversity (Phillips, 2003; Phillips & Loyd, 2006; Phillips, Northcraft, & Neale, 2006; Phillips et al., 2004). In this chapter, we suggest three psychological mechanisms that account for how social category diversity affects people's affective and cognitive functions and their subsequent performance. These mechanisms are intended to help us better understand the widespread assumption about the congruence between social category and informational diversity.

First, individuals *expect* socially similar others to agree with them more on both task-relevant and irrelevant issues with socially dissimilar others (Allen & Wilder, 1979; Phillips, 2003; Phillips & Loyd, 2006; Phillips et al., 2004; Tajfel & Wilkes, 1963). In particular, Phillips and Loyd's (2006) findings support this psychological process by showing the influence of dissenting social majority members in diverse versus homogeneous groups. In two experimental studies they examined two different sources of social category diversity (functional background and geographic affiliation) and argued that expectations can cause diverse groups to benefit from the mere presence of people who are different, regardless of whether those "different" individuals have unique perspectives to share.

In their first study, Phillips and Loyd (2006) told MBA student participants that they would be working in a three-person team composed of the participant and either two other MBA students or one fellow MBA student and a medical student. This led to two conditions: (1) the homogenous condition, in which all members of the team were MBA students (same functional category); and (2) the diverse condition, in which one of the members was a medical student (different functional category). Given the composition of the groups, there was always a majority of MBA students, so the participant was always a member of the social majority. The participants were then told that their opinions about which market to target for a medical device was in disagreement with the opinions of the other two members of the group, who were in agreement with one another. Thus, the participant was always a dissenting social majority member. The findings of this first study revealed that participants expected greater task perspective similarity with socially similar (i.e., MBA students) than with socially dissimilar others (i.e., medical students). In addition, when their expectations for similarity were violated, participants were more surprised and irritated by disagreement from the socially similar individuals (i.e., the other MBA students) in homogeneous settings than with the socially similar individual in diverse settings. Furthermore, participants in diverse groups expected a more positive and accepting group experience than those in homogeneous groups. These findings suggest that task-relevant categorization (functional background) triggers expectations of where task perspective similarities are likely to exist.

In their second study, Phillips and Loyd (2006) explored the possibility that individuals expect greater task perspective similarity with socially similar than socially dissimilar others even when the category is irrelevant to the task at hand. In this study, the task-irrelevant distinction was the side of campus in which the participants lived (north or south campus); in the diverse condition, there was one group member from one side of campus and two from the opposite side of campus, whereas in the homogeneous condition, all group members were from the same side of campus. In addition, interacting groups were brought together to make a decision about the best company for another company to acquire. The task was an information-sharing one that allowed for the exchange of unique information and opinions (McLeod, Baron, Marti, & Yoon, 1997). In both homogeneous and diverse conditions, one of the group members—the dissenting social majority member—held an opinion that was different from that held by the rest of the group because the dissenting social majority member's packet contained information about the companies that was different from that given to the other two members of the group.

The results of this second study suggest that even task-irrelevant characteristics (e.g., geographic location) can trigger expectations of similarity. More specifically, Phillips and Loyd (2006) found that when a member of the social majority voiced a different opinion, homogeneous group members had more negative feelings and engaged less in the task than diverse group members because their expectations that socially similar others would agree with their task perspective were violated. In contrast, when a member of the social majority possessed a different opinion in diverse groups, members perceived the groups as more positive and accepting of alternative viewpoints, there was more persistent and confident voicing of dissenting perspectives, and greater task engagement. These results are consistent with arguments that group members expect differences in knowledge or opinions from individuals who are socially dissimilar (Phillips, 2003; Thomas-Hunt, Ogden, & Neale, 2003). As such, group members seem more likely to consider unique perspectives from socially dissimilar individuals than from socially similar others.

Further evidence for expectations of agreement among socially similar others can be found in Sommers's (2006) research on the effects of racial diversity on jury decision making. Sommers argued that Caucasian jurors in diverse groups cited more case facts and paid more attention to different opinions from other group members than Caucasians in all-Caucasian juries. According to Phillips and Lount's (2007) interpretation regarding Sommers's findings, the Caucasian participants in the homogeneous juries may have been comparatively less focused on information presented during a case because they expected that the homogeneous setting would be characterized by agreement and easy interaction. Conversely, Caucasian participants in diverse settings may have expected more disagreement and divergent opinions about the case, leading them to consider the facts of the case more thoroughly. Thus, Sommers's study indicates that racial diversity in jury decision making can be beneficial as it may allow Caucasian participants to express their opinions and consider information and alternatives that they would otherwise dismiss in homogeneous settings. In addition, Antonio et al.'s (2004) study also supports the idea that social category diversity promotes critical thinking by individuals in groups. They found that individuals displayed more integrative complexity when they had been exposed to more racial diversity in their personal lives (as self-reported on a survey) and in the experiment itself: Following group discussion of a controversial social issue, Caucasians demonstrated more complex thinking in writing an essay when assigned to a diverse group with a Black minority opinion holder than when assigned to a homogeneous group of all Caucasians with a Caucasian minority opinion holder.

Second, individuals *prefer* their opinions and beliefs to be more similar to in-group members than to out-group members (e.g., Allen & Wilder, 1975, 1979; Heider, 1958; Holtz & Miller, 1985; Newcomb, 1968; Tajfel, 1969; Wilder & Allen, 1978). For example, Phillips (2003) argued that diverse groups may be better able to garner the benefits of minority (i.e., disagreeing) perspectives when they stem from out-group rather than in-group members. According to Phillips, because individuals tend to prefer opinions that are similar to those offered by their in-group members, out-group minority members are more likely to state their opinions confidently and influence the group decision more than in-group minority members. Ultimately, this may suggest that categorical diversity among group members can be beneficial to a group, not only because it serves to increase the breadth of knowledge available to its members but also because expectations about those categorical differences facilitate acceptance of differing perspectives.

The third fundamental psychological process underlying the value of social category diversity stems from individuals' motivation to maintain balance in social relationships with socially similar others. Specifically, Phillips, Liljenquist, et al., (2009) argued that the members of the social majority (i.e., in-group members) who agree with out-group members feel socially insecure because an alliance with out-group members threatens their social ties with other in-group members. This threat motivates opinion allies of out-group members to reconcile the divergent opinions in the group (Heider, 1958; Newcomb, 1968). This argument is consistent with Heider's (1958) balance theory, which suggests that people are motivated to maintain their social ties with similar others and to reconcile differences of opinion among socially similar others. The motivation to restore balance with similar others may ultimately improve group performance because members pay more attention to the task in an effort to reconcile the different opinions (Phillips, 2003; Phillips & Loyd, 2006; Phillips et al., 2004; Phillips, Liljenquist, et al., 2009). Thus, even when out-group members do not bring minority viewpoints to the table, the *mere presence* of social category diversity in task groups can fundamentally change the behavior of the social majority and enhance group performance.

Taken together, rather than assuming that people who are socially different will bring different task perspectives to the group, the aforementioned psychological processes may provide alternative explanations about why social category diversity is beneficial in groups. Social category differences trigger expectations that informational and opinion differences may be present in groups and legitimize the expression of unique perspectives and knowledge (Phillips, 2003; Phillips & Loyd, 2006; Phillips et al., 2006; van Knippenberg & Haslam, 2003; van Knippenberg, De Dreu, & Homan, 2004). In addition, the presence of social category diversity can decrease conformity to socially similar others in a group, which ultimately leads them to voice unique perspectives. Furthermore, the desire to restore social ties with the socially similar others can benefit groups by increasing the discussion of differing information and knowledge. Therefore, we propose that when benefits from social category diversity occur:

> Proposition 1: Social category diversity's benefits are not fully accounted for by underlying (and assumed) congruence with informational diversity.

AFFECT AND COGNITION IN DIVERSE GROUPS

Research has shown that when group members have different opinions as to how to perform a task, groups that have social category differences may actually outperform those that have no social category differences (i.e., homogeneous groups). Group members in diverse groups are more likely to consider unique perspectives and engage more in the task to understand the constellation of agreement and disagreement (Phillips, 2003; Phillips & Loyd, 2006; Phillips, Liljenquist, et al., 2009). These interpretations include social concerns about how individuals generally have a differential response to agreement from in-group versus out-group members in diverse group settings. Specifically, agreement with an in-group member may be socially validating (Abrams, Wetherell, Cochrane, Hogg, & Turner, 1990; Deutsch & Gerard, 1955; Festinger, 1954; Heider, 1958), whereas agreement with an out-group member may violate social expectations (Phillips, 2003; Phillips & Loyd, 2006; Phillips, Liljenquist, et al., 2009). Thus, when group members agree with an out-group member, they are more likely to attempt to uncover the roots of their agreement. They are also likely to seek out the reason behind any divergence of opinion between themselves and their in-group members (Phillips, Liljenquist, et al., 2009). Indeed, balance theory suggests that group members should be motivated to reconcile the incongruence they experience between members and to balance social concerns with task focus (Heider, 1958; Phillips, 2003; Phillips et al., 2004).

However, recent research reveals that, although the motivation to resolve imbalance in a group may ultimately enhance group performance, members of diverse groups actually feel less confident about their performance and therefore experience anxiety and discomfort (Phillips, Liljenquist, et al., 2009; Sommers, 2006; Wang, Loyd, Phillips, & Lount, 2009). For example, Phillips, Liljenquist, et al. (2009) examined how homogeneous groups were affected by the addition of either an in-group or an out-group newcomer. They found that the members of the social majority (i.e., in-group members) who agreed with the out-group newcomers (i.e., allies) were more uncomfortable and concerned about maintaining their social ties with existing in-group members. This discomfort and anxiety can cause diverse groups to perceive their outcomes and interactions as less effective than those resulting from homogeneous groups. Ironically, according to Phillips, Liljenquist, et al., the affective discomfort leads diverse groups to engage in more careful processing of information than groups that are socially homogeneous. Presumably, this occurs because allies of out-group newcomers feel less socially validated than the other members of the social majority (i.e., non-allies). Seeking to protect their relationships with in-group members, allies were motivated to examine the root cause of the discrepancies in opinions more carefully and to pay more attention to the perspectives of the newcomer and to the task. Similarly, Sommers (2006) showed that Caucasian jurors in diverse groups engaged in more systematic thought processes and evaluated more available pieces of information than Caucasians in all-White juries. These results suggest that negative affective responses, such as greater anxiety and discomfort in diverse settings can facilitate increased information processing, leading to better performance. Thus, we suggest the following:

> Proposition 2: The affective pain experienced by members of diverse groups can contribute to cognitive gains.

DIVERSITY BELIEFS IN GROUPS

Recent research has focused on the influence of individuals' expectations of working in a diverse group to provide a broader understanding of relationships between affective responses and cognitive functioning. Indeed, some studies suggest that individuals may expect interactions with socially dissimilar others to be less pleasant than those with socially similar others prior to entering the diverse setting, and these expectations may influence their affective consequences and cognitive processes (Antonio et al., 2004; Phillips & Lount, 2007; Sommers, 2006; Wang et al., 2009). For example, Antonio et al.'s (2004) examination of the effects of racial diversity on integrative complexity revealed that Caucasians in a diverse group (including a Black confederate) were more likely to engage in complex thinking about a discussion topic than those in a homogeneous group of all Caucasians prior to discussing that topic. Similarly, Wang et al. (2009) showed that when participants realized that their partner was an out-group member, they displayed more cognitive effort to process information thoroughly prior to any discussion.

Considering the importance of individuals' expectations about diversity, researchers have examined how diversity beliefs, defined as beliefs individuals hold about the value of diversity for task accomplishment (van Knippenberg & Haslam, 2003), influence related constructs of group process and performance in diverse groups (e.g., Cox, 1993; Ely & Thomas, 2001; Hostager & De Meuse, 2002; van Dick, van Knippenberg, Hägele, Guillaume, & Brodbeck, 2008; van Knippenberg, Haslam, & Platow, 2004). For example, van Knippenberg et al. (2004) argued that when people perceived their work group diversity as valuable for their tasks, they were more likely to respond favorably to their diversity and its diverse membership. Consistent with this perspective, they found that diversity beliefs moderated the relationship between diversity and group members' identification with their group. Specifically, when individuals believed in the value of diversity for the task, diversity was positively related to group identification, whereas diversity was negatively related to identification when individuals believed that similarity was more beneficial. Similarly, van Dick et al.'s (2008) longitudinal studies among students working in ethnically diverse project teams indicated that diversity beliefs moderated responses to ethnic diversity. That is, the relationship between subjective diversity (i.e., subjectively perceived differences between group members) and group identification was more positive in ethnically diverse groups when group members held prodiversity beliefs. Furthermore, Homan, van Knippenberg, van Kleef, and De Dreu (2007) examined the effects of diversity beliefs on groups' use of their informational diversity, focusing on groups with a diversity faultline. They suggested that groups were more likely to use their diverse information and perspectives effectively when group members believed in the value of diversity. Thus, even under fault-line conditions, informationally diverse groups performed better in group decision-making contexts when group members believed in the value of diversity rather than similarity, whereas the performance of information-ally homogeneous groups was less affected by diversity beliefs. In addition, the effect of diversity beliefs in informationally diverse groups was medi-ated by group elaboration of task-relevant information. In other words, their study suggests that the disruptive effects of diversity faultlines can be overcome by the value of diversity.

Phillips and Lount (2007) suggested that diversity beliefs may moderate the relationship between diversity and affective tone, although they expect that diversity will generally cause negative affective reactions such as uncer-tainty, anxiety, and discomfort. According to the affective model of diver-sity that Phillips and Lount propose, individuals who believe in the value of diversity may not expect to experience negative emotional responses when anticipating interaction with dissimilar others. Furthermore, individuals with more positive diversity beliefs should be more willing to embrace the negative affect and disagreement that occurs in diverse settings. Meanwhile, diversity beliefs can change depending on an individual's experiences while working in diverse groups. In particular, previous positive interactions in diverse groups may lead individuals to develop positive diversity beliefs, which will subsequently lead to less negative affective reactions. Linking these perspectives to Phillips, Liljenquist, et al.'s (2009) research, although groups with out-group newcomers (i.e., diverse groups) generally experience affective pain, it is possible for diverse groups to minimize that discomfort and anxiety and embrace the process of reconciling divergent opinions if they have the appropriate diversity beliefs.

In short, these findings have important implications for why it is worth-while to study diversity beliefs. Indeed, individuals' diversity beliefs can influence their affective and cognitive reactions, thereby leading differ-ent group processes and performance in diverse settings. Thus, given the

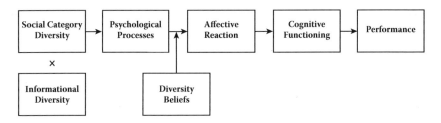

FIGURE 11.1
Model of psychological processes underlying diversity.

potential impact of diversity beliefs on groups, it would seem appropriate to conduct more in-depth research on the nature and antecedents of diversity beliefs to ultimately better understand the benefits of social category diversity in groups (Figure 11.1).

FUTURE RESEARCH

The social psychological study of diversity in groups has recently experienced a resurgence. As reviewed in this chapter, much of the work on diversity in teams had until recently been dominated by organizational scholars using survey methodologies, which left many of the group processes and underlying dynamics unexamined (Williams & O'Reilly, 1998). In this section, we will underscore the changing ways that diversity is being studied and highlight some directions for future research.

Of particular interest here are the varied experiences that individuals may be having inside of a diverse group. Thus, much of the research reviewed in this chapter has examined the influence of diversity in groups at the individual, dyadic, and group levels. For instance, Sommers's (2006) study examined subsets of individuals within the groups and compared their behavior. Likewise, Phillips, Liljenquist, et al. (2009) distinguished between individuals within the group who played different roles because of their structural positions (e.g., old-timers, newcomers, allies to the newcomer). Other researchers have also adopted this multilevel lens in an effort to gain more insight into what is really happening in diverse settings (e.g., Jehn & Greer, 2007; Knight, Klein, & Bates, 2007). This more nuanced approach to studying diversity is critical for developing future research agendas on diversity in groups. Because not all members of the group will be experiencing the same reality, our ability to understand those differences will shed important light on how to capture the potential benefits and minimize the downsides of diversity.

Moreover, there are several directions for future research that deserve further attention. The first draws on the concept of status distance and argues that much diversity research ignores the level of status differentiation associated with the diversity characteristics being examined in a given study (Phillips, Rothbard, & Dumas, 2009). Although we know from much sociological research that characteristics like race and gender are imbued with status expectations (e.g., Ridgeway, 1982, 1991), all groups naturally develop status hierarchies. In some cases, that hierarchy might imbue strong status differences (i.e., high status distance) and create difficulties with sharing information and solving problems in task groups, whereas in other situations the status distance may be lower and facilitate improved group process and performance. Whether the basis of social category diversity is functional background, race, or gender, within a given group in an organization there may be varying status distances that if measured could help explain the varied results we see in diverse groups. Future research on diversity in groups should measure the status distance between individuals to capture a broader and more complete picture of the diversity that exists. To be sure, this variable would be separate from a measure of diversity: Two groups with equal amounts of diversity may have very different levels of status distance and thus entail different psychological processes and performance.

Second, future research should continue to consider the role of expectations and beliefs in diverse settings. The work on congruence and diversity beliefs highlights the fact that the effects of diversity may be in the eye of the beholder. Lount, Phillips, and Rink (2009) recently found that, when given identical transcripts of a discussion attributed either to a socially diverse or homogeneous group, observers report the discussion of the diverse group as having more conflict than the homogenous group. This suggests that some of what has been captured in the study of conflict in groups are measurements of group members' perceptions and interpretations of the conflict and not actual behaviors. This warrants closer examination of groups in terms of the role that diversity beliefs may play to more finely distinguish between reality and perception.

In a related vein, it is worthwhile to examine the effects of diversity beliefs on psychological processes. Previous research suggests that diversity beliefs can lead group members to respond favorably to work group diversity, can reduce negative feelings toward diversity, and can lead to better performance. Earlier in this chapter, we suggested how social category and informational diversity affect three fundamental psychological processes and how these psychological processes influence affective reaction and cognitive processing, ultimately affecting performance (see Figure 11.1). In other words, not only can diversity beliefs influence these psychological mechanisms, but these mechanisms can strongly impact individual beliefs about diversity. For example, group members who believe in the value of diversity may be less inclined to conform with socially similar others. Meanwhile, group members' strong motivation to maintain social ties with socially similar others may weaken their pro-diversity beliefs. Therefore, future research should further investigate how diversity beliefs influence the psychological processes and vice versa and how these effects may ultimately impact group performance.

CONCLUSION

Understanding the value of diversity is an important goal. Not only is it critical for organizations seeking to benefit from the different perspectives, information, and opinions that diverse group members bring to the table, but it is also important for society as a whole. Demographic trends are clear—diversity is here to stay. With this increase in social category diversity there will be an infusion of informational diversity, but we argue here that the value of diversity does not stop there. The value of diversity comes from the increased cognitive processing and vigilance that social category diversity brings to a group. Thus, the ability to benefit from the informational diversity that is present in most task groups may be enhanced and legitimized by the presence of social category diversity (Phillips et al., 2006). Social psychological theory supports this idea. Organizations will hopefully get there.

REFERENCES

Abrams, D. M., Wetherell, M., Cochrane, S., Hogg, M. A., & Turner, J. C. (1990). Knowing what to think by knowing who you are: Self-categorization and the nature of norm formation, conformity and group polarization. *British Journal of Social Psychology,* *29*, 97–119.

Allen, V. L., & Wilder, D. A. (1975). Categorization, belief similarity, and intergroup discrimination. *Journal of Personality and Social Psychology, 32*, 971–977.

Allen, V. L., & Wilder, D. A. (1979). Group categorization and attribution of belief similarity. *Small Group Behavior, 10*, 73–80.

Antonio, A. L., Chang, M. J., Hakuta, K., Kenny, D. A., Levin, S., & Milem, J. F. (2004). Effects of racial diversity on complex thinking in college students. *Psychological Science, 15*, 507–510.

Argote, L., Gruenfeld, D. H., & Naquin, C. (2000). Group learning in organizations. In M. E. Turner (Ed.), *Groups at work: Advances in theory and research* (pp. 369–411). Hillsdale, NJ: Erlbaum.

Chen, F. F., & Kenrick, D. T. (2002). Repulsion or attraction? Group membership and assumed altitude similarity. *Journal of Personality and Social Psychology, 83*, 111–125.

Cox, T. H. (1993). *Cultural diversity in organizations: Theory, research and practice.* San Francisco: Berrett-Koehler.

Cox, T. H., Lobel, S. A., & McLeod, P. L. (1991). Effects of ethnic group cultural differences on cooperative and competitive behavior on a group task. *Academy of Management Journal, 34*, 827–847.

Deutsch, M., & Gerard, H. B. (1955). A study of normative and informational social influences upon individual judgment. *Journal of Abnormal and Social Psychology, 51*, 629–636.

Ely, R., & Thomas, D. (2001). Cultural diversity at work: The effects of diversity perspectives on work group processes and outcomes. *Administrative Science Quarterly, 46*, 229–273.

Festinger, L. (1954). A theory of social comparison processes. *Human Relations, 7*, 117–140.

Gruenfeld, D. H., Mannix, E. A., Williams, K. Y., & Neale, M. A. (1996). Group composition and decision making: How member familiarity and information distribution affect process and performance. *Organizational Behavior and Human Decision Processes, 67*, 1–15.

Harrison, D. A., Price, K. H., & Bell, M. P. (1998). Beyond relational demography: Time and effects of surface- and deep-level diversity on work group cohesion. *Academy of Management Journal, 41*, 96–107.

Heider, F. (1958). *The psychology of interpersonal relations.* New York: Wiley.

Holtz, R., & Miller, N. (1985). Assumed similarity and opinion certainty. *Journal of Personality and Social Psychology, 48*, 890–898.

Homan, A.C., van Knippenberg, D., van Kleef, G.A., & De Dreu, C. K. W. (2007). Bridging faultlines by valuing diversity: Diversity beliefs, information elaboration, and performance in diverse work groups. *Journal of Applied Psychology, 92*, 1189–1199.

Hostager, T. J., & De Meuse, K. P. (2002). Assessing the complexity of diversity perceptions: Breadth, depth, and balance. *Journal of Business and Psychology, 17*, 189–206.

Jackson, S. E., Joshi, A., & Erhardt, N. L. (2003). Recent research on team and organizational diversity: SWOT analysis and implications. *Journal of Management, 29*, 801–830.

Jackson, S. E., May, K. E., & Whitney, K. (1995). Understanding the dynamics of diversity in decision-making teams. In R. A. Guzzo & E. Salas (Eds.), *Team decision-making effectiveness in organizations* (pp. 204–261). San Francisco: Jossey-Bass.

Janis, I. L. (1982). *Victims of groupthink* (2nd ed.). Boston: Houghton Mifflin.

Jehn, K., & Greer, L.L. (2007). *The effects of group composition on dyadic interactions: Relationship quality and status differences.* Paper presented at the annual meeting of the Academy of Management, August, Philadelphia, PA.

Jehn, K., Northcraft, G., & Neale, M. (1999). Why differences make a difference: A field study of diversity, conflict, and performance in workgroups. *Administrative Science Quarterly, 44,* 741–763.

Knight, A., Klein, K., & Bates, A. (2007). *The relationship underpinnings of conflict and cohesion in teams.* Paper presented at the annual meeting of the Academy of Management, August, Philadelphia, PA.

Kochan, T., Bezrukova, K., Ely, R., Jackson, S., Joshi, A., Jehn, K., et al. (2003). The effects of diversity on business performance: Report of the diversity research network. *Human Resource Management, 42,* 3–21.

Lawrence, B. S. (1997). The black box of organizational demography. *Organization Science, 8,* 1–22.

Lount, R. B., Jr., & Phillips, K. W. (2007). Working harder with the out-group: The impact of social category diversity on motivation gains. *Organizational Behavior and Human Decision Processes, 103,* 214–224.

Lount, R. B., Jr., Phillips, K. W., & Rink, F. (2009). *The impact of group diversity and performance on perceptions of conflict and motivation in groups.* Paper presented at the annual meeting of the Academy of Management, Chicago, IL.

Mannix, E. A., & Neale, M. A. (2005). What differences make a difference? The promise and reality of diverse teams in organizations. *Psychological Science in the Public Interest, 6,* 31–55.

McLeod, P., Baron, R., Marti, M., & Yoon, K. (1997). The eyes have it: Minority influence in face-to-face and computer-mediated group discussion. *Journal of Applied Psychology, 82,* 706–718.

Milliken, F. J., & Martins, L. L. (1996). Searching for common threads: Understanding the multiple effects of diversity in organizational groups. *Academy of Management Review, 21,* 402–433.

Newcomb, T. M. (1968). Interpersonal balance. In R. Abelson, E. Aronson, W. McGuire, T. Newcomb, M. Rosenberg, & P. Tannenbaum (Eds.), *Theories of cognitive consistency: A sourcebook.* Chicago: Rand McNally.

Pelled, L. H. (1996). Demographic diversity, conflict, and work group outcomes: An intervening process theory. *Organization Science, 7,* 615–631.

Pelled, L. H., Eisenhardt, K. M., & Xin, K. R. (1999). Exploring the black box: An analysis of work group diversity, conflict, and performance. *Administrative Science Quarterly, 44,* 1–28.

Phillips, K. W. (2003). The effects of categorically based expectations on minority influence: The importance of congruence. *Personality and Social Psychology Bulletin, 29,* 3–13.

Phillips, K. W., Liljenquist, K. A., & Neale, M. A. (2009). Is the pain worth the gain? The advantages and liabilities of agreeing with socially distinct newcomers. *Personality and Social Psychology Bulletin, 35,* 336–350.

Phillips, K. W., & Lount, R. B., Jr. (2007). The affective consequences of diversity and homogeneity in groups. In E. Mannix, M. A. Neale, & C. Anderson (Eds.), *Research on Managing Groups and Teams* (Vol. 10, pp. 1–20). San Diego, CA: JAI Press.

Phillips, K. W., & Loyd, D. L. (2006). When surface and deep-level diversity collide: The effects on dissenting group members. *Organizational Behavior and Human Decision Processes, 99,* 143–160.

Phillips, K. W., Mannix, E., Neale, M., & Gruenfeld, D. (2004). Diverse groups and information sharing: The effects of congruent ties. *Journal of Experimental Social Psychology, 40,* 497–510.

Phillips, K. W., Northcraft, G. B., & Neale, M. A. (2006). Surface-level diversity and decision-making in groups: When does deep-level similarity help? *Group Processes and Intergroup Relations, 9,* 467–482.

Phillips, K. W., Rothbard, N. P., & Dumas, T. L. (2009). To disclose or not to disclose? Status distance and self-disclosure in diverse environments. *Academy of Management Review, 34,* 710–732.

Ridgeway, C. L. (1982). Status in groups: The importance of motivation. *American Sociological Review, 47,* 76–88.

Ridgeway, C. L. (1991). The social construction of status value: Gender and other nominal characteristics. *Social Forces, 70,* 367–86.

Riordan, C. M. (2000). Relational demography within groups: Past developments, contradictions, and new directions. In G. R. Ferris (Ed.), *Research in personnel and human resource management* (Vol. 19, pp. 131–173). Greenwich, CT: JAI Press.

Sommers, S. (2006). On racial diversity and group decision-making: Identifying multiple effects of racial composition on jury deliberations. *Journal of Personality and Social Psychology, 90,* 597–612.

Stasser, G., Stewart, D. D., & Wittenbaum, G. M. (1995). Expert roles and information exchange during discussion: The importance of knowing who knows what. *Journal of Experimental Social Psychology, 31,* 244–265.

Tajfel, H. (1969). Cognitive aspects of prejudice. *Journal of Social Issues, 25,* 79–97.

Tajfel, H. (1972). Some developments in European social psychology. *European Journal of Social Psychology, 2,* 307–322.

Tajfel, H. (1974). Social identity and intergroup behavior. *Social Science Information, 13,* 65–93.

Tajfel, H., & Wilkes, A. L. (1963). Classification and quantitative judgment. *British Journal of Psychology, 54,* 101–114.

Thomas, D. A., & Ely, R. J. (1996). Making differences matter: A new paradigm for managing diversity. *Harvard Business Review, 74,* 79–90.

Thomas-Hunt, M. C., Ogden, T. Y., & Neale, M. A. (2003). Who's really sharing? Effects of social and expert status on knowledge exchange within groups. *Management Science, 49,* 464–477.

Toossi, M. (2006, November). A new look at long-term labor force projections to 2050. *Monthly Labor Review, 129,* 19–39.

Triandis, H. C., Kurowski, L. L., & Gelfand, M. J. (1994). Workplace diversity. In H. C. Triandis, M. D. Dunnette, & L. M. Hough (Eds.), *Handbook of industrial and organizational psychology* (2nd ed., Vol. 4, pp. 769–827). Palo Alto, CA: Consulting Psychologists Press.

Turner, J. C., Hogg, M. A., Oakes, P. J., Reicher, S. D., & Wetherell, M. S. (1987). *Rediscovering the social group: A self-categorization theory.* Oxford, UK: Blackwell.

van Dick, R., van Knippenberg, D., Hägele, S., Guillaume, Y. R. F., & Brodbeck, F. C. (2008). Group diversity and group identification: The moderating role of diversity beliefs. *Human Relations, 61,* 1463–1492.

van Knippenberg, D., De Dreu, C. K. W., & Homan, A. C. (2004). Work group diversity and group performance: An integrative model and research agenda. *Journal of Applied Psychology, 89,* 1008–1022.

van Knippenberg, D., & Haslam, S. A. (2003). Realizing the diversity dividend: Exploring the subtle interplay between identity, ideology and reality. In S. A. Haslam, D. van Knippenberg, M. J. Platow, & N. Ellemers (Eds.), *Social identity at work: Developing theory for organizational practice* (pp. 61–77). New York: Psychology Press.

van Knippenberg, D., Haslam, S. A., & Platow, M. J. (2004). *Unity through diversity: Value-in-diversity beliefs as moderator of the relationship between work group diversity and group identification.* Paper presented at the Society for Industrial and Organizational Psychology 19th Annual Conference, April, Chicago.

van Knippenberg, D., & Schippers, M. C. (2007). Work group diversity. *Annual Review of Psychology, 58,* 515–541.

Wang, C. S., Loyd, D. L., Phillips, K. W., & Lount, R. B., Jr. (2009). *Elaborating more with the out-group: The role of relationship focus and opinion diversity.* Working paper, Northwestern University.

Webber, S. S., & Donahue, L. M. (2001). Impact of highly and less job-related diversity on work group cohesion and performance: A meta-analysis. *Journal of Management, 27,* 141–162.

Wilder, D. A., & Allen, V. L. (1978). Group membership and preference for information about other persons. *Personality and Social Psychology Bulletin, 4,* 106–110.

Williams, K. Y., & O'Reilly, C. (1998). Demography and diversity in organizations: A review of 40 years of research. In B. M. Staw & R. Sutton (Eds.), *Research in organizational behavior* (Vol. 21, pp. 77–140). Greenwich, CT: JAI Press.

12

Antisocial Behavior at Work: The Social Psychological Dynamics of Workplace Victimization and Revenge*

Karl Aquino
Sauder School of Business

Jane O'Reilly
Sauder School of Business

Sally arrived at work in her usual way: haughty, humorless, and eager to begin her daily meetings with clients, which she likened to warfare. She wielded her authority in the office with a pathological zeal. The principal target for her imperial depredations was Karen, her unassuming personal assistant. Each day, Karen would endure Sally's requests to perform menial and irrelevant tasks along with her more consequential duties. Sally would inevitably criticize Karen for failing to accomplish these tasks to her satisfaction, to which the devoted assistant would respond with self-deprecating assurances that she would do better next time. When asked by coworkers why she tolerated her superior's abuse, Karen dismissed their inquiries by saying that working for Sally was better than being unemployed. Yet it was becoming apparent that Sally's relentless criticism was eroding what remained of Karen's faltering dignity. In the evenings Karen went home emotionally exhausted but resigned to playing her role in the relationship she had formed with her boss. Her sleep was often troubled, though, by the disquieting pains and inner longings that mar the dreams of the unworthy.

Three floors down, in another part of the firm, Harrison's agitated steps carried him to the row of cubicles he shared with several other employees who did the same job as he. Harrison was feeling dissatisfied and edgy, which was typical of his state of mind. Every sight, sound, and smell of the

---

* The authors contributed equally to this chapter.

office irritated him, and he let it be known to his coworkers by responding to their morning greetings with a surly glare. As the day progressed, he made contemptuous remarks about one person's lack of taste and the banality of another person's ideas. He had become predictable in the frequency and nature of his personal attacks and often found himself arguing with his cubicle mates over the most trivial matters. Harrison often complained to his friends about his troubles at work. He would tell his friends stories about how he was shunned at parties and gossiped about by envious colleagues. Harrison couldn't understand why he was so unpopular because he saw himself as serving an important function at the firm. He alone among the sycophants who occupied his floor was willing to denounce the incompetence of his superiors and reveal the workplace inefficiencies that only he seemed capable of recognizing. He concluded that everyone around him was simply threatened by his honesty and the enormity of his talents. He appeared confident in this belief while at work, but when he went home Harrison could not dismiss from his mind the possibility that he was a very unlikable person.

The protagonists in these stories share a common experience: They perceive themselves as being the targets of harmful actions emanating from other employees, and it causes them psychological and emotional distress. From this perspective, both can be described as being "victims" of workplace mistreatment. A victim in the most general sense is anyone who experiences a negative outcome as a result of some event, which in the context of this chapter refers to how one is treated by another person or persons within the organization. In this chapter, we explore the concept of *workplace victimization* as a form of antisocial behavior. Like the other chapters in this volume, our exploration will be narrow and emphasize the work conducted by the first author and his colleagues. The chapter summarizes this program of research that has sought to explain why some people become the targets of harmful actions from other employees, be they coworkers or superiors.

Workplace victimization falls within the broader conceptual domain of antisocial workplace behaviors, but its emphasis is on the target of such behaviors rather than on the perpetrator. However, the targets of victimization can sometimes choose to respond aggressively to those who mistreat them, so they then assume the role of perpetrator. Recognizing that workplace victimization can have a dynamic, reciprocal quality, our chapter also explores work by Aquino and his colleagues on another form of antisocial behavior: revenge. Workplace victimization and revenge form an appropriate theoretical marriage because, for every action displayed in the context of ongoing workplace relationships, there is a reaction. Whether this reaction is positive or negative, aggressive or passive, momentary or sustained, subtle or transparent depends on many factors, and we will consider some of these in our chapter.

We begin by reviewing the studies conducted by Aquino and his colleagues on workplace victimization before turning our attention to revenge. When addressing both concepts we follow the same outline. First, we briefly summarize the findings of the most significant studies and identify the social psychological theories that Aquino and his associates have applied to explain the phenomenon of interest. We then offer a theoretical and methodological critique of this program of research and present proposals for advancing future study of these phenomena. By the end of the chapter, we hope to convince the reader of the practical utility of applying social psychology to explaining these two forms of antisocial behavior in organizations.

WORKPLACE VICTIMIZATION

Aquino and Thau (2009) reviewed the state of the literature on aggressive behavior from the victim's perspective and proposed that workplace victimization occurs "when an employee's well-being is harmed by an act of aggression perpetrated by one or more members of the organization" (p. 718). An employee's well-being is harmed when a fundamental psychological need, such as the need to belong, the ability to avoid pain, or the need for control, has been thwarted by these aggressive acts. By this definition, our fictional employees Karen and Harrison can both be characterized as having been targets of workplace victimization because each experienced one or more of these needs as being thwarted. However, the social psychological dynamics that led to their victimization are quite different. Karen's experience results from the misfortune of being the subordinate of a domineering, insensitive boss. Coupled with her lack of assertiveness, she has become a participant in an ongoing pattern of humiliation and debasement that she has, for the moment, chosen to tolerate. Harrison's mistreatment by his coworkers, on the other hand, is primarily the result of how he presents himself at work. By violating commonly recognized norms that prescribe friendliness, cooperation, and mutual respect in social interactions, Harrison has knowingly or unknowingly made himself the target of negative behaviors from his coworkers.

Aquino and his colleagues have examined the personality characteristics that underlie the behaviors of people like Karen and Harrison, factors that have been repeatedly shown to predict who becomes a victim of others' harmful actions. These characteristics are captured by two main types of victims first proposed by Olweus (1978) based on his investigations of schoolyard bullying. Olweus found that the majority of targets of schoolyard bullying were more anxious, quiet, and insecure compared with the other students. They also held more negative views about themselves and were seen by others as being socially inept and unpopular. Olweus labeled this group of targets *submissive victims*. Rather unfortunately, submissive victims passively contribute to their victimization as they are seen as easy targets of others' aggression. In addition to the submissive victims, Olweus also noted that a smaller group of targets fit a very different profile. He labeled these targets *provocative victims*. Provocative victims are described as being hostile, uncompromising, and aggressive. Their antagonistic behavior irritates their peers and elicits aggression as a form of reprisal or as a means of socially controlling their undesirable behavior.

Several studies conducted by Aquino and his colleagues provide evidence of personality predictors of workplace victimization that are consistent with the victim typology proposed by Olweus (1978). Similar to the submissive victim profile, several of their studies show that employees who reported high negative affectivity, a trait associated with the tendency to experience higher levels of negative emotions such as anger and anxiety, also reported being a more frequent target of coworkers' aggressive behaviors (Aquino & Bradfield, 2000; Aquino, Grover, Bradfield, & Allen, 1999). In another study, employees who reported using an "obliging" conflict-resolution style also reported a higher level of victimization (Aquino, 2000). An obliging conflict-resolution style is characterized by being overly concerned with others' needs while having a low concern for one's own needs (Rahim, 1983). Employees who use an obliging style routinely give in to the demands of others and may be perceived as weak and vulnerable to aggressive acts, typical of the submissive victim. In support of the provocative victim profile, Aquino and Bradfield (2000) found that people who report high levels of trait aggressiveness, a predisposition to engaging in aggressive behaviors, also reported a greater amount of victimization.

So where does social psychological theory fit into this work on the relationship between personality and victimization? An implicit assumption of all the previously reported studies is that the personality determinants of observable behavioral patterns that make one a more likely target of victimization occur in the context of social relationships. Thus, two theoretical ideas permeate all of these studies, both of which have their roots in social psychological principles: victim precipitation and symbolic interactionism. According to victim precipitation theory, victims either unknowingly or knowingly participate in the sequences of events that eventually lead up to their experiences of victimization (Amir, 1967; Curtis, 1974). Similar to Olweus's (1978) victim typology, victim precipitation models divide precipitation into two major groupings: *passive* and *active.* Passive precipitation can occur when potential victims fail to protect themselves from becoming a target. For example, potential victims might decide to work in an organization with known destructive interpersonal norms. In this situation, simply being in an environment where people are generally more likely to become targets of victimization increases the chances of being victimized. Furthermore, complementary to the image of a submissive victim, potential targets may passively precipitate their victimization by appearing weak, vulnerable to, or defenseless against aggressive or harmful behavior. In support of the passive victim precipitation model, Tepper, Duffy, Henle, and Lambert (2006) found that subordinates high in negative affectivity were more often the targets of their supervisors' displaced aggression. Active precipitation, on the other hand, suggests that victims engage in behaviors that will elicit direct responses from others. In contrast to the passive victim, who is seen as an easy target, active victims appear as "deserving" of mistreatment. Comparable to Olweus's (1978) provocative victim, active victims engage in threatening or irritating behavior that make them more likely targets of victimization. However, the victim precipitation model goes beyond Olweus's typology of victims by arguing that it is not simply certain personality types that make one a more likely target of victimization. Rather, potential targets engage in certain behaviors and actions that inadvertently or deliberately send signals to observers that they are vulnerable to or deserving of harm. This interaction between victims and their would-be victimizers increases the likelihood that individuals will become the target of victimization.

Elements of the victim precipitation model are also reflected in the symbolic interactionist model of aggression (Felson, 1992; Felson & Steadman, 1983). Symbolic interactionism argues that harmful or aggressive behaviors directed toward a selected target are often intended as a means of social control, to enhance one's social identity, or to achieve retributive justice. In this sense, people are victimized as a form of social punishment. The symbolic interactionist approach also provides a more theoretically detailed explanation for observers' responses to the active precipitation model or the provocative victim profile. Victims are perceived as deserving of harm because they initially breached a social norm. For example, employees who constantly berate their colleagues, complain about minor issues, or fail to go above and beyond their formal work duties to help out their peers in times of need may violate informal norms of courtesy, respect, and teamwork. This behavior can initiate a negative norm of reciprocity with one's peers or superiors and direct negative behavior against the norm violator as a form of social sanctioning, deterrence, or punishment (Gouldner, 1960). Similar to victim precipitation, symbolic interactionism suggests that individuals are more likely to become targets of victimization when their behavior triggers or incites such a reaction from others.

Victim precipitation theory and the symbolic interactionism models both focus on a victim's behaviors and actions toward others; however, another foundational principle of social psychology is that behavior is a function of the person and the situation. Aquino and his colleagues have also incorporated this notion into their research by proposing that, even though certain characteristics might make an employee appear as a vulnerable or deserving target of mistreatment, the nature of the relationship between the perpetrator and the victim may also influence whether in fact an individual actually becomes a target of mistreatment. Aquino and colleagues have focused considerable attention on exploring the moderating effect of an employee's formal status on the relationship between personality factors and experiences of victimization. We review three studies that have examined this relationship.

Hierarchical Status as a Moderator of the Personality–Victimization Relationship

Formal hierarchical status is a form of power. High-status individuals are generally seen as being more deserving of preferential treatment and respect and are generally considered to be more privileged and worthy than low-formal-status employees (Jackson, Schuler, & Rivero, 1989). In addition, high-status individuals often have more control over valued outcomes and resources (Lawler & Yoon, 1993), and, as a result, others in the organization are generally less willing to victimize high-status individuals for fear of reprisal. Thus, because of their position within the social framework of organizations, high-status individuals are seen as less vulnerable to and less deserving of acts of aggression. Based on this reasoning, Aquino and his colleagues have predicted that the empirical relationship between personality factors that generally precipitate victimization and reports of victimization would be stronger for low-status employees than high-status employees. They found support for this assertion in several studies. For example, Aquino, Grover, Bradfield, and Allen (1999) surveyed employees in a public utility as part of an organizational assessment. They found that the relationship between negative affectivity, an individual characteristic previously noted as a precipitating factor of victimization, and victimization was stronger for low-status employees.

Aquino and Bommer (2003) also investigated the effects of formal status on victimization. In this study, rather than looking at the personality or behavioral traits hypothesized to encourage victimization, the researchers looked at employee organizational citizenship behavior (OCB) as a potential factor that would discourage victimization. OCB refers to positive and discretionary employee behavior that is not formally rewarded by an organization and that benefits organizational functioning or performance (Organ, 1988). Aquino and Bommer focused on *interpersonal* OCB: positive behaviors directed toward others in the organization (rather than the organization itself) such as going above and beyond one's formal duties to help a coworker in need and proactively taking steps to prevent interpersonal conflict and problems. They argued that employees who performed frequent OCBs initiated a pattern of positive reciprocity among their peers and supervisors, reducing the likelihood that they would become a target of aggressive or harmful behaviors. They collected self-reports of victimization and supervisor reports of OCB and found that OCB was negatively related to incidences of workplace victimization, but only for those of low formal status. In contrast, those of high status reported low overall levels of workplace victimization. The results suggest that those of high status do not have to engage in OCB to reduce the likelihood of being the target of aggressive behaviors because their high-level positions make them less vulnerable to mistreatment in general.

Finally, Aquino (2000) investigated the moderating effect of status on the relationship between conflict resolution styles and victimization. As already noted, those who used an obliging conflict-resolution style also reported higher levels of victimization. However, this relationship was stronger for those of low status in the organization. Interestingly, this study also found that, while there is no direct relationship between the use of an "integrative" conflict-resolution style and victimization, there is a significantly positive relationship for low-status employees. An integrative conflict-resolution style is characterized by having a high regard for both one's own and the other party's interests in a conflict situation. This result was contrary to what was expected as it was originally hypothesized that the use of an integrative style would be negatively associated with victimization. There are several potential explanations for this finding. First, while low-status individuals may have a concern for their own interests in a conflict, they may also lack the overall power and resources needed to sufficiently protect those interests. As a result, by default they may be forced to use a more obliging conflict-resolution style, even when this may not have been their original intention. Furthermore, research in the conflict-resolution literature suggests that an integrative style is constructive in solving conflict when it is used in conjunction with a dominating style, an approach characterized as having high concerns only for one's own interests in a conflict (van de Vliert, Euwema, & Huismans, 1995). Low-status individuals may not adequately and strategically pair these styles together and as a result appear weak and overly accommodating to the needs of others. Regardless of the underlying reasons, this finding, along with the bulk of this research, suggests that high-status individuals experience less victimization than low-status individuals and can get away with certain behaviors that would normally precipitate victimization for low-status employees.

The Moderating Effect of Demographics

In addition to situational factors, the first author's research has also examined the interaction of personality characteristics and demographic markers of status. Drawing from status characteristics theory

(Berger, Fiske, Norman, & Zelditch, 1977), two studies have investigated how gender and race moderate the relationship among personality characteristics, behavior, and victimization. Social categories, such as race and gender, can informally indicate one's status in the organization (Pettigrew & Martin, 1987). White men are generally perceived as having more power, status, and influence in an organization than minorities or women employees. Status characteristics theory also proposes that people make inferences about the reasons for others' behaviors differently for high-status and low-status individuals. Specifically, bystanders are more likely to attribute the positive behaviors (e.g., good performance) of high-status employees to an underlying individual trait (e.g., intelligence, ability) compared with their attributions of the same behaviors performed by individuals in a social category considered to be low status. Thus, in their study on the relationship between OCB and victimization, Aquino and Bommer (2003) predicted that OCB and victimization would be more strongly and negatively related for White employees compared with racial minorities and for men compared with women. Their results did not support a significant interaction between gender and OCB; however, they did find support for the moderating effects of race. As predicted, they found that, for White employees, engaging in OCB was negatively related to being a target of workplace victimization; however, the benefits of engaging in OCBs on victimization did not carry over for racial minority employees.

Finally, Aquino and Byron (2002) investigated the moderating effect of gender on the relationship between a dominating conflict-resolution style and victimization. In this study, Aquino and Byron collected self-reports of victimization and peer reports of dominating behavior from master's students working together on a course project. They predicted that victimization within the group would be higher for those who were reported by their peers as exhibiting either low or high levels of dominating behavior. They argued that those who exhibit low dominating behaviors may fail to protect their self-interests and are taken advantage of by other group members, thus representing the submissive victim profile. On the other hand, those who exhibit high levels of dominating behavior are likely to be seen as aggravating and uncompromising by their peers and thus to elicit a retaliatory response, fitting the provocative victim profile. The researchers found that the relationship between a dominating style and victimization exhibited the predicted curvilinear pattern, but only for male group members. There was no relationship between dominating behaviors and victimization for women. The researchers offered several explanations for this finding. First, the "chivalry bias" noted in the stereotype literature refers to the common perception that women should be treated with more leniency than men, even when it comes to counterstereotypical behavior (Crew, 1991; Moulds, 1980). Thus, when women exhibit a strong dominating conflict-resolution style, a counterstereotypical behavior, they receive less retaliation than their male counterparts. Another potential explanation is that women face qualitatively different forms of victimization not captured in the study. For example, group members may use more passive or indirect forms of victimization as a means of socially sanctioning women, such as ignoring their ideas or opinions and gossiping behind their backs.

Critique of Research and Future Research Directions

We hope the reader is persuaded that the studies of workplace victimization just reviewed make theoretical and practical contributions to our understanding of harmful workplace behaviors and the victim's role in unintentionally provoking mistreatment. However, this research program is not without limitations. First, most of the studies have used a cross-sectional survey design and have relied on victims' self-perceptions of personality, or behavioral styles, and reports of victimization. These methods are all susceptible to respondent biases. This limitation is particularly salient in the context of workplace victimization, especially when considering the relationship between negative affectivity and victimization. It is possible that, rather than becoming a target of workplace mistreatment as a result of being negative and experiencing high levels of anxiety, fear, and worry, many of the respondents in Aquino and colleagues' studies experience this negative state as a result of being victimized. Other researchers have argued that negative affectivity is a result of experiencing harmful behaviors at work (e.g., Hansen et al., 2006; Mikkelsen & Einarsen, 2002), and none of the studies we reviewed can rule out this possibility.

The self-report method for assessing victimization is also vulnerable to recall and attribution biases (e.g., Blaney, 1986). People high in negative affectivity and aggressive tendencies tend to see the world through a pessimistic lens. They are more likely to focus on or remember negative events and perceive hostile intent in others' actions. Thus, a potential alternative explanation for the results in many of these studies is that certain targets only *perceive* themselves to be targets of victimization when in fact they are not treated, by a more "objective" standard, any different from the other members of the organization.

These limitations do not supersede the basic tenet that the victim *may* contribute, either knowingly or unknowingly, to their own victimization, even if that role is to some degree a subjective perception. To gain a better understanding of the dynamics of victimization, these limitations need to be addressed so that victim precipitation and symbolic interactionist models can be tested more rigorously. Two studies in Aquino and colleagues' research program have addressed these limitations by using multisource respondents (Aquino & Bommer, 2003) and a longitudinal design (Aquino & Byron, 2002). Both provide some evidence that victims behave in ways that are recognized by those around them and that these behaviors influence how they are treated.

Finally, while the victimization literature has built a strong case for the need to understand the victim's role to truly explain workplace victimization, the empirical research on victimization pursued by Aquino and colleagues has largely ignored the role and nature of the perpetrator. It is not necessarily a limitation to ignore the perpetrator depending on the question one seeks to address, but the theoretical framework that guides the work reviewed here clearly implies an interrelationship between victims and their perpetrators. Aquino and Lamertz (2004) proposed a theoretical framework that takes this interrelationship into account to explain different forms of victimization in dyads.

A Relational Model of Workplace Victimization: Uniting the Victim's and the Perpetrator's Perspectives of Victimization

Aquino and Lamertz's (2004) relational model of workplace victimization proposes that employees can occupy certain relational roles within the organization's social system and that the characteristics of these roles can influence patterns of victimization. They suggest that four archetypal relational roles can emerge in organizations based on a combination of two victim types (i.e., submissive and provocative) and two perpetrator types (i.e., domineering and reactive). A domineering perpetrator is someone with a strong desire to dominate, control, or exploit others. A reactive perpetrator is someone who has a propensity to respond aggressively to coercive or norm-violating actions.

Two combinations of relationships can lead to frequent, repeated patterns of victimization and aggression. The first is when a submissive victim forms a relationship with a domineering perpetrator. This combination produces the classic bully–whipping boy relational role. The second type of relational role is one that develops between a reactive perpetrator and a provocative victim. These types play complementary roles in which victimization occurs in a context of frequent and escalating personal conflict between the two role actors. In addition to these two relational roles, less predictable and potentially more explosive victimization events can emerge between a dominating perpetrator and a provocative victim. The interpersonal styles of these two types clash, and dominating perpetrators are likely to perceive some of the behavior of a provocative victim as challenging to their authority or control. This relationship can lead to episodic victimization because provocative victims are willing to defend themselves against such treatment. In addition, given the similarities between the personalities of a dominating perpetrator and a provocative victim, there can be periodic bursts of role reversal between these two. Finally, a relational role can form between a submissive victim and reactive perpetrator. However, given that submissive victims are unlikely to give a reactive perpetrator any reason to respond aggressively to their behavior, this relationship is likely to be characterized by low levels of victimization.

Aquino and Lamertz (2004) do not claim that all employees fit into one of these four types or that they capture all the potential relational roles in organizations. They are ideal types, meant to be abstract, metaphoric, and useful as a way of describing relational patterns that might emerge in organizations. What specific personality or individual difference characteristics map onto each of these types is a question for another theory to address. As we see it, the main contribution of Aquino and Lamertz's model is that it explains how different patterns of victimization result from the roles that different parties in the relationship enact and socially validate through their actions. Whether the theory will have practical value for guiding research remains to be seen.

WORKPLACE REVENGE

On Fridays Sally would sometimes ask Karen to pick up her suits from the dry cleaner. It was not a task in Karen's job description, but she did it anyway to avoid antagonizing her boss. Sally would instruct Karen to take her suits home and bring them back to the office on Monday so she could have a fresh wardrobe available for her afternoon meetings. Sally sometimes changed her clothes during the day to appeal to the imagined tastes of her clients, which she believed would make them more vulnerable to her charm and influence. Karen disliked picking up Sally's suits because it was burdensome to carry these articles along with her other possessions while jostling for space in a crowded, suffocating subway car. Karen was feeling particularly morose about her work situation when Sally stopped by to request that she pick up two pantsuits from the dry cleaner. Karen did as she was told and when she arrived at her apartment after a long commute, she hung Sally's clothes in her closet. She paused for a moment to study them. She noticed the fine material of which they were made and admired how the pleasant colors of their fabrics conveyed a warmth and generosity that belied the true nature of their wearer. She envied the woman who could afford such luxuries and this emotion, mingled with her nascent anger, led her to devise a plan. She went into her sewing box and removed a tiny pair of scissors. Carefully, deliberately, she sliced the threads that bound the seam at the back of one of Sally's custom tailored pants. She cut only a few threads, but enough, she thought, that over the course of a day the pressure from her boss's fleshy rump rising and falling, stretching and turning, would eventually cause the seam to burst.

On Monday, before her afternoon meeting, Sally changed into one of the pantsuits Karen had brought from the cleaner. An hour later, Sally returned from her meeting looking triumphant and self-satisfied. She approached Karen's desk, handed her a list of the day's remaining tasks, and without saying a word walked quickly to her office. Karen examined her carefully and observed that the seam on back of Sally's pants had given way, exposing her diaphanous, lime-green undergarment. Karen smiled. She imagined Sally's clients catching a brief glimpse of the translucent panty in the dimming light of the walnut-paneled meeting room. For a moment, Karen experienced a sweet, liberating feeling of moral equilibrium that eclipsed the otherwise unpleasant sensations that until then had marked every hour of her day.

Tom was a clerk in Harrison's department. He had been a clerk at the firm for many years and though his position held little importance, he had gained some respect from his superiors because of his dedication and attention to detail. Tom accepted his role without complaint for his mind was neither curious nor filled with complex ideas. One day Harrison summoned Tom to his cubicle for what he described as "an urgent task." When Tom arrived, Harrison handed him a stack of documents that needed to be passed on to a superior. He instructed Tom to review them for errors and then deliver them to the appropriate authority. Harrison claimed that he was too busy to review the documents himself, though Tom noticed that his desk was clear and his computer screen was opened to the local newspaper's Web site. Harrison implied that such mindless work was beneath him. "It's a job for an imbecile," he snorted. Tom never liked Harrison. His condescending tone and self-righteous ramblings were irksome to the ear. Now Harrison had amplified these undesirable attributes of his character by making a remark that, for a reason he could not immediately apprehend, Tom found deeply wounding. Perhaps it was because Tom felt insecure in the presence of a senior analyst and to be reminded of his lowly status by giving him a job fit only for an imbecile made him defensive and angry. It was his anger that led him to reply to Harrison in a voice that surprised everyone in the office with the intensity of its defiance. "Then it's the perfect job for you, asshole! Read them yourself." Having made his point, Tom dropped the urgent documents at Harrison's feet, turned his back to the astonished analyst, and walked away. Harrison was perplexed by Tom's impertinence and he scanned the faces of his cubicle mates for any sign of support or understanding. But his colleagues had returned to their work, leaving Harrison to contemplate in isolation what he could possibly have done to deserve such treatment from a lowly clerk.

At some point employees who experience workplace victimization may decide they have had enough. When they do, they might confront the perpetrators to try to resolve the conflict, go to an authority for assistance, withdraw from the situation, or seek revenge. It is the last option that has been the subject of several studies by Aquino and his associates. Aquino, Tripp, and Bies (2001) defined *revenge* as "an action to some perceived harm or wrongdoing by another party that is intended to inflict damage, injury, discomfort, or punishment on the party judged responsible" (p. 53). Some scholars have argued that revenge is not necessarily a negative workplace phenomenon as it can sometimes deter unwarranted mistreatment from others (Bies & Tripp, 1998) and spark a constructive process of organizational change (McLean Parks, 1997). However, others have noted that revenge often leads to counterretaliation and conflict escalation that can damage relationships and impair productivity (Pruitt & Rubin, 1986). For these reasons, we consider revenge to be a form of antisocial behavior.

Turning back to the primary purpose of this chapter: What are the social psychological theories that Aquino and his colleagues have used to explain revenge in an organizational context? First, they have used social psychological theories of self-identity to conceptualize revenge as a response to an identity-threatening provocation (Aquino et al., 2001; Aquino & Douglas, 2003; Aquino, Tripp, & Bies, 2006). Social psychology research has established that people strive to maintain a positive self-identity, which consists of both personal characteristics (e.g., intelligent, caring) and social identities (e.g., gender, ethnicity, nationality) (Steele, 1988; Tajfel & Turner, 1986). A positive self-identity is important for one's overall sense of self-esteem and purpose, and thus we are often highly motivated to defend against social threats that might violate the perception we have of ourselves (Bies, 2001). In general, people expect to be treated with dignity and respect. When people are treated unfairly or poorly by others it conveys a message that they are not worthy of the same courtesy as other valued individuals. Identity threats are actions that challenge a person's sense of dignity and self-worth (Aquino & Douglas, 2003; Bies, 2001; Steele, 1988). When such threats occur, people are motivated to seek revenge against the source.

Aquino and his associates have also drawn from social rank and evolutionary psychology theories to explain the effects of formal status in organizations on one's propensity to seek revenge (e.g., Fournier, Moskowitz, & Zuroff, 2002; Wicklund & Gollwitzer, 1982). By their very nature, organizations are hierarchical social structures. The desire to achieve status within such structures is an extremely powerful human motivation because it is associated with material and social outcomes (Daly & Wilson, 1988). High-status people are privileged; they receive a disproportionally large share of desired social and material outcomes. Low-status people on the other hand tend to receive a disproportionally large amount of undesirable outcomes including being subject to more disrespectful treatment or social invalidation. Daly and Wilson (1988) argue that a prevalent and detrimental result of these status differences is that low-status members of a group are often more aggressive and assertive about defending their position within the social hierarchy, deprived as it may be, against social threats. Aquino and his colleagues have drawn from this notion to explain the somewhat contradictory effects of two different dimensions of status in organizations: *absolute* status (i.e., one's formal level of hierarchy in the organization) and *relative* status (i.e., the status difference between individuals and their offender). The following section discusses how these theories have guided their work.

The Effects of Absolute Status on Revenge

Aquino and colleagues have argued that people with higher formal status in an organization are less likely to engage in revenge and provide two complementary explanations for this assertion. First, the abundance of social and material affirmations high-status individuals receive as a result of their privileged positions provides them with a psychological buffer against identity threats. As a result, high-status individuals are not as strongly motivated to respond aggressively to such threats compared with low-status individuals. On the other hand, low-status individuals are motivated to protect their dignity and honor, even in the face of seemingly minor transgressions. They drew support for their argument from Gilligan's (1996) study of men imprisoned for violent acts. Gilligan found that many of the triggering events that led to violent offenders' imprisonment were rather trivial insults (e.g., being looked at in the "wrong" way; having one's shoes stepped on). However, Gilligan argued that, from the offender's position, these individuals received very little status-enhancing opportunities in life and that aggressive responses were used as a means of defending their self-respect and maintaining what little status they had. There is evidence supporting the notion that low-status individuals are quick to respond to identity threats (e.g., Daly & Wilson, 1988; Gilligan, 1996), but the work by Aquino and his colleagues was some of the first empirical research in an organizational context to show that having high status may actually act as a buffer against threats.

Another explanation offered by Aquino and his colleagues for why high-status people are less likely to exhibit revenge is that they face strong normative pressures discouraging them from acts of petty vengeance (Hogan & Emler, 1981; Tripp & Bies, 1997). Aggressive retaliation by a high-status person can also arouse anger and resentment in others, who might then use the high-status person's behavior as an excuse to usurp their power. For example, Boehm (1993) described a phenomenon he termed "reverse dominance hierarchy," in which the rank-and-file members of a society form a coalition and rebuke the leader's formal power in response to unfair treatment. Low-status members can retaliate publicly by openly criticizing their leader's behavior, or they can decide to retaliate surreptitiously by secretly disobeying the leader's orders or demands. Thus, it is perhaps politically disadvantageous for a leader to enact revenge.

Three studies by Aquino and his colleagues tested and found support for their proposition regarding the role of absolute status as a predictor of revenge. Aquino et al. (2001) surveyed employees of a government service agency. They used the "critical incident technique" to elicit salient workplace offenses by asking participants to think about a time within the past six months in which they had been offended by another member of their organization at work. They were then asked to report their reactions to this offense and the extent to which they sought revenge as a response. The results indicated that those of higher overall status in the organization reported that they sought less revenge than their low-status counterparts. This finding was replicated in another study by Aquino et al. (2006), in which the researchers again used the critical incident technique to survey the employees of a public utility organization. These two studies provide empirical support for the argument that high-status employees engage in less revenge; however, the underlying explanation for this result remains unclear. Are high-status employees buffered against the psychological harm of identity threats, do social norms constrain their behavior, or do both occur and reinforce each other? Unfortunately, neither of these studies examined the motives of avengers, so this question remains open for future research.

Aquino and Douglas (2003) looked at whether antisocial behavior was associated with identity threats. Although they did not ask whether the antisocial behavior was directed specifically against the source of the identity threat, the pattern of their findings converges with that found in the studies of revenge described previously. Aquino and Douglas surveyed employees from three organizations: a transportation company, a public school system, and a municipality. They asked respondents to report the extent to which they faced identity-threatening events at work, such as being embarrassed, judged unfairly, or criticized. They also asked respondents to report the degree to which they engage in, for example, antisocial behavior, negative behavior directed at others in their organization (e.g., saying unkind things to others), and criticizing others at work. Contrary to the studies on direct revenge, the results of the Aquino and Douglas study did not find a main effect of hierarchical status on antisocial behavior. However, the results did show a negative relationship between identity threat and antisocial behavior for high-status employees in environments where the respondents' peers did not engage in high levels of antisocial behavior. In other words, in environments where antisocial behavior was counternormative, high-status individuals exhibited less antisocial behavior than in environments where it was relatively more common. The negative relationship between identity threats and antisocial behavior in this type of environment was not found for low-status employees. The results of this study lend some support to Aquino and colleagues' second explanation for the relationship between absolute status and revenge, namely, that high-status individuals are more constrained by normative social pressures and must refrain from abusing their power.

The Effects of Relative Power on Revenge

Relative power can be captured by differences in status between a harm doer and a would-be avenger as well as by differential capabilities to act on desired goals, to inflict punishment, or to withhold rewards. Aquino and colleagues have argued that having high status relative to an offender is likely to encourage people to seek revenge. They base this assertion on instrumental arguments. Since individuals with high relative status are likely to have more social and material power, it is disadvantageous for an injured party to seek revenge against an offender who is of higher status than him or her. The threat of reprisal, however, is weaker for offenders who are of equal or lower status than a would-be avenger. Two studies by Aquino et al. (2001) and Aquino et al. (2006) empirically assessed the relationship between relative status and revenge to test this hypothesis. Aquino et al. (2001) found a main effect such that those of higher formal status relative to a harm doer were more likely to pursue revenge. Aquino et al. (2006), however, failed to replicate this finding. The results from this study did show that those with high relative status compared with a harm doer were more likely to engage in revenge if they perceived their organizational environment to be procedurally unjust. In other words, when people felt that they had no formal mechanism to seek retribution, they were more likely to take matters into their own hands, but only if the target of their vengeance had lower status relative to their own.

Critique of Research and Future Research Directions

Aquino and colleagues' assertion that employees with high absolute status are less likely to engage in revenge is open to challenge because several theoretical paradigms would suggest the opposite. For example, Keltner, Gruenfeld, and Anderson's (2003) power, approach, and inhibition model argues that more powerful people are chronically motivated by the approach-motivation system and often react quickly with little thought about the consequences of their actions. As a result, high-powered people are more likely to deviate from social norms than low-powered people and can often act aggressively and carelessly. Power and absolute status are not necessarily equivalent constructs, but high-status individuals tend to be awarded with more organizational power and the ability to influence others' outcomes and resources. Furthermore, Hollander's (1958) notion of idiosyncrasy credits suggests that high-status individuals are awarded a degree of leeway and are able to deviate from social norms so long as they do not deviate to such a degree that they use up all their hypothetical credits. Finally, Baumeister, Smart, and Boden (1996) argued that individuals who see themselves as superior to others are more likely to react aggressively to ego threats and to show less remorse for their behavior. Thus, other theories of self-esteem and power argue that high-status individuals are *more* likely to react aggressively to identity threats and are *less* likely to be normatively constrained by social conventions. Future research should be devoted to understanding the nuances of the relationship between absolute hierarchical status and revenge.

Several potential explanations for Aquino et al.'s (2001, 2006) findings that absolute status is negatively related to revenge should be explored in future research. First, it is possible that their finding is an artifact of the methodology used in these studies. Aquino and colleagues have used the critical incident technique to capture personal experiences of offenses and revenge responses. It is possible that high-status individuals experience qualitatively different types of offenses that do not necessarily warrant revenge. For example, perhaps high-status individuals are not faced with offenses that cause a significant degree of instrumental harm and thus are less likely to respond with revenge. The important implication of this explanation is that, if faced with the same situations as high-status employees, low-status employees would also not react vengefully, and, if faced with the same situations as low-status employees, high-status employees would react vengefully.

Another potential explanation for their finding is that high-status employees have more formal or sneaky ways of enacting revenge, and as a result they do not interpret their motives as vengeful. For example, a boss may be able to use passive forms of revenge against an employee who has offended him or her by ignoring emails, refusing to answer the employee's calls, and excluding the employee from his or her social circle. This boss may not consider such actions to be revenge because he or she does not directly and aggressively seek to harm the offender. Alternatively, an offended boss could move an employee to an undesirable work project as a form of retribution but justify such behavior as being necessary for maintaining a productive work environment.

Finally, it is possible that because of their social position high-status individuals are less likely to act vengefully when they are faced with minor transgressions; however, when they are faced with a more extreme transgression, particularly one that attacks their source of status, they are more likely than low-status persons to react directly and aggressively.

CONCLUSION AND FINAL REMARKS

This chapter reviewed the first author's program of research on two forms of antisocial behavior: workplace victimization and revenge. We summarized some of his most relevant published articles and highlighted the social psychological theories that informed the research. We also tried to identify the shortcomings and limitations of this corpus of studies and to offer suggestions for how to settle unanswered theoretical questions, to test alternative explanations, and to improve on the methodologies and designs that have been used so far. We are optimistic that our review will spark further interest in this topic, but we also hope to provoke challenges and improvements to the theoretical arguments that have guided this research agenda.

> Karen's moment of satisfaction at having successfully executed her plan to embarrass her boss passed swiftly and by the next day her life at work resumed its normal pattern. Sally showed no indications of softening and a

series of recent successes only magnified her hubris. One day, after a week of troubling dreams, Karen resolved to take a longer lunch break than usual. She was surprisingly unconcerned about how Sally would react. Karen left her desk promptly at noon and decided not to return for two hours. She took a walk. The day was blustery but the sun was out. She passed by shops she'd never noticed, heard a street musician playing a familiar song, and found herself in front of a school where children were climbing a metallic structure that looked like a large birdcage. She had conquered her fear of a similar structure as a child. Seeing it again reminded her of the first time she experienced the sting of hurtful words that even now reverberated through her interior world. She felt melancholy and debased. But then, strangely, she felt a friendly, comforting sensation begin to swell inside her and she turned away from the school. She took the train home. When she reached her apartment she found it tidy and glowing with sunlight. She noticed a plant on the kitchen table and her morning coffee half finished beside it. She went to her couch and lay down, composing a letter in her mind. The letter finished, she lifted a book she had never read from the shelf and turned the page. That evening, while she slept, she found herself at the center of many fantastical dreams.

Harrison concluded it was time for him to find a job more befitting of his talents. He perceived his office mates as becoming increasingly dull and uninspiring and was convinced that he needed to be around people who were as visionary and ambitious as he. He wanted to remain with the firm so he searched through the internal job postings for an appropriate position. To his delight, he found one. A senior consultant, a woman whose reputation was formidable but who was known to be an extremely difficult boss, was seeking an analyst for her team. Harrison noticed that the woman's office was only a few floors above his, and he began to strategize about how he could introduce himself to her before submitting his resume. He was sure that if she met him in person she would quickly recognize his potential. He felt pleased with himself, and though he did not know her, he sensed that he and the senior consultant would form a perfect union.

REFERENCES

Amir, M. (1967). Victim precipitated forcible rape. *Journal of Criminal Law, Criminology, and Police Science, 58*, 493–502.

Aquino, K. (2000). Structural and individual determinants of workplace victimization: The effects of hierarchical status and conflict management style. *Journal of Management, 26*, 171–193.

Aquino, K., & Bommer, W. H. (2003). Preferential mistreatment: How victim status moderates the relationship between organizational citizenship behavior and workplace victimization. *Organization Science, 14,* 374–385.

Aquino, K., & Bradfield, M. (2000). Perceived victimization in the workplace: The role of situational factors and victim characteristics. *Organization Science, 11,* 525–537.

Aquino, K., & Byron, K. (2002). Dominating interpersonal behavior and perceived victimization in groups: Evidence for a curvilinear relationship. *Journal of Management, 28,* 69–87.

Aquino, K., & Douglas, S. (2003). Identity threat and antisocial behavior in organizations: The moderating effects of individual differences, aggressive modeling, and hierarchical status. *Organizational Behavior and Human Decision Processes, 90,* 195–208.

Aquino, K., Grover, S., Bradfield, M., & Allen, D. G. (1999). The effects of negative affectivity, hierarchical status, and self-determination on workplace victimization. *Academy of Management Journal, 42,* 260–272.

Aquino, K., & Lamertz, K. (2004). A relational model of workplace victimization: Social roles and patterns of victimization in dyadic relationships. *Journal of Applied Psychology, 89,* 1023–1034.

Aquino, K., & Thau, S. (2009). Workplace victimization: Aggression from the target's perspective. *Annual Review of Psychology, 60,* 717–741.

Aquino, K., Tripp, T. M., & Bies, R. J. (2001). How employees respond to personal offense: The effects of blame attribution, victim status and offender status on revenge and reconciliation in the workplace. *Journal of Applied Psychology, 86,* 52–59.

Aquino, K., Tripp, T. M., & Bies, R. J. (2006). Getting even or moving on? Power, procedural justice and types of offense as predictors of revenge, forgiveness, reconciliation and avoidance in organizations. *Journal of Applied Psychology, 91,* 653–668.

Baumeister, R. F., Smart, L., & Boden, J. M. (1996). Relation of threatened egotism to violence and aggression: The dark side of high self-esteem. *Psychological Review, 103,* 5–33.

Berger, J., Fiske, M. H., Norman, R. Z., & Zelditch, M., Jr. (1977). *Status characteristics and social interaction: An expectation-states approach.* New York: Elsevier.

Bies, R. J. (2001). Interactional (in)justice: The sacred and the profane. In J. Greenberg & R. Cropanzano (Eds.), *Advances in organizational behavior* (pp. 89–118). Stanford, CA: Stanford University Press.

Bies, R. J., & Tripp, T. M. (1998). The many faces of revenge: The good, the bad, and the ugly. In R. W. Griffin, A. O'Leary-Kelly, & J. Collins (Eds.), *Monographs in organizational behavior and industrial relations, Vol. 23: Dysfunctional behavior in organizations: Part B. Non-violent dysfunctional behavior* (pp. 49–67). Greenwich, CT: JAI Press.

Blaney, P. H. (1986). Affect and memory: a review. *Psychological Bulletin, 99,* 229–246.

Boehm, C. (1993). Egalitarian behavior and reverse dominance hierarchy. *Current Anthropology, 34,* 227–254.

Crew, B. K. (1991). Sex differences in criminal sentencing: Chivalry or patriarchy? *Justice Quarterly, 8,* 59–83.

Curtis, L. A. (1974). Victim precipitation and violent crime. *Social Problems, 21,* 594–605.

Daly, M., & Wilson, M. (1988). *Homicide.* Hawthorne, NY: Aldine De Gruyter.

Felson, R. B. (1992). "Kick 'em when they're down": Explanations of the relationship between stress and interpersonal aggression and violence. *Sociological Quarterly, 33,* 1–16.

Felson, R. B., & Steadman, H. J. (1983). Situational factors in disputes leading to criminal violence. *Criminology, 21,* 59–74.

Fournier, M. A., Moskowitz, D. S., & Zuroff, D. C. (2002). Social rank strategies in hierarchical relationships. *Journal of Personality and Social Psychology, 83,* 425–453.

Gilligan, J. (1996). *Violence: Our deadly epidemic and its causes.* New York: G.P. Putnam.

Gouldner, A. W. (1960). The norm of reciprocity: A preliminary statement. *American Sociological Review, 25,* 161–178.

Hansen, A. M., Hogh, A., Persson, R., Karlson, B., Garde, A. H., & Orbaek, P. (2006). Bullying at work, health outcomes, and physiological stress response. *Journal of Psychosomatic Research, 60,* 63–72.

Hogan, R., & Emler, N. P. (1981). Retributive justice. In M. J. Lerner & S. C. Lerner (Eds.), *The justice motive in social behavior* (pp. 125–143). New York: Plenum.

Hollander, E. P. (1958). Conformity, status, and idiosyncrasy credit. *Psychological Review, 65,* 117–127

Jackson, S. E., Schuler, R. S.., & Rivero, J. C. (1989). Organizational characteristics as predictors of personnel practices. *Personnel Psychology, 42,* 727–786.

Keltner, D., Gruenfeld, D. H. & Anderson, C. (2003). Power, approach, and inhibition. *Psychological Review, 110,* 265–284.

Lawler, E. J., & Yoon, J. (1993). Power and the emergence of commitment behavior in negotiated exchange. *American Sociological Review, 58,* 465–481.

McLean Parks, J. (1997). The fourth arm of justice: The art and science of revenge. In R. J. Lewicki, R. J. Bies, & B. H. Sheppard (Eds.), *Research on negotiation in organizations* (Vol. 6, pp. 113–144). Greenwich, CT: JAI Press.

Mikkelsen, E. G., & Einarsen, S. (2002). Basic assumptions and symptoms of post-traumatic stress among victims of bullying at work. *European Journal of Work and Organizational Psychology, 11,* 87–111.

Moulds, E. F. (1980). Chivalry and paternalism: Disparities of treatment in the criminal justice system. In S. Datesman & F. Scarpitti (Eds.), *Women, crime, and justice* (pp. 277–299). New York: Oxford.

Olweus, D. (1978). *Aggression in schools: Bullies and whipping boys.* Washington, DC: Hemisphere.

Organ, D. W. (1988). *Organizational citizenship behavior: The good soldier syndrome.* Lexington, MA: Lexington Books.

Pettigrew, T. F., & Martin, J. (1987). Shaping the organizational context for Black American inclusion. *Journal of Social Issues, 43,* 41–78.

Pruitt, D. G., & Rubin, J. Z. (1986). *Social conflict: Escalation, stalemate, and settlement.* New York: Random House.

Rahim, M. A. (1983). A measure of styles of handling interpersonal conflict. *Academy of Management Journal, 26,* 368–376.

Steele, C. M. (1988). The psychology of self-affirmation: Sustaining the integrity of the self. In L. Berkowitz (Ed.), *Advances in experimental psychology* (Vol. 21, pp. 261–302). San Diego, CA: Academic Press.

Tajfel, H., & Turner, J. C. (1986). The social identity theory of intergroup behavior. In S. Worchel & W. G. Austin (Eds.), *Psychology of intergroup relations* (2nd ed., pp. 7–24). Chicago: Nelson-Hall.

Tepper, B. J., Duffy, M. K., Henle, C. A., & Lambert, L. S. (2006). Procedural justice, victim precipitation, and abusive supervision. *Personnel Psychology, 59,* 101–123.

Tripp, T. M., & Bies, R. J. (1997). What's good about revenge?: The avenger's perspective. In R. J. Lewicki, R. J. Bies, & B. H. Sheppard (Eds.), *Research on negotiation in organizations* (Vol. 6, pp. 145–160). Greenwich, CT: JAI Press.

van de Vliert, E., Euwema, M. C., & Huismans, S. E. 1995. Managing conflict with a subordinate or a superior: Effectiveness of conglomerated behavior. *Journal of Applied Psychology, 80,* 271–281.

Wicklund, R. A., & Gollwitzer, P. M. (1982). *Symbolic self-completion.* Hillsdale, NJ: Erlbaum.

13

Creativity in Individuals and Groups: Basic Principles With Practical Implications

Carsten K.W. De Dreu
University of Amsterdam

Bernard A. Nijstad
University of Amsterdam

Matthijs Baas
University of Amsterdam

Creativity is a million-dollar business. A Google Internet search in March 2009, for example, results in more than 27,500 Web sites offering "creativity coaching" and more than 60,000 offering "creativity training." Creativity may be popular in part because we all feel that creativity matters and that improving creativity might be desirable. Indeed, our children follow special artistic creativity classes, and after school we drive them to drama lessons. As managers we subscribe to courses and sessions that putatively stimulate our creative thinking, and our organizations spend large amounts of money to refurnish meeting rooms to stimulate employees' creative thinking and innovative practices. Help books on creativity abound, as are the herbal teas, gemstones, and shampoos that are sold under the pretense that they break us free and stimulate our creativity.

Our desire to be creative matches several functions creativity serves. Creative capabilities help us deal with changes in our environment and with the opportunities and threats of everyday life (e.g., Runco, 2004). However, there are other functions as well. For example, engaging in creative tasks helps to sustain and promote a positive mood and sense of well-being (Hirt, Devers, & McCrea, 2008), it makes people more attractive mating partners (Griskevicius, Cialdini, & Kenrick, 2006), and it helps them to win conflicts and debates (De Dreu & Nijstad, 2008). Creativity also is core to successful entrepreneurship and to establishing and expanding market share (Frese, Chapter 5). In short, creativity helps humans to survive, adapt, and prosper.

Here we take a closer look at what creativity is and at the conditions that facilitate or hinder creative performance at the individual and group level of analysis. Our aim is to connect the social psychological literatures on individual-level creativity with work on group creativity and innovation being conducted primarily in the organizational sciences. We begin with a treatise on what we mean by creativity and innovation. Subsequently, we introduce the Dual Pathway to Creativity Model (De Dreu, Baas, & Nijstad, 2008), a model of the basic principles involved in individual-level creativity. We then move to the group level of analysis, which brings additional complexities, and we use the Motivated Information Processing in Groups (MIP-G) Model (De Dreu, Nijstad, & van Knippenberg, 2008) to understand past research findings on group creativity and innovation. We discuss new evidence for specific implications of MIP-G for group creativity and innovation. We conclude this chapter with a summary of our conclusions and general avenues for new research.

CREATIVITY AND INNOVATION

Creativity and *innovation* are often used interchangeably, but to do so misses some important nuances (e.g., Mumford & Gustafson, 1988; Sawyer, 2006). Creativity can be defined as the generation of ideas, problem solutions, or insights that are novel and appropriate (Amabile, 1996; Runco, 2004). Innovation, however, can be defined as "the intentional introduction and application within a role, group or organization of ideas, processes, products or procedures, new to the relevant unit of adoption, designed to significantly benefit the individual, the group, the organization or wider society" (West & Farr, 1990, p. 9).

These two definitions highlight several critical distinctions between creativity and innovation (Anderson, De Dreu, & Nijstad, 2004). First, creativity requires the idea, insight, or solution to be appropriate, defined as "fitting the problem": Somehow, the idea, insight, or solution has to make sense. Innovations, however, necessitate the new idea, insight, or solution to advance the individual or group by helping, for example, to perform tasks in a more effective or efficient way or to manage social relations better. Thus, in contrast to creativity, innovation requires individuals and groups to overcome a number of "implementation barriers," including resource allocation processes, political games, and human tendencies to resist change (e.g., Klein, Conn, & Sorra, 2001). Second, creativity calls for an idea that is new and original—not many others have had that same idea, insight, or solution. Innovation requires something to be new to the implementing unit: Many others may have had and implemented the same idea, insight, or solution, but implementing it in this particular group or by this particular individual can still be considered novel.

Both creativity and innovation can be considered from a process perspective as well as from an "end-state" or product perspective (Simonton, 2003). The latter refers to the ultimate product that is evaluated in terms of its novelty and appropriateness (in the case of creativity) or usefulness (in the case of innovations). The former tackles the individual as well as group-level processes involved in the generation or implementation of new ideas, insights, or solutions. In the remainder of this chapter we focus on the interplay between individual-level processes on the one hand and group-level processes on the other. After introducing the Dual Pathway to Creativity Model (DPCM; De Dreu, Baas, et al., 2008; Baas, De Dreu, & Nijstad, 2008) we seek to understand creativity in social groups, such as decision-making units and organizational teams. We review evidence and discuss possible connections between individual and group creativity and group-level innovation. The chapter concludes with a section on future research.

DUAL PATHWAY TO CREATIVITY MODEL

Creative performance is often assessed using three indicators: fluency, originality, and flexibility (Guilford, 1967; Torrance, 1966). *Fluency* refers to the generated number of nonredundant ideas, insights, problem solutions, or products. *Originality* is one of the defining characteristics of creativity and refers to the uncommonness or infrequency of the ideas, insights, problem solutions, or products that are being invented (Guilford, 1967). *Flexibility* manifests itself in the use of different cognitive categories and perspectives and the use of broad and inclusive cognitive categories (Amabile, 1996; Mednick, 1962).

Although fluency, originality, and flexibility all are considered to be dimensions of "creative performance," they are not necessarily highly correlated. Fluency and originality may be correlated (e.g., quantity breeds quality; Osborn, 1957), but they need not be. For example, fluency may manifest itself in a relatively large number of solved insight or perception problems, with the solutions themselves not being particularly new or uncommon (Förster, Friedman, & Liberman, 2004). Moreover, states or traits that influence fluency do not necessarily also influence originality and vice versa. Taking different approaches and using more cognitive categories (i.e., high flexibility) will, all other things being equal, be associated with more ideas overall (i.e., increased fluency; Nijstad, Stroebe, & Lodewijkx, 2002, 2003) as well as with the generation of ideas in categories that are not usually considered (i.e., originality; Murray, Sujan, Hirt, & Sujan, 1990). However, it is also possible to generate many ideas without being flexible (e.g., generating many ideas within a limited number of cognitive categories), and some of these ideas may also be original (Rietzschel, Nijstad, & Stroebe, 2007).

To understand creative performance, De Dreu, Baas, et al. (2008) proposed the Dual Pathway to Creativity Model, which defines creative performance in terms of the number and originality of ideas, insights, and solutions. Figure 13.1 shows that both fluency and originality can be achieved through (1) flexible thinking, set breaking, and divergent processing of information; through (2) persistent analytical probing and systematically and incrementally combining elements and possibilities; or through (3) some combination of cognitive flexibility and cognitive persistence. The flexibility route captures set breaking (Smith & Blankenship, 1991) and the use of flat associative hierarchies (Mednick, 1962). The persistence route captures the notion that creative fluency and originality need hard work, perseverance, and the deliberate, persistent, and in-depth exploration of a few cognitive categories or perspectives (Boden, 1998; Simonton, 1997; Schooler, Ohlsson, & Brooks, 1993). Persistence will manifest itself in the generation of many ideas within a few categories (i.e.,

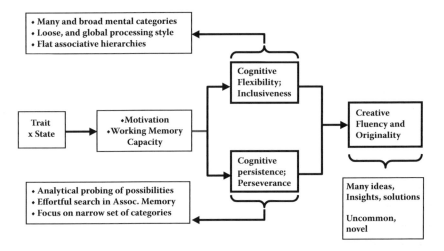

FIGURE 13.1
Dual pathway to creativity model.

within-category fluency; Nijstad & Stroebe, 2006) or in longer time on task (De Dreu, Baas, et al., 2008).

Initial Evidence for DPCM

DPCM argues that for both flexibility and cognitive persistence the individual needs to somehow be cognitively activated (see Figure 13.1). This is a critical deviation from the widely shared notion that creativity results from being relaxed, unfocused, and unengaged (e.g., Bransford & Stein, 1984; Martindale, 1999). Rather, and consistent with the idea that performance curvilinearly relates to stress (Staw, Sandelands, & Dutton, 1981), DPCM proposes that at moderate levels of activation and arousal both cognitive flexibility and persistence can be facilitated more than under excessively low or high activation and arousal. There are two reasons. First, being activated leads to task engagement and motivation to consider the issue at hand (Dietrich, 2004). Second, moderately high levels of cognitive arousal are associated with the release of certain neurotransmitters such as dopamine and noradrenalin in the prefrontal cortex, which improves a number of cognitive functions, including working memory performance, cognitive flexibility, and sustained attention (e.g., Dreisbach & Goschke, 2004).

According to DPCM different traits, states, and their combinations may lead to cognitive activation. More importantly, some traits or states will be mainly of influence on creativity because they impact cognitive flex-ibility. Other traits or states will affect creativity through their effect on cognitive persistence. Two streams of research on mood and creative flow support this basic proposition and will be reviewed in some detail in the next sections.

Mood and Creative Performance

Previous research has shown different effects of hedonic tone (i.e., posi-tive vs. negative moods) on creative performance (e.g., Shalley, Zhou, & Oldham, 2004). In general, positive moods seem to stimulate creativity, but this positive relation has not always been obtained. Effects of negative mood states are even more inconsistent, with some studies finding nega-tive effects, others finding no effects at all, and still others even finding positive effects on creative performance (for a review see Baas et al., 2008). To explain these different findings, De Dreu, Baas, et al. (2008) distin-guished between the *activating* and *deactivating* effects of different mood states (Barrett & Russell, 1998; Gray, 1990; Watson, Clark, & Tellegen, 1988). Activating moods can be positively (e.g., feeling happy or elated) or negatively toned (e.g., anger, fear); similarly, deactivating moods can have positive (e.g., feeling relaxed or serene) or negative (e.g., sadness, feeling down) hedonic tone.

  According to DPCM, both positive and negative activating moods lead to higher creative performance than deactivating moods, but *how* depends on hedonic tone. Specifically, work in both cognitive neurosciences and social cognition suggests that, when feeling positive, the individual feels safe to explore the environment, is more likely to use broad and inclusive cognitive categories, and more easily engages in divergent thinking—a positive feeling engenders cognitive flexibility (e.g., Fiedler, 1988; George & Zhou, 2007; Schwarz & Clore, 2007). These same literatures also suggest that, when feeling negative, the individual becomes more inward focused and more analytical and processes information in a more bottom-up fash-ion—a negative feeling engenders cognitive persistence (e.g., Ambady & Gray, 2002; Derryberry & Reed, 1998; Schwarz & Bless, 1991). Put differ-ently, activating moods lead to more creativity than deactivating moods, but it is because of flexibility when these activating moods are positive in tone and because of persistence when these activating moods are negative in tone.

De Dreu, Baas, et al. (2008) tested this hypothesis in a series of studies using a variety of creativity tasks, including brainstorming and perceptual insight problems. Through self-generated imagery, participants were induced to experience activating or deactivating mood states that were either positive (happy, elated vs. serene, relaxed) or negative (angry, anxious vs. sad, depressed) in tone. Across four studies, results were consistent with the overall hypothesis that activating moods (e.g., anger, fear, happy, elated) lead to more creative fluency and originality than deactivating moods (e.g., sad, depressed, relaxed, serene): People in activating moods generated more ideas that were of greater originality and solved more insight problems than those in deactivating moods. Furthermore, activating moods influence fluency and originality because of enhanced cognitive flexibility when tone is positive but because of enhanced persistence when tone is negative. For example, participants in a positive activating mood tended to use more cognitive categories in a brainstorming task (i.e., flexibility) whereas participants in a negative activating mood tended to explore a few cognitive categories in greater depth (i.e., persistence).

Baas and colleagues (2008) conducted a meta-analysis of the mood-creativity literature to further examine the robustness of these findings. Consistent with DPCM and the findings reported in De Dreu, Baas, et al. (2008), positive effects were found when studies induced activating rather than deactivating mood states. For example, happy but not relaxed mood states were associated with higher levels of creativity. However, an important qualification was that this distinction applied to activating mood states associated with an approach motivation (i.e., happy, angry) and not to activating mood states associated with an avoidance motivation (i.e., fear). Indeed, in the meta-analysis fear associated with reduced cognitive flexibility. Perhaps fear associates with more focused cognitive activity, which may promote creativity through persistence given enough time on task but not through flexibility (De Dreu & Nijstad, 2008).

Flow and Creative Performance

The distinction between two different pathways to creativity should not be taken as if either one or the other pathway is engaged. In fact, creative performance oftentimes requires both pathways, either sequentially or simultaneously. According to DPCM this is especially the case when people are highly engaged in a creativity task. Such engagement is likely when a certain trait or (mental) state fits with the requirement of the creativity task. According to value-from-fit theory (Higgins, 2006) people derive value from the regulatory fit that they experience when their engagement in an activity sustains their goal orientation, mood, or interests regarding that activity. For example, sad people prefer deliberate thinking, whereas happy people prefer intuitive reasoning. De Vries, Holland, and Witteman (2008) asked participants in a sad (happy) mood to make decisions after deliberate (intuitive) reasoning. They found greater satisfaction and subjective value when the thinking strategy matched rather than mismatched the mood state (i.e., sad/deliberate and happy/intuitive > sad/intuitive and happy/deliberate).

Fit-induced engagement is one of the core ingredients of flow—an almost automatic, effortless, yet highly focused state of consciousness (Csikszentmihalyi, 1996, p. 110). Flow in turn has been argued to promote creative performance because it motivates persistent activity and enables cognitive flexibility. In terms of DPCM, flow merges the cognitive flexibility and persistence pathways to creative performance. Indeed, compared with nonfit, regulatory fit increases cognitive flexibility (Worthy, Maddox, & Markman, 2007) as well as cognitive persistence and fluency (Vaughn, Malik, Schwartz, Petkova, & Trudeau, 2006). Likewise, flow is related to greater perceived fit between individuals' skills and task demands, to longer time on task, and to greater fluency (Keller & Bless, 2008). Put differently, fit rather than nonfit produces positive feelings and a sense of engagement that constitutes flow. Flow, in turn, facilitates cognitive flexibility and persistence and should thereby produce more creativity than misfit.

De Dreu, Nijstad, and Baas (2009) tested this "creative flow-from-fit" prediction in a series of experiments focusing on creativity in brainstorming, perceptual insight tasks, and conceptual problem solving. Across studies, results were consistent with the hypothesis that fit produces more creativity than nonfit. For example, individual differences in approach tendencies (i.e., engagement of the Behavioral Activation System, or BAS; Carver & White, 1994) are associated with differences in cognitive processing style, with individuals higher in BAS preferring a global rather than local processing style (e.g., focus on the forest rather than the trees; see Förster & Higgins, 2005). When the creativity task fit their processing style (e.g., an idea generation task that involved a broad topic with many conceptual categories), high-BAS participants were more creative than low-BAS participants. However, when there was a misfit between their global processing style and the creativity task (e.g., an idea generation task on a narrow topic with few conceptual categories), high-BAS participants were somewhat less creative than low-BAS participants. Similar findings were obtained for state- rather than trait-based differences in global versus local processing style. Moreover, fit compared with nonfit triggered both cognitive flexibility and persistence, and this mediated effects of fit on fluency and originality.

Summary and Conclusions on Individual-Level Creativity

Building on a large and diverse literature on the neuropsychological mechanisms involved in creativity, the Dual Pathway to Creativity Model was formulated (De Dreu, Baas, et al., 2008). It proposes that moderate levels of activation and arousal trigger cognitive flexibility, cognitive persistence, or some combination and that these processes in turn facilitate the generation of many and original ideas, insights, and problem solutions. DPCM is consistent with past literatures on creativity and prospective tests fared well. Consistent with DPCM, individuals are more creative because of enhanced flexibility when they are in an activating (rather than deactivating) positive mood, and they are more creative because of enhanced persistence when they are in an activating (rather than deactivating) negative mood (Baas et al., 2008; De Dreu, Baas, et al., 2008). Recent work showed that when individuals experience a fit between their low versus high chronic approach tendencies and externally induced local versus global processing mode, they experience enhanced engagement and flow, allowing them to be flexible and persistent, and thus creative.

GROUP-LEVEL CREATIVITY AND INNOVATION

A core principle in DPCM is that individuals need to be activated for creativity to happen. Antecedent conditions such as one's mood state, personality, or fit and ensuing engagement all are thought to enhance cognitive processes conducive to creative performance. How does this translate to group settings in which a number of individuals interact (i.e., communicate and exchange information) to jointly perform a creative task? This question is the focus of this section, in which we integrate notions on

DPCM with work on motivated information processing in group judgment and decision making. Of course, group-level creativity will generally benefit from the creativity of the members that constitute the group, and group creativity therefore is likely to benefit from factors that make individual group members creative (e.g., task engagement due to fit). However, because group creativity also entails the sharing of ideas and insights in a group setting and combining individual contributions to a group product, other (group- and individual-level) factors are important as well. The Motivated Information Processing in Groups Model aims to identify these additional factors.

Motivated Information Processing in Groups Model

MIP-G (De Dreu, Nijstad, et al., 2008) builds on the view of groups as information processors developed by Hinsz, Tindale, and Vollrath (1997). Both perspectives assume that individual group members search and process information and that through communication individual-level information processing becomes integrated at the group level, where it affects other individuals in the group and gets distorted and ignored or analyzed deliberately. This cycling between individual-level and group-level information processing continues until a decision is reached or some judgment is rendered.

According to MIP-G, information processing at both the individual and the group level can be more or less shallow and heuristic or deliberate and systematic. When individuals or groups engage in systematic rather than heuristic information processing, attention is given to available and new information, additional information is searched, and information is communicated and integrated in a deliberate manner. The extent to which systematic information processing emerges depends on group members' *epistemic motivation*—their willingness to expend effort to achieve a thorough, rich, and accurate understanding of the world, including the group task or decision problem at hand (De Dreu, Nijstad, et al., 2008).

Epistemic motivation is assumed to be higher among individuals with high rather than low openness to experience or among individuals who are either high rather than low in their need for cognition or who are low rather than high in their need for structure and aversion of ambiguity. Although there are differences between the concept of activation in DPCM and epistemic motivation in MIP-G, both have an activating function and stimulate rather than inhibit cognitive processes and information processing. Thus, groups populated by individuals with high openness to experience, high need for cognition, or low ambiguity aversion can be expected to have higher levels of activation and epistemic motivation and, therefore, to engage in more rather than less systematic and deliberate information search and processing.

Epistemic motivation may also be raised or reduced temporarily by situational pressures. For example, time pressure increases people's need for quick solutions and therefore decreases their epistemic motivation (De Dreu, 2003; Kruglanski & Freund, 1983). On the other hand, making people accountable for the decision-making process by asking them to give reasons for their way of handling a task raises epistemic motivation and the tendency to engage in systematic and effortful information processing (Lerner & Tetlock, 1999). Finally, when there is preference diversity within a group and people realize that others hold different opinions and preferences, they become less confident in the accuracy and validity of their opinions and preferences and, as a result, become more motivated to engage in deep and systematic information processing—preference diversity compared with preference homogeneity raises group members' epistemic motivation (Scholten, van Knippenberg, Nijstad, & De Dreu, 2007). In other words, groups working under severe rather than mild time constraints, lacking rather than facing accountability pressures, or being composed of similar rather than different minds can all be expected to have lower epistemic motivation and, therefore, to engage in less rather than more systematic information searching and processing.

Whereas epistemic motivation promotes the depth and care with which information is searched, processed, and communicated and integrated, MIP-G postulates that the kind of information that is searched, processed, and communicated depends on group members' social motivation. Social motivation refers to the individual's preference for outcome distributions between oneself and other group members and can be pro-self (i.e., the individual is concerned with own outcomes only) or prosocial (i.e., the individual is concerned with joint outcomes and fairness). As with epistemic motivation, social motivation can be trait based or state based. For example, people scoring high on agreeableness are cooperative and empathic and are more likely to adopt a prosocial rather than pro-self motivation. Alternatively, a prosocial motivation can be induced by situational cues. Under positive moods people tend to adopt more cooperative attitudes and have a more prosocial motivation (Carnevale & Isen, 1986). And financial incentive schemes based on collective rather than individual performance induce prosocial versus pro-self motivation, respectively (De Dreu, Weingart, & Kwon, 2000).

Important in MIP-G is that social and epistemic motivation codetermine group-level information processing, judgments, and decisions. Prosocially motivated group members focus on harmony, fairness, and collective success, and they will process information in such a way that these collective outcomes are fostered. Pro-self group members, in contrast, focus on power and personal success, and they will process information in such a way that benefits their personal outcomes. These fundamental differences between prosocial and pro-self individuals will be stronger the more systematically information is searched and processed. Put differently, the difference between prosocially motivated groups and pro-self motivated groups will be bigger under high rather than low epistemic motivation. A central prediction of MIP-G therefore is that collective success (as one important collective outcome) is most likely in groups in which high levels of epistemic motivation are coupled with high levels of prosocial motivation. Indeed, cooperative groups make better decisions when members are accountable to the process (Scholten et al., 2007) or when a critical mindset is induced (Postmes, Spears, & Cihangir, 2001). Also, work teams in organizations exchange information better, learn more, and perform more effectively when they perceive cooperative outcome interdependence, but only when they have high task reflexivity (i.e., when they take time to reflect on, e.g., their behaviors, procedures, task) and concomitant high epistemic motivation (De Dreu, 2007). Finally, negotiators develop more trust, engage in more constructive problem solving, and reach more integrative agreements when they have prosocial rather than selfish goals, but again, this is the case only when they are made accountable to the process (De Dreu, Beersma, Stroebe, & Euwema, 2006).

MIP-G and Group Creativity

Work on MIP-G has focused primarily on the ways social motivation interacts with epistemic motivation to affect the quality of group decisions and negotiated agreements. Yet there is reason to assume these two fundamental motivational forces also drive group creativity. Therefore, in this section we do two things. We review work on individual and group creativity through the lens of MIP-G to see whether past research findings can be meaningfully understood in terms of social motivation, epistemic motivation, or some combination of the two. Second, we review in some detail our recent work designed to put implications of MIP-G to the test.

At the individual level of analysis, stressful conditions that are likely to lower epistemic motivation such as time pressure and conflict-related threat reduce creative problem solving (Schultz & Searleman, 1998), lower cognitive complexity and flexibility (Carnevale & Probst, 1998; De Dreu & Nijstad, 2008), and result in less creative task performance (Baer & Oldham, 2006). Traits associated with reduced epistemic motivation, such as need for closure and fear of invalidity, in particular negatively correlate with individual creativity (Chirumbolo, Mannetti, Pierro, Areni, & Kruglanski, 2005; Rietzschel, De Dreu, & Nijstad, 2007), and traits associated with higher epistemic motivation, such as openness to experience, correlate positively with a variety of creativity indicators (Baer & Oldham, 2006; Wolfradt & Pretz, 2001).

At the group level, similar results have been reported. For example, Chirumbolo and colleagues (2005) and Kelly and Karau (1993) found that group members working on a joint task displayed greater levels of creativity when they had low rather than high need for closure or when time pressure was mild rather than acute. Focusing on group heterogeneity, with its putative stimulating effect on epistemic motivation and systematic information processing, Shin and Zhou (2007) uncovered that teams with transformational leaders and greater educational specialization heterogeneity exhibited greater team creativity. These findings together suggest that, much in line with MIP-G, individual group members become more creative when they have high rather than low epistemic motivation. To the extent that group-level creativity is the aggregate of individual performances, groups can be expected to become more creative as the average epistemic motivation in the group is enhanced.

A number of findings point to some boundary conditions of these creativity-enhancing effects of epistemic motivation. For example, Rietzschel, De Dreu, et al. (2007) found that, at the individual level, the creativity-promoting effect of epistemic motivation reversed when group members feared making errors. Along similar lines, Camacho and Paulus (1995) showed that, at the group level, creativity was substantially reduced when group members were concerned about social face and reputation, a finding replicated at the individual level by De Vet and De Dreu (2007). These studies together suggest that group creativity may be severely hurt when the group climate is characterized by interpersonal competition, undue criticism, power struggle, and self-preserving, defensive tendencies (see, e.g., Shin & Zhou, 2007; Taggar, 2002). Because these are precisely the processes that emerge when group members have or adopt a pro-self rather than prosocial motivation, it follows that group creativity is promoted when epistemic motivation is high, provided group members have a prosocial motivation and create a positive group climate.

Bechtoldt, De Dreu, Nijstad, and Choi (in press) tested this prediction in two studies. Both studies involved three-person groups that engaged in a brainstorming session to generate ideas to improve teaching at their university. In the first study, social motivation was manipulated by either telling group members that their individual performance (the number of nonredundant ideas they generated individually) would be converted into lottery tickets, thus providing a chance on an individual reward (pro-self motivation), or that their group performance (the number of nonredundant ideas they generated as a group) would be converted into lottery tickets, thus providing a chance on a group reward (prosocial motivation). In the second study, social motivation was operationalized as the mean level of agreeableness in the group—individuals all filled out a measure tapping into their level of agreeableness, and these individual scores were aggregated to the group level. Epistemic motivation was manipulated by making the group process accountable or not (Study 1) or by inducing low or high time pressure (Study 2).

In both studies, nonredundant ideas were summed within the group and were taken as an indicator of group-level fluency. Each idea was also reliably rated by independent coders for its originality, and ratings were averaged across ideas to arrive at a group-level indicator of originality. In both studies, higher epistemic motivation produced higher originality, but only when group members had a prosocial rather than pro-self motivation. For fluency, a similar effect was obtained in Study 2 (in Study 1, means were as expected but these differences were not as reliable).

Figure 13.2 shows the effects for fluency and for originality averaged across both studies (to facilitate comparison, we standardized study data to allow aggregation across studies). As can be seen, groups produced more nonredundant ideas that were also of higher average originality when they had high rather than low epistemic motivation, but only when

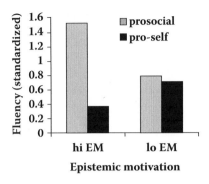

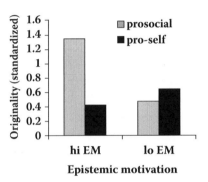

FIGURE 13.2
The influence of social and epistemic motivation on group-level fluency (top chart) and group-level originality (bottom chart). Data refer to standardized averages across studies. (Data derived from Bechtoldt, M. N., De Dreu, C. K. W., Nijstad, B. A., & Choi, H-S., *Journal of Personality and Social Psychology*, in press.)

group members had a prosocial motivation; with a pro-self motivation, lower epistemic motivation seemed to be conducive to group creativity.

The results summarized in Figure 13.2 are in line with MIP-G and thus provide new evidence for the model. More important for the current purposes is that it also means that MIP-G may be a fruitful perspective that allows one to combine and integrate many findings on group creativity uncovered in earlier research. That is, social and epistemic motivation may be the critical mediators between group creativity and antecedent conditions such as time pressure (Kelly & Karau, 1993), mood states (Carnevale & Isen, 1986), and group composition (Shin & Zhou, 2007; Somech, 2006).

It is important to note that the findings in Bechtoldt et al. (in press) relate to individual creativity aggregated to the group level. But there is a difference between individual creativity in a group and group creativity. In the former case, individuals are performing a creativity task, such as generating ideas, in the context of a group, and group processes influence cognitive and motivation processes at the individual level, thereby affecting individual-level creativity. In the latter case, the group as a whole is performing a creativity task, such as creating a new product or making a work of art. Whereas group creativity in the former case is an additive function of individual contributions, group creativity in the latter case has conjunctive as well as disjunctive elements to it (e.g., Steiner, 1972). In creative problem solving (e.g., using insight problems), for example, the group's creativity is a function of the most creative individual—when one individual group member "sees" the solution, the group has achieved its goal. Or when the group makes a joint work of art, the overall product's creative quality is at least partially determined by the inputs of the least creative individual. How such more conjunctive and disjunctive aspects of group creativity are influenced by social and epistemic motivation is a key issue for future research.

Taken together, MIP-G suggests that when individual group members have high epistemic motivation they become more fluent and original in their thinking, leading the group to be relatively more creative. However, this effect emerges to the extent that group members have a prosocial motivation and the group climate is positive and psychologically safe. This prediction is consistent with previous findings on group creativity and a focused test by Bechtoldt and colleagues (in press) provided supportive evidence as well. Future research is needed, in particular, to examine to what extent MIP-G predictions generalize to settings where group members collaboratively produce one single group product. Whereas also in such settings higher epistemic motivation may be more helpful than low epistemic motivation, prosocial motivation may actually promote too much of an "inclusiveness" orientation, allowing poorly performing individuals to disproportionably lower the overall group's creativity.

Another critical issue to be considered in future research is whether the processes delineated in the Dual Pathway to Creativity Model operate at the group level and whether effects of epistemic motivation paired to prosocial rather than pro-self motivation should be understood in terms of enhanced cognitive flexibility, persistence, or some combination. Such research endeavors would allow for a more in-depth connection of DPCM and MIP-G.

MIP-G and Group Innovation

Being creative facilitates innovation, but more creative groups are not necessarily more innovative. First, one can innovate without being creative—for instance, proper scanning of the environment and importing and adopting creative insights, processes, products, or services designed by others suffices to increase one's innovative capacity (e.g., Westphal, Gulati, & Shortell, 1997). Second, even when people are creative, they may not turn their creative ideas into innovative practices. They may have difficulty in identifying their own most original and creative ideas (Rietzschel, Nijstad, & Stroebe, 2006; but see Silvia, 2008) or may fail to overcome certain implementation obstacles. Third, Dailey and Mumford (2006) highlighted that even when people may identify their most novel and creative ideas they may severely overestimate the potential usefulness and underestimate the costs involved in implementing these ideas.

Notwithstanding these conceptual differences between creativity and innovation, work on preference diversity and minority dissent suggests that, much like creativity, group innovation also benefits from high rather than low levels of epistemic motivation combined with a prosocial rather than pro-self motivation. As mentioned, preference diversity reduces individuals' confidence and raises their epistemic motivation and their inclination to systematically search, process, and disseminate information.

A special instance of preference diversity occurs when a minority of group members voices an opinion that deviates from the majority's perspective or way of doing (Schulz-Hardt, Brodbeck, Mojzisch, Kerschreiter, & Frey, 2006). Given that preference diversity activates and enhances epistemic motivation among majority members, it follows that minority dissent has the potential to stimulate group creativity and innovation. Following MIP-G and the work by Bechtoldt et al. (2009), it further follows that such effects of minority dissent come about especially when groups have a prosocial, psychologically safe climate. Indeed, De Dreu and West (2001) found that innovation was higher when teams had high rather than low levels of minority dissent, but especially when they also had high levels of participation in decision making, and Somech (2006) found that team functional heterogeneity promoted group innovation especially when there was a participative rather than directive leadership style (also see Shin & Zhou, 2007). Finally, Nijstad, Selman, and De Dreu (2008) predicted and found among 36 Dutch top-management teams that minority dissent and participative safety interacted on measures of innovation: Minority dissent had a positive relationship with innovation only when participative safety was high but not when participative safety was low. This pattern of results is again consistent with the idea that preference diversity triggers higher epistemic motivation that, in turn, promotes innovations, provided group members have a prosocial motivation.

A final piece of supportive evidence was provided by a study conducted by Choi and Levine (2004). These researchers experimentally studied the effects of newcomers in teams that were engaged in an air surveillance task. After performing one trial, a newcomer entered the group and suggested a new task strategy. The dependent measure was whether the group would adopt this innovation suggested by the newcomer. Choi and Levine found that groups were more likely to adopt the innovation when they were open to new ideas. Thus, groups who had chosen their strategy on the first trial were less likely to adopt the new strategy than groups that were initially given no choice. Similarly, groups that failed on the first trial were more likely to accept newcomer influence than groups who succeeded. This work therefore shows that minorities can stimulate the adoption of innovation and particularly do so when the group is open to new ideas, that is, has high epistemic motivation. Recent work by Kane, Argote, and Levine (2005) reveals that the innovation-promoting effects of newcomers were significantly enhanced when the newcomer shared the same social identity with the other group members compared with when the newcomer was from a different social category. Because a shared social identity is likely to induce prosocial rather than pro-self motivation among group members (De Dreu, Nijstad, et al., 2008), the findings by Choi and Levine and Kane and colleagues strongly suggest that group innovation is indeed a function of high epistemic motivation coupled with a prosocial orientation.

Taken together, there is some initial evidence that factors known to enhance epistemic motivation (e.g., preference diversity) and prosocial motivation (e.g., transformational leadership styles, participative decision making, and shared social identity) jointly predict group innovation. This general pattern—greater group innovation when preference heterogeneity combines with high levels of participative decision making and shared social identity—has been found in field studies with organizational teams as well as in laboratory experiments with ad hoc teams and therefore seems relatively robust and unrelated to specific methodological details.

However, as promising as these findings are, a few critical issues need to be solved in future research. First of all, preference heterogeneity is but one of the many variables putatively raising epistemic motivation, and we need studies showing that antecedents other than (preference) heterogeneity have similar effects on group innovation. Second, and related, is that we should not take the current analysis as suggesting that preference heterogeneity has its effects only because of enhanced epistemic motivation—other processes may be induced by preference heterogeneity, for example, enhanced task conflict (e.g., Nijstad & Kaps, 2008), that can also account for increased group innovation. Third, and finally, new research is needed to specify the intermediating group processes, triggered by the combination of epistemic and social motivation, that account for enhanced group innovation. Likely candidates are better group-level thinking and communication about implementation barriers, smoother coordination to implement new ideas or practices, reduced interpersonal conflicts, and enhanced social support for implementation.

CONCLUSIONS AND AVENUES FOR FUTURE RESEARCH

In this chapter we reviewed two distinct lines of work: (1) basic, individual-level processes driving human creativity; and (2) core motivational antecedents of group-level creativity and innovation. Several important conclusions derive from this review. First, individual creativity, defined as the generation of many and original ideas, insights, and solutions, is a function of cognitive flexibility, cognitive persistence, or some combination of these two pathways. Some factors, such as feeling happy and elated, drive creativity primarily because they promote cognitive flexibility (e.g., Hirt et al., 2008). Other factors, such as feeling angry, drive creativity primarily because they promote cognitive persistence (De Dreu, Baas, et al., 2008). And some factors, such as a fit between task demands and personality, promote creativity because they promote both flexibility and persistence (De Dreu et al., 2009). Thus, the Dual Pathway to Creativity Model is consistent with past work on creativity and allows for new predictions on what drives, or hinders, creative performance among individuals.

Second, our review allows the conclusion that at the group level, both creativity and innovation are enhanced when group members have high rather than low epistemic motivation paired to a prosocial rather than pro-self orientation. High epistemic motivation provides for the cognitive activation and systematic processing of information that facilitates individual creativity. Prosocial orientations provide for the psychologically safe climate needed for self-censorship and ridicule to be reduced or eliminated so that ideas can be voiced; individuals build on each other and benefit from others' inputs. This conclusion suggests two things. First, the Motivated Information Processing in Groups (De Dreu, Nijstad, et al., 2008) applies not only to group judgments (Scholten et al., 2007; Toma & Butera, 2009), bargaining, and negotiation (De Dreu et al., 2006, Halevy, 2008) or overall team effectiveness (De Dreu, 2007), but also to group creativity and innovation (see also Hirst, van Dick, & van Knippenberg, in press). Second, a specific integration of DPCM with MIP-G may provide the theoretical framework for understanding group creativity and innovation that is currently missing. We will return to this but first discuss some issues around individual level creativity.

Individual Creativity: Theoretical and Practical Implications

Over the past decades, much work within social psychology has explored the effects of different personality traits and situational variables on creative performance. For example, social psychological research has shown that creative performance is influenced by dispositional and situationally induced mood states (Baas et al., 2008), by external evaluations and rewards (e.g., Amabile, 1996; Eisenberger & Rhoades, 2001), by situationally induced promotion versus prevention focus (Friedman & Förster, 2001), and by the activation of romantic motives (Griskevicius et al., 2006). The work on the DPCM presented in this chapter contributes to this growing literature in two important ways.

First, DPCM can integrate much of this work within one framework. The model may be used to derive specific predictions about how different variables may relate to either the flexibility or the persistence pathway, and which fit between trait and state might produce engagement and predict creative performance. At the basic level our hypothesis would be that activating approach-related traits (e.g., extraversion, BAS) and states (approach or promotion mindsets, approach-related mood states such as joy and elation) associate with cognitive flexibility and enhance creative performance in situations in which this processing style matches the task constraints. Activating avoidance-related traits (neuroticism, BIS) and states (avoidance and prevention mindsets, avoidance-related mood states such as fear and worries) associate with more systematic processing that can, through persistence, also lead to creativity. Again, this may happen only when this more systematic processing style fits the task constraints. The reason appears to be that fit produces task engagement and improves cognitive functioning.

Second, DPCM implies that certain research findings may depend on the specific circumstances in which a study has been done. For example, Friedman and Förster (2000, 2001) found that situationally induced approach states and promotion focus led to higher levels of creativity than avoidance states and prevention focus. However, if avoidance states and prevention focus are associated with more systematic thinking, potential positive effects on creativity depend on persistence and time on task. Had Friedman and Förster used longer tasks, their effects might not have been obtained. Furthermore, certain creativity tasks might better fit with avoidance than with approach states (e.g., tasks using narrow rather than broad topics) in which case the effects might even be reversed (i.e., people in an avoidance state outperforming those in an approach state).

At a practical level, the model implies that there are very different ways creativity can be stimulated and that the success of a certain intervention might also depend on other factors such as task demands. If one would want to make employees more flexible, one should probably bring them in a happy mood state, emphasize the attainment of positively valued outcomes, or induce a relatively broad mental focus. However, these strategies will work well especially when the creative task is one that fits with such a mental state: broad topics in which many approaches and categories of solutions are possible. Alternatively, when working on a more narrowly defined problem, in which not many categories of solutions or many different perspectives are possible, it might be better to induce a narrow focus, perhaps emphasize the avoidance of negative outcomes, and make people slightly worried rather than happy.

Group Creativity and Innovation: Theoretical and Practical Implications

At the group level, we have argued that creativity and innovation both profit from a combination of high epistemic motivation and prosocial motivation. A critical theoretical issue will be to connect the individual-level DPCM with this group level work. In essence, this entails building theoretical multilevel models, in which creativity at the group level is a function of individual creativity of group members in combination with characteristics at the group level (see also Taggar, 2002). Critical for individual-level creativity to translate to group-level creativity is, in our view, the presence of a cooperative group climate where people trust each other and are willing to contribute toward high group outcomes.

An interesting issue in this regard is that several recent studies on group creativity suggest that it may be important that group members are willing to stand out from the group and differentiate themselves from other members. For example, Beersma and De Dreu (2005) found that groups were more creative after a competitive rather than after a cooperative previous interaction. Nemeth and Ormiston (2007) found that groups were more creative after a change in membership, even though membership change undermined group cohesion. Goncalo and Staw (2006) found that groups in which members were asked to describe how they differed from other people were more creative than groups in which members were asked to describe how they were similar to others. The commonality in these examples is that groups either focused on what members have in common and group harmony or on how members differ and uniqueness. For creativity, it seems that group members should use different approaches and there should be no pressure toward uniformity (also see Chirumbolo et al., 2005; De Dreu, Nijstad, et al., 2008). This is more likely after a competitive negotiation, after membership change, and when individualistic values have been activated.

At first blush these findings appear inconsistent with our view that groups need a cooperative climate. Indeed, a cooperative atmosphere may lead to conformity and low levels of creativity, but this will happen only when epistemic motivation in a group is low. Furthermore, it is perfectly possible to differentiate oneself from other group members in the interest of the group and with prosocial motives (e.g., when one believes that taking a different stand will really help the group to function better). Indeed, our studies on minority dissent suggest exactly this: Standing out from the group helps creativity as long as the group is characterized by a cooperative climate. The practical advice thus is to encourage people to take a different perspective (rather than to conform) but also to ensure a cooperative and safe climate. Leaders have an especially important role in these processes (see, e.g., Shin & Zhou, 2007).

Concluding Thoughts

To understand creativity we began with our Dual Pathway to Creativity Model, in which individual creativity is understood as a function of cognitive flexibility and persistence that in turn are functions of a variety of external states such as the individual's mood state or global mind-set, chronic dispositions such as need for structure and behavioral activation, and their more or less fitting combinations. DPCM offers a straightforward and integrative modeling of individual creativity capturing most past research findings and, at the same time, offering new insights and generating new questions awaiting future research. DPCM also provides a basis for understanding creativity in groups, an area we discussed at length in the second half of this chapter. Integrating DPCM with our work on motivated information processing in groups generated the insight that group creativity not only needs the individuals to be activated but in addition requires the group climate to be constructive, generating the psychological safety needed for members to build on each other, and to open-mindedly generate and disseminate ideas and insights. We suggest new research to focus on the merging of DPCM and models of motivated cognition in groups to further understanding group creativity. Ultimately, this will lead to the much-needed conceptualization of creativity as a multifaceted, multilevel process.

REFERENCES

Amabile, T. M. (1996). *Creativity in context: Update to the social psychology of creativity.* Boulder, CO: Westview.

Ambady, N., & Gray, H. M. (2002). On being sad and mistaken: Mood effects on the accuracy of thin-slice judgments. *Journal of Personality and Social Psychology, 83,* 947–961.

Anderson, N., De Dreu, C. K. W., & Nijstad, B. A. (2004). The routinization of innovation research: A constructively critical review of the state-of-the-science. *Journal of Organizational Behavior, 25,* 147–173.

Baas, M., De Dreu, C. K. W., & Nijstad, B. A. (2008). A meta-analysis of 25 years of mood-creativity research: Hedonic tone, activation, or regulatory focus? *Psychological Bulletin, 134,* 779–806.

Baer, M., & Oldham, G. R. (2006). The curvilinear relation between experienced creative time pressure and creativity: Moderating effects of openness to experience and support for creativity. *Journal of Applied Psychology, 91,* 963–970.

Barrett, L. F., & Russell, J. A. (1998). Independence and bipolarity in the structure of current affect. *Journal of Personality and Social Psychology, 74,* 967–984.

Bechtoldt, M. N., De Dreu, C. K. W., Nijstad, B. A., & Choi, H-S. (in press). Motivated information processing, social tuning, and group creativity. *Journal of Personality and Social Psychology.*

Beersma, B., & De Dreu, C. K. W. (2005). Conflict's consequences: Effects of social motives on post-negotiation creative and convergent group functioning and performance. *Journal of Personality and Social Psychology, 89,* 358–374,

Boden, M. A. (1998). Creativity and artificial intelligence. *Artificial Intelligence, 103,* 347–356.

Bransford, J. D., & Stein, B. S. (1984). *The ideal problem solver.* New York: Freeman.

Camacho, L. M., & Paulus, P. B. (1995). The role of social anxiousness in group brainstorming. *Journal of Personality and Social Psychology, 68,* 1071–1080.

Carnevale, P. J. D., & Isen, A. M. (1986). The influence of positive affect and visual access on the discovery of integrative solutions in bilateral negotiation. *Organizational Behavior and Human Decision Processes, 37,* 1–13.

Carnevale, P. J. D., & Probst, T. M. (1998). Social values and social conflict in creative problem solving and categorization. *Journal of Personality and Social Psychology, 74,* 1300–1309.

Carver, C. S., & White, T. L. (1994). Behavioral inhibition, behavioral activation, and affective responses to impending reward and punishment: The BIS/BAS scales. *Journal of Personality and Social Psychology, 67,* 319–333.

Chirumbolo, A., Mannetti, L., Pierro, A., Areni, A., & Kruglanski, A. W. (2005). Motivated closed-mindedness and creativity in small groups. *Small Group Research, 36,* 59–82.

Choi, H-S., & Levine, J. M. (2004). Minority influence in work teams: The impact of newcomers. *Journal of Experimental Social Psychology, 40,* 273–280.

Csikszentmihalyi, M. (1996). *Creativity: Flow and the psychology of discovery and invention.* New York: HarperCollins.

Dailey, L., & Mumford, M. D. (2006). Evaluative aspects of creative thought: Errors in appraising the implications of new ideas. *Creativity Research Journal, 18,* 385–390.

De Dreu, C. K. W. (2003). Time pressure and closing of the mind in negotiation. *Organizational Behavior and Human Decision Processes, 91,* 280–295.

De Dreu, C. K. W. (2007). Cooperative outcome interdependence, task reflexivity, and team effectiveness: A motivated information processing perspective. *Journal of Applied Psychology, 92,* 628–638.

De Dreu, C. K. W., Baas, M., & Nijstad, B. A. (2008). Hedonic tone and activation level in the mood–creativity link: Toward a dual pathway to creativity model. *Journal of Personality and Social Psychology, 94,* 739–756.

De Dreu, C. K. W., Beersma, B., Stroebe, K., & Euwema, M. C. (2006). Motivated information processing, strategic choice, and the quality of negotiated agreement. *Journal of Personality and Social Psychology, 90,* 927–943.

De Dreu, C. K. W., & Nijstad, B. A. (2008). Mental set and creative thought in social conflict: Threat rigidity versus motivated focus. *Journal of Personality and Social Psychology, 95,* 648–661.

De Dreu, C. K. W., Nijstad, B. A., & Baas, M. (2009). *Creative flow-from-fit: The role of behavioral inhibition, approach tendency, and processing mode.* Unpublished manuscript, University of Amsterdam.

De Dreu, C. K. W., Nijstad, B. A., & van Knippenberg, D. (2008). Motivated information processing in group judgment and decision making. *Personality and Social Psychology Review, 12,* 22–49.

De Dreu, C. K. W., Weingart, L. R., & Kwon, S. (2000). The influence of social motives on integrative negotiation: A meta-analytic review and test of two theories. *Journal of Personality and Social Psychology, 78,* 889–905.

De Dreu, C. K. W., & West, M. A. (2001). Minority dissent and team innovation: The importance of participation in decision making. *Journal of Applied Psychology, 86,* 1191–1201.

De Vet, A. J., & De Dreu, C. K. W. (2007). The influence of articulation, self-monitoring ability, and sensitivity to others on creativity. *European Journal of Social Psychology, 37,* 747–760.

De Vries, M., Holland, R. W., & Witteman, C. L. M. (2008). Fitting decisions: Mood and intuitive versus deliberative decision strategies. *Cognition and Emotion, 22,* 931–943.

Derryberry, D., & Reed, M. A. (1998). Anxiety and attentional focusing: Trait, state, and hemispheric influences. *Personality and Individual Differences, 25,* 745–761.

Dietrich, A. (2004). The cognitive neuroscience of creativity. *Psychonomic Bulletin & Review, 11,* 1011–1026.

Dreisbach, G., & Goschke, T. (2004). How positive affect modulates cognitive control: Reduced perseveration at the cost of increased distractibility. *Journal of Experimental Psychology: Learning, Memory, and Cognition, 30,* 343–353.

Eisenberger, R., & Rhoades, L. (2001). Incremental effects of reward on creativity. *Journal of Personality and Social Psychology, 81,* 728–741.

Fiedler, K. (1988). Emotional mood, cognitive style, and behavior regulation. In K. Fiedler & J. P. Forgas (Eds.), *Affect, cognition, and social behavior* (pp. 100–119). Toronto, Ontario: Hogrefe.

Förster, J., Friedman, R. S., & Liberman, N. (2004). Temporal construal effects on abstract and concrete thinking: Consequences for insight and creative cognition. *Journal of Personality and Social Psychology, 87,* 177–189.

Förster, J., & Higgins, E. T. (2005). How global vs. local processing fits regulatory focus. *Psychological Science, 16,* 631–636.

Friedman, R. S., & Förster, J. (2000). The effects of approach and avoidance motor actions on the elements of creative insight. *Journal of Personality and Social Psychology, 79,* 477–492.

Friedman, R. S., & Förster, J. (2001). The effects of promotion and prevention cues on creativity. *Journal of Personality and Social Psychology, 81,* 1001–1013.

George, J. M., & Zhou, J. (2007). Dual tuning in a supportive context: Joint contributions of positive mood, negative mood, and supervisory behaviors to employee creativity. *Academy of Management Journal, 50,* 605–622.

Goncalo, J. A., & Staw, B. M. (2006). Individualism–collectivism and group creativity. *Organizational Behavior and Human Decision Processes, 100*, 96–109.

Gray, J. A. (1990). Brain systems that mediate both emotion and cognition. *Cognition and Emotion, 4*, 269–288.

Griskevicius, V., Cialdini, R. B., & Kenrick, D. T. (2006). Peacocks, Picasso, and parental investment: The effects of romantic motives on creativity. *Journal of Personality and Social Psychology, 91*, 63–76.

Guilford, J. P. (1967). *The nature of human intelligence*. New York: McGraw-Hill.

Halevy, N. (2008). Team negotiation: Social, epistemic, economic, and psychological consequences of subgroup conflict. *Personality and Social Psychology Bulletin, 34*, 1687–1702.

Higgins, E. T. (2006). Value from hedonic experience and engagement. *Psychological Review, 113*, 439–460.

Hinsz, V. B., Tindale, R. S., & Vollrath, D. A. (1997). The emerging conceptualization of groups as information processors. *Psychological Bulletin, 121*, 43–64.

Hirst, G., van Dick, R., & van Knippenberg, D. (in press). A social identity perspective on leadership and employee creativity. *Journal of Organizational Behavior.*

Hirt, E. R., Devers, E. E., & McCrea, S. M. (2008). I want to be creative: Exploring the role of hedonic contingency theory in the positive mood–cognitive flexibility link. *Journal of Personality and Social Psychology, 94*, 214–230.

Kane, A. A., Argote, L., & Levine, J. M. (2005). Knowledge transfer between groups via personnel rotation: Effects of social identity and knowledge quality. *Organizational Behavior and Human Decision Processes, 96*, 56–71.

Keller, J., & Bless, H. (2008). Flow and regulatory compatibility: An experimental approach to the flow model of intrinsic motivation. *Personality and Social Psychology Bulletin, 34*, 196–209.

Kelly, J. R., & Karau, S. J. (1993). Entrainment of creativity in small groups. *Small Group Research, 24*, 179–198.

Klein, K. J., Conn, A. B., & Sorra, J. S. (2001). Implementing computerized technology: An organizational analysis. *Journal of Applied Psychology, 86*, 811–824.

Kruglanski, A. W., & Freund, T. (1983). The freezing and unfreezing of lay inferences: Effects on impressional primacy, ethnic stereotyping, and numerical anchoring. *Journal of Experimental Social Psychology, 19*, 448–468.

Lerner, J. S., & Tetlock, P. E. (1999). Accounting for the effects of accountability. *Psychological Bulletin, 125*, 255–275.

Martindale, C. (1999). Biological bases of creativity. In R. J. Sternberg (Ed.), *Handbook of creativity* (pp. 137–152). Cambridge, UK: Cambridge University Press.

Mednick, S. A. (1962). The associative basis of the creative process. *Psychological Review, 69*, 220–232.

Mumford, M. D., & Gustafson, S. B. (1988). Creativity syndrome: Integration, application, and innovation. *Psychological Bulletin, 103*, 27–43.

Murray, N., Sujan, H., Hirt, E. R., & Sujan, M. (1990). The influence of mood on categorization: A cognitive flexibility interpretation. *Journal of Personality and Social Psychology, 59*, 411–425.

Nemeth, C. J., & Ormiston, M. (2007). Creative idea generation: Harmony versus stimulation. *European Journal of Social Psychology, 37*, 524–535.

Nijstad, B. A., & Kaps, S. C. (2008). Taking the easy way out: Preference diversity, decision strategies, and decision refusal in groups. *Journal of Personality and Social Psychology, 94*, 860–870.

Nijstad, B. A., Selman, F., & De Dreu, C. K. W. (2008). *Innovation in top management teams: A motivated information processing approach.* Working paper, University of Amsterdam.

Nijstad, B. A., & Stroebe, W. (2006). How the group affects the mind: A cognitive model of idea generation in groups. *Personality and Social Psychology Review, 10,* 186–213.

Nijstad, B. A., Stroebe, W., & Lodewijkx, H. F. M. (2002). Cognitive stimulation and interference in groups: Exposure effects in an idea generation task. *Journal of Experimental Social Psychology, 38,* 535–544.

Nijstad, B. A., Stroebe, W., & Lodewijkx, H. F. M. (2003). Production blocking and idea generation: Does blocking interfere with cognitive processes? *Journal of Experimental Social Psychology, 39,* 531–548.

Osborn, A. F. (1957). *Applied imagination* (2nd ed.). New York: Scribner's.

Postmes, T., Spears, R., & Cihangir, S. (2001). Quality of decision making and group norms. *Journal of Personality and Social Psychology, 80,* 918–930.

Rietzschel, E. F., De Dreu, C. K. W., & Nijstad, B. A. (2007). Personal need for structure and creative performance: The moderating influence of fear of invalidity. *Personality and Social Psychology Bulletin, 33,* 855–866.

Rietzschel, E. F., Nijstad, B. A., & Stroebe, W. (2006). Productivity is not enough: A comparison of interactive and nominal brainstorming groups on idea generation and selection. *Journal of Experimental Social Psychology, 42,* 244–251.

Rietzschel, E. F., Nijstad, B. A., & Stroebe, W. (2007). Relative accessibility of domain knowledge and creativity: The effects of knowledge activation on the quantity and originality of generated ideas. *Journal of Experimental Social Psychology, 43,* 933–946.

Runco, M. A. (2004). Creativity. *Annual Review of Psychology, 55,* 657–687.

Sawyer, R. K. (2006). *Explaining creativity: The science of human innovation.* New York: Oxford University Press.

Scholten, L., van Knippenberg, D., Nijstad, B. A., & De Dreu, C. K. W. (2007). Motivated information processing and group decision making: Effects of process accountability on information processing and decision quality. *Journal of Experimental Social Psychology, 43,* 539–552.

Schooler, J. W., Ohlsson, S., & Brooks, K. (1993). Thoughts beyond words: When language overshadows insight. *Journal of Experimental Psychology: General, 122,* 166–183.

Schulz-Hardt, S., Brodbeck, F. C., Mojzisch, A., Kerschreiter, R., & Frey, D. (2006). Group decision making in hidden profile situations: Dissent as a facilitator for decision quality. *Journal of Personality and Social Psychology, 91,* 1080–1093.

Schultz, P. W., & Searleman, A. (1998). Personal need for structure, the Einstellung task, and the effects of stress. *Personality and Individual Differences, 24,* 305–310.

Schwarz, N., & Bless, H. (1991). Happy and mindless, but sad and smart? The impact of affective states on analytic reasoning. In J. P. Forgas (Ed.), *Emotion and social judgments* (pp. 55–71). Elmsford, NY: Pergamon Press.

Schwarz, N., & Clore, G.L. (2007). Feelings and phenomenal experiences. In E. T. Higgins & A. Kruglanski (Eds.), *Social psychology. A handbook of basic principles* (2nd ed., pp. 385–407). New York: Guilford Press.

Shalley, C., Zhou, J., & Oldham, G. (2004). The effects of personal and contextual characteristics on creativity: Where should we go from here? *Journal of Management, 30,* 933–958.

Shin, S. J., & Zhou, J. (2007). When is educational specialization heterogeneity related to creativity in research and development teams? Transformational leadership as a moderator. *Journal of Applied Psychology, 92,* 1709–1721.

Silvia, P. J. (2008). Discernment and creativity: How well can people identify their most creative ideas? *Psychology of Aesthetics, Creativity, and the Arts, 2,* 139–146.

Simonton, D. K. (1997). Creative productivity: A predictive and explanatory model of career trajectories and landmarks. *Psychological Review, 104,* 66–89.

Simonton, D. K. (2003). Scientific creativity as constrained stochastic behavior: The integration of product, person, and process perspectives. *Psychological Bulletin, 129,* 475–494.

Smith, S. M., & Blankenship, S. E. (1991). Incubation and the persistence of fixation in problem solving. *American Journal of Psychology, 104,* 61–87.

Somech, A. (2006). The effects of leadership style and team process on performance and innovation in functionally heterogeneous teams. *Journal of Management, 32,* 132–157.

Staw, B. M., Sandelands, L. E., & Dutton, J. E. (1981). Threat-rigidity effects in organizational behavior: A multilevel analysis. *Administrative Science Quarterly, 26,* 501–524.

Steiner, I. D. (1972). *Group process and productivity.* New York: Academic Press.

Taggar, S. (2002). Individual creativity and group ability to utilize individual creative resources: A multilevel model. *Academy of Management Journal, 45,* 315–330.

Toma, C,, & Butera, F. (2009). Hidden profiles and concealed information: Strategic information sharing and use in group decision making. *Personality and Social Psychology Bulletin, 35,* 793–806.

Torrance, E. P. (1966). *Torrance tests of creativity.* Princeton, NJ: Personnel Press.

Vaughn, L. A., Malik, J., Schwartz, S., Petkova, Z., & Trudeau, L. (2006). Regulatory fit as input for stop rules. *Journal of Personality and Social Psychology, 91,* 601–611.

Watson, D., Clark, L. A., & Tellegen, A. (1988). Development and validation of brief measures of positive and negative affect: The PANAS scales. *Journal of Personality and Social Psychology, 54,* 1063–1070.

West, M. A., & Farr, J. L. (1990). Innovation at work. In M. A. West & J. L. Farr (Eds.), *Innovation and creativity at work: Psychological and organizational strategies* (pp. 3–13). Chichester, UK: Wiley.

Westphal, J. D., Gulati, R., & Shortell, S. M. (1997). Customization or conformity? An institutional and network perspective on the content and consequences of TQM adoption. *Administrative Science Quarterly, 42,* 366–394.

Wolfradt, U., & Pretz, J. E. (2001). Individual differences in creativity: Personality, story writing, and hobbies. *European Journal of Personality, 15,* 297–310.

Worthy, D. A., Maddox, W. T., & Markman, A. B. (2007). Regulatory fit effects in a choice task. *Psychonomic Bulletin & Review, 14,* 1125–1132.

14

A Social Identity Approach to Workplace Stress

S. Alexander Haslam
University of Exeter

Rolf van Dick
Goethe University Frankfurt

Stress is one of the major topics in the field of industrial and organizational psychology. As Haslam (2004) observes, there are at least four good reasons for this. First, stress can be seen as a "downside" to many of the other important topics in which industrial and organizational psychologists are interested and that are studied extensively in the organizational field. Accordingly, while topics like leadership, motivation, communication, negotiation, and productivity are typically investigated and promoted as valuable organizational processes, it is also clear that each of these can have secondary consequences ("side effects") that impact adversely on employees' well-being. For example, leaders who works hard to initiate change may place a heavy psychological burden both on themselves and on those they lead (Quick, Cooper, Gavin, & Quick, 2002; Terry, Carey, & Callan, 2001). Likewise, motivational and productivity demands may put staff under extreme pressure (Bourassa & Ashforth, 1998; Parker, 1993). At the same time, when it comes to a number of key organizational topics, stress can be seen as another key part of the analytic equation. For instance, it can be seen as a counterweight to trust and lack of perceived justice (see Chapter 9 by Dirks & De Cremer in this volume), as something that can be ameliorated by prosocial behavior (see the chapter by Aquino & O'Reilly), or as a consequence of conflicts at work (see Chapter 12 by Rispens & Jehn and Chapter 10 by Flynn).

Second, there are also grounds for believing that these unwanted pressures have increased dramatically in recent years (e.g., Kompier,

Cooper, & Guerts, 2000; Paoli, 1997). Indeed, a plethora of commentators have argued that the productivity gains witnessed toward the end of the 20th century (e.g., as a function of goal setting, team working, and labor-force flexibility), were achieved only by placing increasing psychological strain on employees and thereby putting their welfare at greater risk (e.g., Martin, 1997; Micklethwait & Wooldridge, 1997; Warhurst & Thompson, 1998). In particular, the last four decades have seen a number of significant changes to the nature of work including globalization, advances in information technology (e.g., arising from the advent of e-mail, teleworking, and computer-based work), the increased flexibility of employee contracts and tenure (Sparks, Faragher, & Cooper, 2001), and ongoing restructuring. Speaking to the last of these factors, the uncertainty and upheaval associated with merger and acquisition activity have been found to be a major source of stress for contemporary workforces (Cartwright & Cooper, 1992; Terry et al., 2001).

Researchers and commentators argue that all of these elements have an impact on stress and well-being. In particular, this is because they are associated with heightened job insecurity, longer working hours, lowered levels of perceived control, and increasingly interventionist managerial styles (e.g., just-in-time production systems, total quality management, incentivization schemes). It would also seem likely that these issues will move further to the fore now that the world is in global recession, and companies and their staff are under increasing pressure to compete in contracting markets—where the fear of failure is both immediate and very real (Catalano, 1991).

A third reason workplace stress is the focus of so much research is that it is situated at the crossroads of a number of key subdisciplines in psychology. In particular, physiological, clinical, social, and organizational psychologists have all brought large and distinct bodies of knowledge to bear on the topic. Moreover, the debate that this promotes clearly has the capacity to enhance the discipline as a whole, not least because it touches on fundamental questions concerning the nature of the relationship between mind and body.

Finally, stress is a widely researched phenomenon because it is a concern for anyone who is keen to promote and enhance employee welfare. Moreover, it makes financial sense to be interested in such matters as the economic toll of stress is immense. Although estimates vary wildly, assessors suggest that stress-related costs arising from absenteeism, inefficiency, and demands on health care may account for up to 1% of national gross domestic product and 5% to 10% of company profit (Martin, 1997). Part of this cost arises because employers can now be held liable for psychological injury to employees and, if found negligent, forced to pay damages. In recent years individual settlements around the world have routinely involved six-figure sums (in U.S. dollars). As a result, employers are keen to support research in this area both to demonstrate sensitivity to the issues and to provide answers to critical organizational questions: Is a particular organizational environment damaging? If so, how and why? And how might it be improved? Indeed, one of our own recent studies involved formulating a response to the first Stress Improvement Notice issued by the United Kingdom's Health and Safety Executive (HSE) with a view to providing answers to precisely such questions (O'Brien & Haslam, 2003). Evidence suggests that research of this form can be financially as well as intellectually rewarding because psychological work to ameliorate workplace stress has been found to produce a fivefold yield on investment (Martin, 1997).

In this chapter we will look at the new answers to these questions that have been provided by social psychologists—specifically those who have worked from a *social identity* perspective. Whereas most approaches to the study of stress argue that this is a phenomenon grounded in the psychology of the individual *as an individual*, this approach suggests that group memberships are central to people's experiences of, and reactions to, social and environmental stressors (Branscombe, Schmitt, & Harvey, 1999; Haslam, 2004; Haslam, O'Brien, Jetten, Vormedal, & Penna, 2005; Ryan, Haslam, Hersby, Kulich, & Wilson-Kovacs, 2009; Sassenberg & Woltin, 2008; Terry et al., 2001; van Dick & Wagner, 2002; van Dick, Wagner, & Lemmer, 2004). As we will see, a key point here is that group life plays a key role in shaping the psychology of stress through its capacity to inform and structure our sense of self—and the sense of belonging, worth, purpose, and potential that goes with it. Most particularly, the sense of social identity that underpins group membership plays a key role in determining whether stressful conditions change us (for the worse) or we combine with others to change them (for the better).

DOMINANT APPROACHES TO STRESS

Before outlining what the social identity approach is and how it can be applied to the analysis of stress, it is useful first to provide a brief overview of some of the approaches that dominate contemporary understanding of this topic. This is important as a means of understanding both the range of phenomena that need to be explained and, ultimately, what a new approach has (and needs) to offer.

The Physiological Approach

Since initial work in the 1930s, theories of stress have been heavily influenced by physiological conceptions that characterize the phenomenon as the *response* of an organism to unbearable demands. This idea is central to the medical approach pioneered by Cannon (1929) and Selye (1946, 1956). Selye famously argued that stress could be understood in terms of a *general adaptation syndrome* (GAS). This syndrome envisaged stress as having three distinct stages: *shock, countershock,* and *resistance.* It was suggested that if a person works through the full stress process this can mean that, ultimately, the experience is positive as it can promote a person's growth and development and also enhance performance (in the Nietzschian sense whereby "that which does not kill me makes me stronger"). However, Selye argued that this will not be the case if the process of resistance depletes a person's energy as this will result in *exhaustion* that is likely to have adverse long-term health outcomes (e.g., increasing the likelihood of heart disease, strokes, failure of the immune system, cancer; Eyer & Sterling, 1977).

One extreme form that this depletion takes is *burnout.* This syndrome represents the most chronic form of workplace stress and is typically associated with people who work in human service professions (e.g., nursing and teaching). As well as exhaustion, the other two components of the syndrome are *lack of accomplishment* and *callousness* (or depersonalization); when combined these are seen to represent a potent threat to both individual health and organizational functioning (e.g., Jackson, Schwab, & Schuler, 1986; Schulz, Greenley, & Brown, 1995).

Notwithstanding its success in describing important features of the stress process, two key limitations of the physiological approach are that it is apsychological and acontextual (Cooper, Dewe, & O'Driscoll, 2001). This means that it fails to answer a number of key "when" and "why" questions relating to the emergence and impact of stress. To address these we need to attend both to the workings of employees' minds and to the world within which they operate.

The Individual Difference Approach

One very popular way of attempting to come to terms with the psychological dimensions of stress has involved attempting to clarify the psychological profile of the stress-prone person. The most influential work in this area has built on the early work by Rosenman and Friedman (Rosenman et al., 1964), which distinguished between *Type A* and *Type B* behavior patterns (TABP, TBBP). Such work deploys tools like the Jenkins Activity Survey to differentiate between those whose approach to work tasks is rushed and intense (and who are believed to be particularly prone to stress-related illness as a result) and those who are more laid back (Jenkins, Zyzansky, & Rosenman, 1979).

However, despite its enduring popularity, reviews of the reliability and efficacy of this approach provide little evidence that it is either empirically robust or practically useful (e.g., Cooper et al., 2001; Ganster, Schaubroeck, Sime, & Mayes, 1991). Most particularly, this is because the correlations between various measures of personality and key outcomes (e.g., relating to health and work performance) vary widely and are typically very low (e.g., see Myrtek, 2001).

As in other areas of organizational psychology, faced with unimpressive evidence of this form, most researchers who continue to use personality as a basis for understanding stress have moved toward a contingency approach. This suggests that personality factors (e.g., TABP) moderate the relationship between features of the environment and stress reaction such that where particular features of the workplace tend to produce stress their impact will be especially pronounced for people with a particular personality type.

Yet even in this qualified form the personality approach still runs into problems. In particular, the correlational nature of most work makes it unclear whether personality is a *cause* or a *product* of stress and poor health. As well as this, there is a clear sense in which the personality factors that are implicated in the stress process (e.g., Type-A behavior, lack of hardiness, negative affectivity, low self-esteem, pessimism) are circular in the sense that they simply *redescribe* some of its salient features. Accordingly, while personality approaches provide us with a language that is helpful when it comes to describing stress reactions, like work in the physiological tradition, they are not much use when it comes to explaining them. Clearly too the personality approach provides no clear avenues for lowering stress and reducing its adverse consequences.

The Stimulus-Based Approach

If one questions the idea that stress is peculiar to particular types of people, an obvious alternative is to suggest that it is a product of particular features of the organizational environment. Among researchers who have pursued this idea, their key strategies have involved trying to quantify the amount of stress that is likely to arise from both (1) particular life events (e.g., losing one's job, retiring, conflict with one's boss) and (2) having particular occupations. This activity results in different forms of a stress table (e.g., Holmes & Rahe, 1967) frequently reproduced in textbooks and that often inform lay discussions of this issue (e.g., in the media). Yet although this approach generates interesting data that can have some utility for actuarial purposes, it is apparent that such lists are very context specific (e.g., in being restricted to a particular culture at a particular point in time), and that there is at least as much variation in stressfulness *within* particular events and occupations as there is difference *between* them. And again, they are theoretically limited in failing to explain what it is about particular events or particular jobs that makes them stressful.

In an attempt to answer such questions, researchers have attempted to break down the experience of work into its constituent components to identify which of these are primarily responsible for stress. For example, Cartwright and Cooper (1997; see Cooper et al., 2001) differentiate between six major categories of stressors in the workplace, and these criteria commonly are used to assess stress in the workplace. In particular, such work argues that stress tends to be a product of (1) high demand, (2) lack of say in one's work, (3) lack of support from colleagues and superiors, (4) exposure to unacceptable behavior (e.g., bullying), (5) lack of role clarity, and (6) lack of involvement in organizational change. Although these can clearly be distinguished from each other, one feature that these six categories of stressor share is that they all involve some sense of perceived *unfairness* (procedural or distributive; De Cremer, 2006; Tyler & Blader, 2000).

Although it might appear self-evident that such features have the capacity *in and of themselves* to place an excessive strain on employees, it would appear, however, that this is far from universally true. As we will discover later in this chapter, it is not hard, for example, to find situations in which workers thrive under conditions of high demand, limited control, and lack of role clarity. Again, then, despite an impressive amount of research showing that an array of organizational stimuli *can* contribute to stress at work there is a lack of properly integrated theory to explain *when* and *why* they do.

The Transactional Approach

Bearing in mind the weaknesses associated with personality and stimulus-based approaches, stress researchers have increasingly recognized the need to see stress as something that is *psychologically mediated*. In this vein, most contemporary researchers define stress as the strain imposed on a person by stressors in the environment that is *perceived* by them to be threatening to their well-being (e.g., Folkman et al., 1966). The critical point here is that whether a stressor is seen to be problematic depends on the cognitions of the perceiver. As William Shakespeare's Hamlet put it, "There is nothing either good or bad but thinking makes it so" (van Steenbergen, Ellemers, Haslam, & Urlings, 2008). Supporting this idea, classic studies by Lazarus and his colleagues demonstrated that participants' experience of stress is always dependent on their *appraisal* of a particular stimulus situation. Gory images, for example, are found to cause viewers more stress if they are believed to be real rather than staged (Lazarus, 1966).

Elaborations of the transactional approach differentiate between two components of appraisal: (1) *primary appraisal*, which involves evaluation of the significance of an event or situation for the individual's well-being; and (2) *secondary appraisal*, which involves a person's assessment of his or her capacity to cope with a given stressor. This is an evaluative process that draws on beliefs about the self, the environment, and the availability of resources. It includes assessment of the coping options that are available (e.g., reframing, avoidance), the likelihood that a given coping strategy will be effective, and confidence that one can apply the strategy competently (Lazarus & Folkman, 1984). Although coping strategies are not always effective (and some, like denial and avoidance, can actually increase stress in the long run; Carver, 1995), a stress reaction is likely to develop more quickly if coping resources are perceived to be inadequate. Among other things, this is because primary and secondary appraisal are dynamically interrelated, so that negative secondary appraisal ("I can't cope") adversely affects primary appraisal ("This is stressful").

Along these lines, considerable research has focused on *social support* as a key mechanism that helps people to cope with stress (Aspinwall & Taylor, 1997; Cohen & Wills, 1985; Underwood, 2000; van Dick & Wagner, 2001). Here researchers argue that a social support network (e.g., composed of one's friends, family, and colleagues) has the potential to reduce the harmful effects of stress by providing people with (1) concrete aid, material resources, and financial assistance (instrumental support), (2) a sense of acceptance and self-worth (emotional support), (3) affiliation and contact with others (social companionship), and (4) information useful in understanding and coping with stressful events (informational support).

The importance of this general line of inquiry is emphasized by the fact that most stressors have the potential to be a source not only of distress but also of *eu*stress (i.e., leading to a positive rather than a negative stress reaction). Moreover, it is apparent that over time the same person (or the same group of people) can often redefine the stressfulness of a particular stimulus. Stressors are thus rather faddish (Suedfeld, 1997). This is seen in the way epidemics of work-based stress (including burnout, sick building syndrome, and repetitive strain injury) are found to be specific to a particular time and to a particular culture (Bartholomew & Wessely, 2002).

A key point about many such stressors, then, is that they are part of a collective, *shared* experience of the workplace. For example, discrimination, lack of recognition and opportunity, and poor working conditions are not things that people always suffer alone. On the contrary, they are perceived injustices that people often suffer as members of particular social groups and *because* they are members of those groups (e.g., women, members of an ethnic minority or working class; Branscombe et al., 1999; De Cremer, 2006; Ryan et al., 2009). This in turn points to the fact that there is a significant *social* dimension to stress. To date, though, theorizing about these social aspects of stress has tended to be rather limited (Hart & Cooper, 2001). Moreover, the existing theories tend to be appended as something of an afterthought to individualistic models of cognition that focus on the individual *as an individual* (Folkman & Moskowitz, 2004). There is a general failure, then, to see group life as in any way central to individuals' psychological experiences of stress (Levine & Reicher, 1996; Thoits, 1991). Thus, although the transactional approach makes an essential contribution to our understanding, there is scope for its insights to be accommodated within a complementary but broader theoretical framework that integrates *and explains* both personal and social aspects of the stress process. This is where the social identity approach comes in.

THE SOCIAL IDENTITY APPROACH: SOME KEY CONCEPTS AND PREMISES

This is not the place to provide an expansive or definitive statement about the social identity approach (for extensive recent treatments see Ashforth, Harrison, & Corley, 2008; Haslam, 2004; Haslam & Ellemers, 2005; van Dick, 2001, 2004). Nevertheless, before we outline its relevance to the analysis of stress, we need to start by summarizing some of the main premises of the two theories that together comprise this approach: *social identity theory* (SIT) and *self-categorization theory* (SCT).

Social Identity Theory

Social identity theory was originally formulated by Henri Tajfel and John Turner at the University of Bristol in the 1970s (e.g., Tajfel & Turner, 1979). One of its foundational insights is that in many significant social contexts people's sense of self ("who they think they are") is defined by their group membership. This means that rather than being purely personal (e.g., seeing the self as "I") people's sense of identity can also be social (so that the self is as defined by a sense of "us"). The core notion of social identity thus refers to self-definition in group-based terms.

SIT hypothesizes that people's evaluations of the groups to which they see themselves as belonging (i.e., in-groups) are relative in nature. Our sense of who we are is enhanced by knowing not only that we belong to certain groups (e.g., as academics, as psychologists) but also that we are different from members of other groups (e.g., administrators, doctors). These in-group–out-group (us vs. them) distinctions not only help us understand ourselves but also affect people's self-evaluation and sense of worth. In particular, an in-group's perceived superiority relative to other groups in a relevant domain (achieved through positive intergroup comparisons) should tend to enhance self-esteem and well-being (Haslam, Jetten, Postmes, & Haslam, 2009). In contrast, if individuals belong to a group that is perceived to be in some way inferior to others (e.g., because it is disadvantaged or stigmatized), then negative intergroup comparison is likely to pose a threat to well-being and be a potential source of stress. In line with this point, three particular sources of stress in the workplace are sexism, ageism, and racism (e.g., Barreto, Ryan, & Schmitt, 2009; McCann & Giles, 2002; Watts & Carter, 1991).

There is thus more to social identity than the sociological or demographic groupings that might be used to classify an individual (e.g., as a woman, as a professional). Social identities are relative, they differ in the extent to which individuals perceive them as psychologically meaningful descriptions of self (i.e., they are more or less central to our self definition), and their function and meaning can change over time. Within SIT, though, it is the theorizing surrounding these dynamics that makes the notion of social identity a particularly powerful tool in helping researchers go beyond alternative approaches that treat social groups simply as one of many demographic factors that are associated with physical and mental health. Specifically, social identity theory helps to explain how social identities can be associated with positive or negative health outcomes by focusing on the way individuals understand and respond to the social structural conditions in which they find themselves (Jetten, Haslam, & Haslam, in press).

In particular, the theory focuses on the importance of three key structural elements: the perceived *permeability* of group boundaries and the perceived *stability* and *legitimacy* of an in-group's position in relation to other groups (Tajfel & Turner, 1979; see also Ellemers, 1993; Reicher & Haslam, 2006). Without going into too much detail, if members of low-status groups believe that group boundaries are *permeable*, then to deal with negative intergroup comparisons they should favor strategies of *individual mobility* whereby they try to dissociate themselves from a negative or stigmatized group. Yet if individuals perceive group boundaries to be impermeable (so that group membership is fixed and one's low status is inescapable) such strategies are ruled out. Here, if social relations are *secure* (in the sense of being seen as both stable and legitimate), members of low-status groups are predicted to engage in *social creativity*. However, if relations are impermeable and *insecure* (i.e., seen to be unstable or illegitimate), then members of low-status groups are more likely to define themselves in terms of their group membership and strive to achieve some form of *social change*. Among other things, this may involve participation in political action designed to secure improved rights or better treatment for one's in-group (Branscombe et al., 1999).

Importantly, if individuals perceive group boundaries to be impermeable they are more likely to define themselves in terms of social identity (i.e., to show relatively high levels of *social identification*) and hence to act in line with their social demographic status (e.g., as a woman). However, this is less likely to be true when boundaries are perceived to be permeable (particularly if the in-group has low status), since here the relevant group membership tends not to inform individuals' self-definitions and hence their behavior. For the purposes of the present chapter, the important point to take from this is that an appreciation of the way social contextual factors determine individuals' internalization of particular social identities is critical for understanding the meaning of sociodemographic factors and individuals' responses to the various stressors and threats with which those factors are associated (Haslam & Reicher, 2006a). In line with our critique of the stimulus-based approach to stress, this means, for example, that whether or not the work associated with a particular occupation (e.g., teaching) proves to be stressful will depend very much on the nature and strength of employees' identification with this occupation and their perceptions of the status relations between this occupational group and others (e.g., students, parents, managers; van Dick & Wagner, 2002).

Self-Categorization Theory

Self-categorization theory (Turner, 1982, 1985; Turner, Hogg, Oakes, Reicher, & Wetherell, 1987; Turner, Oakes, Haslam, & McGarty, 1994) expands on the insights that social identity theory provides by probing further into the social psychological dynamics of the self. When do we define ourselves as group members rather than as individuals? What determines which group memberships define our sense of self in any given context? What are the consequences of self-definition in group-based terms?

The theory's answer to such questions builds on three key insights. As we have already intimated, the first of these is that social identity is what allows group behavior to occur at all. As Turner (1982) famously put it, "Social identity is the cognitive mechanism that makes group behavior possible" (p. 21). A second core insight is that the self-system reflects the operation of a categorization process whereby, depending on the context in which they are embedded, people see themselves as either sharing category membership with others (i.e., in terms of a shared social identity, "us") or not (seeing those others either as "them" [vs. us] or "you" [vs. me]; Turner, 1985). Whether, and which, social identities become salient is seen to be a product of (1) the fit of a particular categorization and (2) a person's readiness to use it (Oakes, Haslam, & Turner, 1994). For example, a person is more likely to define himself or herself as an employee of Company X (sharing category membership with other Company X employees) if this self-categorization maps on to what he or she sees and understands about the patterns of similarity and difference between people in Company X and those in Company Y (e.g., in terms of work practices, norms, values) and if Company X has some prior meaning for them (e.g., because they have worked there for a long time; Jetten, O'Brien, & Trindall, 2002).

Following up on these ideas, a third insight is that shared social identity is the basis for mutual *social influence* (Turner, 1991). When people perceive themselves to share group membership with other people in a given context they are motivated to strive actively to reach agreement with them and to coordinate their behavior in relation to activities that are relevant to that identity. Again, they do this because it is the group that defines their sense of self. In advancing the group (and its members) they are therefore acting *for* the self, not against it.

For this reason, perceptions of shared social identity can be seen as the basis for all forms of productive social interaction between people, including leadership, motivation, communication, cooperation, helping, trust, and organization (Ellemers, De Gilder, & Haslam, 2004; Haslam, 2004; Haslam, Postmes, & Ellemers, 2003; Postmes, 2003; Reicher, Haslam, & Hopkins, 2005; Turner & Haslam, 2001; van Dick, Grojean, Christ, & Wieseke, 2006). In relation to the analysis of stress, a critical point is that shared social self-categorization is also the basis for effective social support—so that seeing oneself as sharing social identity with another person increases the likelihood (1) that you will offer them support, (2) that they will offer it to you, and (3) that you will both interpret each other's acts in the intended way (i.e., constructively; Levine, Prosser, Evans, & Reicher, 2005). As a corollary, in the absence of shared identity there is a far greater likelihood that support will fail to be provided and be misinterpreted when it is. Among other things, this helps explain why supportive acts that occur across social category boundaries (or faultlines; Lau & Murnighan, 1998; e.g., those of ethnicity, culture, and class) tend to be less effective than those that occur within those boundaries (Nadler, Fisher, & Streufert, 1974).

A SOCIAL IDENTITY APPROACH TO STRESS

Earlier in the chapter we noted that most researchers have tended to conceptualize stress as a very personal phenomenon. At the same, time, though, it was clear that stress has some very important social dimensions. In particular, people's experience of stress is often bound up with the existence of groups and their membership of them. In the workplace this means, among other things, that stress can arise from the activities that particular occupational groups have to perform (e.g., policing, teaching), from the way groups are treated (e.g., by managers), from a person's relationship to a group (e.g., as someone who bullies other group members or is bullied by them), and from norms that develop within a group (e.g., to interpret particular events and situations as stressful). However, building on a range of points that we made in the previous section, we are now in a position to flesh out in more detail some of the important implications of social identity and self-categorization theories for issues of stress in the workplace.

Social Identity and Primary Stress Appraisal

One of the most basic predictions that flows from principles articulated within the social identity approach is that if a person's social identity is salient then his or her *appraisal* of social stressors will be influenced by the perspective and condition of his or her in-group. Consistent with this suggestion, a growing body of research has confirmed that social identity is an important determinant of *primary appraisal* (i.e., whether a given stressor is seen as threatening to self; Lazarus & Folkman, 1984). For example, in experimental research by Levine and Reicher (1996), female athletes found the threat of a knee injury more stressful than the threat of a facial scar when their identity as athletes was made salient, but the opposite pattern emerged when their gender identity was salient. Along related lines, research by St. Claire, Clift, and Dumbelton (2008) showed that people are far more likely to report symptoms of a cold and to request medication if they are first primed to self-categorize as cold sufferers (see also St. Claire & He, 2009).

Other work has also shown that employees are far less likely to respond positively to organizational stressors if they perceive themselves to share a sense of identity with the organization that is the source of those stressors. As a corollary, though, employees with low levels of organizational identification are likely to react less positively to workplace stressors. Support for this hypothesis comes from a number of recent studies we have conducted with colleagues. For example, in a survey of 161 call center workers, Wegge, van Dick, Fisher, Wecking, and Moltzen (2006) found that low levels of organizational identification were a key predictor of the perceived stressfulness of the work environment. Likewise, in studies of schoolteachers in Germany, van Dick and Wagner (2002) found that low levels of organizational identification were correlated with teachers' tendency to report physical symptoms of stress, as were low levels of identification with their work team. And in a study of 154 airline pilots in Thailand, Peters, Tevichapong, Haslam, and Postmes (in press) found that flight attendants who worked for low-cost airlines—which were perceived to have lower status than those who worked for a full-service airline—reported lower levels of organizational identification, and that this in turn was associated with a tendency to find their work much more stressful.

In a similar vein, Knight and Haslam (in press[a]; in press[b]) conducted a program of studies that examined reactions to office space in more than 2,000 employees. They found that, over and above any "objective" features of the work environment, low levels of organizational identification (associated with a lack of control over their workspace) were a significant independent predictor of employees' tendency to find physical features of their work environment stressful. Importantly, this research was both experimental as well as survey based, and a particular strength of the experimental studies was that they were able to control these objective features of the work environment. Here, then, when workers were given no say over their workspace, they reported lower levels of organizational identification and were much more likely to report symptoms of sick office syndrome (e.g., finding the room stuffy and the air stale, akin to sick building syndrome).

We noted earlier that one important feature of phenomena like sick building syndrome is that they are typically shared among members of a particular work community. In line with principles articulated within self-categorization theory (e.g., Turner, 1991), a key reason for this, we suggest, is that members of these communities perceive themselves to share social identity and on this basis are likely to shape each others' appraisal of their work environment through processes of social influence. In contrast to the picture that might emerge from stimulus-based or transactional approaches, it is typically not the case, then, that individuals appraise particular stressors from a position of isolation in which they mechanically process information in a dispassionate, uninvolved manner (e.g., by consulting stress tables) and then decide matter-of-factly whether a particular stimulus is threatening. Instead, they talk to their peers and come to shared understandings about the meaning and significance of their experiences. And it is on this basis that they come to see the air as stale or fresh, the work demands as unreasonable or reasonable, their manager as a bully or a buddy.

Evidence of the role that social identity plays in such appraisals emerges from another of our studies in which, before completing a fairly difficult arithmetic task, university students were exposed to a video-recorded message in which a person who purported to have completed the exercises previously described them as either (1) stressful or (2) challenging (Haslam, Jetten, O'Brien, & Jacobs, 2004). The message was delivered by the same person in each condition, but in different experimental conditions the participants were told that this person was either a university student (i.e., a fellow in-group member) or someone with a stress disorder (an out-group member). Here we predicted that, when they completed the task themselves, the students would be more likely to see the task as a positive challenge rather than as a source of distress when information to this effect was provided by someone they believed to be an in-group rather than an out-group member. This was exactly what we found. As predicted, the in-group member thus exerted influence over stress appraisal in a way that the out-group did not. Following self-categorization theory (Turner, 1991), we suggest that this is because the in-group member was perceived to share the same identity-based perspective as perceivers and hence was seen to be more qualified to inform them about the meaning of the social reality they confronted.

Social Identity and Secondary Stress Appraisal

As well as affecting primary appraisal, social identity salience also serves as a basis for *secondary appraisal* (i.e., coping processes; Lazarus & Folkman, 1984). In particular, this is because, as argued in the previous section, a person's sense of shared group membership is central to the dynamics of *social support* (i.e., whether they give and receive assistance from others, and how they respond to it; Underwood, 2000). Evidence consistent with this hypothesis is provided by a number of studies indicating that a sense of shared social identity helps to buffer groups—especially those with low status—from adverse environmental threats. In particular, this has been found in studies of the work-related stress experienced by minority ethnic groups (James, 1995, 1997) and in studies of Black Americans' responses to discrimination and prejudice (Branscombe et al., 1999; Postmes & Branscombe, 2002).

Our own research with bomb disposal experts and bar staff also supports suggestions that shared social identity has a positive impact on stress because it serves as a basis for the receipt of effective support from ingroup members (Haslam et al., 2005). More specifically, in this research employees' identification with their colleagues was found to be significantly correlated with job satisfaction, and this relationship was mediated by the perception that those colleagues were an important source of material, emotional, and intellectual support.

Interestingly too, this same research also generated evidence that employees' assessment of their capacity to cope with particular stressors was structured by their membership of specific occupational groups. Thus, while bar staff reported that handling bombs would be much more problematic than doing bar work, bomb disposal experts reported the very opposite pattern. Bar staff were thus relatively unfazed by the stresses of bar work and bomb handlers by the stresses of handling bombs. It seems plausible that this pattern of findings reflects the fact that both groups' collective experiences (e.g., during training and in the course of actually doing their job) had allowed them to *normalize* aspects of work that might be quite abnormal and threatening to the uninitiated (Ashforth, 2001). As one of the senior bomb disposal officers put it during postexperiment discussions: "You expect what you see, so it's not so stressful. Disposing with bombs is something you do, not something out of the ordinary." Indeed, because handling bombs *is* more "out of the ordinary" than working behind a bar, normalization processes of this form are likely to be particularly important in preparing people for this type of work (Haslam et al., 2005, p. 365).

More generally, though, these findings suggest that (1) the nature and strength of a person's workgroup identity and (2) the meaning of a specific stressor in relation to that identity are both very important determinants of any given stressor's impact. If one were to rely on objective indices (e.g., of the form that stress tables provide), it seems highly likely that the job of handling bombs would come close to the top of any list of stressful occupations. Nevertheless, it is clear that whether our participants felt they could cope with this work depended very much on what their occupational group membership was and whether this group membership was self-defining.

Social Identity and Burnout

Our work with bomb disposal officers suggests that social identity can play a key role in protecting individuals from extreme stressors that might otherwise be seen as both very self-threatening and as exceeding their capacity to cope. Generally, though, the research we have discussed thus far was conducted with opportunity samples of "normal" workers and hence provides insight into stress only of a relatively unexceptional nature. A key question, then, is whether the analysis we have provided is of any relevance to work environments where stressors are much more toxic. In particular, can the social identity approach help us to understand the dynamics of the burnout process described by researchers like Selye (1946) and Maslach and Leiter (1996)?

Some preliminary evidence that it might comes from two studies that we and our colleagues have conducted. The first of these was O'Brien and Haslam's (2003) study of the organization that had been issued with the first Stress Improvement Notice by the U.K. Health and Safety Executive, previously alluded to. In this we found that low levels of social identification (at both the team level and the organizational level) were a significant independent predictor of worker's burnout levels (which in some workgroups were extremely high). Moreover, along the lines of Haslam et al.'s (2005) study, this relationship between low identification and burnout was found to be mediated by a lack of social support. In other words, there was evidence that workers experienced high levels of burnout because their psychological connection to the organization was very weak, and as a result they found themselves to be both isolated and unsupported. Interestingly, too, this idea fits with a body of recent epidemiological work suggesting that social isolation poses a health risk that is far greater than that associated with traditional medical risk factors (e.g., poor diet, lack of exercise; Ertel, Glymour, & Berkman, 2008; for a discussion see Jetten, Haslam, Haslam, & Branscombe, 2009).

A second study providing evidence of the role that a sense of shared social identity can play in protecting workers from burnout comes from a longitudinal exploration of patterns of group identification, work-related attitudes, and burnout within two teams that we monitored over the course of their work on different theater productions (Haslam, Jetten, & Waghorn, 2009). As predicted, over the course of the study individuals who identified highly with the production team were more likely than those with low levels of identification to perform acts of citizenship that involved helping out other people on the team. Moreover, the former participants were less likely to experience burnout during the most demanding phases of the production (i.e., dress rehearsal and performance). Additional statistical analysis also indicated that the willingness of high identifiers to engage in acts of citizenship was attributable to the fact that their high levels of team identification protected them from burnout during these demanding periods. In this way, the study's results suggest that social identification not only motivates individuals to contribute to group success but also protects them from the stressors they encounter in the process of making that contribution.

Yet as with most of the previous work on burnout (see Cooper et al., 2001), a general problem with these two studies (like the majority of others on this topic) is that they employed a correlational design in which key variables were measured rather than manipulated. As a result, while they show that social identification is associated with variation in burnout, they fail to establish that it plays a causal role. Indeed, in both studies it is plausible (and quite likely) that reduced social identification was as much a *consequence* of burnout as a cause.

A study with the potential to overcome this limitation and to integrate the analysis of stress and burnout with a broader examination of group functioning was conducted by Haslam and Reicher (2006a) in collaboration with the BBC (Koppel & Mirsky, 2002; see also Haslam & Reicher, 2006b; Reicher & Haslam, 2006). In this, 15 participants were randomly assigned to one of two groups—as Prisoners or Guards—within a simulated prison environment, and their behavior was studied closely over a period of 8 days. The goal of the research was to manipulate factors that would impact upon the Prisoners' degree of social identification and to examine the impact of this on their and the Guards' behavior as well as on the functioning of the system as a whole.

A key point to recognize here is that the study was not motivated by a particular or specific interest in issues of prison life. For this reason its aim was not to simulate a prison per se but rather to create an institution that also had important features of other hierarchical institutions (e.g., a school, an office, a barracks) so that we might investigate the behavior of groups that were unequal in terms of their power, status, and resources. What is critical, then, is not that the environment replicated a real prison (which it never could) but that it created inequalities between groups that were real to the participants. Importantly, it was this feature that allowed us to test theoretical ideas derived from SIT and SCT in novel and meaningful ways, and it is on the basis of support for these hypotheses that we seek to generalize its findings (Reicher & Haslam, 2006; Turner, 1981).

So how did we do this? At the start of the study, participants were led to believe that the boundaries between high- and low-status groups were permeable and that it was possible to be promoted from Prisoner to Guard. In line with social identity theory, at this stage it was expected that Prisoners would adopt an individual mobility strategy and would seek to enhance their status by working individually to gain favor with the Guards. Following this, though, opportunities for promotion were ruled out (i.e., group boundaries were rendered impermeable), and it was expected that this would increase Prisoners' social identification and encourage collective responses to their situation.

In addition to behavioral observation, measures were obtained on a number of social, organizational, and clinical measures throughout the study. As predicted, it was clear from these that Prisoners' social identification increased over the course of the study in response to structural changes in the prison. Moreover, as Prisoners' social identification increased they started to resist the Guards' authority (a pattern confirmed on measures of compliance and organizational citizenship), and ultimately their resistance contributed to a breakout which made the Guards' regime unworkable. In the process of arriving at this outcome, the Guards also became increasingly apprehensive about their authority, and this, combined with the Prisoners' insurrection, contributed to a steady decline in their sense of shared social identity.

In line with the general arguments previously outlined (and findings reported by Branscombe et al., 1999; Haslam et al., 2005), it was clear from both psychological and physiological data as well as from behavioral observation that higher levels of social identification were generally associated with more positive stress-related outcomes. As events unfolded, the Prisoners' enhanced identification with their group thus led them to become increasingly resistant to the strains of their predicament (e.g., physical confinement, poor diet, lack of privileges) and increasingly willing to impose strain on the Guards (e.g., by challenging their position, by subjecting them to humiliation and bullying). At the same time, as the Guards' sense of shared identity declined they became increasingly distressed—not least because they became increasingly isolated and failed to provide each other with the support necessary to maintain their authority and resist the various challenges posed by the Prisoners. Ultimately too, the Guards' failure to run the prison effectively led them to experience high levels of burnout—to the extent that, after their regime had collapsed, two of the Guards exercised their right to withdraw from the study.

In its entirety, the BBC prison study thus allowed for an integrated examination of the complex roles that social identification and emergent intra- and intergroup dynamics play in the stress process. On the one hand, the experiences of the Prisoners show how an emergent sense of shared social identity allows individuals to resist strain and to turn adversity into advantage. On the other hand, the experiences of the Guards show how the erosion of social identity exposes individuals to stress and how, to the extent that it contributes to collective failure, it can ultimately pave the way to burnout.

Moreover, by providing a longitudinal analysis of the interwoven processes that contribute to both resistance and exhaustion, the study also helps develop a theoretical framework for a *social psychological* understanding of the physiology of stress (e.g., as described by Selye, 1946). In the first instance it demonstrates that physiology neither follows a generalized trajectory nor is a fundamental property of any individual's personality or biology (e.g., as suggested by the individual differences approach). Instead, the physiology of stress can be seen as one aspect of a social contextual process that derives from, and helps shape, the conditions of group life. In these terms, stress is not primarily a problem of biology, physiology, or personality. It is a problem of *group life*, yet, at the same time, group life is the key to its reduction.

CONCLUSION: WORKPLACE STRESS AS A SOCIAL AND POLITICAL PROCESS

For a field that has tended to see stress very much as an individual-level phenomenon, we believe that the social identity approach has a lot to offer. At the most general level, it makes the point that it can be a mistake to ground one's appreciation of the stress process—and one's responses to stress-related problems—in the psychology of individuals *as* individuals (Haslam, 2004). The validity of this idea is perhaps seen most clearly in the BBC prison study (Reicher & Haslam, 2006) where formal clinical assessment and scores on standard clinical tests indicated that all of the participants in this study were normal, well-adjusted, healthy adults (Haslam & Reicher, 2006a). All had considerable prior experience of exposure to, and management of, stress. Yet it was neither their predetermined resilience nor their prior experience that primarily determined their responses to stress in this study. Instead, these were largely determined by their group memberships and the capacity for those groups to furnish them and their colleagues with a sense of shared identity and purpose in the situation that they found themselves.

At an applied level, the ideas we have presented and the range of studies that support them suggest that practitioners who are interested in understanding and managing the stress process and its outcomes would, at the very least, be well advised to complement individual-based analysis and interventions with activities that are targeted at a group level. Indeed as Ganster and Murphy (2000) note, a failure to do this can mean not only that key phenomena are misunderstood but also that the locus of attention (and blame) shifts from social-structural factors to individual dysfunction and pathology. Rather than attempting to deal with stress-related problems at this personalized level (by which time one is likely to be addressing the consequences of stress not its causes), the social identity approach suggests that an alternative is to create viable, fulfilling, and sustainable groups that provide their members with the psychological and material resources to manage stress effectively and appropriately (Haslam, Eggins, & Reynolds,

2003). This, of course, is no easy task, and an appreciation of its dimensions requires engagement with thorny political issues of leadership, power, and intergroup relations (for a fuller discussion see Haslam, 2004; Reicher et al., 2005; Turner, 2005). Do those in authority want low-status groups to be empowered? Is stress encouraged (or at least tolerated) because it keeps individuals (and therefore groups) "in their place"? Does treating stress as an individual-level problem allow managers to avoid having to recognize and deal with group-level realities? In many organizational contexts, the answer to such questions is yes, and accordingly, it is apparent that here stress is as much a political problem as a social psychological one.

Clearly our analysis calls for further research to explore these social and political dimensions of the stress process much more closely. Ideally, this will involve studies that improve on the various studies that we have reported in a range of ways—for example, by incorporating superior measures, larger samples, and enhanced experimental control. However, we suggest that in future work what will prove to be much more important than all these things is a commitment to large-scale research that involves intense, ongoing social interaction and that moves the field beyond its reliance on self-report measures that individuals complete alone and removed from the hurly-burly of organizational life. For one of the key problems with these standard methodological approaches is that they easily feed into *theories* of stress that are similarly asocial, apolitical, and "dead" (i.e., nondynamic). Whatever else it is, the psychology of stress is not these things. As we have endeavored to document, it is social, it is political, and it is very much alive.

REFERENCES

Ashforth, B. E. (2001). *Role transitions in organizational life: An identity-based perspective.* Mahwah, NJ: Erlbaum.

Ashforth, B. E., Harrison, S. H., & Corley, K. G. (2008). Identification in organizations: An examination of four fundamental questions. *Journal of Management, 34,* 325–374.

Aspinwall, L. G., & Taylor, S. E. (1997). A stitch in time: Self-regulation and proactive coping. *Psychological Bulletin, 121,* 417–436.

Barreto, M., Ryan, M. K., & Schmitt, M. (Eds.) (2009). *The glass ceiling in the 21st century: Understanding barriers to gender equality.* Washington, DC: American Psychological Association.

Bartholomew, R. E., & Wessely, S. (2002). Protean nature of mass sociogenic illness: From possessed nuns to chemical and biological terrorism fears. *British Journal of Psychiatry, 180,* 300–306.

Bourassa, L., & Ashforth, B. E. (1998). You are about to party defiant style: Socialization and identity onboard an Alaskan fishing boat. *Journal of Contemporary Ethnography, 27,* 171–196.

Branscombe, N. R., Schmitt, M. T., & Harvey, R. D. (1999). Perceiving pervasive discrimination among African Americans: Implications for group identification and well-being. *Journal of Personality and Social Psychology, 77,* 135–149.

Cannon, W. B. (1929). *Bodily changes in pain, hunger, fear and rage.* New York: Appleton.

Cartwright, S., & Cooper, C. L. (1992). *Mergers and acquisitions: The human factor.* Oxford, UK: Butterworth-Heinemann.

Cartwright, S., & Cooper, C. L. (1997). *Managing workplace stress.* Thousand Oaks, CA: Sage.

Carver, C. S. (1995). Stress and coping. In A. S. R. Manstead & M. R. C. Hewstone (Eds.), *The Blackwell encyclopedia of social psychology* (pp. 635–639). Oxford, UK: Blackwell.

Catalano R. (1991). The health effects of economic insecurity. *American Journal of Public Health, 81,* 1148–1152.

Cohen, S., & Wills, T. A. (1985). Stress, social support and the buffering hypothesis. *Psychological Bulletin, 98,* 310–357.

Cooper, C. L., Dewe, P. J., & O'Driscoll, M. P. (2001). *Organizational stress: A review and critique of theory, research and applications.* London: Sage.

De Cremer, D. (2006). Unfair treatment and revenge taking: The roles of collective identification and feelings of disappointment. *Group Dynamics: Theory Research and Practice, 10,* 220–232.

Ellemers, N. (1993). The influence of socio-structural variables on identity enhancement strategies. *European Review of Social Psychology, 4,* 27–57.

Ellemers, N., De Gilder, D., & Haslam, S. A. (2004). Motivating individuals and groups at work: A social identity perspective on leadership and group performance. *Academy of Management Review, 29,* 459–478.

Ertel, K., Glymour, M. M., & Berkman, L. F. (2008). Social integration and memory loss over six years of follow-up in the Health and Retirement Study. *American Journal of Public Health, 98,* 1215–1220.

Eyer, J., & Sterling, P. (1977). Stress-related mortality and social organization. *Review of Radical Political Economics, 9,* 1–44.

Folkman, S., Chesney, M., McKusick, L., Ironson, G., Johnson, D., & Coates, T. (1991). Translating coping theory into an intervention. In J. Eckenrode (Ed.), *The social context of coping* (pp. 239–260). New York: Plenum Press.

Folkman, S., & Moskowitz, J. T. (2004). Coping: Pitfalls and promise. *Annual Review of Psychology, 55,* 745–774.

Ganster, D. C., & Murphy, L. (2000). Workplace interventions to prevent stress-related illness: Lessons from research and practice. In C. L. Cooper & E. A. Locke (Eds.), *Industrial and organizational psychology: Linking theory with practice* (pp. 34–51). Oxford, UK: Blackwell.

Ganster, D. C., Schaubroeck, J., Sime, W., & Mayes, B. (1991). The nomological validity of the type A personality among employed adults. *Journal of Applied Psychology, 76,* 143–168.

Hart, P. M., & Cooper, C. L. (2001). Occupational stress: Toward a more integrated framework. In N. Anderson, D. S. Ones, H. K. Sinangil, & C. Viswesvaran (Eds.), *Handbook of industrial, work and organizational psychology* (vol. 2, pp. 93–114). London: Sage.

Haslam, S. A. (2004). *Psychology in organizations: The social identity approach* (2nd ed.). London: Sage.

Haslam, S. A., Eggins, R. A., & Reynolds, K. J. (2003). The ASPIRe model: Actualizing Social and Personal Identity Resources to enhance organizational outcomes. *Journal of Occupational and Organizational Psychology, 76*, 83–113.

Haslam, S. A., & Ellemers, N. (2005). Social identity in industrial and organizational psychology: Concepts, controversies and contributions. In G. P. Hodgkinson & J. K. Ford (Eds.), *International Review of Industrial and Organizational Psychology* (Vol. 20, pp. 39–118). Chichester, UK: Wiley.

Haslam, S. A., Jetten, J., O'Brien, A., & Jacobs, E. (2004). Social identity, social influence, and reactions to potentially stressful tasks: Support for the self-categorization model of stress. *Stress and Health, 20*, 3–9.

Haslam, S. A., Jetten, J., Postmes, T., & Haslam, C. (2009). Social identity, health and well-being. *Applied Psychology: An International Review, 58*(Special Issue), 1 23.

Haslam, S, A., Jetten, J., & Waghorn, C. (2009). Social identification, stress, and citizenship in teams: A five-phase longitudinal study. *Stress and Health, 25*, 21–30.

Haslam, S. A., O'Brien, A., Jetten, J., Vormedal, K., & Penna, S. (2005). Taking the strain: Social identity, social support and the experience of stress. *British Journal of Social Psychology, 44*, 355–370.

Haslam, S. A., Postmes, T., & Ellemers, N. (2003). More than a metaphor: Organizational identity makes organizational life possible. *British Journal of Management, 14*, 357–369.

Haslam, S. A., & Reicher, S. D. (2006a). Stressing the group: Social identity and the unfolding dynamics of responses to stress. *Journal of Applied Psychology, 91*, 1037–1052.

Haslam, S. A., & Reicher, S. D. (2006b). Social identity and the dynamics of organizational life: Insights from the BBC Prison Study. In C. Bartel, S. Blader, & A. Wrzesniewski (Eds.), *Identity and the modern organization* (pp. 135–166). New York: Erlbaum.

Holmes, T. H., & Rahe, R. H. (1967). The social readjustment rating scale. *Journal of Psychosomatic Research, 11*, 213–218.

Jackson, S. E., Schwab, R. L., & Schuler, R. S. (1986). Toward an understanding of the burnout phenomenon. *Journal of Applied Psychology, 71*, 630–640.

James, K. (1995). Social identity, work stress, and minority workers' health. In G. Puryear Keita & S. L. Sauter (Eds.), *Job stress 2000: Emerging issues* (pp. 127–145). Washington, DC: American Psychological Association.

James, K. (1997). Worker social identity and health-related costs for organizations: A comparative study between ethnic groups. *Journal of Occupational Health Psychology, 2*, 108–117.

Jenkins, C. D., Zyzansky, S. J., & Rosenman, R. H. (1979). *The activity survey for health prediction: Form N.* New York: Psychological Corporation.

Jetten, J., Haslam, C., & Haslam, S. A. (Eds.) (in press). *The social cure.* New York: Psychology Press.

Jetten, J., Haslam, C., Haslam, S. A., & Branscombe, N. (2009). The social cure. *Scientific American Mind, 20*, 26–33.

Jetten, J., O'Brien, A., & Trindall, N. (2002). Changing identity: Predicting adjustment to organizational restructure as a function of subgroup and superordinate identification. *British Journal of Social Psychology, 41*, 281–297.

Knight, C., & Haslam, S. A., (in press [a]). *Your place or mine? Organizational identification and comfort as mediators of relationships between the managerial control of workspace and employees' motivation and well-being.* Manuscript under review, University of Exeter.

Knight, C., & Haslam, S. A., (in press [b]). *Lean, green or chosen? Examining the impact of office space management strategies on organizational identification, well-being and productivity.* Manuscript under review, University of Exeter.

Kompier, M. A. J., Cooper, C. L., & Geurts, S. A. E. (2000). A multiple case study approach to work stress prevention in Europe. *European Journal of Work and Organizational Psychology, 9,* 371–400.

Koppel, G. (Series producer) & Mirsky, N. (Executive producer) (2002, May 14, 15, 20, 21). *The experiment.* London: British Broadcasting Corporation.

Lau, D. C., & Murnighan, K. (1998). Demographic diversity and faultlines: The compositional dynamics of organizational groups. *Academy of Management Review, 23,* 325–340.

Lazarus, R. S. (1966). *Psychological stress and the coping process.* New York: McGraw-Hill.

Lazarus, R. S., & Folkman, S. (1984). *Stress, appraisal and coping.* New York. Springer Publishing Company.

Levine, R. M., Prosser, A., Evans, D., & Reicher, S. D. (2005). Identity and emergency intervention: How social group membership and inclusiveness of group boundaries shape helping behavior. *Personality and Social Psychology Bulletin, 31,* 443–453.

Levine, R. M., & Reicher, S. D., (1996). Making sense of symptoms: Self-categorization and the meaning of illness and injury. *British Journal of Social Psychology, 35,* 245–256.

Martin, P. (1997). *The sickening mind: Brain, behaviour, immunity and disease.* London: Flamingo.

Maslach, C., & Leiter, M. P. (1996). *The truth about burnout: How organizations cause personal stress and what to do about it.* San Francisco, CA: Jossey Bass.

McCann, R., & Giles, H. (2002). Ageism in the workplace: A communication perspective. In T. D. Nelson (Ed.), *Ageism: Stereotyping and prejudice against older persons* (pp.163–200). Cambridge, MA: MIT Press.

Micklethwait, J., & Wooldridge, A. (1997). *The witch doctors: What the management gurus are saying, why it matters and how to make sense of it.* London: Random House.

Myrtek, M. (2001). Meta-analyses of prospective studies on coronary heart disease, type A personality, and hostility. *International Journal of Cardiology, 79,* 245–251.

Nadler, A., Fisher, J. D., & Streufert, S. (1974). Donors' dilemma: Recipients' reactions to aid from friend or foe. *Journal of Applied Social Psychology, 4,* 275–285.

Oakes, P. J., Haslam, S. A., & Turner, J. C. (1994). *Stereotyping and social reality.* Oxford, UK: Blackwell.

O'Brien, A. T., & Haslam, S. A. (2003). *Shaping the future (Report in response to the issuing of a Stress Improvement Notice from the UK Health and Safety Executive).* Exeter, UK: School of Psychology, University of Exeter.

Paoli, P. (1997). *Second European survey on working conditions, 1996.* Dublin: European Foundation for the Improvement of Living and Working Conditions.

Parker, M. (1993). Industrial relations myth and shop floor reality: The team concept in the auto industry. In N. Lichtenstein & J. H. Howell (Eds.), *Industrial democracy in America* (pp. 249–274). Cambridge: Cambridge University Press.

Peters, K., Tevichapong, P., Haslam, S. A., & Postmes, T. (in press). *Making the organization fly: Organizational identification, citizenship, and stress in full-service and low-cost airlines.* Manuscript under review, University of Exeter.

Postmes, T. (2003). A social identity approach to communication in organizations. In S. A. Haslam, D. van Knippenberg, M. J. Platow, & N. Ellemers (Eds.), *Social identity at work: Developing theory for organizational practice* (pp. 81–97). New York: Psychology Press.

Postmes, T., & Branscombe, N. (2002). Influence of long-term racial environmental composition on subjective well-being in African Americans. *Journal of Personality and Social Psychology, 83,* 735–751.

Quick, J. D., Cooper, C. L., Gavin, J. H., & Quick, J. C. (2002). Executive health: Building self-reliance for challenging times. *International Review of Industrial and Organizational Psychology, 17,* 187–216.

Reicher, S. D., Cassidy, C., Wolpert, I., Hopkins, N., & Levine, M. (2006). Saving Bulgaria's Jews: An analysis of social identity and the mobilisation of social solidarity. *European Journal of Social Psychology, 36,* 49–72.

Reicher, S. D., & Haslam, S. A. (2006). Rethinking the psychology of tyranny: The BBC Prison Study. *British Journal of Social Psychology, 45,* 1–40.

Reicher, S. D., Haslam, S. A., & Hopkins, N. (2005). Social identity and the dynamics of leadership: Leaders and followers as collaborative agents in the transformation of social reality. *Leadership Quarterly, 16,* 547–568.

Rosenman, R., Friedman, M., Straus, R., Wurm, M., Kositchek, R., Hahn, W., et al. (1964). A predictive study of coronary heart disease. *Journal of the American Medical Association, 189,* 15–22.

Ryan, M. K., Haslam, S. A., Hersby, M. D., Kulich, C., & Wilson-Kovacs, M. D. (2009). The stress of working on the edge: Examining the implications of glass cliffs for both women and organizations. In M. Barreto, M. K. Ryan, & M. Schmitt (Eds.), *The glass ceiling in the 21st century: Understanding barriers to gender equality* (pp.153–169). Washington, DC: American Psychological Association.

Sassenberg, K., & Woltin, K. (2008). Group-based self-regulation: The effects of regulatory focus. *European Review of Social Psychology, 19,* 126–164.

Schulz, R., Greenley, J., & Brown, R. (1995). Organization, management, and client effects on staff burnout. *Journal of Health and Social Behavior, 36,* 333–345.

Selye, H. M. D. (1946). The general adaptation syndrome and dissonances of adaptation. *Journal of Clinical Endocrinology, 6,* 118–135.

Selye, H. M. D. (1956). *The stress of life.* New York: McGraw-Hill.

Sparks, K., Faragher, B., & Cooper, C. L. (2001). Well-being and occupational health in the 21st century workplace. *Journal of Occupational and Organizational Psychology, 74,* 489–509.

St. Claire, L., Clift, A., & Dumbelton, L. (2008). How do I know what I feel? Evidence for the role of self-categorisation in symptom perceptions. *European Journal of Social Psychology, 38,* 173–186.

St. Claire, L., & He, Y. (2009). How do I know if I need a hearing aid? Further support for the self-categorization approach to symptom perception. *Applied Psychology: An International Review, 58,* 24–41.

Suedfeld, P. (1997). The social psychology of "Invictus": Conceptual and methodological approaches to indomitability. In C. McGarty & S. A. Haslam (Eds.), *The message of social psychology: Perspectives on mind in society* (pp. 328–341). Oxford, UK: Blackwell.

Tajfel, H., & Turner, J. C. (1979). An integrative theory of intergroup conflict. In W. G. Austin & S. Worchel (Eds.), *The social psychology of intergroup relations* (pp. 33–47). Monterey, CA: Brooks/Cole.

Terry, D. J., Carey, C. J., & Callan, V. J. (2001). Employee adjustment to an organizational merger: An intergroup perspective. *Personality and Social Psychology Bulletin, 27,* 267–280.

Thoits, P. A. (1991). On merging identity theory and stress research. *Social Psychology Quarterly, 54,* 101–112.

Turner, J. C. (1981). Some considerations in generalizing experimental social psychology. In G. M. Stephenson & J. H. Davis (Eds.) *Progress in applied social psychology* (Vol. 1, pp. 3–34). Chichester, UK: Wiley.

Turner, J. C. (1982).Towards a cognitive redefinition of the social group. In H. Tajfel (Ed.), *Social identity and intergroup relations* (pp. 15–40). Cambridge, UK: Cambridge University Press.

Turner, J. C. (1985). Social categorization and the self-concept: A social cognitive theory of group behavior. In E. J. Lawler (Ed.), *Advances in group processes* (vol. 2, pp. 77–122) Greenwich, CT: JAI Press.

Turner, J. C. (1991). *Social influence.* Milton Keynes, UK: Open University Press.

Turner, J. C. (2005). Explaining the nature of power: A three-process theory. *European Journal of Social Psychology, 35,* 1–22.

Turner, J. C., & Haslam, S. A. (2001). Social identity, organizations and leadership. In M. E. Turner (Ed.), *Groups at work: Theory and research* (pp.25–65). Hillsdale, NJ: Erlbaum.

Turner, J. C., Hogg, M. A., Oakes, P. J., Reicher, S. D., & Wetherell, M. S. (1987). *Rediscovering the social group: A self-categorization theory.* Oxford, UK: Blackwell.

Turner, J. C., Oakes, P. J., Haslam, S. A., & McGarty, C. A. (1994). Self and collective: Cognition and social context. *Personality and Social Psychology Bulletin, 20,* 454–463.

Tyler, T. R., & Blader, S. (2000). *Cooperation in groups: Procedural justice, social identity and behavioral engagement.* Philadelphia, PA: Psychology Press.

Underwood, P. W. (2000). Social support: The promise and the reality. In V. H. Rice (Ed.) *Handbook of stress, coping and health* (pp. 367–391). Thousand Oaks, CA: Sage.

van Dick, R. (2001). Identification in organizational contexts: Linking theory and research from social and organizational psychology. *International Journal of Management Reviews, 3,* 265–283.

van Dick, R. (2004). My job is my castle: Identification in organizational contexts. *International Review of Industrial and Organizational Psychology, 19,* 171–203.

van Dick, R., Grojean, M. W., Christ, O., & Wieseke, J. (2006). Identity and the extra mile: Relationships between organizational identification and organizational citizenship behaviour. *British Journal of Management, 17,* 283–301.

van Dick, R., & Wagner, U. (2001). Stress and strain in teaching: A structural equation approach. *British Journal of Educational Psychology, 71,* 243–259.

van Dick, R., & Wagner, U. (2002). Social identification among school teachers: Dimensions, foci, and correlates. *European Journal of Work and Organizational Psychology, 11,* 129–149.

van Dick, R., Wagner, U., & Lemmer, G. (2004). The winds of change: Multiple identifications in the case of organizational mergers. *European Journal of Work and Organizational Psychology, 13,* 121–138.

van Steenbergen, E. F., Ellemers, N., Haslam, S. A., & Urlings, F. (2008). There is nothing either good or bad but thinking makes it so: Informational support and cognitive appraisal of the work–family interface. *Journal of Occupational and Organizational Psychology, 81,* 349–367.

Warhurst, C., & Thompson, P. (1998). Hands, hearts and minds: Changing work and workers at the end of the century. In P. Thompson & C. Warhurst (Eds.), *Workplaces of the future* (pp. 1–24). Houndmills, UK: Macmillan.

Watts, R. J., & Carter, R. T. (1991). Psychological aspects of racism in organizations. *Group and Organization Management, 16,* 328–344.

Wegge, J., van Dick, R., Fisher, G. K., Wecking, C., & Moltzen, K. (2006). Work motivation, organizational identification, and well-being in call centre work. *Work and Stress, 20,* 60–83.

15

When Good People Do Wrong: Morality, Social Identity, and Ethical Behavior

Madan M. Pillutla
London Business School

Social psychologists have recently begun to pay serious attention to ethical behavior and judgment in organizations. By applying their theories and methods, they have contributed to real progress in understanding the dynamics of business ethics. Prior to this new movement, scholarly studies of business ethics had been grounded in the cognitive development tradition (Kohlberg, 1984), which approached ethical behavior by focusing on the processes of ethical judgment. Because social psychological theory and research have often found a large gap between judgment and behavior (Ajzen, 1985), they have challenged this approach and questioned the utility of focusing on individuals' ethical judgments. In contrast to early studies on ethical judgment, social psychological studies of business ethics have focused on behavior, investigating the conditions that contribute to the emergence of ethical or unethical behavior.

The main theoretical advance in recent research has been in understanding how people act unethically despite being fully aware that they are being unethical. This contrasts with models rooted in the developmental literature that make the implicit assumption that people behave unethically only when they are unaware they are doing so. It is important to acknowledge that none of the scholars from this tradition made this claim explicitly. Nevertheless, models whose central tenet is that the sophistication of individuals' moral reasoning predicts their moral behavior (cf. Kohlberg, 1984; Kohlberg & Kramer, 1969) do suggest that moral behavior results from people being made aware of moral dilemmas.

This assumption—that people will not behave unethically if they are aware that their act is unethical—appears to be fairly reasonable: Most people want to have a positive view of themselves and would therefore not willfully do something to harm that positive, ethical self-view. However, recent advances in social psychology, especially those related to our understanding of how human beings regard themselves, suggest that people structure their self-concepts in ways that allow them to knowingly act immorally without damaging their views of themselves as ethical people.

In this chapter, I use these ideas, the result of research on social identity, to build a compensatory model of unethical behavior. Social identity theory scholars have highlighted the role of the self-concept in regulating moral behavior and have noted how people's views of themselves influence the gap between their ethical judgments and their ethical behaviors. I push the model a step further to argue that a robust, ethical self-concept may actually facilitate unethical behavior in some situations. (I use the terms *moral* and *ethical* behavior interchangeably in the chapter and define them in the next section.)

A MODEL OF ETHICAL DECISION MAKING

According to Rest (1986), ethical decision making is a four-step process. The first step is moral awareness; that is, how much an individual understands that a situation involves ethics or morality. The second step involves the individual making a moral judgment. The third step is the moral decision-making process; that is, how intentions will be translated into action. The final step is the act itself.

This model recognizes that real ethical dilemmas are ambiguous and that many individuals look past them, unaware that they even exist. For example, when a legitimate authority makes a request, individuals tend not to process the situation as one involving a choice; they may not even realize that they can (and possibly should) ask whether they "want" to perform the requested act (Kelman & Hamilton, 1989). In other words, automatic compliance to orders from authority figures can prevent individuals from viewing an unethical action demanded by a legitimate authority as involving an ethical dilemma because they may not even perceive that they have a decision to make or that ethics are involved. Moral awareness also depends on an actor's willingness to expend cognitive effort, which can be determined by situational factors like personal relevance and accountability and by personal factors like the need for cognitive closure (Street, Douglas, Geiger, & Martinko, 2001). People may not be aware of the moral implications of their actions when they don't make the cognitive effort and act automatically.

Models of progressive moral development also suggest that individuals' moral judgments are influenced by two primary factors: (1) the stage of cognitive moral development of the individual decision maker, and (2) the moral intensity of their potential act. Morally intense acts contain an element of moral imperative, which is determined by the magnitude of the consequences of the action, the existence of social consensus, the temporal closeness of the act, the social, cultural, or psychological proximity of those affected by the act, and the concentration of the consequences of the act (Jones, 1991). These models suggest that people will act morally if they judge the moral intensity of their potential actions to be high.

When intensity is low, possibly because of a lack of social consensus, the moral development of the individual decision maker becomes relevant. This is because people at higher stages of Kohlberg's (1984) hierarchy of cognitive moral development are less reliant on the expectations of others and more on universal moral principles in forming moral judgments (Rest, 1986). Thus, moral intensity will not matter as much to them, and they will act ethically even when moral intensity is low. The person–situation interaction can range from individuals at an early stage of moral development facing a situation that has minimal moral consequences to individuals at advanced stages of moral development facing a situation that has obvious, strong moral consequences. According to the developmental models, as one or the other of the two factors increases, so will the likelihood of moral awareness and moral action.

Even though the developmental models accord a central place to ethical judgments, they recognize that the intention that follows moral judgment may differ from the judgment itself. This is because they recognize that people have motivations other than ethical considerations. For example, an individual might recognize that an action is unethical but may decide to do it anyway because some other factor (e.g., need) justifies or outweighs any ethical concerns. In addition, moral action may differ from intentions if intended actions are not actually implemented (which can occur for many reasons).

Rest's (1986) model of the ethical decision-making process makes clear predictions about the probability of ethical action: People will act ethically when they recognize that an act involves ethics; they may act unethically when they don't see the act as unethical, either because they view the situation as one that does not involve ethics or because they do not judge the act in question as unethical. These conditions outline a set of contingencies in which individuals' actions can have no impact on their self-concept; that is, they can continue to view themselves as ethical people despite taking actions that others may consider to be unethical.

In addition, years of research showing that people are particularly good at self-justification suggest that the likelihood of unethical behavior should also increase when people can justify acting unethically (e.g., Holland, Meertens & Van-Vugt, 2002; I discuss this in more detail in the next section). When people take actions that they themselves see as unethical, however, the previously described models suggest that they will damage their views of themselves as ethical even when they can find strong justifications for their actions. Unlike these models, I argue that unethical actions need not damage the self-concept when people are aware that their actions are unethical and when they have no strong justifications for their unethical actions. I develop this argument beginning with a discussion of recent research on moral identity in the next section.

MORAL IDENTITY

A fundamental motive in personality functioning is psychological self-consistency, the notion that people are highly motivated to be consistent in their judgments and actions. This consistency is almost always at stake when individuals face potentially moral actions. Blasi (1980, 1984) noted that the push to be self-consistent results in a deeply felt and expressed need to appear, in our own eyes and those of others, highly moral (sometimes even in the face of overwhelming evidence to the contrary). People often resort to biased justifications to distort reality to allow them to defend and maintain a personal sense of integrity. Bandura (1999, 2002), for instance, identified several processes that people use to selectively disengage from moral self-sanctions, such as cognitive reconstruals (via moral justifications, exonerating comparisons, and sanitizing language), minimizing personal causal agency (via the displacement and diffusion of responsibility), distorting and disregarding harmful consequences, and blaming and devaluing victims.

Blasi (1995) argued that these processes of moral self-deception will be less likely for individuals who have progressed to more mature levels of moral development and for individuals who hold morality central to their self-definitions. He further argued that the combination of a compelling motivation to perceive oneself and to be regarded by others as a moral person and the chance that one could resort to self-deceiving rationalizations and defense mechanisms strongly suggests that the field of moral psychology would benefit greatly from the systematic study of the role of the self in moral functioning. His view was that such research, which distinguishes between individuals who use defensive strategies (and self-deceiving rationalizations) and individuals who do not, would help us understand the gap between ethical judgments and ethical action.

Following Blasi (1984), Colby and Damon (1992) noted that some people seem to act as if morality were their most important concern, consistently, passionately, and even heroically over a lifetime. Based on interviews with 23 such "moral exemplars," Colby and Damon emphasized that the characteristic seeming to distinguish them from others is an exceptionally strong unity between their self-perceptions and morality: "all these men and women have vigorously pursued their individual and moral goals simultaneously, viewing them in fact as one and the same.... Rather than denying the self, they define it with a moral center.... None saw their moral choices as an exercise in self-sacrifice" (p. 300). Thus, Colby and Damon viewed moral identity as the degree of unity between an individual's perception of self and morality; they suggested that when moral identity is strong, "judgment and conduct are directly and predictably linked and action choices are made with great certainty" (p. 150).

For Blasi (1995) and Colby and Damon (1992), moral identity can explain the gap between moral judgment and moral behavior: Morally mature people (or moral exemplars, in Colby and Damon's terminology) behave morally in most situations and avoid the distorting rationalizations and defensive justifications that Bandura (1999, 2002) identified. They do this because they have internalized moral ideals and because their actions are consistent with their conception of their morality-infused selves. In contrast, moral judgment may not correlate with moral behavior for people whose moral identities are not central to their conceptions of self.

Aquino and Reed (2002) and Reed and Aquino (2003) developed these ideas further by suggesting that moral identity refers to the degree to which an individual's self-concept and behavior include characteristically moral traits (see also Chapter 12 in this volume). Following the traditions of social cognition research (cf. Lapsley & Lasky, 2001), they suggest that people for whom moral identity is central have moral schemas that are chronically accessible, readily primed, and easily activated for evaluating social situations. Thus, moral individuals are more likely to see situations as having moral implications; they are also more likely to behave morally in a wide variety of situations. Aquino, Reed, and their colleagues (Aquino & Reed, 2002; Reed & Aquino, 2003; Reed, Aquino, & Levy, 2007) have also developed a measure of moral identity that differentiates people based on their moral schemas; this measure is meant to be used as a predictor of people who will act morally and people who will not.

Aquino and Reed (2002) also offered the intriguing proposition that people may use their moral identities to construct their self-definitions, that is, people may derive a sense of self by belonging to a "moral group." Though their approach is primarily trait based, as they define and measure moral identity as a self-conception organized around a set of moral traits, Aquino and Reed suggested that "moral identity may have a social referent that could be a real membership group (e.g., fellow Peace Corp volunteers)" (p. 1424). The idea that a person's moral identity can act as a form of social identity is important because it suggests the possibility that individuals' moral identities (like other forms of social identity) can vary as their goals and situations change; in other words, actions may differ depending on the salience of a person's moral identity. This allows for intraindividual consistency and interindividual differences in the relationship between an individual's moral and self-identities. In addition, people can vary depending on the centrality as a feature of their self-definitions in relation to other elements that are also important to their identities.

SOCIAL IDENTITY

Tajfel and Turner's social identity theory (Tajfel, 1981; Tajfel & Turner, 1986) adopts the view that social identity is an extension of the self-concept that shifts the focus of self-representation from the individual self to the collective self. When social identities are activated, group memberships are not simply a component of the individual's self-concept; instead, people perceive themselves as part of a larger collective unit. Social identity theory inspired the view that people possess two distinct and relatively independent kinds of identities—personal and social—and both identities play distinct and important roles in people's behaviors (Pelham & Hetts, 1999).

Social identity is the individual's self-concept that results from perceived membership in social groups (Hogg & Vaughan, 2002); it is an individual-based perception of what defines the "us" in any internalized group membership. Personal identity, in contrast, refers to self-knowledge that derives from the individual's unique attributes. This approach views the self as two distinct, coexisting, and interacting elements that can vary depending on the situation. Thus, for example, different social contexts can trigger an individual to think, feel, and act on the basis of his personal, family or national "self" (Turner, Hogg, Oakes, Reicher, & Wetherell, 1987).

An alternative conceptualization (Markus & Kitayama, 1991) views the "self" as an individual with multiple "social identities." For example, people who are doctors and value their membership in the category of doctors may also be mothers and may simultaneously value their membership in that category. But all aspects of a person's identity are not equally accessible at any given time: An individual's past expectations, current motives, and goals and cues, as stimulated by the social context, influence the relative accessibility of one identity (e.g., doctor or parent) or its level (Yale graduate versus college graduate) in the working self-concept. Thus, Americans who are also White may think of themselves as Americans when abroad and as White when a minority among African American colleagues.

A shift in identity or level of identity shifts the accessibility of associated expectations, motives, and goals (cf. Baumeister, 1999; Brewer, 1991; McGuire, McGuire, & Cheever, 1986; Turner, 1999) as well as behaviors. For example, Pillutla and Chen (1999) found that people were more cooperative in social dilemma experiments when their identities as social agents were made salient compared with when their identities as economic agents were made salient.

Roccas and Brewer (2002) suggested the possibility that multiple identities are salient at any given time. How do people reconcile expectations, values, and goals of these different identities? Roccas and Brewer proposed that, while the degree of overlap among a person's social categories may vary considerably from complete embeddedness (e.g., Catholics and Christians) to complete orthogonality (e.g., Muslims and women; p. 89), it may not be reflected in individuals' subjective representations of the interrelationships among their multiple group identities. Some people may be comfortable with, recognize, and reconcile the differing values, norms, and other characteristics of the groups of which they are simultaneously members while others are not. Roccas and Brewer referred to this difference as social identity complexity and appeared to suggest that people at the highest level of complexity are most comfortable with multiple group memberships.

The idea of multiple simultaneous social identities is similar to notions by Stryker and his colleagues (e.g., Stryker, 1980; Stryker & Statham, 1985) of role identities, which refer to individuals' self-perceptions in a particular social position in relation to others who occupy different roles within the same system (e.g., parent, employer, teacher). According to role identity theory, each individual occupies multiple roles arranged hierarchically in order of salience (Figure 15.1). The left-hand side of the figure represents an individual whose employee role is salient; the right side represents an individual whose parent role is salient.

The logic of social identity theory indicates that strong identification leads people to behave as though they are an extension of their group rather than as autonomous actors. This suggests that the norms, values, expectations, motives, and goals associated with the currently salient role should dominate an individual's cognitions and behaviors. For the person

Parent role is salient in the self–concept   Employee role is salient in the self–concept

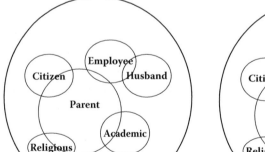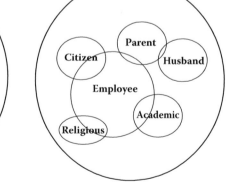

FIGURE 15.1
Role identity salience.

on the left in Figure 15.1, this would be the role of employee; for the person on the right, this would be the role of parent. In other words, salient role identities can depersonalize individuals so that they don't process information, form attitudes, and act as individuals as much as they act as members of their salient social category.

SOCIAL IDENTITY AND MORAL BEHAVIOR

Given this discussion of social identity theory, social identity formulation has two possible implications for our understanding of moral behavior. The first and most straightforward conceptualization would be to identify the social group associated with morality. In other words, moral identity refers to membership in groups whose central feature is adherence to a moral code. Such groups could be one's religion or a secular organization like the Peace Corps. Membership in these social groups should influence an individual's self-concept and direct attention to self-relevant information. When these identities are salient, people will behave as they expect members of that social collective (e.g., fellow religionists or members of the Peace Corps) to behave. Thus moral identity, in this sense, is equivalent to one's identity derived from membership in groups that have important moral dimensions. This conceptualization runs into problems when people are members of groups that have different moral imperatives. What is moral identity here, and how does it explain behavior in this situation? Specifically, what does the notion of moral identity add above and beyond what we can predict about an individual's actions from knowledge of membership and salience of the identity derived from these groups?

A second formulation that views morality as a feature of other social identities may help overcome this problem. Following Blasi (1980, 1984) and Aquino and Reed (2002), I assume that people differ in their perceptions of the centrality of morality to their self-concept; this is the concept of moral identity. Also, following Aquino and Reed, I suggest that a strong moral identity is predictive of moral behavior. Unlike them, however, I don't consider moral identity to be a form of social identity. Instead, I view it as part of the self-concept derived from behaviors in various social roles that individuals play.

Specifically, people view themselves as moral people depending on their morality as, for example, a parent, an employee, or a citizen. As noted, they differ in the degree to which a particular role is salient to their self-concept and, therefore, an important aspect of their social identity (Roccas & Brewer, 2002; Stryker, 1980; Stryker & Statham, 1985). The role most salient to people—the one from which they derive their self-concept—should therefore play a large role in their view of themselves as moral people, and this can shift from one social context to another. If a person's role as a parent is more important to his or her self-concept than his or her role as an employee, then the person's morality in the domain of parenthood should have a greater influence on his or her notions of morality than his or her notions of morality in the domain of employment. In other words, moral identity is jointly determined by the importance of morality to the self-concept and by the social identity that is the most important contributor to the self-concept.

Figure 15.2 depicts four different representations of moral identity salience. The top two diagrams represent relatively low moral identity (i.e., people for whom morality is not an important part of their self-concept); the bottom two represent relatively high moral identity (i.e., people for whom morality is an important part of their self-concept). The diagrams on the left represent individuals whose role as a family member (and presumably identification with their family) is an important aspect of their

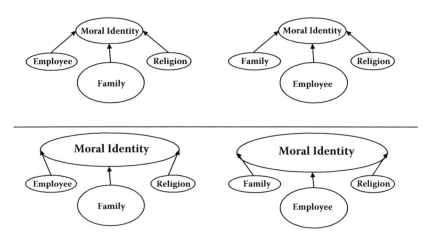

FIGURE 15.2
Determinant and salience of moral identity.

self-concept; the diagrams on the right represent individuals whose role as an employee is an important part of their self concept.

At first, the simple prediction that follows from this representation is that people with stronger moral identities will engage in more ethical behavior than people with weaker moral identities. Thus, the individuals who are represented by the bottom two diagrams in Figure 15.2 should be more ethical than individuals represented by the top two diagrams. This is consistent with the predictions of Aquino and Reed (2002), Blasi (1984), and Colby and Damon (1992). The more interesting differences are those between the individuals represented on the left and the right. In these two cases, situational forces may be a primary determinant of ethical behavior. People who derive their sense of self from being employees may be more ethical at work than individuals who derive their sense of self from their familial roles, and people who derive their sense of self from their families may be more ethical at home than individuals who derive their sense of self from being an employee.

More generally, the prediction is that people who derive their sense of self from a particular domain will be more ethical in that domain compared with individuals who do not derive their sense of self from that domain. This is because individuals can behave unethically in domains that are not strongly implicated in their self-concept; these are situations in which their actions have relatively little consequence to them in terms of their view of themselves as moral people. This option is not available to people who derive their sense of self from that domain. For example, employees who find their work meaningless can justify (to themselves) taking bribes or cheating on their expense accounts because their work life has little meaning for them; employees who find their work truly meaningful, however, cannot use this excuse.

This prediction may sound counterintuitive, as I am suggesting that people will behave more unethically in situations that don't matter to them, which by definition, are domains in which getting ahead or doing well are unimportant. This seems to fly in the face of evidence that people act unethically when the stakes are high rather than low (e.g., Hegarty & Sims, 1978). It is therefore important to note the qualifier. People will find it difficult to behave unethically in domains that they care about (compared with domains that they do not care about) only *if morality is an important part of their identity*. If it is not, people may actually be more unethical in these domains. Thus, the salience of moral identity is expected to moderate the relationship between importance of a particular domain and the likelihood of unethical behavior in that domain.

Another implication of this conceptualization is that strong identification with one particular role can enable unethical behaviors in other roles. To return to the example of taking bribes, people who derive their sense of self from their family may be more inclined to take bribes at work as the bribes help them to be better providers to their family. In other words, unethical behavior in one domain may actually help them perform their roles better in their more important domains. This will be particularly true if they are failing to meet their obligations in the important domain. Specifically, if a parent fails to provide adequately for his or her family and his or her role as a parent is very important for his or her sense of self, the parent is at most risk of unethical behavior. Thus, being a good parent provides both a justification and a reason for being an unethical employee.

Another implication is derived from the self-affirmation literature (cf., Sherman & Cohen, 2006), which asserts that affirming alternative sources of self-integrity when the image of self-integrity is threatened can lead to nondefensive reactions. Thus, affirming people's valued domains (e.g., as a parent) may actually prevent them from doing something unethical when there is conflict between two domains. For example, if the importance of being a good parent leads a person to take a bribe, affirmation of the positive role as a good parent could prevent this from happening. In contrast, unethical behavior in one domain may have fewer negative implications for the self-concept when the valued domain is affirmed. Specifically, unethical behavior as an employee may not have negative implications for the self if it affirms a person's role as a parent.

The final implication comes from an understanding that, in many situations, the role requirements of one role may conflict with the role requirements of other roles (i.e., what is considered ethical may differ from one role to another), and that they may sometimes be in conflict (e.g., Haidt, 2007; Pillutla & Chen, 1999). For example, Haidt (2007) suggested that people's intuitions about morality are grounded in their notions about "ought" and "should" in interpersonal treatment (i.e., how people ought to treat each other) and group behavior (i.e., about how to be a part of a group and especially a group that is in competition with other groups). Thus, people's moral intuitions can be classified as broadly referring to (1) harm, care, and altruism (i.e., people are vulnerable and often need protection); (2) fairness, reciprocity, and justice (i.e., people have rights to certain resources or kinds of treatment); (3) in-group–out-group dynamics and the importance of loyalty; (4) authority and the importance of respect and obedience; and (5) bodily and spiritual purity and the importance of living in a sanctified rather than a carnal way.

Specific identities could lead to the prominence of one of these intuitions over the others, which might then conflict with expectations based on other roles. For example, the role of an employee may lead a person to focus on loyalty or on respect and obedience as guiding moral principles, and this could come into conflict with moral behavior concerned with the avoidance of harm, care, and altruism that would be expected in the role as a member of a liberal political organization. When role requirements conflict and ethical behavior in one role necessarily means unethical behavior in the other, people may choose to be unethical in the domain that has the least implications for their self-concept. Thus, people may choose to be knowingly unethical in one domain (e.g., by being disloyal) in order to be ethical in another domain that they consider more important (e.g., avoidance of harm, fairness, and altruism). This could be the reason people blow the whistle on organizational malpractice and justify (to themselves) their disloyalty to their organization in terms of their desire to adhere to a greater principle derived from being a responsible member of society.

This discussion points to the important counterintuitive implications that can be derived from conceptualizing moral identity as a joint function of the centrality of specific roles or domains in one's self-concept and the centrality of morality in one's identity. Such a conceptualization allows us to understand the following:

- It is possible to retain a sense of morality despite acting unethically in some roles as long as the role is not an important part of one's self-concept.
- Strong identification with one domain may provide the freedom to act unethically in other domains without major implications to the self.
- When being moral in one role conflicts with being moral in another, people will behave unethically in the role that has less importance to their self-concept.
- This tendency may be reduced when the important role is affirmed.
- The negative self-implications of being unethical in a relatively unimportant role can be further attenuated by affirming valued roles.

RELATIONSHIP TO OTHER COMPENSATORY ETHICS MODELS

This conceptualization of moral identity, and the importance of social identities, suggests a compensatory model of ethical behavior that allows people to justify unethical behavior in one domain by their ethical behavior in others. The model is therefore similar to other compensatory models such as moral licensing (Brown, 2000; Monin & Miller, 2001), moral equilibria (Jordan, Mullen, & Murnighan, 2009), and moral compensation (Zhong & Liljenquist, 2006; Zhong, Ku, Lount, & Murnighan, 2010). However, it does differ in some important respects.

The moral licensing and moral equilibrium models suggest that people act as though any good behavior earns them credits they can spend, typically by behaving less ethically in the future than people who have not been good. In one example of this line of research, Monin and Miller (2001) found that experimental participants who had been led to select a clearly qualified ethnic minority for a job, and therefore made their moral credentials clear, subsequently revealed themselves to be more prejudiced in their attitudes toward minorities than participants who had not earned similar moral credentials. The moral compensation model also proposes that people attempt to compensate for bad behavior by being more willing to perform ethical behavior in the future. Jordan et al. (2009) found that participants who had recalled a time when they had acted morally in the past reported weaker prosocial intentions than participants who had recalled neutral information.

In contrast to these compensatory models, the current model does not require any compensation: Unethical behaviors in domains that have little impact on the self-concept do not require the emergence of subsequent ethical acts. Ethical behavior in an important domain can certainly facilitate unethical behavior in unimportant domains (through the process of licensing), but it is not necessary. Another difference is that the licensing, equilibrium, and compensatory models are dynamic: They suggest that individuals balance their virtues and sins across time. The model I am proposing suggests that individuals can balance their ethical identity across domains—by being unethical in some and not in others. Thus, the current model complements the other compensatory models and, along with them, serves as a distinct explanation for unethical behavior even when people are aware that their actions are unethical.

CONCLUSION

I began with the claim that social psychological concepts have helped us understand much about ethical behavior by releasing the field from the central dogma that people behave unethically only when they are unaware of their unethical behavior. By acknowledging that people can behave unethically despite possessing the knowledge and motivation to make ethical judgments, the field is now in a better position to create tools to educate people to behave ethically. Rather than relying on improving people's awareness of and judgments about ethical behavior, new education programs should focus on making people aware of defensive rationalizations and subconscious compensatory mechanisms that can undermine people's good intentions to behave ethically.

The work by Blasi (1995) and others brought ideas about the self to the foreground and has helped bridge the judgment–action gap in two distinct ways. The first is in the development of individual difference variables such as moral identity, which explain why some people act according to their ethical judgments and others don't. The second is in trying to understand how individuals' mental accounting strategies allow them to make conscious unethical choices while retaining their self-integrity. Both of these approaches provide a better understanding of ethical and unethical behaviors. This enhanced understanding should eventually lead to better training and education programs for our students and for ourselves.

REFERENCES

Ajzen, I. (1985). From intentions to actions: A theory of planned behavior. In J. Kuhl & J. Beckman (Eds.), *Action control: From cognition to behavior* (pp. 11–39). Heidelberg, Germany: Springer.

Aquino, K., & Reed II, A. (2002). The self-importance of moral identity. *Journal of Personality and Social Psychology, 83,* 1423–1440.

Bandura, A. (1999). Moral disengagement in the perpetration of inhumanities. *Personality and Social Psychology Review, 3*, 193–209.

Bandura, A. (2002). Selective moral disengagement in the exercise of moral agency. *Journal of Moral Education, 31*, 101–119.

Baumeister, R. F. (Ed.). (1999). *The self in social psychology.* Philadelphia, PA: Psychology Press (Taylor & Francis).

Blasi, A. (1980). Bridging moral cognition and moral action: A critical review of the literature. *Psychological Bulletin, 88*, 1–45.

Blasi, A. (1984). Moral identity: Its role in moral functioning. In W. Kurtines & J. Gewirtz (Eds.), *Morality, moral behavior and moral development* (pp. 128–139). New York: Wiley.

Blasi, A. (1995). Moral understanding and the moral personality: The process of moral integration. In W. Kurtines & J. Gewirtz (Eds.), *Moral development: An introduction* (pp. 229–254). Needham Heights, MA: Allyn & Bacon.

Brewer, M. (1991). The social self: On being the same and different at the same time. *Personality and Social Psychology Bulletin, 77*, 475–482.

Brown, B. R. (2000). When moral entitlement leads to immoral acts. (Doctoral dissertation, Stanford University, 2000). *Dissertation Abstracts International: Sciences and Engineering, 61*, 1132.

Colby, A., & Damon, W. (1992). *Some do care: Contemporary lives of moral commitment.* New York: Free Press.

Haidt, J. (2007). The new synthesis in moral psychology. *Science, 316*, 998–1002.

Hegarty, W. H., & Sims, H. P. (1978). Some determinants of unethical decision behavior: An experiment. *Journal of Applied Psychology, 63*(4), 451–457.

Hogg, M. A., & Vaughan, G. M. (2002). *Social Psychology*, 3rd ed. London: Prentice Hall.

Holland, R. W., Meertens, R. M., & van Vugt, M. (2002). Dissonance on the road: Self-esteem as a moderator of internal and external self-justification strategies. *Personality and Social Psychology Bulletin, 28*, 1713–1724.

Jones, T. M. (1991). Ethical decision making by individuals in organizations: An issue-contingent model. *Academy of Management Review, 16*, 366–395.

Jordan, J., Mullen, E., & Murnighan, J. K. (2009). Moral Miscreants and Immoral Angels: A Model of Moral Equilibrium, unpublished manuscript.

Kelman, H. C., & Hamilton, V. L. (1989). *Crimes of obedience: Toward a social psychology of authority and responsibility.* New Haven, CT: Yale University Press.

Kohlberg, L. (1984). Moral stages and moralization: The cognitive developmental approach. In L. Kohlberg (Ed.), *Essays on moral development: Vol 2. The psychology of moral development: The nature and validity of moral stages* (pp. 170–205). San Francisco: Harper & Row.

Kohlberg, L., & Kramer, R. (1969). Continuities and discontinuities in childhood and adult moral development. *Human Development, 12*, 93–120.

Lapsley, D. K., & Lasky, B. (2001). Prototypic moral character. *Identity, 1*(4), 345–363.

Markus, H. R., & Kitayama, S. (1991). Culture and the self: Implications for cognition, emotion, and motivation. *Psychological Review, 98*, 224–253.

McGuire, W. J., McGuire, C. V., & Cheever, J. (1986). The self in society: Effects of social contexts on the sense of self. *British Journal of Social Psychology, 25*, 259–270.

Monin, B., & Miller, D. T. (2001). Moral credentials and the expression of prejudice. *Journal of Personality and Social Psychology, 81*(1), 33–43.

Pelham, B. W., & Hetts, J. J. (1999). Implicit and explicit personal and social identity: Toward a more complete understanding of the social self. In T. R. Tyler, R. M. Kramer & O. P. Johns (Eds.), *The psychology of the social self.* Mahwah, NJ: Erlbaum.

Pillutla, M., and Chen, X. P. (1999). Social norms and cooperation in social dilemmas. *Organizational Behavior and Human Decision Processes, 78*(2), 81–103.

Reed II, A., & Aquino, K. (2003). Moral identity and the expanding circle of moral regard toward out-groups. *Journal of Personality and Social Psychology, 84,* 1270–1286.

Reed II, A., Aquino, K., & Levy, E. (2007). Moral identity and judgments of charitable behaviors. *Journal of Marketing, 71,* 178–193.

Rest, J. R. (1986). *Moral development: Advances in research and theory.* New York: Praeger.

Roccas, S., & Brewer, M. B. (2002). Social identity complexity. *Personality & Social Psychology Review, 6*(2), 88–106.

Sherman, D. K., & Cohen, G. L. (2006). The psychology of self-defense: Self-affirmation theory. In M. P. Zanna (Ed.), *Advances in experimental social psychology* (Vol. 38, pp. 183–242). San Diego, CA: Academic Press.

Street, M., Douglas, S. C., Geiger, S. W., & Martinko, M. J. (2001). The impact of cognitive expenditure on the ethical decision-making process: The cognitive elaboration model. *Organizational Behavior and Human Decision Processes, 86*(2), 256–277.

Stryker, S. (1980). *Symbolic interactionism: A social structural version.* Menlo Park, CA: Benjamin/Cummings.

Stryker, S., & Statham, A. (1985). Symbolic interaction and role theory. In G. Lindzey & E. Aronson (Eds.), *The handbook of social psychology* (pp. 311–378). New York: Random House.

Tajfel, H. (1981). *Human groups and social categories.* Cambridge, UK: Cambridge University Press.

Tajfel, H., & Turner, J. C. (1986). The social identity theory of inter-group behavior. In S. Worchel & L. W. Austin (Eds.), *Psychology of intergroup relations.* Chicago: Nelson-Hall.

Turner, J. C. (1999). Some current issues in research on social identity and self-categorization theories. In N. Ellemers, R. Spears, & B. Doosje (Eds.), *Social identity: Context, commitment, content* (pp. 6–34). Oxford, UK: Blackwell.

Turner, J. C., Hogg, M. A., Oakes, P. J., Reicher, S. D., & Wetherell, M. S. (1987). *Rediscovering the social group: A self-categorization theory.* Oxford, UK: Basil Blackwell.

Zhong, C. B., Ku, G., Lount Jr., R. B., & Murnighan, J. K. (2010). Compensatory ethics. *Journal of Business Ethics, 92*(3), 323–339.

Zhong, C. B., & Liljenquist, K. (2006). Washing away your sins: Threatened morality and physical cleansing. *Science, 313*(8), 1451–1452.

16

Culture and Creativity: A Social Psychological Analysis

Kwok Leung
City University of Hong Kong

Michael W. Morris
Columbia University

While employee creativity is an increasingly studied topic (Zhou & Shalley, 2003), there is limited research investigating it outside of Western cultures or comparatively across cultures. Nonetheless, journalists frequently invoke connections between culture and creativity, although not always in consistent ways. For instance, one *New York Times* article suggested that the Japanese culture may suppress creativity in scientific discovery (French, 2001), yet a subsequent article on other trends in Japan asserted that "a tradition of tinkering and building has made Japan welcoming to experimental ideas, no matter how eccentric" (Fackler, 2007). This more optimistic assessment of creativity in Japan is not sheer imagination. A recent study ranks Japan as the most innovative country in the world in terms of the amount of time needed for new products to take off (Chandrasekaran & Tellis, 2008). To foster a more nuanced popular understanding of cultural influences on creativity, it is worthwhile to integrate and summarize what research has learned thus far.

This chapter provides a cultural perspective on creativity and innovativeness, with a contrast between East Asia and the West. The chapter begins with an exploration of how culture may influence the perceived importance of creativity and innovativeness and the criteria used to evaluate them. The relationship between specific cultural constructs and creativity is then probed, followed by a discussion of how experiencing multiple cultures may enable creativity. The chapter concludes with major directions for future research. In our discussion, *creativity* refers to the generation of novel ideas, whereas *innovativeness* focuses more on generating creative outcomes, such as creating a new product. Our analysis is at the individual level, not at the firm level, and we are concerned with societal culture not organizational or team culture.

PRIORITIZATION AND CONCEPTUALIZATION OF CREATIVITY

Cultures may differ, at a fundamental level, in how they prioritize and conceptualize creativity. Niu and Sternberg (2001) analyzed the artwork that Chinese and American students produced and found that Chinese were less creative in the absence of instructions to be creative but that they improved more from the instructions than did Americans. These findings suggest that in the absence of prompting, Chinese may be less motivated to be creative than Americans. In fact, Rudowicz and Yue (2000) found that Chinese in mainland China, Hong Kong and Taiwan regarded creative characteristics such as "have original ideas" and "innovative" as relatively unimportant.

Culture also shapes how creativity is conceptualized and the criteria used for its evaluation. Creativity typically involves the generation of novel and appropriate (useful) solutions to problems (e.g., Amabile, 1996; see also De Dreu et al., Chapter 13 in this volume). In evaluating creativity, Westerners emphasize novelty more, and appropriateness less, than non-Westerners (Lubart, 1999). Consistent with this view, Yue and Leung (2003) surveyed the motives and attitudes underlying creativity among Hong Kong and mainland Chinese undergraduates and found that extrinsic and instrumental rewards like social responsibility and contributions were more emphasized than intrinsic rewards such as personal satisfaction. Creativity is seen more as a means to an end, supporting the notion that Chinese tend to emphasize the appropriateness dimension of creativity. Nouri, Erez, Rockstuhl, and Ang (2008) found that, in a creative task, Israeli dyads scored higher in originality (number of original ideas), but Singaporean dyads scored higher in elaboration (amount of detail provided for an idea). The most direct evidence is provided by Bechtoldt, De Dreu, Nijstad, and Choi (2009), who found that, when solving creativity tasks under high epistemic and prosocial motivation, Dutch groups emphasized novelty more and appropriateness less than Korean groups; this difference can be attributed to differences in individualism-collectivism.

An ecological account may provide one explanation of why creativity—particularly novelty—is less emphasized in non-Western cultures. Most non-Western cultures are less affluent, so the dominant ethos channels people's attention and energy toward survival needs rather than the pursuit of novelty and stimulation. In line with this reasoning, Schwartz and Sagie (2000) found that across 42 societies, socioeconomic development was positively related to self-direction, which involves the values of creativity and curiosity.

An interesting extrapolation of this ecological argument is that affluent non-Western groups should place more emphasis on novelty and creativity. Indeed, Shimai, Otake, Park, Peterson, and Seligman (2006) found that American and Japanese young adults were equal in their endorsement of creativity as a self-description. In an experiment, Paletz and Peng (2008) manipulated the novelty and appropriateness of different products and asked university students from China (Beijing), Japan (Tokyo and Osaka), and the United States (Berkeley and Chapel Hill) to indicate their desirability. Surprisingly, Chinese were more influenced by novelty and less by appropriateness in their desirability ratings than both Japanese and Americans. Perhaps because Beijing has undergone phenomenal economic growth in the past decade, its norms have shifted toward an emphasis on novelty.

Cultures also differ in the specific criteria used to evaluate creativity. Chan and Chan (1999) found that Hong Kong teachers regarded "quick in responding" as a creative attribute, whereas "self-centered" was mentioned by U.S. teachers. In summary, there seems to be significant cultural differences in the prioritization and conceptualization of creativity, yet the evidence is far from clear, calling for more research on this topic.

CULTURAL DIFFERENCES IN CREATIVE PERFORMANCE

Asians are sometimes characterized as less proficient than Westerners in tasks requiring creativity (e.g., Ng, 2001). To evaluate the validity of this claim, we first consider whether the meaning and measurement of creative performance has sufficient cross-cultural equivalence to warrant meaningful comparisons across cultures (Leung & van de Vijver, 2008).

Conceptual and Measurement Issues

The fundamental question of what constitutes creativity has puzzled researchers for decades. Guilford (1950) viewed creativity as a personality trait, but other researchers have viewed it as a social process (e.g., Amabile, 1996) involving cognitive, motivational, and social components. Csikszentmihalyi (1990) took a systemic perspective and argued that "creativity is not an attribute of individuals but of social systems making judgments about individuals" (p. 198). This relativist view of creativity suggests that Western creativity tests may be biased against non-Western groups (Niu & Sternberg, 2002). It is entirely possible that Western creativity tests may not capture attributes that are regarded as creative in non-Western cultural contexts, particularly the social side of creative output, such as whether an idea is socially acceptable.

To broaden the measurement of creativity, less structured creativity tests, such as drawings, and the use of raters to evaluate the outputs have been introduced (e.g., Niu & Sternberg, 2001). However, these more subjective methods are susceptible to bias associated with the culturally based values and implicit theories of the raters. As in the case of intelligence tests, creativity tests valid across cultures and contexts have yet to be developed, posing a serious threat to valid cross-cultural comparison of creativity.

Are Some Cultures More Creative Than Others?

Accepting for the moment the validity of comparing creative performance across cultures, does the literature show consistent patterns of differences? Leung, Au, and Leung (2004) reviewed the literature and failed to identify reliable East–West differences in creativity. A number of studies document the superiority of Western students in standard Western creativity tests. For instance, Jellen and Urban (1989) assessed children from 11 countries with the Test for Creative Thinking–Drawing Production and found that children from Western countries such as England, Germany, and the United States obtained significantly higher overall creativity scores and unconventional scores (reflecting nonstereotypical usage of a given fragment) than those from Asian countries such as China, India, and Indonesia. Based on the Torrance Test, Saeki, Fan, and van Dusen (2001) found that Japanese students scored lower in elaboration and abstractness than American students, but there was no cultural difference in other dimensions. Niu and Sternberg (2001) asked American and Chinese college students to produce two artworks, which were then evaluated by judges from both cultures. Judges of both groups rated the American artworks as more creative, aesthetically pleasing, and technically advanced than the Chinese artworks.

Yet many findings contradict the generalization of higher creative performance by Westerners (Niu & Sternberg, 2002). For instance, Japanese (Torrance & Sato, 1979) and Hong Kong Chinese (Rudowicz, Lok, & Kitto, 1995) were found to outperform their American counterparts in creativity tests. Chan, Cheung, Lau, Wu, Kwong, and Li (2001) found that Hong Kong Chinese scored higher in ideational fluency than did Americans as reported by Wallach and Kogan (1965), although it may be problematic to compare findings across three decades. Chen, Kasof, Himsel, Greenberger, Dong, and Xue (2002) asked European American and Chinese university students to provide drawings of geometric shapes, which were than evaluated by judges from both cultures. There was no significant cultural difference in the creativity of the drawings as rated by the judges. More recently, Nouri et al. (2008) did not find any difference between Singaporeans and Israelis in the overall performance on a creative test derived from the Torrance test.

Even if we do not question the validity of Western creativity tests for Asians, there is no conclusive evidence that Westerners are more creative than Asians. Perhaps the large number of culturally related determinants of creativity (Zhou & Shalley, 2003) makes comparative performance levels contingent on many situational factors. To illustrate, consider collectivism and uncertainty avoidance. Collectivism is widely believed to suppress creativity through prioritizing conformity (e.g., Goncalo & Staw, 2006), whereas low uncertainty avoidance promotes creativity because it is associated with the tolerance of risk (e.g., Shane, 1995). Chinese are higher on collectivism but lower on uncertainty avoidance than are Americans. In a situation in which conformity is detrimental to creativity, Americans are likely to outperform Chinese. In contrast, in a situation in which risk taking is conducive to creativity, Chinese may be in an advantageous position. Another complicating factor is that, in the work context, organizational culture tends to overwhelm the effect of societal culture on innovation (Tellis, Prabhu, & Chandy, 2009). Creative performance may be the result of so many different processes that cultural differences in performance are unlikely to be constant across a wide range of situations. The search for sweeping, cross-situational cultural differences in creativity is probably unproductive (see also Westwood & Low, 2003).

Unpackaging the Influence of Culture

We argue that a more productive approach is to "unpackage" the influence of culture into the influence of specific cultural constructs (Leung & van de Vijver, 2008). This approach explores the role of specific cultural constructs in accounting for cultural differences in creativity and innovativeness. We illustrate this approach by several studies conducted in the Chinese context in the following sections.

Extending Western Research on Innovativeness to the Chinese Context

One approach to assess the influence of culture on innovativeness is to examine and extend Western theories in the Chinese context. Research in the West suggests that learning-goal orientation, which emphasizes learning and knowledge acquisition, is conducive to innovative behavior (Payne, Youngcourt, & Beaubien, 2007). In contrast, performance-goal orientation, which emphasizes the attainment of performance targets, suppresses innovative behavior (Payne et al., 2007; Shalley, 1991). Lu, Lin, and Leung (2009) examined this framework in the Chinese context and argued that the positive effect of learning-goal orientation on innovative behavior would be mediated by knowledge sharing—that is, the tendency to exchange knowledge and skills with coworkers—whereas the negative effect of performance-goal orientation would be mediated by lower perceived autonomy. A survey of midlevel employees in the Shanghai area showed that, as expected, knowledge sharing partially mediated the relationship between learning-goal orientation and innovative behavior. Performance-goal orientation was negatively related to perceived autonomy, which was positively related to innovative behavior. Because performance-goal orientation did not show a significant effect on innovative behavior, its effect on innovative behavior was indirect and through perceived autonomy.

These results are consistent with Western theorizing about goal orientation and raise several interesting issues about cultural differences in innovativeness. First, it is interesting to see if Chinese firms differ in learning orientation from Western firms. If Chinese firms are lower in learning-goal orientation, the innovativeness of their employees may suffer. Second, Chinese students emphasize academic performance more than their Western counterparts (e.g., Stevenson & Lee, 1996), but it is unclear if this cultural difference generalizes to the work setting. Interestingly, American firms are more likely to pursue short-term performance goals than Japanese firms (e.g., Ueno & Sekaran, 1992), and this specific cultural difference may disadvantage American firms in their innovativeness, an idea worth examining. Third, Lu et al. (2009) found that both knowledge sharing and perceived autonomy are positively related to innovative behavior. Cultural characteristics that influence these two variables may therefore elevate employee innovativeness. For instance, Chinese emphasize *guanxi* (i.e., interpersonal connection), which is positively related to knowledge sharing between employees (Huang, Davison, & Gu, 2008) and firms (Ramasamy, Goh, & Yeung, 2006). The emphasis on *guanxi* by Chinese may promote their innovativeness through knowledge sharing. In addition, paternalistic leadership is prevalent in the Chinese context (e.g., Cheng, Chou, Wu, Huang, & Farh, 2004), which tends to reduce employee autonomy. Chinese employees are likely to experience less autonomy than their Western counterparts, resulting in lower innovativeness. We note, however, that Chinese employees seem to react less negatively to low autonomy compared with Westerners (Hui, Au, & Fock, 2004), and this cultural difference may buffer them against a less autonomous environment.

In a second study extending Western theories to China, Lu, Zhou, and Leung (in press) explored different types of conflict as antecedents of innovative behavior. Task conflict refers to disagreement about how work should be accomplished, whereas relationship conflict refers to personal clashes and criticism (De Dreu & Weingart, 2003). Although task conflict in a group may give rise to innovative solutions (Jehn, 1994; Kurtzberg & Mueller, 2005), meta-analyses raise questions about the robustness of this effect (De Dreu & Weingart, 2003). Task conflict may have both positive and negative consequences, which are moderated by contextual factors. In a survey conducted in Shanghai, Lu et al. (2009) found that task conflict was positively related to innovative behavior, but the relationship was weaker when support for innovation was lower.

Cultural differences in people's responses to these two types of conflict may play a role in cultural differences in creativity. Tse, Francis, and Walls (1994) found that, compared with Canadians, mainland Chinese reacted more negatively to relationship conflict but less negatively to task conflict. The stronger negative reaction to relationship conflict by Chinese is consistent with their cultural collectivism, which emphasizes harmonious interpersonal relationships. The stronger negative reaction of Canadians to task conflict may be a function of their cultural individualism. Individualism is characterized by competitiveness (Morris et al., 1998), and individualists may react more negatively to task conflict because they view group discussions as a competition between individuals to offer the winning idea.

These cross-cultural differences give rise to an interesting conjecture. If Chinese culture disposes people to react less negatively to task conflict, then task conflict may be more conducive to innovativeness for Chinese. Future research should explore whether the positive effect of task conflict on employee innovativeness is stronger in Chinese cultural contexts than in the West.

Innovativeness From a Chinese Perspective

While the previously reviewed studies are based on Western theorizing, innovativeness can also be studied from a Chinese perspective. Yao, Yang, Dong, and Wang (in press) argued that Chinese may be unwilling to express creative ideas because of the collectivist pressure for conformity and the need to take instructions from superiors as a result of high power distance. In line with this argument, research in China shows that the positive relationship between creative ideas and innovative behavior was moderated by *zhong yong*, the preference for moderation and the avoidance of extreme positions (Yao et al., in press), and shyness (Yao, Wang, & Wang, 2009). Specifically, high *zhong yong* and shyness tend to suppress the expression of creative ideas.

Leung, Chen, Zhou, and Lim (2009) examined the implications of two Chinese cultural constructs, face and *renqing*, for innovative behavior. Face refers to the concern for a positive self- and public image, and *renqing* refers to the tendency to be compassionate toward others and to offer them favors. People with a positive face are likely to offer and receive *renqing*, and these two constructs are often viewed as two related facets of the Chinese relational orientation (Cheung et al., 1996). Leung et al. argued that face–*renqing* should be negatively related to innovative behavior because innovation attempts often fail, causing a loss of face and favor. Indeed, Leung et al. found that face–*renqing* was negatively related to fear of failure and innovative behavior. Similarly, Huang et al. (2008) found that face concern among Chinese employees was negatively related to the intention to share knowledge with coworkers. As discussed before, knowledge sharing is conducive to innovativeness, and this finding suggests that face concern can lower innovativeness by suppressing knowledge sharing.

Leung et al. (2009) also examined the moderating role of two contextual factors, innovative climate and autocratic leadership, an aspect of paternalistic leadership. As expected, the negative relationship between face–*renqing* and fear of failure was attenuated when innovative climate was high. Also, fear of failure was related to low innovative behavior only when innovative climate was low. Thus, face–*renqing* seems to have negative consequences for innovative behavior, but its influence can be ameliorated by a climate that explicitly supports innovation.

A striking finding is that innovative climate and autocratic leadership interact, such that innovative behavior is highest when both innovative climate and autocratic leadership are high. This finding contradicts the widely held belief that autocratic leadership is detrimental to innovativeness (e.g., Kanter, 1983). One way to account for this paradoxical finding is to assume that autocratic leadership, coupled with a strong innovative climate, provides clarity and motivation for subordinates to strive for innovativeness. In the Western cultural context, West et al., (2003) found that leadership clarity (i.e., the presence of a clear leader) predicted team innovation, and the effect was mediated by positive processes such as clearer objective setting and fuller team participation. Kahai, Sosik, and Avolio (2004) further found that directive leadership (similar to autocratic leadership) positively predicted participation by subordinates, an antecedent of innovativeness. Perhaps autocratic leadership may not be as detrimental to innovativeness as assumed in Western research, especially in high-power distance societies. This possibility deserves careful scrutiny in future research.

In sum, the studies reviewed illustrate how research on culture and innovativeness can enrich theorizing in each area. When creativity and innovativeness are viewed through a cultural lens, novel antecedents may emerge, such as face and *renqing*. The cultural perspective also stimulates theory development by calling received generalizations into question.

MULTICULTURAL EXPERIENCE AND CREATIVITY

The foregoing review concerns the effects of people's primary or first cultural heritage on their creative style. However, in this era many individuals have significant life experience with other cultures beyond their first culture. Some are permanent immigrants; some are "sojourners" who plan to return home after living abroad; and an increasing fraction are "transnationals" who maintain an ongoing life in two countries through travel and technology (see, e.g., Berry, Kim, Minde, & Mok, 1987; Ward & Kennedy, 1994). Still other individuals experience multiple cultures without emigrating, as they reside in multicultural families or communities. Hence, in addition to considering how particular cultural traditions shape creativity, researchers have begun to explore how exposure to multiple cultures enables creativity.

Multicultural experience can be thought of as cultural diversity within a person's life experience, and there is much evidence at different levels of analysis that cultural diversity potentiates creativity. At the level of world history, creativity increases after civilizations open themselves to outside cultural influences (Simonton, 1997). In organizations and teams, creativity increases with heterogeneous composition and norms fostering the expression of heterogeneous opinions (e.g., Guimera, Uzzi, Spiro, & Amaral, 2005; Levine & Moreland, 2004; Nemeth & Wachtler, 1983). Likewise, immigrants and ethnic minority group members, who experience the mix of their heritage culture and the mainstream host culture, tend to show high creativity (Lambert, Tucker, & d'Anglejan, 1973; Simonton, 1997, 1999). While such findings suggest that multicultural experience may well be associated with creativity, they do not reveal the mechanisms involved in how an individual's creative range is broadened or deepened through exposure to multiple cultures.

Recent research probing this matter elucidates two general ways that multicultural experience fosters greater creativity. We use the term *creative versatility* to describe the range of one's creative powers. Some kinds of multicultural experiences enable people to effortlessly switch between qualitatively different cultural styles, much like a bilingual can switch languages. We use the term *creative virtuosity* to describe the quality of creative performance, which can be assessed by criteria such as novelty, usefulness, and fluency. Some but not all kinds of multicultural experience enable this through increasing access to ideas, unconventional associations, and novel conceptual combinations. Our focus is identifying the critical aspects of multicultural experience in fostering these advantages of creativity.

VERSATILITY

Individuals who live between two cultures often describe themselves as having two distinct cultural identities (Phinney & Devich-Navarro, 1997). Studies of identification level confirm that a new cultural identity need not replace or weaken a person's first cultural identity (Ryder, Alden, & Paulhus, 2000). A distinctive phenomenon identified among biculturals is frame switching, the tendency to process information through the lenses of culture A in one situation and then through the lenses of culture B in a subsequent situation (LaFromboise, Coleman, & Gerton, 1993). For example, an Asian American may think and act according to Asian schemas and scripts when at home with family and then automatically switch to mainstream American schemas and scripts upon arriving to work.

A cognitive account for this phenomenon (Hong, Morris, Chiu, & Benet-Martinez, 2000) proposes that cultures are represented in memory as distinct networks of associated nodes (identities, schemas, and scripts) that dynamically activate in response to situational cues. This account has been tested through experiments that expose biculturals to cultural symbols (pictorial or verbal stimuli centrally associated with one of the cultures) and assess the accessibility of schemas from the primed culture (Fu, Chiu, Morris, & Young, 2007). Exposure to primes has tangible consequences such as shifting biculturals' biases in social judgments (Hong et al., 2000) and person memories (Morris & Mok, 2010).

Interestingly, however, different bicultural experiences give rise to different directions of frame switching. Some biculturals experience their two cultures as compatible, whereas others experience them as conflicting. Conflicted identity structures are associated with more stressful acculturation experiences (Benet-Martinez & Haritatos, 2005) and more culturally segregated social networks (Mok, Morris, Benet-Martinez, & Karakitapoglu-Aygun, 2007). Studies of attribution bias found that compatibles frame switch in the assimilative direction, shifting toward norms of the cued culture, whereas conflicted biculturals switch in the contrastive direction, shifting away from the cued cultural norm (Benet-Martinez, Leu, Lee, & Morris, 2002). This reversal in the direction of frame switching as a function of bicultural identity structure replicates in other kinds of social judgments, such as appraising job performance (Mok, Cheng, & Morris, 2010) and forecasting social behavior (Mok & Morris, 2010). Similar moderation effects on frame switching occur with variables conceptually related to identity, including beliefs about the separateness of races (No et al., 2008) and feelings of disidentification with one's cultures (Zou, Morris, & Benet-Martinez, 2008). The psychological mechanism operating in conflicted biculturals seems to be unconscious reactance in which the biases invited by the situational cue are suppressed in favor of the opposite biases (Mok & Morris, 2009).

Frame switching may enable Asian American biculturals to shift in their style of creative performance between Asian and American modes, the latter prioritizing novelty to a greater extent. Compatible biculturals would assimilate to the cued cultural norm (generating more novel ideas in an American versus Asian setting), whereas conflicted biculturals would react against it (generating fewer novel ideas in an American versus Asian setting).

Mok and Morris (in press) demonstrated this pattern in several priming experiments. In Experiment 1, Asian Americans were shown a picture of either Asian or Caucasian businesspeople before being asked to generate names for new products (e.g., cocktail) as part of a marketing interview, after being given an example (e.g., martini). Novelty was measured by the number of answers that did not share verbal properties with the examples (i.e., "bartini" is less novel than "bloodlust"). Participants with compatible identities generated more novel ideas after American versus Asian priming (i.e., assimilating to the cultural norm), whereas those with conflicted identities generated fewer novel labels after American versus Asian priming (i.e., contrasting against the cultural norm). Similar results were obtained in Experiment 2, with a task requiring participants to provide examples with categories (e.g., fruit).

In sum, frame switching studies identify two distinct directions in which biculturals shift their styles of creative performance in response to situational primes or cues. Either one—assimilative or contrastive shifting—could be adaptive, depending on the creativity challenge a person faces. Bicultural individuals who succeed in diplomacy or politics, such as

Mahatma Gandhi or Barack Obama, may do so through chameleon-like assimilative shifts to mesh with different cultural audiences. Biculturals who succeed across cultures in the arts, such as I. M. Pei or Ravi Shankar, may be more likely to engage in contrastive shifts that confront each audience with unfamiliar and intriguing ideas from the other culture.

VIRTUOSITY

The notion that exposure to different cultures stimulates or liberates creative abilities is an age-old truism. Stories of formerly blocked successful émigré artists can be cited for almost any nation, medium, and era. Yet in these tales of escaping the familiar for the exotic, the underlying dynamics are not always clear. Contemporary research (for a review see Leung, Maddux, Galinsky, & Chiu, 2008) has probed these dynamics, concluding that multicultural experience can foster better creative performance through (1) broader access to ideas, (2) unconventional associations, and (3) novel conceptual combinations.

However, these optimistic findings have to be reconciled with other findings about negative cognitive consequences of exposure to unfamiliar cultures, such as culture shock, a paralyzing state of anxiety, and disorientation (Ward, Bochner, & Furnham, 2001). Even within one's home country, exposure to artifacts of foreign cultures can sometimes evoke xenophobic fear or disgust rather than cosmopolitan curiosity (Chiu & Cheng, 2007). Encountering differences can spur rigid and close-minded responses rather than the open, unconventional, and complex responses required for creativity. Hence, for each mechanism of creativity gain from multicultural experience it is important to analyze the conditions under which it is most likely to occur.

Broad Access to Ideas

A person is more likely to devise creative solutions to the extent that the person draws from a broad pool of ideas. Experience in a new culture exposes one to novel artifacts and events such as designs, flavors, fashions, recipes, and games. Creativity can occur simply through importing foreign forms or structures and presenting them to new audiences. This straightforward process can be seen in many stories of innovators' epiphanies abroad, such as chief executive officer Howard Schultz's vision of the Starbucks experience when stopping in a café during a visit to Milan (Schultz & Yang, 1997). Indeed, Leung and Chiu (in press) found that European American undergraduates with greater multicultural experience were more likely to devise novel solutions to creativity problems. They also found that greater multicultural experience engenders increased tendency to search for information from culturally foreign sources, which suggests that a more enduring advantage in access to ideas comes from the cosmopolitan tastes that multicultural experience instills. Multicultural exposure tends to create an appetite for diversity—curiosity for a taste of the flavors, designs, and ideas of other cultures.

These gains do not come equally for everyone, however. Leung and Chiu (in press) found that individuals high on the personality dimension of openness gain from multicultural exposure more than individuals low on openness. Related to openness, another necessary condition for accessing ideas from intercultural experiences is affective trust. An important form of multicultural exposure for contemporary businesspeople is one's professional network. A culturally heterogeneous network potentially exposes one to a broader range of ideas than a homogenous network (Chua, Morris, & Ingram, in press). Yet not all businesspeople who are embedded in diverse networks reap the innovation advantage from them. Chua and Morris (2009) proposed that such shortfalls may reflect deficits in "innovation communication." Some individuals do not share ideas as freely in their intercultural relationships as in intracultural relationships, because sharing new ideas with another makes one vulnerable and requires trust. Some individuals have intercultural anxiety, which inhibits information sharing or disclosure in one's intercultural relationships (Stephan, Helms, & Haynes, 1995).

To test this affective mechanism, Chua and Morris (2009) measured the affect-based trust (rapport) in relationships controlling for cognition-based trust (perceived competence and reliability; see McAllister, 1995). In a survey of business executives with culturally diverse networks, they found that individuals lower on a dispositional measure of cultural intelligence (Ang et al., 2007) tended to experience less innovation communication specifically in their *inter*cultural ties, not in their intracultural ties. Mediational analyses confirmed that this effect on innovation communication was accounted for by a deficit in affect-based trust, not cognition-based trust. That is, low culturally intelligent individuals have a deficit in affect-based trust that appears specifically in their intercultural relationships, and this mechanism inhibits their access to innovation-relevant ideas from the other cultures.

Other literatures focused on occupational success as a function of intercultural experience suggest similar effects of affective orientations. Affective attitudes toward the host culture have been implicated in the success of expatriate managers (Bhaskar-Shrinivas, Harrison, Shaffer, & Luk, 2005) and of immigrant groups (Sowell, 1996). For reluctant expatriates and nonvoluntary immigrants, exposure to another culture is inevitable, but learning from this exposure is not. When personal openness and trust in the host culture are lacking, multicultural exposure spurs retreat into the comfort zone of one's familiar heritage culture rather than increased access to a broader pool of ideas.

Unconventional Associations

A basic function of cultures is to provide conventional ways of thinking about situations or problems; individuals adhere to culturally conventional biases in their thoughts and actions to be understood and accepted by in-group others (Fu et al., 2007). However, conventional answers to questions can become so automatic, habitual, and crystallized in our thinking that we lose the ability to think differently and imagine alternative solutions. Experience in other cultures breaks down the conventionalized associations inculcated by one's first culture. For instance, Leung and Chiu (in press) asked students varying in multicultural experience to list ideas for gifts and found those with more multicultural experience provided more unconventional suggestions.

This idea is further illustrated in a particularly important type of creativity involving improvising solutions with limited materials, such as imagining how an available object can be repurposed for a different function. Living in multiple cultures enables one to see that the same object or action can be used for different functions; it breaks down form–function fixedness in one's assumptions. Maddux and Galinsky (2009) gave MBA students the Duncker candle problem, which requires imagining how a particular form (the cardboard box holding some tacks) could be repurposed for an unconventional function (used as a candleholder). Interestingly, the advantage of foreign exposure only came from living abroad; vacation travel abroad had no effect. Maddux and Galinsky reasoned that escaping from form–function fixedness may come only from experiences requiring adapting to the other culture. In a follow-up study, they measured the degree to which people had adapted to the host culture in their foreign stays and found that this indeed mediated the effect. Finally, in a study that supports the hypothesized direction of the causal relationship, Maddux and Galinsky observed creativity differences after priming participants to think of experiences of either living abroad or adapting to a new culture but not after priming them to think of experiencing travel abroad or adapting to things other than a new culture.

Novel Conceptual Combinations

For the mechanisms reviewed heretofore—access to new ideas and unconventional associations—several of the preconditions are orientations toward the second culture such as trust and adaptation; in short, they require getting close to the other culture. For the final mechanism—novel combination—the key is simultaneous closeness to both cultures: one's first and second culture. Leung and Chiu (in press) exposed European American undergraduates to a 45-minute cultural slideshow before encountering some creativity problems. In the control condition, there was no slideshow. In the American culture condition, the slideshow featured images of American culture (i.e., arts, architecture, and food). In the Chinese culture condition, it featured images of Chinese culture. In the juxtaposed cultures condition, it featured adjacent images of American and Chinese cultures. In the fusion condition, it featured images of products and artworks combining elements of the two cultures (e.g., fashion and music combining Chinese and Western elements). The results showed a creativity advantage in the juxtaposed and fusion conditions over the unicultural conditions and the control condition. Content analysis of participants' thoughts about the slideshow showed that in the juxtaposed and fusion conditions participants analyzed the similarities and differences between the cultures and generated new ideas through combining them. In this way, simultaneous engagement with ideas from two cultures triggers creative conceptual expansion (Wan & Chiu, 2002).

Some creative tasks, which can be called creative fusion problems, specifically demand combining elements from two disparate cultures. Cheng, Sanchez-Burks, and Lee (2008) found that Asian Americans with blended cultural identities as opposed to separated identities performed better in such a task (e.g., designing recipes for Asian–Western fusion cuisine) but not in control tasks (e.g., designing purely Asian or Western recipes). For this type of task, bicultural experience is insufficient; the advantage comes only to bicultural individuals who have integrated their two identities and hence can simultaneously access constructs and schemas from the two cultures.

The advantages gained from simultaneous access to two cultures may extend beyond fusion problems, explicitly requiring content from both cultures. Building on Wan and Chiu's (2002) idea of novel conceptual combination from the immigration experience, Tadmore and Tetlock (2006) theorized that immigrants with bicultural identities differ from those with unitary identities (assimilationists who maintain only the host identity, and separatists who maintain only the heritage identity). Those with simultaneous strong dual identification chronically encounter conflicts between the two cultures that can be resolved only through integrating different ideas in novel and complex ways. This integrative complexity then becomes habitual for biculturals and enables creativity on a variety of tasks that reward complex thinking. Consistent with this claim is the finding of Benet-Martinez, Lee, and Leu (2006) that Chinese American biculturals, compared with monoculturals, exhibited more complex thinking about culture-related topics yet not about non-culture-related topics. Likewise Tadmor, Tetlock, and Peng (2009) found that, among Israeli Americans and Asian Americans, biculturals expressed more integratively complex thoughts about culture and work-related topics than assimilationists or separatists. In the first incisive test of the hypothesis, Tadmor, Maddox, and Galinksy (2010) had participants generate novel uses for a brick (Guilford, 1950) and measured the number of uses generated (i.e., fluency), the number of different categories of uses generated (i.e., flexibility), and originality or novelty of the uses. In a sample of MBA students with multiple cultural experiences, they found greater fluency, flexibility, and novelty for biculturals than assimilated or separated individuals. To confirm that the causal direction runs from dual identification to integrative complexity, Tadmor et al. (2010) conducted an experiment with Asian American participants primed to think of themselves as bicultural versus assimilated or separated and found that priming the bicultural identity indeed induced greater complexity of thought.

This account has interesting implications for the literature investigating predictors of work performance of expatriates. The past literature has focused on emotional adjustment as the key driver of success (e.g., Berry et al., 1987; Ward & Kennedy, 1994). However, the evidence shows that high performance is only modestly associated with emotional adjustment (e.g., Bhaskar-Shrinivas et al., 2005) and is sometimes shown by those employees with more initial culture shock (Kealey & Ruben, 1983; Tung, 1998). Tadmor et al. (2010) suggested that the key to this puzzle may be whether employees maintain a high identification with both their heritage cultures and strive to integrate the ideas and norms from both cultural sources. Tadmor et al. (Study 2) followed 100 Israeli professionals working in the United States and found that those who identified with both American and Israeli cultures achieved higher promotion rates and more positive performance-related reputations than assimilated or separated individuals. Further follow-up analyses found that this effect was indeed mediated by greater levels of integrative complexity.

In summary, multicultural experience can elevate one's creativity by expanding one's idea repertoire and breaking the yoke of conventional wisdom, and these two mechanisms depend on personal openness as well as trust and adaptation toward the second culture. The third mechanism, novel conceptual combination, depends on simultaneous engagement with the first and second cultures, which can be facilitated situationally and tends to be the case for individuals having cultural identities that are strong and integrated with each other. As Figure 16.1 shows, these three processes that expand creative virtuosity each have distinct antecedents, and these antecedents partially overlap with these of the aforementioned processes that enable cultural versatility.

CONCLUSION

Research on culture and creativity can shed new light on theorizing about culture and about creativity via two approaches. The first approach examines the relationship between constructs salient in a culture and the creativity it fosters. We have noted that these constructs range from the indigenous and idiosyncratic to the pancultural and general. The second approach assesses the impact of multicultural experience

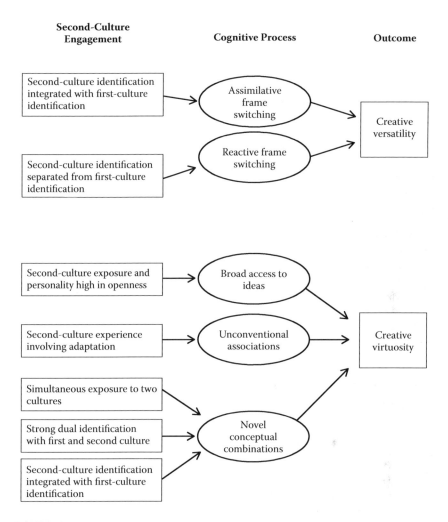

FIGURE 16.1
Mechanisms for creativity gain from second-culture experience.

on creativity. We have noted mechanisms involved in enhancing creative versatility and virtuosity. Both approaches have unraveled novel antecedents and processes of creativity as well as new mechanisms to account for cultural differences in creativity. Despite the short history of this research area, many intriguing findings have been reported, but many more important questions remain unanswered. Hopefully, this chapter will provide some signposts for future research and stimulate more interest in this research area.

REFERENCES

Amabile, T. M. (1996). *Creativity in context: Update to "The Social Psychology of Creativity."* Boulder, CO: Westview Press.

Ang, S., van Dyne, L., Koh, C., Ng, K. Y., Templer, K. J., Tay, C., et al. (2007). Cultural Intelligence: Its measurement and effects on cultural judgment and decision making, cultural adaptation and task performance. *Management and Organization Review, 3,* 335–371.

Bechtoldt, M. N., De Dreu, C. K. W., Nijstad, B. A., & Choi, H.-S. (2009). *Motivated Information processing and group creativity.* Manuscript submitted for publication.

Benet-Martinez, V., & Haritatos, J. (2005). Bicultural Identity Integration (BII): Components and psychosocial antecedents. *Journal of Personality, 73,* 1015–1050.

Benet-Martinez, V., Lee, F., & Leu, J. (2006). Biculturalism and cognitive complexity: Expertise in cultural representations. *Journal of Cross-Cultural Psychology, 37,* 386–407.

Benet-Martinez, V., Leu, J., Lee, F., & Morris, M. W. (2002). Negotiating biculturalism: Cultural frame switching in biculturals with oppositional versus compatible cultural identities. *Journal of Cross-Cultural Psychology, 33,* 492–516.

Berry, J. W., Kim, U., Minde, T., & Mok, D. (1987). Comparative studies of acculturative stress. *International Migration Review, 21,* 491–511.

Bhaskar-Shrinivas, P., Harrison, D. A., Shaffer, M. A., & Luk, D. M. (2005). Input-based and time-based models of international adjustment: Meta-analytic evidence and theoretical extensions. *Academy of Management Journal, 48,* 257–281.

Chan, D. W., & Chan, L-K. (1999). Implicit theories of creativity: Teachers' perception of student characteristics in Hong Kong. *Creativity Research Journal, 12,* 185–195.

Chan, D. W., Cheung, P-C., Lau, S., Wu, W. Y. H., Kwong, J. M. L., & Li, W-L. (2001). Assessing ideational fluency in primary students in Hong Kong. *Creativity Research Journal, 13,* 359–365.

Chandrasekaran, D., & Tellis, G. J. (2008). Global takeoff of new products: Culture, wealth, or vanishing differences? *Marketing Science, 27,* 844–860.

Chen, C., Kasof, J., Himsel, A. J., Greenberger, E., Dong, Q., & Xue, G. (2002). Creativity in drawings of geometric shapes: A cross-cultural examination with the consensual assessment technique. *Journal of Cross-Cultural Psychology, 33,* 171–187.

Cheng, B-S., Chou, L-F., Wu, T-Y., Huang, M-P., & Farh, J-L. (2004). Paternalistic leadership and subordinate responses: Establishing a leadership model in Chinese organizations. *Asian Journal of Social Psychology, 7,* 89–117.

Cheng, C-Y., Sanchez-Burks, J., & Lee, F. (2008). Connecting the dots within: Creative performance and identity integration. *Psychological Science, 19,* 1178–1184.

Cheung, F. M., Leung, K., Fan, R. M., Song, W-Z., Zhang, J-X., & Zhang, J-P. (1996). Development of the Chinese Personality Assessment Inventory. *Journal of Cross-Cultural Psychology, 27,* 181–199.

Chiu, C-Y., & Cheng, S. Y-Y. (2007). Toward a social psychology of culture and globalization: Some social cognitive consequences of activating two cultures simultaneously. *Social and Personality Psychology Compass, 1,* 84–100.

Chua, R. Y. J., & Morris, M. W. (2009). *Innovation communication in multicultural networks: Deficits of affect-based trust and idea sharing in intercultural relationships.* Unpublished manuscript, Harvard Business School, Boston, MA.

Chua, R. Y. J., Morris, M. W., & Ingram, P. (in press). Embeddedness and new idea discussion in professional networks: The mediating role of affect-based trust. *Journal of Creative Behavior*.

Csikszentmihalyi, M. (1990). The domain of creativity. In M. A. Runco & R. S. Albert (Eds.), *Theories of creativity* (Vol. 115, pp. 190–212). Thousand Oaks, CA: Sage Publications.

De Dreu, C. K. W., & Weingart, L. R. (2003). Task versus relationship conflict, team performance, and team member satisfaction: A meta-analysis. *Journal of Applied Psychology, 88,* 741–749.

Fackler, M. (2007, October 20). Fearing crime, Japanese wear the hiding place. *New York Times*. Retrieved from http://www.nytimes.com

French, H. W. (2001, August 7). Hypothesis: A scientific gap; Conclusion: Japanese custom. *New York Times*. Retrieved from http://www.nytimes.com

Fu, H-Y., Chiu, C-Y., Morris, M. W., & Young, M. (2007). Spontaneous inferences from cultural cues: Varying responses of cultural insiders, outsiders, and sojourners. *Journal of Cross-Cultural Psychology, 38,* 58–75.

Goncalo, J. A., & Staw, B. M. (2006). Individualism–collectivism and group creativity. *Organizational Behavior and Human Decision Processes, 100,* 96–109.

Guilford, J. P. (1950). Creativity. *American Psychologist, 5,* 444–454.

Guimera, R., Uzzi, B., Spiro, J., & Amaral, L. A. N. (2005). Team assembly mechanisms determine collaboration network structure and team performance. *Science, 308,* 697–702.

Hong, Y-Y., Morris, M. W., Chiu, C-Y., & Benet-Martinez, V. (2000). Multicultural minds: A dynamic constructivist approach to culture and cognition. *American Psychologist, 55,* 709–720.

Huang, Q. V., Davison, R. M., & Gu, J. B. (2008). Impact of personal and cultural factors on knowledge sharing in China. *Asia Pacific Journal of Management, 25,* 451–471.

Hui, M. K., Au, K., & Fock, H. (2004). Empowerment effects across cultures. *Journal of International Business Studies, 35,* 46–60.

Jehn, K. A. (1994). Enhancing effectiveness: An investigation of advantages and disadvantages of value-based intragroup conflict. *International Journal of Conflict Management, 5,* 223–238.

Jellen, H. G., & Urban, K. (1989). Assessing creative potential world-wide: The first cross-cultural application of the Test for Creative Thinking–Drawing Production (TCT-DP). *Gifted Education International, 6,* 78–86.

Kahai, S. S., Sosik, J. J., & Avolio, B. J. (2004). Effects of participative and directive leadership in electronic groups. *Group & Organization Management, 29,* 67–105.

Kanter, R. (1983). *The change masters*. New York: Simon and Schuster.

Kealey, D. J., & Ruben, B. D. (1983). Cross-cultural personnel selection criteria, issues, and methods. In D. Landis & R. W. Brislin (Eds.), *Handbook of intercultural training* (Vol. 1, pp. 155–175). New York: Pergamon Press.

Kurtzberg, T. R., & Mueller, J. S. (2005). The influence of daily conflict on perceptions of creativity: A longitudinal study. *International Journal of Conflict Management, 16,* 335–353.

LaFromboise, T., Coleman, H. L. K., & Gerton, J. (1993). Psychological impact of biculturalism: Evidence and theory. *Psychological Bulletin, 114,* 395–412.

Lambert, W. E., Tucker, G. R., & d'Anglejan, A. (1973). Cognitive and attitudinal consequences of bilingual schooling. *Journal of Educational Psychology, 65,* 141–159.

Leung, A. K-Y., & Chiu, C-Y. (in press). Multicultural experience, idea receptiveness, and creativity. *Journal of Cross-Cultural Psychology.*

Leung, A. K-Y., Maddux, W. W., Galinsky, A. D., & Chiu, C-Y. (2008). Multicultural experience enhances creativity—The when and how. *American Psychologist, 63,* 169–181.

Leung, K., Au, A., & Leung, B. W. C. (2004). Creativity and innovation: East–West comparisons with an emphasis on Chinese societies. In S. Lau, A. N. N. Hui, & G. Y. C. Ng (Eds.), *Creativity: When East meets West* (pp. 113–135). Singapore: World Scientific Publishing.

Leung, K., Chen, Z., Zhou, F., & Lim, K. (2009). *Relationship between traditional culture and innovative performance in China: The role of face and* renqing. Manuscript submitted for publication.

Leung, K., & van de Vijver, F. J. R. (2008). Strategies for strengthening causal inferences in cross cultural research: The consilience approach. *International Journal of Cross Cultural Management, 8,* 145–169.

Levine, J. M., & Moreland, R. L. (2004). Collaboration: The social context of theory development. *Personality and Social Psychology Review, 8,* 164–172.

Lu, L., Lin, X. W., & Leung, K. (2009). *Effects of learning and performance goal orientations on routine and innovative job performance.* Manuscript submitted for publication.

Lu, L., Zhou, F., & Leung, K. (in press). Effects of task and relationship conflict on work behavior. *International Journal of Conflict Management.*

Lubart, T. I. (1999). Creativity across cultures. In R. J. Sternberg (Ed.), *Handbook of creativity* (pp. 339–350). New York: Cambridge University Press.

Maddux, W. W., & Galinsky, A. D. (2009). Cultural borders and mental barriers: The relationship between living abroad and creativity. *Journal of Personality and Social Psychology, 96,* 1047–1061.

McAllister, D. J. (1995). Affect- and cognition-based trust as foundations for interpersonal cooperation in organizations. *Academy of Management Journal, 38,* 24–59.

Mok, A., Cheng, C. Y., & Morris, M. W. (2010). Matching versus mismatching cultural norms in performance appraisal: Effects of the cultural setting and bicultural identity integration. *International Journal of Cross-Cultural Management, 10,* 17–35.

Mok, A., & Morris, M. W. (in press). Assimilation versus reactance to cultural norms in creative expression: The role of cultural cues and biculturals' identity conflict. *Management and Organization Review.*

Mok, A., & Morris, M. W. (2009). Cultural chameleons and iconoclasts: Assimilation and reactance to cultural cues in biculturals' expressed personalities as a function of identity conflict. *Journal of Experimental Social Psychology, 45,* 884–889.

Mok, A., & Morris, M. W. (2010). *Forecasting others' behavior: Assimilation and contrast responses to cultural primes as a function of bicultural identity integration.* Manuscript in preparation.

Mok, A., & Morris, M. W. (2010). *Isolating effects of cultural conceptions: Shifts in Asian-Americans' person-description and memory biases in response to cultural priming.* Manuscript in preparation.

Mok, A., Morris, M. W., Benet-Martinez, V., & Karakitapoglu-Aygun, Z. (2007). Embracing American culture: Structures of social identity and social networks among first-generation biculturals. *Journal of Cross-Cultural Psychology, 38,* 629–635.

Morris, M. W., Williams, K. Y., Leung, K., Larrick, R., Mendoza, M. T., Bhatnagar, D., et al. (1998). Conflict management style: Accounting for cross-national differences. *Journal of International Business Studies, 29,* 729–747.

Nemeth, C. J., & Wachtler, J. (1983). Creative problem solving as a result of majority versus minority influence. *European Journal of Social Psychology, 13*, 45–55.

Ng, A. K. (2001). *Why Asians are less creative than westerners.* Singapore: Prentice Hall.

Niu, W., & Sternberg, R. J. (2001). Cultural influences on artistic creativity and its evaluation. *International Journal of Psychology, 36*, 225–241.

Niu, W., & Sternberg, R. J. (2002). Contemporary studies on the concept of creativity: The East and the West. *Journal of Creative Behavior, 36*, 269–288.

No, S., Hong, Y-Y., Liao, H., Lee, K., Wood, D., & Chao, M. M. (2008). Lay theory of race affects and moderates Asian Americans' responses toward American culture. *Journal of Personality and Social Psychology, 95*, 991–1004.

Nouri, R., Erez, M., Rockstuhl, T., & Ang, S. (2008, August). Creativity in multicultural teams: The effects of cultural diversity and situational strength on creative performance. Paper presented at the Academy of Management Conference, Anaheim, CA.

Paletz, S. B. F., & Peng, K. (2008). Implicit theories of creativity across cultures: Novelty and appropriateness in two product domains. *Journal of Cross-Cultural Psychology, 39*, 286–302.

Payne, S. C., Youngcourt, S. S., & Beaubien, J. M. (2007). A meta-analytic examination of the goal orientation nomological net. *Journal of Applied Psychology, 92*, 128–150.

Phinney, J., & Devich-Navarro, M. (1997). Variations in bicultural identification among African American and Mexican American adolescents. *Journal of Research on Adolescence, 7*, 3–32.

Ramasamy, B., Goh, K. W., & Yeung, M. C. H. (2006). Is Guanxi (relationship) a bridge to knowledge transfer? *Journal of Business Research, 59*, 130–139.

Rudowicz, E., Lok, D., & Kitto, J. (1995). Use of the Torrance tests of creative thinking in an exploratory study of creativity in Hong Kong primary school children: A cross-cultural comparison. *International Journal of Psychology, 30*, 417–430.

Rudowicz, E., & Yue, X-D. (2000). Concepts of creativity: Similarities and differences among mainland, Hong Kong and Taiwanese Chinese. *Journal of Creative Behavior, 34*, 175–192.

Ryder, A. G., Alden, L. E., & Paulhus, D. L. (2000). Is acculturation unidimensional or bidimensional? A head-to-head comparison in the prediction of personality, self-identity, and adjustment. *Journal of Personality and Social Psychology, 79*, 49–65.

Saeki, N., Fan, X., & van Dusen, L. (2001). A comparative study of creative thinking of American and Japanese college students. *Journal of Creative Behavior, 35*, 24–36.

Schultz, H., & Yang, D. J. (1997). *Pour your heart into it: How Starbucks built a company one cup at a time.* New York: Hyperion.

Schwartz, S. H., & Sagie, G. (2000). Value consensus and importance: A cross-national study. *Journal of Cross-Cultural Psychology, 31*, 465–497.

Shalley, C. E. (1991). Effects of productivity goals, creativity goals, and personal discretion on individual creativity. *Journal of Applied Psychology, 76*, 179–185.

Shane, S. (1995). Uncertainty avoidance and the preference for innovation championing roles. *Journal of International Business Studies, 26*, 47–68.

Shimai, S., Otake, K., Park, N., Peterson, C., & Seligman, M. E. P. (2006). Convergence of character strengths in American and Japanese young adults. *Journal of Happiness Studies, 7*, 311–322.

Simonton, D. K. (1997). *Genius and creativity: Selected papers.* Greenwich, CT: Ablex.

Simonton, D. K. (1999). *Origins of genius: Darwinian perspectives on creativity.* Oxford, UK: Oxford University Press.

Sowell, T. (1996). *Migrations and cultures: A world view.* New York: Basic Books.

Stephan, C. W., Helms, M. M., & Haynes, P. J. (1995). Inter-cultural anxiety: Implications for improving expatriate selection for Japan. *Cross Cultural Management: An International Journal, 2,* 25–32.

Stevenson, H. W., & Lee, S-Y. (1996). The academic achievement of Chinese students. In M. H. Bond (Ed.), *The handbook of Chinese psychology* (pp. 124–142). New York: Oxford University Press.

Tadmor, C. T., Maddox, W., & Galinksy, A. (2010). *Biculturalism: Dual identification with home and host cultures predicts creative and professional performance.* Unpublished manuscript.

Tadmor, C. T., & Tetlock, P. E. (2006). Biculturalism: A model of the effects of second-culture exposure on acculturation and integrative complexity. *Journal of Cross-Cultural Psychology, 37,* 173–190.

Tadmor, C. T., Tetlock, P. E., & Peng, K. (2009). Acculturation strategies and integrative complexity: The cognitive implications of biculturalism. *Journal of Cross-Cultural Psychology, 40,* 105–139.

Tellis, G., Prabhu, J., & Chandy, R. (2009). Radical innovation in firms across nations: The pre-eminence of corporate culture. *Journal of Marketing, 73,* 3–23.

Torrance, E. P., & Sato, S. (1979). Figural creative thinking abilities of United States and Japanese majors in education. *Creative Child & Adult Quarterly, 4,* 216–221.

Tse, D. K., Francis, J., & Walls, J. (1994). Cultural differences in conducting intra- and inter-cultural negotiations: A Sino-Canadian comparison. *Journal of International Business Studies, 25,* 537–555.

Tung, R. L. (1998). American expatriates abroad: From neophytes to cosmopolitans. *Journal of World Business, 33,* 125–144.

Ueno, S., & Sekaran, U. (1992). The influence of culture on budget control practices in the USA and Japan: an empirical study. *Journal of International Business Studies, 23,* 659–74.

Wallach, M. A., & Kogan, N. (1965). A new look at the creativity-intelligence distinction. *Journal of Personality, 33,* 348–369.

Wan, W. W. N., & Chiu, C-Y. (2002). Effects of novel conceptual combination on creativity. *Journal of Creative Behavior, 36,* 227–240.

Ward, C., Bochner, S., & Furnham, A. (2001). *The psychology of culture shock* (2nd ed.). Hove, UK: Routledge.

Ward, C., & Kennedy, A. (1994). Acculturation strategies, psychological adjustment, and sociocultural competence during cross-cultural transitions. *International Journal of Intercultural Relations, 18,* 329–343.

West, M. A., Borrill, C. S., Dawson, J. F., Brodbeck, F., Shapiro, D. A., & Haward, B. (2003). Leadership clarity and team innovation in health care. *Leadership Quarterly, 14,* 393–410.

Westwood, R., & Low, D. R. (2003). The multicultural muse: Culture, creativity and innovation. *International Journal of Cross Cultural Management, 3,* 235–259.

Yao, X., Wang, Z., & Wang, L. (2009). *The influence of shyness on innovation behavior of individuals with different levels of creative ability: A moderating effect model.* Unpublished manuscript, Peking University.

Yao, X., Yang, Q., Dong, N., & Wang, L. (2010). The moderating effect of *zhong yong* on the relationship between creativity and innovation behavior. *Asian Journal of Social Psychology, 13,* 53–57.

Yue, X. D., & Leung, K. (2003). Values for creativity: A study among undergraduates in Hong Kong and Guangzhou. *New Horizons in Education, 47,* 1–5 (in Chinese).

Zhou, J., & Shalley, C. E. (2003). Research on employee creativity: A critical review and directions for future research. *Research in Personnel and Human Resources Management, 22,* 165–217.

Zou, X., Morris, M. W., & Benet-Martinez, V. (2008). Identity motives and cultural priming: Cultural (dis)identification in assimilative and contrastive responses. *Journal of Experimental Social Psychology, 44,* 1151–1159.

Author Index

Subject Index